Police and International Peacekeeping Missions

Garth den Heyer • James F. Albrecht
Editors

Police and International Peacekeeping Missions

Securing Peace and Post-conflict Rule of Law

Springer

Editors
Garth den Heyer
School of Social and Behavioral Science
Walden University
Minneapolis, MD, USA

James F. Albrecht
Department of Criminal Justice and
Homeland Security
Pace University
New York, NY, USA

ISBN 978-3-030-77899-6 ISBN 978-3-030-77900-9 (eBook)
https://doi.org/10.1007/978-3-030-77900-9

This Springer imprint is published by the registered company Springer Nature Switzerland AG
The registered company address is: Gewerbestrasse 11, 6330 Cham, Switzerland

This book is dedicated to police officers across the globe, who continue to make personal sacrifices to ensure that society remains safe and secure and particularly to those who have lost their lives while serving their communities and in post-conflict peacekeeping missions.
"Blessed are the peacemakers, for they shall be called the children of God."
Matthew 5:9—King James Bible
This book is dedicated to my two grandsons, Liam and Joshua.
Garth den Heyer
This book is dedicated to my two children, Jimmy and Kristiana, who continue to provide me with continuous motivation through their unlimited sense of curiosity and their enthusiasm for learning.
James F. Albrecht

Foreword

Securing Peace explains the role and contribution of the police in international peacekeeping and post-conflict rule of law and stability. The editors and contributors, Garth den Heyer and James Albrecht, combine their extensive experiences from the United States, New Zealand, and throughout the world. As such, they have advanced significantly our knowledge about the achievements of the police toward the goal of peacekeeping. While there is an extensive literature on the influence of the military in peacekeeping, prior to this volume there has been precious little information on the role of the civilian police in global post-conflict criminal justice reform.

den Heyer and Albrecht, two pracademics with a vast knowledge base and real-world experience, provide the reader with new information on policing and peacekeeping by way of survey data and a collection of chapters written by renown experts. There is a strong reliance on the successes of New Zealand and American police agencies, but the book reaches far beyond those borders to assess the contributions made by North American, European, and the United Nations police.

One of the important features of the book is the chapter (Section 4) that looks at the challenges and lessons learned from mentoring the Haitian Police. In other words, the reader is able to understand the impact of the influencers on the influenced and vice versa. This two-way mirror provides the reader with a view of international peacekeeping from several perspectives. The editors provide various ideas and perspectives with a conclusion that links them all together.

We learn very quickly that peacekeeping involves the deployment of international police personnel directly to a post-conflict zone. In order for a post-conflict society to be safe and begin its reconstruction, police must assist in the establishment of a secure and stable environment. We learn a great deal about the development and rebuilding of police capacity in post-conflict and developing countries and regions.

Securing Peace traces the history of peacekeeping and the consequences of its proper and also ineffective planning, organization, and deployment. A critical comparison presented here is the difference between police reform and security in advanced and developing countries and those in compromised ones. The strengths, weaknesses, and threats of deploying civilian police as a critical part of peacekeeping has become a common strategy throughout this text.

This volume adds to the literature on policing and democratic reform, which has often skipped many countries in need. *Securing Peace* has the strong potential to influence the growth and development of police agencies around the world. den Heyer and Albrecht stress the importance of evidence-based policy development, and they have set the stage to engage a variety of stakeholders in such critical reform efforts. One of the remarkable programs that has helped increase research capabilities of law enforcement officers and agencies in the United States and other countries is the National Institute of Justice's (NIJ) Law Enforcement Advancing Data and Science (LEADS) Program. Developing such a program in other countries and linking and developing partnerships between police agencies and researchers in academic institutions will go a long way to assist agencies understand and improve their roles and better influence change.

In conclusion, den Heyer and Albrecht have put together an important book for anyone interested in learning about civilian policing globally and the mission of peacekeeping. They have brought together top scholars, who have engaged in effective critical thinking and provided valuable insight into rule of law and post-conflict peacekeeping endeavors. Academics, researchers, practitioners, government officials, and policy makers will gain key insight and important perspectives from this highly informative and comprehensive volume. It clearly will provide a valuable contribution to this field, and one that will have a lasting impact on democracy, rule of law, criminal justice, and policing reform.

Department of Criminology and Criminal Justice Geoffrey P. Alpert
University of South Carolina
Columbia, SC, USA

Contents

About the Authors

James F. Albrecht is a professor in the Department of Criminal Justice and Homeland Security at Pace University in New York City. Jimmy received a prestigious Fulbright Fellowship in 1998 and worked as a professor at the National Police College of Finland. He is also the recipient of a 2013 Embassy Policy Specialist Fellowship (USDOS/IREX) and was tasked with conducting research and making recommendations to improve law enforcement effectiveness and legitimacy in Ukraine. Police Chief Albrecht served in the European Union Rule of Law Mission (EULEX) in Kosovo (former Yugoslavia) as the head of the EULEX Police Executive Department, in charge of criminal investigations and coordinating international law enforcement cooperation and intelligence analysis from 2008 through 2010. He had previously served in the United Nations Mission in Kosovo Police from 2007 to 2008. Jimmy is also a 23-year veteran of the NYPD who retired as the Commanding Officer of NYPD Transit Bureau District 20, tasked with the prevention of crime and terrorism in the subway and commuter transit system in New York City. He was a first responder and incident command manager at the September 11, 2001, terrorist attack on the World Trade Center and developed the counter-terrorism strategic plan for the subway system in the borough of Queens, New York City.

Garth den Heyer is a professor with Arizona State University and a senior research fellow with the Police Foundation. He is also a contributing faculty member at Walden University and an associate with the Scottish Institute of Policing Research. He served with the New Zealand Police for 38 years, retiring as Inspector and Manager: National Security. He also spent more than 20 months as a strategic advisor to the Regional Assistance Mission to the Solomon Islands. His main research interests are policing, militarization, service delivery efficacy, policy development, strategic thinking, and organizational reform.

Salih Hakan Can began his career in law enforcement in 1984 as a police chief in the Turkish National Police. Upon graduation from the police academy, where he earned a Bachelor of Science degree in criminal justice and law, Hakan was promoted to ranking officer and worked in many divisions including Interpol, Narcotics

Investigations, and Financial Crimes. As part of Turkish National Police's international police collaboration, he worked or joined law enforcement operations in Germany, Spain, Netherlands, Switzerland, Russia, Azerbaijan, Kosovo, Bosnia, Bulgaria, Romania, and Albania. Dr. Can received his master's degree from the University of North Texas and a Ph.D. from Sam Houston State University. While he was working at the Law Enforcement Management Institute of Texas, he established a program called "Incident Command Simulation," which received funding and great recognition from the US Department of Homeland Security. Hakan currently works on multiple projects with the United Nations, Interpol, the National Sheriffs Association, and the International Association of Chiefs of Police. Dr. Can has published 6 books and 62 articles, 48 of which were peer reviewed.

Benoit J. S. Maure is a serving Peace Officer with the Royal Canadian Mounted Police (RCMP). His 32-year police career within the RCMP took him from patrolling the streets of Surrey, British Columbia, Canada, to investigating drugs and organized crimes, economic crimes, and terrorism. In 1999, Ben completed a 1-year tour of duty as a United Nations Peacekeeper in Quetzaltenango, Guatemala. Between 2009 and 2013, Ben reached the coveted position of Canadian diplomat (first secretary) and police liaison officer at the Embassy of Canada in the Dominican Republic. He holds a Bachelor of Technology degree from the British Columbia Institute of Technology and a Master of Arts degree in Social Justice from the University of the Fraser Valley. Ben's interests are national security and international policing. He is also the recipient of a Meritorious Service Cross (M.S.C.) for work done in Afghanistan.

Robert Peacock recently transitioned to academia after spending a decade as a consultant to transitional governments in East Europe and Central Asia and the prior decade as an intelligence analyst with the US Department of State. Dr. Peacock has an M.B.A. in finance from Ohio University and a B.A. in public policy from the University of Michigan, prior to receiving a Ph.D. in criminal justice from Michigan State University.

Dr. Peacock's research interests are in the role of corruption in law enforcement and security agencies, particularly those in East Europe and Central Asia. Dr. Peacock currently serves on USAID's first cybersecurity advisory group and is developing the Florida International University (FIU) led program to support cyber security education in developing countries. Over his first **2** years at FIU, Dr. Peacock was the principal investigator for a US Department of Justice grant to provide strategic reform assistance to new police agencies in Ukraine and Armenia. Dr. Peacock is fluent in Russian and has an intermediate level in the Ukrainian l**anguage.**

Michael Raymond Sanchez has 23 years of experience in the criminal justice system. Dr. Sanchez served for 4 years as an international police officer for the United Nations. Dr. Sanchez served in the United Nations Mission in Kosovo (UNMIK) Police as an investigator on a counter-terrorism task force, as an international police and firearms instructor, as the deputy chief of training, and ultimately as the director of personnel and administration in the United Nations Mission in Kosovo Police in Kosovo. In this position, Dr. Sanchez was a member of the UNMIK police commissioner's senior staff.

Dr. Sanchez also served as an international police officer for the United Nations Stabilization Mission in Haiti from **2009–2010**. Starting out in the field as a police mentor, zone commander, deputy regional commander, and ultimately he served as the regional commander for the Les Cayes Region of Haiti. Dr. Sanchez was in Haiti when the **12** January **2010** earthquake struck Haiti. He commanded his region through the recovery and normalization **effort.**

Dr. Sanchez currently teaches criminal justice at the University of Texas Rio Grande Valley in Brownsville**, Texas.**

Part I
Introduction to the Police in International Peacekeeping

Chapter 1
Introduction to International Peacekeeping and Post-Conflict Democratic Reform

Garth den Heyer

Introduction

Countries such as Australia, Canada, New Zealand, Norway, the United Kingdom, and the United States have a long history of involvement in peacekeeping activities. The majority of peacekeeping missions that have taken place since the Second World War have been led by the United Nations or by regional organizations such as the North Atlantic Treaty Organization (NATO), the African Union, or the South Pacific Leaders Forum.

The original mandate of the United Nations was "to save succeeding generations from the scourge of war" (United Nations, 1945). Historically, United Nations peacekeeping missions have been established on the principles of consent, impartiality, and not using force, except in self-defense (Capie, 2012). Such missions are different from peace enforcement missions, which involve the use of coercive measures to bring an end to hostilities, while peacemaking missions comprise diplomatic actions that have been designed to bring conflict to a negotiated end (Capie, 2012).

The deployment of international police to a post-conflict zone is a fundamental part of peacekeeping and is vital for the commencement of the reconstruction of a society. The police play a central role in establishing a sense of security and stabilizing the lives of people living in post-conflict nations. According to Schmidl (1998), "[p]olice play a crucial role in securing the transfer from war to peace, enabling the people to return to their 'normal' lives" (p. 3).

The police were first deployed by the United Nations to a post-conflict zone in July 1960. Following a lull of approximately two decades, the number of police involved in peacekeeping operations increased from 1677 officers in 1994 to more than 11,000 officers in 2020 (United Nations Peacekeeping, 2021). The role of the

G. den Heyer (✉)
School of Social and Behavioral Science, Walden University, Havelock North, New Zealand

G. den Heyer, J. F. Albrecht (eds.), *Police and International Peacekeeping Missions*, https://doi.org/10.1007/978-3-030-77900-9_1

police has continued to broaden, from one of monitoring general elections and providing training and basic security to one of patrolling and developing the capacity[1] of local police.

The reform of local police is a crucial element when establishing a sense of security and developing a post-conflict nation. Although the principles and practices of capacity development can be applied in most development assistance programs, there are some additional challenges to developing or rebuilding police capacity in weak, post-conflict, and failed countries. In these situations, rapid capacity development is critical, but the environment is not conducive to success or to the evaluation of these technical assistance programs.

Despite the extensive literature that has examined the role of the military in peacekeeping and intervention operations, little literature or information that investigates the role and the work of the police or the methods that they use to assist in the reformation of local police is available. The lack of literature that examines the contribution of the police to international peacekeeping creates a gap in our history and in our understanding of the cultural and social benefits to such deployments.

Peacekeeping and Its Continual Evolution

Since the emergence of peacekeeping in the mid-1950s, United Nations peacekeeping missions have evolved through two phases; the first being classical or traditional, and the second being multidimensional. They are now in a third phase, of which the structure is unclear and has been contested (Woodhouse & Ramsbotham, 2005). The evolution in peacekeeping has come about because of the changes in the form and size of civil wars and the 9/11 terrorist attacks in the United States.

Civil war has been the most important and most troubling problem for underdeveloped and developing nations. Apart from the killing and injuring of innocent civilians, violent civil conflict makes it is difficult to solve problems such as state collapse, corruption, and the lack of security. Howard (2008) cautioned that if these problems are not resolved then they could lead to renewed conflict, international crime, and terrorist activity.

The 9/11 attacks validate this claim. Following the terrorist attacks and the subsequent "war on terror," it was implied that there was a link between the security of a state and that state's capability (Dinnen, 2007). Previously, "state failure" had been viewed in humanitarian terms, but following the war on terror, any failure was viewed as being a major security threat to the developed world. Building an effective state would be an answer "to actual and potential state failure and its [possible] contagious effects" (Dinnen, 2007, p. 256). It was also claimed that the large number of state-building exercises that were conducted between 2002 and 2015 were

[1] Capacity development is the process or method by which "individuals, organizations, institutions, and societies develop (individually and collectively) to perform functions, solve problems, and set and achieve objectives" (United Nations Development Programme, 1997, p. 5).

undertaken "with a sense of urgency and pronounced concern for security" (Dinnen, 2007, p. 256).

Multidimensional peacekeeping operations were designed to rebuild the basic institutions of a state. These types of peacekeeping operations are typically large and complex and require a substantial amount of input and deployment of political, military, civilian police, refugee, humanitarian, electoral, and often, human rights personnel and resources (Howard, 2008).

Gauging the success of these forms of peacekeeping missions is, however, problematic. To measure a mission's success, a mission needs to be examined from a number of different perspectives (Ratner, 1995). It was easier to measure the success of first-generation operations or traditional missions as they had clear benchmarks set as to what they were to achieve, which was notably to maintain the conditions of a ceasefire. It is not so easy to measure the success of second-generation or multidimensional missions as they had a number of different political and social agendas. Another difficulty with multidimensional peacekeeping missions is that they are conceptual rather than practical, which adds to the difficulty in measuring their success.

Whether multidimensional missions are a suitable response to state corruption and breakdown has not yet been determined (Howard, 2008). To date, other than deploying the military and civilian police, no other ideas or practices to respond to state breakdowns have been identified. Howard (2008) maintained that the lack of initiatives creates an impression of incremental development and adaption.

The civilian police component of peacekeeping missions has not enjoyed great success (Howard, 2008). This is despite the importance that civilian policing plays in multidimensional peacekeeping operations. Howard (2008) maintains that the concept of civilian policing was developed as a response to the need for security and national development leading up to the separation of Namibia from South Africa in 1990. To assist with the separation, the United Nations deployed the United Nations Transitional Assistance Group (UNTAG), which included a civilian police (CIVPOL) division to monitor and retrain the Namibian police. The mission was deemed to be a success.

Following the use of civilian police in United Nations Transitional Assistance Group, the CIVPOL division was deployed in 1993 as a component of the United Nations Transitional Authority in Cambodia (UNTAC). The division comprised the same police chief and many of the same officers and was given a similar mandate to observe and retrain the local police in the same manner as it had done in the previous United Nations Transitional Assistance Group mission. The police in Cambodia were, however, different from those in Namibia, in that the Namibian police were disciplined and spoke a common language (Howard, 2008), whereas the Cambodian police were untrained, did not speak a common language, and were not well equipped. As a result of the differences between the Namibian and Cambodian police, the same monitoring and evaluation procedures could not be used. The problems that were initially encountered with the Namibian police, such as a lack of basic police training, were replicated in Cambodia, but with more intensity (Howard,

2008). Subsequently, the mission in Cambodia failed as a result of these difficulties.

Following the civilian policing missions in Namibia and Cambodia, missions in Croatia, Mozambique, and Bosnia have been more effective in implementing their mandates, and as a result, the United Nations began to deploy civilian police to post-conflict nations. The success of these civilian police missions needs to be balanced with the cases of extreme state failure, such as those in parts of Sierra Leone, the Democratic Republic of Congo, and Haiti. The mandate for deploying the civilian police to these failed states was different from the mandates used for missions to countries that have suffered conflict. The development of any future mandates for police reform should take into account the differences between nations that have suffered conflict and those where the state has failed. It is important that the police reform model takes these two situations into account.

Concerns have also been raised about the United Nations using the same type of mandate for civilian policing that was developed for use in Namibia and in other missions where the state had broken down (Howard, 2008). A mandate should be specifically designed for each mission and should not be reused. Each conflict is unique, and a mandate should be specifically tailored to address the reasons why a conflict has occurred. Mandates have been reused despite substantial amounts of aid being donated, donor governments expressing their disappointment in the terms of the mandate, and the limited impact that traditional approaches to development assistance have had in strengthening weak, recipient institutions and improving the living standards of those who live in these nations. Critics have also argued that international aid and peacekeeping missions have "become part of the problem by increasing levels of dependency and fuelling corruption among political and bureaucratic elites" (Dinnen, 2007, pp. 256–257).

Implementing multidimensional operations is often fraught with difficulties because they are staffed by civilian police who are often undertrained and underequipped and often come themselves from states where authoritarian regimes rule (den Heyer, 2013). This implies that they should not be expected to assist in rebuilding state institutions and promoting democratic policing (den Heyer, 2013). Another difficulty in the staffing of the police component of multidimensional missions is that there are very few good police officers and the countries that have them are reluctant to send them abroad, instead preferring to keep them for use at home (den Heyer, 2013; Howard, 2008). If peacekeeping missions are to be effective, then politicians and decision-makers need to understand that using undertrained civilian police officers could influence the outcome of a mission.

There are concerns as to the circumstances under which the United Nations or other regional bodies should deploy a multidimensional peacekeeping mission (Ratner, 1995) and how they should staff and resource such a mission. A review of previous peacekeeping missions reveals that there are two core issues in determining whether to and how to develop and implement a mission: whether the participants in a conflict are amenable to outsider involvement in finding a solution to the conflict and whether the contributing country will be valuable in the endeavor to resolve the conflict (Ratner, 1995). If the need for peacekeeping missions continues, then contributing countries can expect to have to engage in a continuous process of decision-making as to whether to contribute to a mission and how it should be implemented. The development and implementation of a multidimensional peacekeeping mission will not only demand expertise from the military and the police but will also necessitate political and economic resources from the contributing countries (Ratner, 1995). If these demands are recognized, they will form a framework that will enable objectives and performance measures to be developed for an intended mission and will enable a mission to be flexible so that it can respond to the evolving security, political, and social situation in a post-conflict country.

Police Reform as a Component of Peacekeeping

The frequency and intensity of peacekeeping missions and state-building interventions have increased markedly since the end of the Cold War in 1989 (Dinnen, 2007). The central feature of modern peacekeeping missions is that it has focused on ending a conflict and restoring law and order, and this has led to an emphasis being placed on strengthening the rule of law. Law and order has become a necessary condition for all aspects of state building and development, and modern missions bestow police officers with executive powers and the decree to develop the capacity of the local police and justice institutions (Dinnen, 2007).

The change in emphasis of peacekeeping missions has been supported by a change in academic thinking. Since the early 1990s, scholars of civil–military relations and peacekeeping, along with academics in international relations, have turned their attention to policing and police reform and the contribution it makes to establishing security and nation building in post-conflict countries. It was during this period that the value of deploying police officers as a component of peacekeeping missions was recognized (Greener, 2009). Following the successful experience in Namibia, police began to be deployed to peacekeeping missions in larger numbers and with specific reform remits.

The interest in the role of the police in nation building increased because justice and law enforcement institutions in many parts of world were not able "to address basic public safety and human security issues in a fair, effective, credible, and transparent manner" (Griffiths et al., 2005). To address this, the involvement of the police in peacekeeping operations broadened and deepened, and by the late 1990s, civilian police were included in missions to countries where the criminal justice system had totally collapsed. The role and the responsibilities of the police in assisting with state building have been described as changing from one of policing to one of law enforcement (Greener, 2009).

The development or reform of the police in a post-conflict nation has been identified as an important "point of entry" for security sector development and is a prerequisite for the establishment of democratic accountability (Griffiths et al., 2005). The deployment of civilian police signifies that a mission is civil and demilitarized and there are benefits to deploying civilian police to a post-conflict nation. Civilian police are able to assist with bringing different groups and communities together to foster the cooperation that is necessary for the establishment of relationships that reduce ethnic tensions (Wiatrowski & Pino, 2008).

Despite the increase in the number of peacekeeping missions, their success has been both minimal and disappointing (Botes & Mitchell, 1995). In the former Yugoslavia and throughout large parts of Africa, for example, peace operations have failed, and even where an uncertain truce existed, it was sustained more by the threat of force than by any persistent search for genuine peace and security (O'Connor, 2006).

Reforming the local police and creating security so that a nation can develop are paramount in post-conflict environments. Policing, in general, is a difficult and complex task (Jones & Newburn, 2005; Jones et al., 2005; Stone & Ward, 2000), even in developed countries. The police usually lack resources, function in a continually changing legislative environment, have weak public support, and face criticism from governments. Whether in a developed nation or in a post-conflict environment, such as Kosovo, Haiti, Iraq, Afghanistan, or the Solomon Islands, the cultural, institutional, and political challenges make effective police reform complicated and the challenges great. More than just financial assistance is required if a competent level of success is to be reached (Bajraktari et al., 2006).

Difficulties have been encountered when developing the police in post-conflict nations, and one area that needs to be addressed is the difficulty in delivering sustainable reforms (Griffiths et al., 2005). Sustainable reforms have been difficult to achieve despite the United Nations focusing on a "SMART" model of civilian policing in post-conflict nations – "SMART' meaning Support, Monitoring, Administering, Reporting, and Training (Greener, 2009). The difficulty in not being able to design and implement sustainable police reform solutions results from the lack of two elements. The first is the lack of reliable crime data and information that pertains to the police of the post-conflict nation (den Heyer, 2013; Griffiths et al., 2005), and the second is that data regarding the performance of the police and justice agencies are not available (den Heyer, 2013; Griffiths et al., 2005). These two factors, along with the fact that police reform programs are rarely systematically evaluated, mean that there is very little reliable information available that would prove whether a method of reform has been effective (Griffiths et al., 2005).

Another problem that is encountered is that the countries that contribute to peacekeeping missions do not see police reform as being a long-term commitment. Reforming the justice and security sectors requires an intervention over the longer term so that social, cultural, structural, organizational, and technological transformation can be encouraged and supported (Griffiths et al., 2005).

By the mid-2000s, police reform in post-conflict nations was beginning to change (Greener, 2009). There was a move away from police reform that had focused primarily on technical and structural organizational issues, such as the ideal size of an organization and providing equipment to one that focused on building the public's confidence in the local police (den Heyer, 2010; Greener, 2009). Focusing on police reform through capacity development became known as democratic policing.

The Increase in the Involvement of the Police in Peacekeeping and Nation Building

Prior to the early 2000s, civilian police were a neglected and underutilized component of peacekeeping, but following the 9/11 terrorist attacks, military and academic researchers considered the civilian police to play a vital role in stabilizing a post-conflict nation (Greener, 2009). Recognizing that civilian policing was a vital part of peacekeeping missions represented a significant change from times when "civilian police issues were typically more of an afterthought" (Greener, 2009, p.2).

The deployment of civilian police as a component of a peacekeeping mission has reached a level where the phrase "international police peacekeeping" is now in common use (Greener, 2011). Greener (2011) also claimed that civilian police not only performed their traditional policing duties but also assumed peace enforcement and peace-building tasks. Although civilian police bring new skills and capabilities to a mission, there are often weaknesses in the capabilities of some of the deployed officers and there can be difficulties in sourcing an appropriate number of police officers (den Heyer, 2012, 2013; Greener, 2011). There are also concerns regarding the models of policing that are being used to reform police organizations in post-conflict countries. The models used do not take into consideration local, cultural issues (den Heyer, 2010, 2012).

The demand for the civilian police to be a part of a peacekeeping mission increased markedly between the late 1990s and 2010, especially in state building and preventing conflict. The increase in demand arose because of the training that the police receive and their underlying philosophy of policing by consent. These factors placed the civilian police in a unique position of being able to embed certain values within post-conflict communities (den Heyer, 2010; Greener, 2011).

The increase in demand for the civilian police to be included as a part of a peacekeeping mission not only led to an increase in the number of civilian police being deployed but also led to an increase in the amount of assistance and support given by private sector organizations (Greener, 2011; Scahill, 2007). As well as an increase in the number of civilian police deployed, there was also a change in the role of the civilian police. They had been deployed in an executive, inline policing role, but this changed to one that included reforming and mentoring the local police (den Heyer, 2012).

The number of civilian police deployed by the United Nations grew from 35 in 1988 to 9000 in February 2000 and from 7300 in August 2006 to approximately 14,000 in September 2010 (International Peacekeeping Institute, 2019), with just more than 11,000 deployed in December 2020 (United Nations Peacekeeping, 2021). Regional contributing bodies also increased their contribution of civilian police officers during the period 2000–2008, while the European Union only increased their contribution to executive missions in 2008 (Greener, 2011). It was during this period that the New Zealand Police had approximately 150 personnel deployed on peacekeeping missions in Afghanistan, Timor-Leste, and a number of Pacific Island countries. The increase in the number of civilian police deployed, the expansion of their role, and the increase in the number of private sector organizations providing support implied that there was a new era in international policing (Greener, 2009).

The Problems of Civilian Police and Peacekeeping

A number of problems come to light when civilian police are considered for use in peacekeeping missions. The first is that police officers are usually a local, state, or national resource and are not housed or stationed in camps or barracks. In Western nations, they live in local communities, which means that they are not usually a part of a standing reserve force who are waiting to be deployed to a peacekeeping mission. There are some police units, however, that are a standing force and are able to be deployed quickly to high-end violent situations, for example, the French Gendarmerie and Italian Carabinieri (den Heyer, 2011).

Another problem with deploying civilian police on peacekeeping missions is that each officer is employed to fill a role in their local police force and are, therefore, not easily replaced. Generally, police forces are understaffed. Compounding this issue is that peacekeeping missions usually require experienced officers with at least 5 years' service and sometimes require officers who have special capabilities, such as investigators or forensic specialists. These types of officers are usually highly valued by their own police force and are not willingly made available for deployment. As a result, the deployment of civilian police becomes a political decision (Greener, 2011).

Civilian police forces do not generally have an expeditionary capability and typically do not have the understanding or training to undertake a peacekeeping mission role. Nor do they have any experience in post-conflict situations (den Heyer, 2012; Greener, 2011). They do not usually have any capability in areas such as logistics, transport, engineering, medical, and catering (Greener, 2011). Consequently, the civilian police often rely on the military component of a peacekeeping mission to supply these capabilities.

In summary, not only is it difficult to obtain an adequate number of civilian police for a peacekeeping mission, it is also difficult to obtain officers who possess the skills needed. These problems are compounded during a mission by the number of different national civilian police forces who are participating in the mission and the varying levels of leadership (den Heyer, 2013).

The Change in the Role of Police Peacekeeping Missions

The role of civilian police in peacekeeping missions has broadened and deepened from one of monitoring local elections to one that includes reforming and training the local police. The role of modern, civilian police deployed on a peacekeeping mission usually comprises a number of different functions. One function includes arresting and detaining offenders, undertaking patrol, and providing on-the-job mentoring, advising, and training, and offering support to the local police. Another function includes providing operational support and public order and crowd control to the local community. They also undertake capability building, mentoring, and training, and provide protection for United Nations personnel and facilities. In addition, civilian police reform, restructure, and rebuild the local police force. Civilian police also assist "with other rule of law agencies in helping to provide legislation, systems, procedures, codes, values, organisation, management, vetting, training, basic material, logistics and communications" (Greener, 2009, pp. 111–112).

The change in the role of the civilian police was underlined when the United Nations developed a model for using the civilian police in peacekeeping missions. Prior to the late 1990s, the civilian police that were deployed by the United Nations used the SMART (support, monitoring, administering, reporting, and training) model of civilian policing as a part of their strategic approach to peacekeeping (Hartz, 2000). However, as the United Nations civilian police gained experience in reforming the police in Bosnia and Cambodia and during the state-building missions in Kosovo and Timor-Leste, they changed the policing model to the "three Rs" – reforming, restructuring, and rebuilding (Greener, 2011). The role of the civilian police changed again following the 9/11 terrorist attacks in the United States and the subsequent invasions of Afghanistan and Iraq. A number of commentators argued that the main focus of both the Afghanistan and Iraq missions should have included "police-keeping" rather than peacekeeping during the stabilization and transition phases of the mission (Day & Freeman, 2003).

The changes in the role of civilian police mean that at a political level countries appear to be willing to deploy their police officers to peacekeeping missions that comprise more proactive roles "in the name of humanitarian aid, risk management, or the preservation of order" (Greener, 2009, p. 109). This implies that the civilian police undertake a larger role in responding to the security challenges that are presented as part of a mission. It is also their role to address the security gap in a mission (den Heyer, 2011; Greener, 2009).

The Issue of Police-Building

Following the use of the term police-keeping after the invasion of Afghanistan and Iraq and subsequent peacekeeping missions, another term for describing police-keeping was developed for the missions in the Pacific (Dinnen et al., 2008). The Pacific missions were called police-building, which was used to describe the 2003 regional police-led mission to the Solomon Islands [called the Regional Assistance Mission to the Solomon Islands (RAMSI)]. This mission was led by the Participating Police Force (PPF). The Participating Police Force was granted extensive executive powers and was given autonomy and immunity by the Solomon Islands government. This was granted to help establish law and order, purge the corrupt factions within the local police, and create a new police force (den Heyer, 2008, 2010; Greener, 2011).

RAMSI was described as a successful mission (den Heyer, 2008, 2010; Dinnen, 2007; Dinnen et al., 2006; Dinnen et al., 2008). The success of this mission, according to Glenn (2007) and Fullilove (2006), was attributed to the mission being led by the police and not the military. The military only played a minor role in stabilizing the Solomon Islands and resolving the conflict. This approach highlights the importance of establishing law and order, the rebuilding of the state, and the keeping of human rights. Critics, however, have claimed that the mission focused too much on restoring the police and should have included a Solomon Islands cultural aspect in the policing model used (den Heyer, 2008, 2010; Greener, 2011).

The Structure of This Book

Examining changes in policing in post-conflict or transitioning countries could measure whether any state consolidation has been reflected in these countries. There are many ways in which such empirical evidence of change in policing in post-conflict or transitioning countries can be observed. The most obvious is actual, sustained change in actions. Measuring a police officer's attitude and their expectations of their deployment and across the different stages of the democratic consolidation of the country may be one approach in gauging the success of a mission. Determining how police officers experienced a mission and how they facilitated the strategic objectives of a mission can lend evidence and context to policy deliberations on how to define, create, implement, and sustain styles of policing that, in turn, contribute to a country's new goals (Bayley, 1995, 2006).

This book will present three fairly distinct but overlapping strands. A discussion pertaining to the principal factors of police reform and development in post-conflict nations forms the basis of Chap. 2. The role of the New Zealand Police in peacekeeping and their deployment to Afghanistan, Bougainville, the Solomon Islands, and Timor-Leste is discussed and examined in Chap. 2. The New Zealand Police case studies are followed by case studies on the Canadian police experience in peacekeeping, the rule of law in Kosovo, and the challenges experienced in Haiti. The final chapters comprise a discussion on the acculturation of police in peacekeeping, the understanding of the stressor faced by police in peacekeeping, and a survey of the New Zealand Police members who have been deployed on peacekeeping missions. In the concluding section, the main themes of the case studies and the surveys are drawn together and thoroughly discussed.

Conclusion

The role of the police and their experiences while deployed on peacekeeping missions have changed from one of mainly monitoring elections to the complex task of reforming national and local police agencies. However, it should be noted that policing and police reform cannot be separated from other forms of mission assistance, such as economic, military stabilization, and those that relate to state institution building and political development. It is also important to note that the police are an important component of peacekeeping missions and should be treated as such by mission planners.

As discussed in this chapter, in spite of the number of completed peacekeeping missions and the tendency to include the police and the reformation of the security sector in reconstruction efforts, the role of the police within peacekeeping remains something of an under-researched area. It is hoped that this research and book will go some way in rectifying this deficiency.

References

Bajraktari, Y., Boutellis, A., Gunja, F., Harris, D., Kapsis, J., Kaye, E., & Rhee, J. (2006). *The PRIME system: Measuring the success of post-conflict police reform*. United Nations.

Bayley, D. (1995). A foreign policy for democratic policing. *Policing and Society, 5*, 79–94.

Bayley, D. (2006). *Changing the guard: Developing democratic police abroad*. Oxford University Press.

Botes, J., & Mitchell, C. (1995). *Constraints on third party flexibility*. The ANNALS of the American Academy of Political and Social Science. Sage Publications.

Capie, D. (2012). Peacekeeping - New Zealand's involvement in peacekeeping. *Te Ara: The Encyclopaedia of New Zealand*. Retrieved from http://www.TeAra.govt.nz/en/peacekeeping/.

Day, G. & Freeman, C. (2003). Policekeeping is the key: Rebuilding the internal security architecture of post-war Iraq. *International Affairs, 79*(2), pp.299–313.

den Heyer, G. (2008). Evaluating police reform in post conflict nations: A Solomon Islands case study. *International Journal of Comparative and Applied Criminal Justice, 34*(1), 213–234.

den Heyer, G. (2010). Measuring capacity development and reform in the Royal Solomon Islands Police Force. *Policing and Society, 20*(3), 298–315.

den Heyer, G. (2011). Filling the security gap: Military versus civilian police. *Police Practice and Research: An International Journal, 12*(6), 460–473.

den Heyer, G. (2012). *The role of civilian police in peacekeeping 1999–2007*. Police Foundation.

den Heyer, G. (2013). Police as nation builders: Distinguishing between countries that contribute police officers to United Nations peace operations. *International Journal of Peacekeeping, 17*(1–2), 74–115.

Dinnen, S. (2007). A comment on state-building in Solomon Islands. *The Journal of Pacific History, 42*(2), 255–263.

Dinnen, S., McLeod, A., & Peake, G. (2006). Police-building in weak states: Australian approaches in Papua New Guinea and Solomon Islands. *Civil Wars, 8*(2), 87–108.

Dinnen, S., McLeod, A., & Peake, G. (2008). Police-building in weak states: Australian approaches in Papua New Guinea and Solomon Islands. In G. Peake, E. Sheye, & A. Hills (Eds.), *Managing insecurity: Field experiences of security sector reform* (pp. 1–22). Routledge.

Fullilove, M. (2006). *The testament of Solomons: RAMSI and international state-building*. Lowy Institute for International Policy.
Glenn, R. (2007). Counterinsurgency in a test tube: Analysing the success of the Regional Assistance Mission to Solomon Islands (RAMSI). Rand Corporation.
Greener, B. (2009). *The new international policing*. Palgrave Macmillan Publishers Limited.
Greener, B. (2011). The rise of policing in peace operations. *International Peacekeeping, 18*(2), 183–195.
Griffiths, C., Dandurand, Y., & Chin, V. (2005). Development assistance and police reform: Programming opportunities and lessons learned. *Canadian Review of Policing Research*. Retrieved from http://crpr.icaap.org/index.php/crpr/article/view/32/40.
Hartz, H. (2000). CIVPOL: The UN instrument for police reform. In T. Holm & E. Eide (Eds.), *Peacebuilding and police reform* (pp. 27–42). Frank Cass.
Howard, L. M. (2008). *UN peacekeeping in civil wars*. Cambridge University Press.
International Peacekeeping Institute (2019). To serve and protect: The role of UN police in protecting civilians. Retrieved from: https://theglobalobservatory.org/2019/09/to-serve-and-protect-the-role-of-un-police-protecting-civilians/
Jones, T., & Newburn, T. (2005). Transformation of policing? Understanding current trends in policing systems. In T. Newburn (Ed.), *Policing: Key readings* (pp. 733–750). Willan.
Jones, S., Wilson, J., Rathmell, A., & Riley, J. (2005). *Establishing law and order after conflict*. RAND.
O'Connor, V. (2006). Rule of law and human rights protections through criminal law reform: Model codes for post-conflict criminal justice. *International Peacekeeping, 13*(4), 517–530.
Ratner, S. (1995). *The New UN peacekeeping: Building peace in lands of conflict after the cold war*. St. Martin's Press.
Scahill, J. (2007). *Blackwater: The rise of the world's most powerful mercenary army*. Serpent's Tail.
Schmidl, E. (1998). Police functions in peace operations: An historical overview. In R. Oakley, M. Dziedzic, & E. Goldberg (Eds.), *Policing the new world order: Peace operations and public security* (pp. 19–40). National Defense University Press.
Stone, C., & Ward, H. (2000). Democratic policing: A framework for action. *Policing and Society, 10*(1), 11–45.
United Nations. (1945). *UN Charter (full text)*. Retrieved from: https://www.un.org/en/sections/un-charter/un-charter-full-text/
United Nations Development Programme. (1997). *Capacity development: Technical advisory paper 2*. Management Development and Governance Division, United Nations.
United Nations Peacekeeping. (2021). *UN Police*. Retrieved from: https://peacekeeping.un.org/en/un-police#:~:text=Global%20contribution%20to%20peace%20and%20security&text=The%20number%20of%20UNPOL%20officers,increased%20demand%20for%20policing%20expertise.
Wiatrowski, M. & Pino, N. (2008). Policing and intermediate forces during democratic transitions. Unpublished manuscript. Texas State University–San Marcos.
Woodhouse, T., & Ramsbotham, O. (2005). Cosmopolitan peacekeeping and the globalization of security. *International Peacekeeping, 12*(2), 139–156.

Chapter 2
Police Reform and Development Within the Context of Peacekeeping Deployments

Garth den Heyer

Introduction

The United Nations undertook a number of successful peacekeeping missions prior to the early 1990s. However, the Somalia mission, which took place in September–October of 1993, led to the United Nations becoming dysfunctional (Howard, 2008) and inward looking. The United Nations then turned away from undertaking peacekeeping missions, and between 1995 and 1998, there were no new multidimensional peacekeeping missions except for the Eastern Slavonia operation that took place during 1996 and 1997 (Howard, 2008). By late 1999, as a result of the leadership and stewardship of the then United Nations Secretary General, Kofi Annan, four missions had begun in Kosovo, Sierra Leone, Congo, and East Timor (Howard, 2008). This was driven principally by the culmination of several peace processes coming to fruition at once.

A second wave of missions was established during 2003 and 2004, and these were driven by the convergence of three factors. The first was a change in policy by the United States toward supporting United Nations peacekeeping missions, the second was a change in opinion by the United Nations in relation to the augmented role of peacekeeping following a number of civil wars (Howard, 2008), and the third was the 9/11 terrorist attacks in the United States with the subsequent invasions in Afghanistan and Iraq.

Following the September 11, 2001, terrorist attacks in the United States, governments from all around the world had to adjust to the new realities of the war on terrorism (Howard, 2008). The adjustments were made because of al-Qaeda and their presence in Afghanistan and Somalia. The perpetrators of the 9/11 attacks, al-Qaeda, had been training fundamentalist terrorists in Afghanistan and Somalia. Afghanistan and Somalia had also been identified as failed states. Failed states and

G. den Heyer (✉)
School of Social and Behavioral Science, Walden University, Havelock North, New Zealand

G. den Heyer, J. F. Albrecht (eds.), *Police and International Peacekeeping Missions*, https://doi.org/10.1007/978-3-030-77900-9_2

civil war create a fertile ground for training terrorists. It was at this time that the United States realized that more effort must be made to stop states from failing, and in order to undertake this work, the United States would need allies to assist with rebuilding such states.

This chapter examines the reform and the development of police agencies as a component of peacekeeping missions in post-conflict countries. The first section provides a short history of the changes made in peacekeeping missions, and the second section discusses the approaches taken to reforming police organizations in post-conflict nations. The following section examines the weaknesses encountered in building transnational police organizations and in providing capacity development. The last section analyzes, in detail, the methods used to reform police organizations in post-conflict nations and the deployment of gendarmerie-type police to post-conflict nations.

A Short History of International Peacekeeping Endeavors

By the late 1980s and the end of the Cold War, a new form of peacekeeping had been implemented on a seemingly permanent basis to respond to changes in the international order (Ratner, 1995). Peacekeeping had been developed originally as a temporary option to maintain peace or to monitor a ceasefire between two hostile armies, but following the end of the Cold War, peacekeeping evolved into a method for implementing an agreed-upon political solution to the underlying reasons for a conflict and for implementing strategic, political, and social goals, such as the maintenance of civil order and domestic tranquility, and upholding human rights and economic and social development (Ratner, 1995).

The United Nations realized that there was a need for a more sustainable peacebuilding and state-building effort if peace and security were to be realized. The United Nations believed that by rebuilding a post-conflict state any potential threats that could arise from a security vacuum following the ceasing of hostilities would be removed (Greener, 2009).

The first post-Cold War United Nations peacekeeping mission was to Namibia in 1989. Prior to this mission, the police contingent of a peacekeeping mission usually comprised only a few police officers within a military-led mission. These police officers provided support and training to the local police (Greener, 2009). They also provided advice and monitored the election process. The mission to Namibia was the first mission where a police commissioner had led the police contingent rather than the police contingent reporting to a military commander. The Namibia mission was deemed to be a watershed in terms of who was to control a police contingent (Greener, 2009).

This approach was a positive development and formed the basis for determining how to assist with restructuring war-torn nations. Other than the successful Namibia mission, other missions unfortunately have not been viewed as being successful. Ratner (1995) claimed that other missions did not achieve anything other "than freezing conflicts in place" (p. 10). Ratner (1995) explained that the lack of success in these early missions was because the United Nations had limited the function of the missions to observing the peace rather than keeping the peace. Ratner (1995) also claimed that the presence of the United Nations in post-conflict nations may have even "prolonged the underlying conflict by removing any incentives to settle it" (p. 10).

Reforming Police Organizations in Post-Conflict Nations

When considering public sector or police reform, it is important to note that there are differences between developing or transitioning countries and developed countries. As Varenik (2003) noted, often the most dramatic governmental restructuring programs tend to occur in nations during independence, post conflict, or following a regime change, as happened, for example, after the collapse of the Soviet Union post 1989. While developing and transitional nations have a comprehensible wish to hasten reform, they have attempted to do this by implementing advanced managerial enhancements that have been designed by developed countries (Schick, 1998). Care needs to be taken when implementing these enhancements because they have been based on Western values and not on the values that are embraced by the post-conflict nation. If enhancements are to be adopted, then they need to be carefully adapted to local conditions and cultures (den Heyer, 2011b).

The reform of the police in developing, transitioning, or post-conflicting nations tends to be based on the desire to create a new, professional police (Varenik, 2003) force or service with formal independence from the military. The separation of the police from the military usually includes the promotion of democratic policing, that is, policing that seeks to complement democratic institutions rather than to undermine them (Ellison & Pino, 2012). The majority of police reform programs have been based on a Western model of policing. Such policing models draw on the principles of Community Policing and include upholding laws that protect basic rights and provide for a broader social order. This means that police officers are given autonomy and can act independently and are able to function in a less hierarchical atmosphere. At the organizational level, the police seek to instill problem and community-oriented policing, which are proactive and preventive programs. Adopting such programs is the first step toward creating a democratic police organization that can be held accountable for its actions. However, implementing these first steps is fraught with difficulty because of the fractured nature of institutions, the lack of political will, and because such reforms are often beyond a developing country's reach (Schick, 1998).

It was not until the publication and release of the Brahimi report in 2000 that the United Nations called on member states to "establish a national pool of civilian police officers that would be ready for deployment to UN peace operations on short notice" (quoted in Greener, 2009, p. 26). The report also called for a "doctrinal shift" in the deployment of police officers to post-conflict nations to reflect the need for missions to focus on strengthening human rights and the rule of law (Greener, 2009). The call for a shift came about because of the way in which the police operate within societies; they have the ability to shape societies in which they deliver their services (Greener, 2009). The shift highlighted the relevance of the fundamental role that the police play in international peacekeeping (Greener, 2009), which was originally to observe the local police. The police are now given executive policing powers and are expected to restructure a local police organization (United Nations, 2000).

The Brahimi report also noted that the reform of the police in a post-conflict nation could not be undertaken in isolation from reforming other justice sector agencies. The report stressed that there was little sense in reforming the local police in the absence of legal and constitutional reform as it was from these institutions that the police derive their powers and mandate. The report also concluded that the judicial system and the civil–military relationship needed to be factored into an overall police reform program (Ellison & Pino, 2012).

At about the same time that the Brahimi report was released, both the European Council and the European Commission increased their involvement in peacekeeping and international policing (Greener, 2009). The activities of the European Council were directed primarily toward the peace and security tasks assigned to it under the Second Pillar of the European Union's European Security and Defence Policy (ESDP) or Common Security and Foreign Policy (CSFP) (Greener, 2009). A number of police missions for the European Security and Defence Policy have taken place, such as those in Bosnia, Georgia, former Yugoslavian Republic of Macedonia (FRYOM), Kosovo, Afghanistan, Iraq, Palestinian territories, Congo, and in Aceh, Indonesia (Greener, 2009). None of these missions had executive policing components.

The challenge for the police in adopting and implementing organizational reform in developing or transitional nations is that the restructuring process should be extended to the entire justice sector, not just the police (Das, 2000; den Heyer, 2011b). The criminal justice sector is seamless, and reform cannot focus on one justice sector agency to the exclusion of all others (Bayley, 2006). The most critical element that must be considered when reforming the police in developing and transitioning countries is that of corruption (den Heyer, 2011b). If corruption is widespread and "there is no culture of accountability or transparency in public or private organizations, it is unlikely that there will be meaningful police reform" (Casey, 2009, p. 61). To address corruption, it is essential that a country has a noncorrupt and accountable police and criminal justice sector already in place (Casey, 2009).

The Weaknesses in Transnational Police Building and Capacity Development

Recognizing that police reform is the foundation for rebuilding a state has been the catalyst for identifying three problems. The first is, because police reform has been "given scale, priority and prominence," it has placed a burden on the capacity and capability of donor governments and agencies to respond adequately and appropriately (Goldsmith & Dinnen, 2007, p. 1106). The second problem is that the police have become drawn into the political environment, at both the national and international levels, "for which it is typically poorly prepared" (Goldsmith & Dinnen, 2007, p. 1106). The third problem is that local public support for deploying police to post-conflict nations can be fragile or nonexistent (Goldsmith & Dinnen, 2007).

As mentioned earlier, the number of peacekeeping and police reform missions increased during the late 1990s (Bayley, 2006; Goldsmith & Sheptycki, 2007; Jones et al., 2005; Marenin, 2005). This was despite a lack of understanding as to how such capacity-building and development activities should proceed (Goldsmith & Dinnen, 2007). While the literature that is available on international police reform discusses the importance of the local context and the political character of policing (e.g., see Bayley, 2006; den Heyer, 2010, 2012; Marenin, 2005), there are very few publications that include a detailed analysis of the specific settings in which the police reform should be undertaken (Goldsmith & Dinnen, 2007). This is notwithstanding the fact that since the mid-1980s peacekeeping missions have been needed because of "the collapse of local police authority and the ensuing disorder" (Fukuyama, 2006, p. 11). According to Hopp and Kloke-Lesch (2005) and Paris (2004), the implementation of police reform in post-conflict countries is still not well understood and therefore the appeal made in the Brahimi report for "the modern role of civilian police in peace-building .... to be better understood" (United Nations, 2000, p. 7) has still not been realized.

This has not been helped by the limited amount of engagement by scholars in the fields of transnational, comparative and developmental policing (Goldsmith & Sheptycki, 2007; Ellison, 2007). Some authors claim that lessons have been learned from police reform missions (Bayley, 2006; Marenin, 2005; Mobekk, 2005) and have provided a basis for the further development of policing in post-conflict nations. Regardless, a more detailed analysis of how police reform should be instituted in post-conflict countries is needed.

The literature that is available has acknowledged the informal relationship of politicians and senior police officers in many non-Western societies and how these informal relationships affect the goals, tasks, and achievements of any intended police reform. While these problems create weaknesses or fragility from a state-centric governance perspective (Chandler, 2006), the elimination of such relationships as part of an intended police reform can seem intimidating or insulting to local politicians and police officers (Goldsmith & Dinnen, 2007).

Another weakness relates to the concerns that Western politicians have with failed or failing states (Chesterman et al., 2005). Donor countries are often apprehensive about the state's political and economic viability (Goldsmith & Dinnen, 2007) and stability. State building has now become, according to Goldsmith and Dinnen (2007), more about donor nations responding to internal security fears than about transnational crime and terrorism. The flow on effect of this perspective is that the development of a post-conflict nation has become more focused on security (Duffield, 2001; Chandler, 2006) and has become a balancing act between maintaining political stability and implementing police reform. Maintaining political neutrality is challenging owing to the character of the politics in the post-conflict country and the dominant role of the police in the donor country (Goldsmith & Dinnen, 2007).

Police reform in post-conflict nations shares similar weaknesses with other aspects of nation-building in post-conflict states (Goldsmith & Dinnen, 2007). The most prominent being a lack of a historical and cultural knowledge as well as a lack of understanding of reform in post-conflict settings (Dodge, 2003). Another is the complexity of the task. Peacekeeping and police reform in post-conflict nations are new roles for the police and challenge the traditional notion of policing. It raises questions as to the suitability of Western ideals of policing, such as the separation of powers and impartial policing (Goldsmith & Dinnen, 2007) and whether the model is suitable for post-conflict nations.

There are five factors that must be included in an implementation plan if a reform is to be successful. These are as follows:

1. Learning about the post-conflict nation in detail. A comprehensive threat assessment should be undertaken before engagement with the country involved. Consultation with local groups and those with expertise in the area should be included in any briefings.
2. Presenting a degree of reflexivity and humility about the objectives behind the intended police reform and how these might be perceived and responded to locally.
3. Adopting a practice that is flexible and adaptive to local circumstances and develop appropriate implementation procedures and measures that include deferring to local knowledge and methods.
4. Instituting a type of organizational reform that is not limited to the short-term technical aspects of police service delivery and encompasses a broader set of political and community elements.
5. Establishing and implementing oversight and auditing mechanisms that are supported by a performance measurement framework (adapted from Goldsmith & Dinnen, 2007, pp. 1106–1107).

The Limitations in the Current Method of Providing Assistance to Post-Conflict Nations

The main limitation in the current method of providing assistance to post-conflict nations is that donor countries primarily export what Western nations view as a universal policing standard (Ellison & Pino, 2012). This standard of policing seeks to instill Western social and moral values on the post-conflict nation, and these values are often not applicable to most of these nations. These standards are usually intertwined with promoting the donor country's own foreign policy objectives (Hills, 2009).

Another limitation is that often the result of a police reform program does not match the reform objectives that were predetermined at the initial deployment of international police officers. According to Hills (2009), the gap between what is achieved and what was meant to be achieved results from not including the political, historical, and cultural dynamics when preparing for or during the implementation of a reform program.

Given these limitations, a number of researchers have developed a number of ideas for a participatory governance of reform policing programs. Methods that traverse the difficulties in top-down, state-centered development programs have been proposed (Cain, 2000; Davis & Trebilcock, 2001; den Heyer, 2012; Ghani & Lockhart, 2008; Kaldor 2007; McEvoy & McGregor, 2008; Pino & Wiatrowski, 2006; Rose, 1998; Shearing, 2001). These ideas seek to develop bottom-up strategies to strengthen the society of a post-conflict nation and use local solutions for "local problems by drawing on indigenous knowledge and civil society strengths while accounting for the diversity of the country or region" involved (Ellison & Pino, 2012, pp. 31–32). The ideas that researchers have developed are as follows:

1. Establish a more effective governance structure by incorporating and working within neoliberal globalized approaches and Western foreign policy objectives, primarily through top-down strategies.
2. Strengthen the capacity of the donor state to provide security and reduce the role of private providers .
3. Develop a global transnational ethic for the provision of security.
4. Establish bottom-up strategies for the security sector and other reforms that strengthen the capacity of the post-conflict nation's civil society (adapted from Ellison & Pino, 2012, p. 28).

Post-Conflict Police Reform

Little theory has been developed as to what the police role is in a post-conflict nation and even less on how to implement a reform (Pino & Wiatrowski, 2006). As a result, there is little evidence that police reform and capacity development have resulted in sustainable outcomes (Griffiths et al., 2005). This is because effective reforms are difficult to implement and institutions take time to develop to a level where they are confident in the delivery of their services. Furthermore, police reform programs that were designed to improve capacity or service effectiveness have not produced any measurable outcomes. The usual way to measure the success of a reform program is to examine how the police conduct routine policing activities (Jackson & Lyon, 2002) and it is not from the application of a performance measurement framework.

Measuring the process and the impact that police reform initiatives have had complicates the reform of the police. Usually government donors and interested parties rely on a mixture of anecdotal and ad hoc reports to measure the progress made. However, this form of reporting does not provide a systematic analysis of the police service as a whole and does not fully convey any outcomes achieved.

It is important that the reform of the police in a post-conflict nation is not undertaken in isolation from other justice sector and economic and political reforms that seek to alleviate socioeconomic inequalities and enhance the position of women, minorities, and young people (Ellison & Pino, 2012). The way that post-conflict development is currently conceptualized and promoted by Western states is often in conflict with the democratic goals of post-conflict nations. Furthermore, the way that assistance is conceptualized by Western nations can lead to structural conditions of inequality and create problems for introducing democratic policing (den Heyer, 2012).

The process of reforming the police in a post-conflict nation should begin with an appreciation of the effect that a positive change to a police force will have on the public's perception of security (Peake, 2004). Five other factors should also be considered:

1. The police are the most visible and immediately present representative of government and the state security system.
2. The performance of the police is crucial to the performance and credibility of the criminal justice sector.
3. The archaic practices, poor human rights records, outdated methods, and aggressive practices of the police add to the public's perception of the police being corrupt and self-serving.
4. The police are often used to control civil disorder at the discretion of the political elite.
5. The police are in a unique position of being able to provide a foundation for the stability, security, and confidence in the state (adapted from Peake, 2004; Griffiths et al., 2005).

The complexity of post-conflict police reform led Jean Francois Bayart (1993) to create the term "Rhizome state" to describe patrimonial state structures in Africa, in that such states are similar to a tangled underground root system, which has "no central axis, no unified point of origin, and no given direction or growth" (quoted in Grosz, 1994, p. 199). Goldsmith (2002) noted that such an entity has little in common with the "Weberian ideal state with its impartial, merit-based bureaucracy, commitment to the Rule of Law and monopoly of legitimate violence" (p. 15). These observations mean that planners of police reform programs need to understand how complex the task can be and that any reform program developed must be appropriate for the situation. If the model of reform is inappropriate for the police organization in a post-conflict nation, then there will be implications when implementing police reform (Ellison & Pino, 2012). An inappropriate model will also have implications for the structure of the police organization that is to be reformed. An effective model would include the aim and intended outcomes of the reform and the techniques and technologies that will be adopted to achieve the outcome (Ellison & Pino, 2012).

The Approach Taken to Reform Police

Given the obstacles to reforming the police in post-conflict nations, program planners and decision-makers must consider several factors that influence the success of an intervention (Jackson & Lyon, 2002). The main factor that should be considered is the choice of policing model that will be used for reforming the police of a post-conflict nation. As discussed previously in this chapter, Community Policing is the reform model of choice of Western donor nations. According to Ellison and Pino (2012), the use of Community Policing as a basis for a reform model "has little relevance to the vagaries of transitional and post-conflict states" (p. 80). Furthermore, a number of researchers would argue that there is little evidence that Community Policing works in Western democracies (Brogden, 2002, 2005; Brogden & Nijkar, 2005; Pino & Wiatrowski, 2006; Hinton & Newburn, 2009). Implementing a democratic form of policing can also be difficult in post-conflict environments and some would argue logically impossible (see, for instance, Manning, 2010) if the social, legal, and political institutions are not supportive of democratic rights and ideals (Ellison & Pino, 2012).

There is no single model of police reform that can be transferred from Western nations to post-conflict nations, and there is no guarantee that what works in the policing of Western nations will work in the policing of post-conflict nations. The inability to transfer policing models occurs because reforming a nation's police is a highly dependent process. The reform needs to be based on a constitutional and political framework and on an established functioning economic system (Ellison & Pino, 2012).

The operating environment and weaknesses in the institutions of a post-conflict nation mean that the best that can be expected of any police reform is that the community of the post-conflict nation feels an increased sense of security. The reform of the police, however, may not be able to establish the type of security that exists in a Western nation. The reform cannot be undertaken without considering the reform of other state institutions (Loader & Walker, 2001), and without an assessment of what developmental processes of societies in post-conflict nations comprise and what the processes are expected to achieve. Community Policing has been used as a model for police reform because our understanding of the police developmental process is limited (Ellison & Pino, 2012). According to Ellison and Pino (2012), the use of the concept of Community Policing in the reform process follows "the line of least resistance and create[s] the illusion of doing something but leaving the larger structural problems largely unacknowledged" (p. 80).

The Problems in Implementing Police Reform

A number of problems may be encountered when implementing an effective police reform program in a post-conflict nation. Difficulties may be encountered because the implementation of such a program requires the input of various institutions and the planning of the reform concept needs to be based on an analysis and understanding of the complexity of organizational relationships (Call, 2003).

The first problem is the need for a method to identify a reform model that balances the reform of the local police with maintaining security. The second problem is that police reform is not understood in the context of globalization and the dependency of the post-conflict state. The problem is exacerbated by the uneven implementation of development projects, the underdevelopment of nations, and the history of colonization (Ellison & Pino, 2012). The third problem is that policing in post-colonial states tends to emulate the structures and style of policing that has been introduced by former colonial powers. There is usually a legacy of paramilitarism and police institutions that are characterized by a centralized and "bureaucratic system that [is] inefficient, undisciplined, lacking in appropriate equipment and filled with line officers that [are] under-paid and dissatisfied with their jobs" (Hills, 2000, p.7).

The problem with using a colonial style of policing in a post-conflict nation is that its failings become intensified once independence has been established. After independence has been gained, the police in a post-conflict nation will have adapted to the change, not by adopting Western policing values but by adjusting to political events and accommodating politicians or administrations. This means that after a nation has gained independence there may be no significant change in the delivery of policing (Hills, 2000). This is intensified by the fact that post-conflict nations do not usually establish democratic state institutions or create legal frameworks that support the reform of the police (Ellison & Pino, 2012).

The fourth problem is that the control over the police is usually "personalistic" (Hinton & Newburn, 2009), which means that the police are under the control or influence of a powerful person either a relational or tribally related politician rather than being held to institutional forms of accountability (Hinton & Newburn, 2009).

The fifth problem stems from the fact that the structures of the majority of police forces in post-conflict countries are centralized. Centralized police forces, according to Hinton and Newburn (2009), are often less able to respond to and manage local problems. These types of structures make it difficult to ensure that the local police are held accountable and that their performance can be monitored. This is owing to the lack of availability of good quality statistical data and inadequate resourcing.

The sixth problem is that there is a large variation in what is deemed to be a successful reform of the police in a post-conflict country. It is difficult to identify the strategies and initiatives that work in a successful police reform because what may have been successful in one country may not be successful in another. The difference in the outcome of a reform can be caused by a number of social, cultural, or structural factors, which include extremes in wealth and poverty, the historical relationship of the police with the community, civil society, the presence of ethnic or racial problems, and the financing of the reform (Ellison & Pino, 2012).

The final problem to be discussed is that there is no accepted definition of the term "police reform." Practitioners, policymakers, and academics have sought to define the term "police reform," but there is no single, widely shared understanding of the concept (Call, 2003). The lack of definition means that policymakers and practitioners have difficulty in designing, developing, and implementing police reform strategies.

The Use of the Gendarmerie in Post-Conflict Nations

When assisting a nation in its post-conflict reconstruction, the period between the cessation of hostilities and establishing a stable environment is important (Dziedzic & Stark, 2009; Wiatrowski & Pino, 2008). After the fighting has ceased and immediately after a mission has been deployed, there is a window of opportunity for establishing a sense of security (Blume, 2008; Stromseth et al., 2006). Security must be established in order for the reconstruction of political and economic systems to take place. The window of opportunity is known as the security gap. The security gap is important as establishing and maintaining a stable environment is the foundation for "sustainable development, democracy, peace and security" (Hanggi & Scherrer, 2008, p. 486) and the failure to fill the security gap can impact negatively on state building, establishing law and order and deterring organized crime, terrorism, and insurgency.

One approach that can be taken to fill the security gap is to deploy gendarmerie-type police units or formed police units. Gendarmerie-type police units or formed police units can be used for providing security as they have been trained and equipped to respond to serious internal disturbances and violent civil disorder (Lutterbeck, 2004; den Heyer, 2011a). Such units are not, however, involved in the process of reforming the police. Gendarmerie units may be involved in the initial stages of a deployment by providing training to the local police in how to respond to civil disorder and riots and in the use of firearms. They are also able to provide border control and are a mobilized response to the challenges that are involved in upholding security (Lutterbeck, 2004).

It is unclear as to whether the deployment of gendarmerie types of police forces to post-conflict situations is effective (den Heyer, 2011a). The crises in the Solomon

Islands, Timor-Leste, and Bougainville (Papua New Guinea) in the late 1990s have shown that the use of gendarmerie police forces to solve law and order problems leads to confusion in the community, mistrust of the police and the national government, and destabilizes the situation further. The reason for this is because the operations of the gendarmerie tend to undermine Community Policing efforts as they are perceived to be more aligned to the military rather than to the police.

While the gendarmerie types of forces have some policing skills and have been trained to use less-then-lethal force, their history indicates that they are military units rather than civilian police. Both the Italian Carabinieri and the French National Gendarmerie were formed as military war units and have fought in several wars over their respective 200-year histories. Although these forces may be better at de-escalating violence than at peacekeeping, "they are also prone to using more heavy tactics than civilian police forces, as shown in East Timor" (Friesendorf & Penksa, 2008, p. 691).

While the deployment of gendarmerie- or paramilitary-type police forces will fill a security gap, their utilization can be seen as an anomaly (Bayley, 1985; Bigo, 2000; den Heyer, 2011a). Their presence represents a military or quasi-military perspective to security, and as a result of their militarized actions, they are also often associated with authoritarian or repressive tendencies and can be a threat to civil liberties (Lutterbeck, 2004). The use of gendarmerie in peacekeeping missions, however, has increased since the late 1990s, primarily because they possess a combination of both policing and militaristic characteristics.

Conclusion

The reform of the police in post-conflict nations involves a number of inherent challenges. These challenges can come from the identifying and sourcing the needed number of international police with the appropriate skills to assist with the reform of the police to being able to develop an appropriate policing model for the nation involved. Other challenges emerge from the post-conflict state seeking to reform or establish a more democratic police service.

References

Bayart, J. (1993). *The state in Africa: The politics of the belly*. Polity.

Bayley, D. (1985). *Patterns of policing: A comparative international analysis*. Rutgers University Press.

Bayley, D. (2006). *Changing the guard: Developing democratic police abroad*. Oxford University Press.

Bigo, D. (2000). When two become one: Internal and external securitisations in Europe. In M. Kelstrup & M. Williams (Eds.), *International relations theory and the politics of European integration, power, security and community* (pp. 171–205). Routledge.

Blume, T. (2008). Security, justice and the rule of law in peace operations. *International Peacekeeping, 15*(5), 713–721.

Brogden, M. (2002). Implanting community policing in South Africa: A failure of history. Of context and of theory. *Liverpool Law Review, 24*, 157–218.
Brogden, M. (2005). Horses for courses and thin blue lines: Community policing in transitional society. *Police Quarterly, 8*(1), 64–98.
Brogden, M., & Nijkar, P. (2005). *Community policing: National and international models and approaches*. Willan Publishing.
Cain, M. (2000). Orientalism, occidentalism and sociology of crime. *British Journal of Criminology, 40*, 239–260.
Call, C. (2003). *Challenges in police reform: Promoting effectiveness and accountability*. Retrieved from: https://www.ipinst.org/wp-content/uploads/publications/challenges_in_police.pdf.
Casey, J. (2009). *Policing the world: Theory and practice of international policing*. Carolina Academic Press.
Chandler, D. (2006). *Empire in denial: The politics of state-building*. Pluto Press.
Chesterman, S., Ignatieff, M., & Thakur, R. (Eds.). (2005). *Making states work: State failure and the crisis of governance*. United Nations University Press.
Das, D. (2000). Challenges of policing democracies: A world perspective. In D. Das & O. Marenin (Eds.), *Challenges of policing democracies: A world perspective* (pp. 3–22). Gordon and Breach Publishers.
Davis, K., & Trebilcock, M. (2001). Legal reforms and development. *Third World Quarterly, 22*(1), 21–36.
den Heyer, G. (2010). Measuring capacity development and reform in the Royal Solomon Islands Police Force. *Policing and Society, 20*(3), 298–315.
den Heyer, G. (2011a). Filling the security gap: Military versus civilian police. *Police Practice and Research: An International Journal, 12*(6), 460–473.
den Heyer, G. (2011b). New public management: A strategy for democratic police reform in transitioning and developing countries. *Policing: An International Journal of Police Strategies and Management, 34*(3), 419–433.
den Heyer, G. (2012). *The role of civilian police in peacekeeping 1999–2007*. Police Foundation.
Dodge, T. (2003). *Inventing Iraq: The failure of nation building and a history denied*. Columbia University Press.
Duffield, M. (2001). *Global governance and the new wars: The merging of development and security*. Zed Books.
Dziedzic, M., & Stark, C. (2009) *Bridging the public security gap*. Retrieved from www.usip.org.
Ellison, G. (2007). Fostering a dependency culture: The commodification of community policing in a global marketplace. In A. Goldsmith & J. Sheptycki (Eds.), *Crafting transnational policing: Police capacity-building and global police reform* (pp. 203–242). Hart Publishing.
Ellison, G., & Pino, N. (2012). *Globalization, police reform and development: Doing it the western way?* Palgrave Macmillan.
Friesendorf, C., & Penksa, S. (2008). Militarised law enforcement in peace operations: EUFOR in Bosnia and Herzegovina. *International Peacekeeping, 15*(5), 677–694.
Fukuyama, F. (Ed.). (2006). *Nation-building: Beyond Afghanistan and Iraq*. Johns Hopkins University Press.
Ghani, A., & Lockhart, C. (2008). *Fixing failed states: A framework for rebuilding a fractured world*. Oxford University Press.
Goldsmith, A. (2002). Policing weak states: Citizen safety and state responsibility. *Policing and Society, 13*(1), 3–21.
Goldsmith, A., & Dinnen, S. (2007). Transnational police building: Critical lessons from Timor-Leste and Solomon Islands. *Third World Quarterly, 28*(6), 1091–1109.
Goldsmith, A., & Sheptycki, J. (Eds.). (2007). *Crafting global policing: Police capacity-building and global police reform*. Hart Publishing.
Greener, B. (2009). *The new international policing*. Palgrave Macmillan Publishers Limited.
Griffiths, C., Dandurand, Y., & Chin, V. (2005). Development assistance and police reform: Programming opportunities and lessons learned. *Canadian Review of Policing Research*. Retrieved from http://crpr.icaap.org/index.php/crpr/article/view/32/40.

Grosz, E. (1994). A thousand tiny sexes: Feminism and rhizomatics. In C. Boundas & D. Olkowski (Eds.), *Gilles Deleuze and the theatre of philosophy* (pp. 182–211). Routledge.
Hanggi, H., & Scherrer, V. (2008). Towards an integrated security sector reform approach in UN peace operations. *International Peacekeeping, 15*(4), 486–500.
Hills, A. (2000). *Policing Africa: Internal security and the limits of liberalisation*. Lynne Rienner.
Hills, A. (2009). The possibility of transnational policing. *Policing and Society, 19*(3), 300–317.
Hinton, M., & Newburn, T. (Eds.). (2009). *Policing developing democracies*. Routledge Publishing.
Hopp, U., & Kloke-Lesch, A. (2005). External nation-building vs endogenous nation-forming – A development policy perspective. In J. Hippler (Ed.), *Nation-building: A key concept for peaceful conflict transformation* (pp. 137–150). Pluto Press.
Howard, L. M. (2008). *UN peacekeeping in civil wars*. University Press.
Jackson, A., & Lyon, A. (2002). Policing after ethnic conflict: Culture, democratic policing, politics and the public. *Policing: An International Journal of Police Strategies and Management, 25*(2), 221–241.
Jones, S., Wilson, J., Rathmell, A., & Riley, J. (2005). *Establishing law and order after conflict*. RAND.
Kaldor, M. (2007). Human security: Reflections on globalization and intervention. Polity Press.
Loader, I., & Walker, N. (2001). Policing as public good: Reconstituting the connections between policing and the state. *Theoretical Criminology, 1*(5), 9–35.
Lutterbeck, D. (2004). Between police and military: The new security agenda and the rise of Gendarmeries. *Cooperation and Conflict: Journal of the Nordic International Studies Association, 39*(1), 45–68.
Manning, P. (2010). *Democratic policing in a changing world*. Paradigm.
Marenin, O. (2005). *Restoring policing systems in conflict torn nations: Process, problems, prospects*. Occasional Paper no 7. Geneva Centre for the Democratic Control of Armed Forces.
McEvoy, K., & McGregor, L. (2008). *Transitional justice from below: Grassroots activism and the struggle for change*. Hart Publishing.
Mobekk, E., (2005). Transitional justice in post-conflict societies - Approaches to reconciliation. In A. Ebnother & P. Fluri (Eds.), After Intevention: Public Security Management in Post-Conflict Societies - From Intervention to Sustainable Local Ownership. Geneva Centre for the Democratic Control of Armed Forces (DCAF), Geneva.
Paris, R. (2004). *At war's end: Building peace after civil conflict*. Cambridge University Press.
Peake, G. (2004). *Police reform*. Presented at the Security Network Symposium, Global Facilitation Network for Security Reform, Kingston, Jamaica, April 20–21.
Pino, N., & Wiatrowski, M. (2006). *Democratic policing in transitional developing countries*. Ashgate Publishing Limited.
Ratner, S. (1995). *The New UN peacekeeping: Building peace in lands of conflict after the cold war*. St. Martin's Press.
Rose, C. (1998). The 'new' law and development movement in the post-cold war era: A Vietnam case study. *Law and Society Review, 32*(1), 93–140.
Schick, A. (1998). Why most developing countries should not try New Zealand's reforms. *The World Bank Observer, 13*(1), 123–131.
Shearing, C. (2001). A nodal conception of governance: Thoughts on a policing commission. *Policing and Society, 11*(3–4), 259–272.
Stromseth, J., Wippman, D., & Brooks, R. (2006). *Can might make rights? Building the rule of law after military interventions*. Cambridge University Press.
United Nations. (2000). *Report of the panel on United Nations peace operations*. A/55/305, S/2000/809. United Nations.
Varenik, R. (2003). *Exploring roads to police reform: six recommendations*. Project on reforming the administration of justice in Mexico Centre for US-Mexican Studies, USMEX 2003–2004 Working Paper Series, La Jolla, California.
Wiatrowski, M. & Pino, N. (2008). *Policing and intermediate forces during democratic transitions*. Unpublished manuscript. Texas State University–San Marcos.

Part II
The New Zealand Police Role in Post-conflict Peacekeeping Missions

Chapter 3
The Role of the New Zealand Police in International Peacekeeping and in Providing Post-Conflict Assistance

Garth den Heyer

Introduction

New Zealand has a long history of involvement in peacekeeping activities. As a small nation, New Zealand has a strong interest in a rules-based international order and peaceful resolutions to disputes. This can be demonstrated by the fact that the country was a founding member of the United Nations in 1945 (Capie, 2012).

According to Capie (2012), New Zealand has been continuously involved in United Nations peacekeeping activities since the 1950s. The New Zealand Government, however, prefers the broader term of "peace-support operations" to describe the form of mission that they support and commit resources to. These missions usually include United Nations peacekeeping missions, but also peace enforcement and other forms of military deployments that are based on alliances and other political or bilateral ties (Capie, 2012). While peacekeeping is usually seen as a military activity, civilian police have been involved in post-conflict situations, with New Zealand Police personnel being deployed to Cyprus (1964–1967), Namibia (1989–1990), East Timor (1999–2015), Bougainville (since 2000), the Solomon Islands (2003–2015), Afghanistan (2005–2012), and Tonga (since 2006).

During the period 1964–2018, the New Zealand Police supported nine peacekeeping missions in seven different countries. These countries and the missions are presented in Table 3.1.

Since 1964, the New Zealand Police have sent more than 1000 police officers and civilian staff to peacekeeping missions in Europe, Africa, Afghanistan, and the Asia-Pacific (New Zealand Police, 2018a). They have been sent to assist in a humanitarian response by the New Zealand Government or in response to a United Nations request. The character of each mission has been different, and each mission has demanded that the New Zealand Police undertake a variety of roles, ranging

G. den Heyer (✉)
School of Social and Behavioral Science, Walden University, Havelock North, New Zealand

G. den Heyer, J. F. Albrecht (eds.), *Police and International Peacekeeping Missions*, https://doi.org/10.1007/978-3-030-77900-9_3

Table 3.1 New Zealand Police mission countries and years deployed

Mission country	Mission year
Afghanistan	2005–2012
Bougainville	1998–2001/2002 to present
Cyprus	1964–1967
Namibia	1989–1990
Solomon Islands – International Peace Monitoring Team (IPMT)	2000–2001
Solomon Islands – Policing Project	November 2002 to July 2003
Solomon Islands – Regional Assistance Mission (RAMSI)	2003–2017
Timor-Leste	1999–2001/2002–2015
Tonga	2006 to present

from responding to a disaster and providing investigation assistance to the mentoring and capacity building of local police officers.

The staff deployed from the New Zealand Police to the various missions have contributed to restoring stability in conflict and post-conflict affected situations. The demonstration of community-based approaches to policing has borne results in highly challenging and often unstable and changing environments, usually in complex multidonor environments (Law & Development Partnership, 2013). Assistance that has been provided by the New Zealand Police is generally unilateral, which involves the provision of assistance from one police service to another. This entailed officers to perform the following:

- Establishing close, professional relationships with partner country police forces
- Adopting flexible and pragmatic approaches to problems
- Proactively demonstrating how to engage with communities (e.g., through youth or sports clubs, and women's groups)
- Adopting culturally sensitive approaches
- Demonstrating an outgoing "user-friendly" style to local police forces more attuned to paramilitary policing approaches (Law & Development Partnership, 2013, p. 2)

The largest number of New Zealand Police deployments to post-conflict missions took place during the period 2000–2012, with approximately 150 personnel deployed on peacekeeping missions to Afghanistan, Timor-Leste, and a number of Pacific Island countries. The number of deployments increased over this period for a number of reasons, but primarily because (i) of the changes in the security environment following the 9/11 terrorist attacks; (ii) an increase in the understanding of the role that security and justice plays in the stabilization and development of post-conflict nations and fragile states by the international development community; (iii) New Zealand's desire to be a good global and regional citizen and to work in solidarity with Australia and in line with its commitment to the Pacific Forum (Solomon Islands), the United Nations (Timor-Leste), and the international community (Afghanistan); and (iv) the increase in concern about New Zealand's security in the wake of 9/11, the Bali bombings, and the instability in the Pacific region.

This chapter discusses the approach that has been taken by New Zealand to international peacekeeping and the role that the New Zealand Police performed. Two main problems that the New Zealand Police encountered when deploying personnel on international missions will be examined, and the first two missions undertaken by New Zealand Police officers – Cyprus (1964–1967) and Namibia (1989–1990) – will be presented, which will provide the context for the Afghanistan, Bougainville, Solomon Island, and Timor-Leste case studies.

Background

The New Zealand Police is a part of a whole-of-government approach to contributing to international security and development, where all of the government departments and services work collaboratively toward securing an international environment in support of New Zealand's security interests. The New Zealand Government has outlined a number of broad strategic national security outcomes that they wish to achieve and to which the New Zealand Police contributes the following:

1. a secure New Zealand including its people, land, territorial waters, exclusive economic zone, natural resources, and critical infrastructure
2. a strong strategic relationship with Australia in support of common interests for a secure and peaceful region
3. a political environment in the South and West Pacific in which national economies, societies, and identities continue to evolve in a climate of good governance and internationally agreed standards of compliance with human rights
4. an expanding role in the regional dialogue of South East and North East Asia and, where appropriate, a role in regional security consistent with New Zealand's interests and capabilities
5. a global approach that supports New Zealand's position in an international community committed to the maintenance of human rights and the collective security responsibilities enshrined in the United Nations Charter and that strengthens New Zealand's international economic linkages (New Zealand Police, 2009c)

The *Pacific Plan,*[1] *Pacific Security Strategy,*[2] and the strategies outlined in the Official Development Assistance (ODA) document by New Zealand Aid (NZAID) provide guidance for the New Zealand Police in undertaking international aid and development. The overarching goal of the Pacific Plan is to "enhance and stimulate economic growth, sustainable development, good governance and security for

[1]The Pacific Plan, endorsed by Leaders (including New Zealand) at the Pacific Islands Forum meeting in October 2005, forms the basis of the ongoing strengthening of regional cooperation and integration for the benefit of the people of the Pacific to achieve the Leaders' Pacific Vision.

[2]There are four strategic objectives to the Pacific Plan: economic growth, sustainable development, good governance, and security.

Pacific countries through regionalism." There are two objectives that the New Zealand Police are required to achieve as part of the Pacific Plan:

- Improved transparency, accountability, equity, and efficiency in the management and use of resources in the Pacific
- Improved political and social conditions for stability and safety (New Zealand Police, 2009c)

In parallel, the New Zealand Police supports New Zealand's national security and developmental interests by delivering services to achieve the following five objectives:

1. Maintaining a secure New Zealand through Safer Communities Together
2. Maintaining a close relationship with Australian and Pacific police authorities in pursuit of common law enforcement and security interests
3. Supporting New Zealand's foreign policy objectives in the Pacific and beyond and through providing assistance
4. Collaborating with other countries' police services in order to assist law enforcement in New Zealand and to contribute to the maintenance of security in the Asia-Pacific region
5. Contributing to global law enforcement, counter-terrorism, and security through participation in peace support and peacekeeping operations at the direction of the New Zealand Government (New Zealand Police, 2009c)

To implement these objectives, the New Zealand Police has four international roles (adapted from New Zealand Police, 2009c):

Role 1: Furthering New Zealand's Law Enforcement Interests Internationally.

To accomplish this role, the New Zealand Police undertakes activities such as the exchange of police intelligence, supporting New Zealand Police investigations, and collaboration with other countries' police services in order to detect, prevent, and investigate transnational crime and terrorist-related activities. Examples of this are the New Zealand Police overseas liaison posts, working with the Indonesian Policing on countering terrorism, the secondment of a New Zealand Police Officer to the Honolulu-based Joint Interagency Task Force, and the deliberate development of relationships with other countries' law enforcement agencies to facilitate information sharing and cooperation.

Role 2: Supporting the Government's Foreign Policy in the Pacific and Beyond Through Police Activities.

To support this role, the New Zealand Police seconds senior staff members to police services and delivers capacity-building programs such as the Pacific Prevention of Domestic Violence Program and the Pacific Police Dog Programmes. These activities support the New Zealand Government's foreign policy objectives in the Pacific region and beyond by capacity building and cooperative law enforcement initiatives.

Role 3: Contributing to Global Peace Support Operations.

The third role is to contribute police personnel at the direction of the government to peace support and peacekeeping operations. Examples are New Zealand Police contributions to Bougainville, the Solomon Islands, Afghanistan, Timor-Leste, and Tonga.

Role 4: Contributing to Disaster and Emergency Response and Other Tasks as Required.

This role includes short-term deployment activities such as security liaison roles for major events (e.g., annual celebrations in Gallipoli, Turkey, and the Olympics Games) and crisis response activities such as disaster relief operations such as the extreme weather incidents in the South Pacific or in Asia.

The New Zealand Approach to International Peacekeeping

This section discusses the New Zealand approach to peacekeeping. The first section outlines how New Zealand decides on whether to contribute staff and resources to an international peacekeeping mission. The second section examines the rationales that New Zealand considers during the decision-making process of whether to deploy staff and resources. The third section discusses the barriers for New Zealand when contributing staff and resources, and the fourth section highlights the current challenges for New Zealand when contributing staff and resources to international peacekeeping missions.

New Zealand's Decision-Making Process

The ultimate decision-making authority as to whether the New Zealand Government will deploy staff and resources sits with the prime minister after the decision has been approved by the Cabinet. This process was established and approved by the Cabinet on 19 November2011, in recognition of the complex nature of multiagent, international peace operations (New Zealand Police, 2009c). The approval process now includes a more systematic whole-of-government approach to engaging in peace support operations. The coordination of the approval process and the strategic management of the deployment and staff is provided through the Officials Committee for Defence and External Security Coordination (Governance),[3] who is tasked with providing cross-ministerial strategic policy advice on security and intelligence matters (Department of the Prime Minster and Cabinet, 2016; Greener, 2018).

In response to the initial deployments of staff and resources to the Solomon Islands, Timor-Leste, and Afghanistan in the early 2000s, the New Zealand

[3] ODESC(G) is chaired by the chief executive of the Department of the Prime Minister and Cabinet. Membership includes the Department of the Prime Minister and Cabinet, State Services Commission, Treasury, Ministry of Foreign Affairs and Trade, New Zealand Defence Force, Ministry of Health, Ministry of Defence, Ministry for Primary Industries, New Zealand Police, and Crown Law (Department of the Prime Minister and Cabinet, 2016).

Government developed four criteria on which to base decisions about future deployments to peace operations:

1. Strategic implications of the operation, including its effect on security, the humanitarian situation, and New Zealand's relationships with other countries
2. The nature of the mission – the legality of the proposed mission and the proposed mandate under international law
3. Repercussions for New Zealand agencies involved in the proposed peace support operation
4. Whether New Zealand can assist the fragile or post-conflict state in other ways (New Zealand Police, 2009c; Capie, 2012)

The four decision criteria are also applied to any United Nations requests that the New Zealand Government may receive. In considering requests from the United Nations for contributions where New Zealand has the capability to respond, an interdepartmental process is initiated, and this entails the development of a joint Ministry of Foreign Affairs and Trade/Defence/Police discussion paper. The paper includes comments from New Zealand Permanent Missions (embassies and high commissions) and is sent to the relevant Ministers of Foreign Affairs and Trade, Defence and Police, as well as the prime minister (Department of the Prime Minister and Cabinet, 2016). The paper advises how the request measures up against the agreed upon criteria for such missions, and following the decision by government to engage in a peace support operation, it then informs Parliament. The government has often requested and received a formal parliamentary vote for support in undertaking a peace operation, but as the government holds a majority in Parliament, there is no requirement for formal parliamentary approval (Greener, 2018).

Rationale for Contributing Staff and Resources to International Peacekeeping Missions

Similar to that of other developed nations, New Zealand has five different forms of rationale for committing personnel and resources to international peacekeeping and assistance missions: political, economic, security, institutional, and normative. Each of these rationales is discussed below.

1. Political Rationale

All of the previous governments in New Zealand believe that United Nations and non-United Nations international peacekeeping contributions can strengthen New Zealand's international influence and help build its relationship with like-minded countries (Henderson & Watson, 2005). Furthermore, contributing New Zealand personnel and resources to such missions is seen as a way for New Zealand to "lead by example" and to be a "good international citizen" (Hobbs, 2005).

New Zealand recognizes the need to be seen as contributing to international peacekeeping and assistance missions. New Zealand's contribution to peacekeeping has been discussed in depth in the Ministry of Defence, 2016 Defence white paper. The paper notes that "New Zealand actively supports the rules based international order through its support for institutions and arrangements that reinforce global stability, including the United Nations" (Ministry of Defence, 2016, p. 4).

2. Economic Rationale

According to Hobbs (2005), the economic rational factors are not significant in the decision-making process as New Zealand sees itself as a good international neighbor and will assist others in an emergency. Economics is not considered in the decision-making process because the reimbursement for international peacekeeping missions that the United Nations makes does not cover the full cost of contributing personnel and equipment.

3. Security Rationale

Security rationale do not play a significant role in the decision-making process (Henderson & Watson, 2005; Greener, 2018). Because New Zealand is geographically isolated from other nations, with large oceans forming a significant physical barrier, the risk of refugees or other threats and "spill overs" from armed conflict in other nations is minimal (Greener, 2018). The primary reason why New Zealand supports peace and stability in the South Pacific is because the country relies on trade and secure trade routes for its exports (Henderson & Watson, 2005; Greener, 2018).

4. Institutional Rationale

Institutional considerations do have a level of influence on New Zealand's decisions to contribute to peace operations (Henderson & Watson, 2005; Ministry of Defence, 2016; Greener, 2018). This influence is owing to the fact that the government does not primarily visualize the military as being a fighting force, but as a peacekeeping force (Henderson & Watson, 2005; Ministry of Defence, 2016; Greener, 2018).

5. Normative Rationale

This is the most significant reason for New Zealand's engagement in United Nations peacekeeping operations (Greener, 2018). According to Greener (2018), New Zealand has long viewed itself as being a "good international citizen." Successive New Zealand governments have advanced and encouraged the country's support for the United Nations and have urged the United Nations to play a more comprehensive part in international policy and affairs (Greener, 2018).

Constraints to Contributing to United Nations Peacekeeping Missions

There are a number of constraints to New Zealand contributing personnel and resources to United Nations peacekeeping missions. These constraints are as follows:

- Clashing political or strategic priorities – differing government priorities at the same time as a proposed United Nations mission.
- Financial costs – excessive cost of deploy personnel and resources for the benefit to be gained by New Zealand.
- Difficult domestic politics – the government is unable to obtain agreement for supporting the peacekeeping mission within its own party.
- Logistical obstacles – New Zealand is unable to provide a logistical structure for the proposed deployment (adapted from Greener, 2018).

Challenges to Contributing to United Nations Peacekeeping Missions

The biggest challenges to contribution to United Nations peacekeeping missions are economic or financial (Greener, 2018) and the availability of staff and resources. Government departments in New Zealand have been restructured a number of times since the early 1990s, and their purpose or objective restricts them to their core role. This means that there are often not enough military or police personnel available to be deployed.

The second challenge is balancing New Zealand's ongoing contributions to any new or proposed United Nations peacekeeping mission with those missions that they are already contributing to. Owing to restricted departmental budgets, the government would review their current contribution commitments prior to contributing personnel and resources to a new mission.

The New Zealand Police

The New Zealand Police has a substantial presence in the South Pacific and provides regional policing support to a number of overseas assistance programs. The role of the New Zealand Police in these missions has changed over time with missions prior to the turn of the century being based on the SMART model (support, monitoring, advising, reporting, training) and more modern missions comprising the three Rs (reforming, restructuring, and rebuilding the local police) (Capie, 2012). In general terms, staff that are deployed are involved in investigative support, post-conflict capacity building, advising and mentoring, and longer-term capability development roles (New Zealand Police, 2009b). The deployment of police officers often leads to longer-term capacity-building programs, which require sustained commitment over several years, and are difficult to manage on an ad hoc basis without impacting on domestic policing (New Zealand Police, 2009b).

The number of New Zealand Police personnel who are deployed to international missions has also changed. By the end of 2017, the New Zealand Police had contributed to six long-term and three short-term capability development programs that involved approximately 50 staff (New Zealand Police, 2018a). This was a significant decrease from the mid-2000s when the police had more than 75 members deployed to three main missions: Afghanistan, the Solomon Islands, and Timor-Leste (Ministry of Foreign Affairs and Trade, 2014).

The New Zealand Police has a history of providing trusted, capable, and professional personnel to a variety of types of peace support missions, and it retains a strategic rationale for continuing involvement in these operations (New Zealand Cabinet External Relations and Defence Committee, 2013). New Zealand's peace support priorities will continue to focus on the South Pacific and discretionary peace support operations further afield should not affect New Zealand's capacity to respond to an emerging crisis in the South Pacific (New Zealand Cabinet External Relations and Defence Committee, 2013). As the mandates and conditions in peace support operations continue to grow more complicated, there is an expectation that New Zealand would, along with Australia, play a leading role in responding to any conflict or crisis in the South Pacific region (New Zealand Cabinet External Relations and Defence Committee, 2013). This means that the New Zealand Police would need to retain sufficient capacity for non-discretionary regional engagement in the South Pacific while still maintaining its domestic capability.

The New Zealand Police had previously recognized the value in operating in offshore peacekeeping and assistance operations and the high regard with which the 'NZ Police brand' is held internationally (New Zealand Cabinet External Relations and Defence Committee, 2013). The Commissioner of Police must, however, balance domestic requirements with the desire to deploy police personnel on peace support activities and is more likely to favor deployments to the Asia-Pacific region. This means that in the future the New Zealand Police will likely only have the capacity to deploy small teams or individual officers to peacekeeping or assistance missions, but in the case of an emergency, the police would have the capability to deploy up to 20 people internationally for short periods of time (New Zealand Cabinet External Relations and Defence Committee, 2013).

Problems with International Deployments

Two major problems occurred within the New Zealand Police during the mid-2000s owing to the large number of personnel being deployed to international peacekeeping and assistance missions. These issues were the borrowing of personnel from police districts and service centers from around the country and that of funding.

The Problem of Borrowing Personnel

The primary problem was the practice of taking police personnel out of the existing personnel baseline (New Zealand Police, 2009c). At this time, the staffing and resourcing of police international deployments was on an ad hoc, case-by-case basis, and the staff that were selected for deployment were requested and removed from front-line duties in police districts as the need of each deployment was determined.

The practice of deploying staff overseas from baseline resources caused tension with police district and area commanders and, occasionally, with local government leaders. The tension arose from the fact that personnel were often away from their assigned domestic role for up to 9 months (Capie, 2012), and this challenged the ability of some of the police districts to maintain coverage of front-line policing services. It also caused problems with selecting staff for deployment because of the need to distribute the impact of the staff selections geographically or equitably across the country.

The officers and members of the police that were sought for overseas deployment were of a high caliber and were often valued for their domestic operational, front-line abilities (New Zealand Police, 2009c). Retaining staff by the police districts also had an effect on the selection process of staff members to be deployed and for the planning of the mission, which caused delays in finalizing mission commitments.

During the mid-2000s, the police were being increasingly called on, often at short notice, to assist in the restoration of law and order in Pacific and South East Asian countries, as well as participating in long-term capacity development programs (New Zealand Police, 2009b). In 2005, it was identified by the police that in order to maintain overseas deployment numbers a ratio of approximately 2.5 staff members for every 1 staff member deployed offshore for each 6-month rotation was needed, placing pressure on district staffing (New Zealand Police, 2009c). The ratio of 1:2.5 persons did not take into account any annual leave that was accrued during the deployment, average sick leave levels, or other down time (New Zealand Police, 2009c).

At the beginning of 2006, 47 police staff were deployed offshore, and by 1 December 2006, this figure had increased to 126 staff (New Zealand Police, 2009b). The increase in staff deployed was owing to the police sending two contingents to the Solomon Islands to respond to the civil unrest in Honiara and deploying 45 staff to Tonga to assist with the restoration of law and order following the riots in Nuku'alofa (New Zealand Police, 2009b). Another nine staff members were also deployed to Fiji in late 2006 to support the consular activities of the Ministry of Foreign Affairs and Trade and in respect to the security of the New Zealand High Commission and residence in Suva (New Zealand Police, 2009b). By 1 February 2009, however, the number of staff deployed offshore had dropped back to 79 (New Zealand Police, 2009b).

Prior to 2006, the police had also contributed staff to international emergency and disaster relief efforts. For example, 30 staff members of the New Zealand Police were deployed to Phuket, Thailand, to assist with victim identification and provide consular support after the 2004 Asian Tsunami. Monthly rotations were then established of between 25 and 30 officers and forensic experts, and in total, 160 New Zealand Police staff were deployed to Thailand over the period of a year (New Zealand Police, 2009b).

It was realized by the executive of the New Zealand Police in late 2005 that the selection and deployment arrangements for maintaining New Zealand Police overseas deployments were not efficient or sustainable, and that if the participation of the New Zealand Police in New Zealand's international security efforts were to be effective, then the selection and deployment process needed to be based on stable, continuing structures and funding (New Zealand Police, 2009b). The police were not structured or resourced to provide for any sustained overseas deployments in peacekeeping, law enforcement, or capacity-building roles that it had been asked to undertake. Establishing a permanent overseas deployment pool at this time would have been an effective solution.

The method that was considered to overcome this problem was to establish a permanent deployment pool of police staff that would involve New Zealand Aid covering the direct costs of the pool and the police absorbing the indirect costs from baseline funding (New Zealand Police, 2009c). It was proposed that the pool would be approximately 2.5 times the number of staff deployed overseas and would provide the following benefits:

- At a strategic level, a basis for ministers to assess priorities and achieve a balance of deployments according to New Zealand's interests.
- A configuration for the rapid deployment of staff to an international crisis or emergency.
- The domestic impact from having police staff deployed offshore could be effectively minimized.
- Staff would be trained, inoculated, and security cleared for international deployment prior to being required to be deployed.
- Assist in the management of the myriad of one-off, day-to-day, staffing pressures in maintaining ongoing deployments.
- The good reputation of New Zealand as contributing constructively with its traditional partners at the time of crisis would be enhanced (New Zealand Police, 2009c).

On 17 May 2006, the Cabinet External Relations and Defence committee noted that the police relied on a case-by-case approval of additional funds to their baseline or funding from New Zealand Aid for each overseas staff deployment (New Zealand Police, 2009b). The Cabinet committee invited the then Minister of Police to present a paper to the committee so that they could consider creating a dedicated resource for any New Zealand Police overseas deployments (New Zealand Police, 2009b).

The New Zealand Police proposed that the overseas deployment pool would be implemented incrementally over a period of 3 years and that any staff who were deployed overseas at that time would be counted as being a part of the proposed pool of 250 personnel (New Zealand Police, 2009b). It was also proposed that the permanent deployment pool would be based on staff who were allocated to the pool remaining in their home locations when not deployed and would, in most cases, return there when their deployment tenure had been completed (New Zealand Police, 2009b). On return from a deployment, a reintegration process would ensure that there was a smooth transition back to home locations and pool members could provide additional policing capacity back in the police districts (New Zealand Police, 2009b).

The paper that proposed the establishment of a permanent deployment pool was submitted to the Cabinet committee in July 2006. Although the committee acknowledged the difficulties that the police faced, it was decided that the pool would not be funded at that time. The paper did receive some support, but a decision was deferred, pending further analysis in relation to possible funding options for identifying the police staff numbers required to establish the pool. Time and changes in the New Zealand Government and the international security space removed the need for the police to establish a permanent deployment pool. As at the date of writing, the police do not have an alternative plan for deploying staff on international missions other than continuing with finding suitable staff from baseline resources.

The Problem of Funding Deployed Personnel

The second problem that the police faced in relation to the deployment of personnel to international peacekeeping and assistance missions was that of funding. The police did not have a separate budget for overseas deployment operations, although a separate budget for such commitments was available, though the establishment of such a framework was suggested following the Solomon Islands and Timor-Leste deployments (New Zealand Police, 2009c). This meant that districts, service centers, and Police National Headquarters carried the overhead costs for offshore deployments.

As a result of the police not having a separate budget for international deployments, each mission was funded on a case-by-case basis either from the police baseline or with assistance from New Zealand Aid. This meant that there was no forward or strategic planning of missions and that the police were required to coordinate with a number of different agencies to arrange funds for offshore activities (New Zealand Police, 2009c).

The Beginning: Cyprus (1964–1967)

The United Nations Peacekeeping Force in Cyprus (UNFICYP) is one of the longest running United Nations Peacekeeping missions. Attempts to solve the Cyprus conflict and reunify the island have to date been without result, although relations between the north and south populations of the island have improved over the years (United Nations Peacekeeping Force in Cyprus, 2019a).

The internal strife in Cyprus was first brought to the notice of the United Nations Security Council on 26 December 1963 in a letter from the Government of Cyprus, which listed perceived acts and threats against the territorial integrity and sovereignty of Cyprus and requested the United Nations to protect the country from unilateral military intervention (Aksu, 2013). The Cyprus Government, which was by then exclusively in the hands of Greek Cypriots, declared that it feared a Turkish invasion (Aksu, 2013).

The first overseas deployment of New Zealand Police Officers to a United Nations peacekeeping mission was to Cyprus in 1964 under United Nations Security Council Resolution 186. The mission was established as a response to the conflict on the island following Cyprus gaining independence from Britain in 1960 (New Zealand Police Association, 2014). Following independence, violence broke out between the larger Greek Cypriot community and the Turkish Cypriot community (New Zealand Police Association, 2014). After the failure to restore peace, the United Nations Security Council unanimously adopted Resolution 186 (1964), which recommended that a United Nations Peacekeeping Force be established in Cyprus. The mission's mandate was to perform the following:

- Prevent a recurrence of fighting
- Contribute to the maintenance and restoration of law and order
- Contribute to a return to normal conditions (United Nations Peacekeeping Force in Cyprus, 2019d)

According to Aksu (2013), the mandate was not clearly defined and resulted in the United Nations issuing a clearer set of guidelines and objectives. These documents provided guiding principles as to the command structure of the mission and the principles of self-defense (Aksu, 2013). The documents also highlighted that the mission would be a limited-scope security mission (Aksu, 2013).

The mission's responsibilities expanded in 1974, following a coup d'état by elements favoring a union with Greece and the subsequent military intervention by Turkey, whose troops had established control over the northern part of the island (United Nations Peacekeeping Force in Cyprus, 2019a).

Following a request from the United Nations, the New Zealand Police deployed 20 police officers as a part of the United Nations Peacekeeping Force in Cyprus

(McLintock, 1966; New Zealand Police Association, 2014; New Zealand Police, 2014, 2018b). According to McLintock (1966) and the New Zealand Police (2014, 2018b), the contingent reached Cyprus on 21 May 1964, which was during a period of serious fighting between Greek Cypriots and Turkish Cypriots. By 8 June 1964, the mission had reached a strength of 6411, which included military personnel from Austria, Canada, Denmark, Finland, Ireland, Sweden, and the United Kingdom, and civilian police units from Australia, Austria, Denmark, New Zealand, and Sweden (United Nations Peacekeeping Force in Cyprus, 2019c).

According to the New Zealand Police (2014), the idea of traveling to Cyprus was popular, with more than 350 applications for 13 constable vacancies in the first contingent. A number of officers served in up to four contingents. The first contingent met the prime minister, Keith Holyoake, following a week-long selection and training at Trentham (New Zealand Police Association, 2014). The contingent was deployed for 6 months and was initially stationed in the Nicosia Hotel and then in the Curium Palace Hotel in Limasol, where they acted as liaison between Greek Cypriot and Turkish Cypriot police and investigated incidents between the two populations (McLintock, 1966; New Zealand Police Association, 2014; New Zealand Police, 2014, 2018b).

The mission's contingents were deployed throughout the island, and an effort was made as far as possible to match each contingent area of responsibility (zones or districts) with the island's administrative district boundaries (United Nations Peacekeeping Force in Cyprus, 2019d). This was meant to facilitate a close working relationship with the district officers of the Cyprus Government and the local Turkish Cypriot leaders (United Nations Peacekeeping Force in Cyprus, 2019b).

All Cyprus districts were covered according to the intensity of the armed confrontation. The capital, Nicosia, was initially staffed by two UNFICYP contingents (Canadian and Finnish) and was organized in a single Nicosia zone under a Canadian commander (United Nations Peacekeeping Force in Cyprus, 2019d). The districts of Kyrenia and Lefka were each managed by a contingent, and the other two contingents covered the districts of Larnaca, Limassol, and Paphos (United Nations Peacekeeping Force in Cyprus, 2019b). The New Zealand contingent was assigned to the Limasol sector.

The mandate for the mission was comprehensive, and as a result, the mission became involved, from its inception, in carrying out a vast array of activities that affected almost every aspect of life in Cyprus, often in difficult conditions (Aksu, 2013; United Nations Peacekeeping Force in Cyprus, 2019b). According to McLintock (1966) and Henn (2004), the New Zealand contingent was primarily tasked with overseeing the roadblocks set up by the Greek Cypriots, escorting Red Crescent convoys through them and supervising the stevedoring and convoying of cargoes of firearms. All of the UNFICYP's functions were of necessity carried out in consultation with the government of Cyprus and the Turkish Cypriot authorities, and also, on many occasions, with the governments of Greece and Turkey (United Nations Peacekeeping Force in Cyprus, 2019b).

New Zealand police officers were well-received by both sides – by the Greeks because of the contribution made by New Zealand to Greece in World War II, and by the Turkish because of New Zealand's association with the invasion of Gallipoli during World War I (New Zealand Police, 2014). In total, 79 New Zealand police officers served in six United Nations peacekeeping missions between 1964 and 1967 when the last New Zealand police contingent left the island (New Zealand Police Association, 2014; New Zealand Police, 2014). The United Nations Peacekeeping Force in Cyprus continues to this day.

Namibia (1989–1990)

In 1966, the United Nations terminated the South Africa's League of Nations mandate over Namibia (the legal source for South Africa's administrative authority since 1920) and placed the territory under direct United Nations administration (Ratner, 1995). Under a 1967 resolution, which was later endorsed by the Security Council, the United Nations created the United Nations Council on Namibia "[to] administer South West Africa until independence, with the maximum possible participation of the people of the Territory" (quoted in Ratner, 1995, p. 102). The Council "would promulgate any necessary laws or regulations, maintain law and order, ensure the removal of South African civilians, police, and military forces, and set up a constituent assembly to draft a constitution pending elections and independence" (Ratner, 1995, p. 102). The approach, however, was not agreed to by South Africa, who refused to cede any control to the Council (Ratner, 1995).

In 1966, the military wing (known as People's Liberation Army of Namibia or PLAN) of the South West Africa People's Organisation (SWAPO), a Namibian liberation movement, began to launch guerrilla attacks from Zambia (Ratner, 1995; Howard, 2008). The first attack took place on 26 August 1966 at Omugulugwombashe, and the conflict became known as the Namibian war of independence (Howard, 2008). Over the next few years, there were a series of General Assembly resolutions in relation to Namibia, condemning the South African occupation and calling for free elections (Ratner, 1995).

On 30 January 1976, the Security Council adopted Resolution 385, which declared that it was imperative to hold free elections under United Nations supervision and control for the whole of Namibia as one political entity (United Nations, 1976). Later in 1978, the United Nations Security Council approved a resolution with a specific, timetabled plan for the withdrawal of the South African Defence Force and for the holding of the Namibian elections. The United Nations also authorized the establishment of the United Nations Transition Assistance Group (UNTAG), with a combined military and civilian force, to facilitate the transition to independence at this time (United Nations, 1978; Ratner, 1995). The mission, however, stalled for more than a decade because of the civil war in Angola (Ratner, 1995).

The UNTAG in Namibia was established on 16 February 1989 by Resolution 632 (1989) to ensure the early independence of Namibia through free and fair elections under the supervision and control of the United Nations (United Nations Transition Assistance Group, 2018). The mission was established on the following four principal components: (1) overall establishment of UNTAG offices, (2) military disarmament and civilian policing, (3) refugee return, and (4) preparation for, and the holding of, elections (Ratner, 1995; Howard, 2008). The mission was also to ensure that all hostile acts ended; troops confined to base, and, in the case of the South Africa, the ultimate withdrawal from Namibia; all discriminatory laws repealed, political prisoners released, Namibian refugees permitted to return, intimidation of any kind prevented, and that law and order is impartially maintained (Ratner, 1995; United Nations Transition Assistance Group, 2018).

According to Howard (2008), the mission differed from all previous United Nations peacekeeping operations in that its primary means and purpose was political and was to monitor the democratic transition and electoral process, rather than it being a military intervention and overseeing a ceasefire agreement. The mission also provided the origin for a number of peacekeeping innovations that are still in use today including "a western 'Contact Group,' an elaborate 'information program,' and most significantly, United Nations 'civilian policing' in its current form" (Howard, 2008, p. 52).

The mission was the United Nations' first multidimensional peacekeeping mission after the unsuccessful operation in the Congo in 1964 (Ratner, 1995; Howard, 2008). The mission started on 1 April 1989 and ended in March 1990 and was made up of people from 109 contributing countries (Ratner, 1995; Howard, 2008; United Nations Transition Assistance Group, 2018). The authorized strength of its military component was 7500, supported by almost 2000 international civilian and local staff, and 1500 police officers (Howard, 2008; United Nations Transition Assistance Group, 2018).

In order to establish the mission, staff from the United Nations were to interact as much as possible with the local population (Howard, 2008). Staff were to exercise "moral" rather than "executive" authority by helping to create "a new atmosphere and climate of reconciliation" (Howard, 2008, p. 68).

The police role within the mission included the monitoring of the electoral process and also the monitoring and supervision of the South African police (Ratner, 1995). To complete this role, the mission police accompanied the South African police on patrol and "worked alongside them to induce respect for the integrity of the political process and the rights of Namibians" (Ratner, 1995, p. 120). Ratner (1995) claimed that the presence of the police in the mission led to an immediate improvement in the behavior of the South West African Police, although the extent of their improvement varied across the country. The mission police also assisted the South West African Police with providing security patrols as the election date neared and as the threat of violence increased (Ratner, 1995).

There is no literature that examines or discusses the role of the New Zealand Police in the mission of the United Nations Transition Assistance Group nor has the experiences of the members of the police been documented. The lack of information from the police perspective extended to official information and documents at Police National headquarters. After an extensive search, the only information that was located was that there were 32 police members deployed to the mission (United Nations, 1990). It is not known whether this was one contingent or a number of contingents and whether the deployment was for the full 12 months or for a lesser period.

Overall, the operation was successful on a number of fronts. The first was that the mission was successful in implementing its mandate. Second, the mission was able to create the conditions for political stability in post-independence Namibia (Howard, 2008). The third was the success in the holding of elections between 7 and 11 November 1989, with a voter turnout of 97 percent (United Nations Transition Assistance Group, 2018). Personnel from the mission monitored the ballot and the counting of votes, and on 14 November, the United Nations declared that the elections had been free and fair (United Nations Transition Assistance Group, 2018). The police component of the mission, while less successful at fulfilling their mandate, achieved most of the tasks that were assigned to them (Howard, 2008).

On 21 March 1990, the South African flag was lowered over Namibia for the last time and the country became the world's newest state, which ended a 70-year-old dispute originating from the League of Nations mandate identifying the territory for self-determination (Ratner, 1995). The most interesting component of the mission, according to Howard (2008), was the organizational changes to the perspective of deploying civilian police within peacekeeping missions. Previously, civilian police had not been deployed to engage in policing tasks in a peacekeeping operation as they had been in Namibia (Howard, 2008).

Organizational learning was at the heart of the mission's success (Howard, 2008). The mission took its cues from local events and political occurrences, rather than from the United Nations Headquarters in New York (Howard, 2008). This approach ensured that the mission was better integrated with its environment and was able to learn from it (Howard, 2008). The success of the mission also provided two indictors that would be used to form the new approach to peacekeeping (Ratner, 1995). The first indicator depends on all parties being willing to end a dispute (Ratner, 1995), and the second was that only qualified personnel who have knowledge of the country in which they are to be deployed to and have political experience are to be deployed to the mission (Ratner, 1995).

The most important legacy of the mission is that it established a link between the operational aspects of earlier missions and the multifunctional mandates that define second-generation peacekeeping and assistance missions (Ratner, 1995). The operational complexity of the mission exceeded previous peacekeeping missions, and as a result, "expanded the concept of peacekeeping to include electoral matters, police, human rights, and education functions" (Ratner, 1995, p. 123).

Conclusion

The intention of this chapter was to provide a background to the New Zealand approach to supporting peacekeeping missions and to the deployment of New Zealand Police Officers and staff on such missions. What follows in subsequent chapters are case studies based on the deployment of New Zealand Police to Afghanistan, Bougainville, the Solomon Islands, and Timor-Leste.

References

Aksu, E. (2013). The UN in the Cyprus conflict: UNFICYP. In E. Aksu (Ed.), *The United Nations, intra-state peacekeeping and normative change* (pp. 130–154). Oxford University Press.

Capie, D. (2012). Peacekeeping - New Zealand's involvement in peacekeeping. *Te Ara: The Encyclopaedia of New Zealand*. Retrieved from http://www.TeAra.govt.nz/en/peacekeeping/.

Department of the Prime Minister and Cabinet. (2016). *National security system handbook*. Department of the Prime Minister and Cabinet.

Greener, B. (2018). *Peacekeeping contributor profile: New Zealand*. Retrieved from: http://www.providingforpeacekeeping.org/2014/04/03/contributor-profile-new-zealand/.

Greener-Barcham, B. (2005). The New Zealand experience. In J. Henderson & G. Watson (Eds.), *Securing a Peaceful Pacific* (pp. 215–218). Canterbury University Press.

Henderson, J., & Watson, G. (Eds.). (2005). *Securing a peaceful Pacific*. Canterbury University Press.

Henn, F. (2004). *A business of some heat: The United Nations force in Cyprus 1972–74*. Pen & Sword Military.

Hobbs, M. (2005). Securing a peace: New Zealand's role. In J. Henderson & G. Watson (Eds.), *Securing a Peaceful Pacific* (pp. 20–25). Canterbury University Press.

Howard, L. (2008). *UN peacekeeping in Civil Wars*. Cambridge University Press.

Law & Development Partnership. (2013). *Strategic evaluation of police work funded under the New Zealand aid program, 2005–2011*. Wellington: New Zealand Ministry of Foreign Affairs and Trade.

McLintock, A. (1966). *An encyclopaedia of New Zealand*. R. E. Owen, Government Printer.

Ministry of Defence. (2016). *Defence white paper*. Ministry of Defence.

Ministry of Foreign Affairs and Trade. (2014). *Peace support operations*. Retrieved from: http://www.mfat.govt.nz/Foreign-Relations/1-Global-Issues/International-Security/4-Peacekeeping-Operations.php.

New Zealand Cabinet External Relations and Defence Committee. (2013). *Peace Support Operations Review*. ERD Min (13) 11/3. Cabinet Office.

New Zealand Police. (2009b). *Briefing for the Minister of Police: New Zealand Police proposed overseas deployment pool*. Reference BR/09/41, 13 February. New Zealand Police.

New Zealand Police. (2009c). *International commitments*. New Zealand Police.

New Zealand Police. (2014). Cyprus: Keeping the peace. *Ten-One*, Issue No. 383, page 9, August. Retrieved from: http://www.ten-one.police.govt.nz/tenone/August14National6.htm.

New Zealand Police. (2018a). *Annual report 2017/2018*. New Zealand Police.

New Zealand Police. (2018b). *Past ISG deployments*. Retrieved from http://www.police.govt.nz/about-us/programmes-initiatives/isg/past-deployments.

New Zealand Police Association. (2014). Mission to Cyprus. *Police News*, July, p. 145. New Zealand Police Association.

Ratner, S. (1995). *The New UN peacekeeping: Building peace in lands of conflict after the cold war*. St. Martin's Press.

United Nations. (1976). *United Nations Security Council Resolution 385*. Retrieved from: http://unscr.com/en/resolutions/385.

United Nations. (1978). *United Nations Security Council Resolution 435*. Retrieved from: http://unscr.com/en/resolutions/435.

United Nations. (1990). *Namibia facts and figures*. Retrieved from: https://www.un.org/en/peacekeeping/missions/past/untagF.htm.

United Nations Peacekeeping Force in Cyprus. (2019a). *About*. Retrieved from: https://unficyp.unmissions.org/about.

United Nations Peacekeeping Force in Cyprus. (2019b). *Deployment and organisation*. Retrieved from: https://unficyp.unmissions.org/deployment-and-organisation.

United Nations Peacekeeping Force in Cyprus. (2019c). *Establishment of UNFICYP*. Retrieved from: https://unficyp.unmissions.org/establishment-unficyp.

United Nations Peacekeeping Force in Cyprus. (2019d). *UNFICYP mandate*. Retrieved from: https://unficyp.unmissions.org/unficyp-mandate.

United Nations Transition Assistance Group. (2018). *Namibia – UNTAG*. Retrieved from: https://peacekeeping.un.org/sites/default/files/past/untagM.htm.

Chapter 4
The Role of the New Zealand Police in Police Reform and International Peacekeeping in Afghanistan

Garth den Heyer

Introduction

The modern history of Afghanistan is well known. Following the al-Qaeda attacks on the Twin Towers and the Pentagon on 11 September 2001, the United States and its allies invaded Afghanistan on 7 October 2001. The Taliban were driven from power, and by 17 December 2001, the military of the United States and its allies were establishing bases near the major cities in Afghanistan.

After the end of the Taliban regime and more than 20 years of internal conflict, the Afghanistan Police Force was in a state of disarray, which reflected years without systemic training and a lack of equipment and resources. It was estimated that there were approximately 70,000–80,000 "police" in Afghanistan at this time – many of whom were mujahidin or former combatants, who had little formal police training or supervision.

The reconstruction of Afghanistan's police began in February 2002 with a conference being held in Germany to discuss support from the international community for the Afghanistan police. A comprehensive plan to create a national Afghanistan Police Force was presented at another conference, which was held 1 month later in Berlin (Jones et al., 2005). The plan was based on a lead nation being responsible for the coordination and delivery of each of the five main pillars:

1. Law enforcement (Germany)
2. Judiciary (Italy)
3. Counter-narcotics (the United Kingdom)
4. Afghanistan National Army (the United States)
5. Disarmament, demobilization, and reintegration of militia forces (Japan) (Greener, 2009).

G. den Heyer (✉)
Walden University, Minneapolis, ML, USA

G. den Heyer, J. F. Albrecht (eds.), *Police and International Peacekeeping Missions*, https://doi.org/10.1007/978-3-030-77900-9_4

On 13 October 2006, the Joint European Union Assessment Mission to Afghanistan presented a report to the Council of the European Union's Political and Security Committee, which detailed an analysis of the state of the rule of law in Afghanistan. The report contained a number of recommendations that would strengthen the European Union's strategic contribution to the law enforcement sector in Afghanistan, and it recommended that consideration be given to the European Union "contributing support to the police sector through a police mission." To explore the feasibility of such a mission, the report recommended that a fact-finding mission be sent to Afghanistan (Council of the European Union, 2007a).

The fact-finding mission visited Afghanistan between 27 November and 14 December 2006. From this mission, the council "approved the crisis management concept (CMC) for an EU police mission to Afghanistan in the field of policing that would have linkages to the wider rule of law. It was agreed that the mission would provide added value" (Council of the European Union, 2007b). The council noted that the mission would be a long-term commitment that would aid in reforming the Afghan police force. The reform would be based on local ownership, have respect for human rights, and would operate within the framework of the rule of law. The mission would build on international efforts and would follow a comprehensive and strategic approach. In adopting this program of reform, the mission would "address issues of police reform at central, regional, and provincial levels" (Council of the European Union, 2007a).

On 23 April 2007, the council approved the Concept of Operations for a European Union Police Mission to Afghanistan (EUPOL Afghanistan), which would cover the entire country (Council of the European Union, 2007b) and would include a police reform program with links to the wider rule of law (Council of the European Union, 2007b). The council noted that the proposed mission would build on the efforts of the German Police Project Office and would be set in the wider context of the "international community's effort to support the Government of Afghanistan in taking responsibility for strengthening the rule of law and in particular, in improving its civil police and law enforcement capacity" (Council of the European Union, 2007b).

The council identified that the minimum time frame of EUPOL Afghanistan would be 3 years. The council also determined that the mission would require close coordination with other international actors, including the International Security Assistance Force (ISAF). The council also noted that because the environment was so unpredictable the mission would need to take a flexible approach.

Police Reform in Afghanistan

There were two countries that were primarily involved in reforming the Afghanistan police in early 2004. Germany was the lead country for the reform of the police force and had deployed 29 police officers to advise the Afghanistan Transitional Authority (Ministry of Interior) on the rebuilding of a professional, ethnically balanced, national police force (Ministry of Foreign Affairs and Trade, 2004). Working from a newly rebuilt National Afghanistan Police Academy in Kabul, German police officers focused on training police recruits to a university degree level.

The second country involved in reforming the Afghanistan police was the United States, who were based at a Central Training Centre (CTC) in Kabul. This center focused on providing basic police training, upgrading the skills of existing police officers who were at the constable level and training police instructors. In addition to three American instructors at the Kabul Center, there were two instructors from the United Kingdom, one from Sweden, and one from Slovenia.

The Afghanistan police training project aimed to train 50,000 new Afghanistan police officers (including 12,000 border police) by the end of 2005 (Ministry of Foreign Affairs and Trade, 2004). A training curriculum was developed jointly by German and American police officers. The curriculum emphasized respect for human rights and the role of the police in a democratic state, which is governed by the rule of law.

The New Zealand Police Mission to Afghanistan

On 23 June 2004, the New Zealand Police drafted a report to the Minister of Police to seek approval to deploy two New Zealand Police Officers to the Regional Police Training Centre in Bamiyan,[1] Afghanistan, in association with the New Zealand-led Provincial Reconstruction Team (PRT) (New Zealand Police, 2004b). The deployment of the two officers was subject to a final decision by the Commissioner of the New Zealand Police, who would base his decision on the level of threat in Afghanistan and the implementation of measures for managing any risks. The initial deployment of the two officers would be for six-months and they would be accommodated at the Provincial Reconstruction Team base with assistance provided by the New Zealand Defence Force. The costs associated with the police deployment were to be met by the New Zealand Agency for International Development (Ministry of Foreign Affairs and Trade, 2004).

According to the report, the New Zealand Police had been approached by the United States head of the Afghanistan Police Training Project to provide police assistance at the Regional Training Centre (RTC) in Bamiyan. The reason that the approach was made was because New Zealand was leading a Provincial Reconstruction team at Bamiyan and that support for the Police Training Centre would add value to New Zealand's profile as a country committed to enhancing security in Afghanistan (New Zealand Police, 2004b). Support for the Police Training Centre would also be consistent with New Zealand's contribution of development assistance and for other programs that were being undertaken in Bamiyan.

[1] Bamiyan can also be spelt as Bamian or Bamyan.

Reconnaissance Mission to Afghanistan

Following the approach that was made by the head of the United States Afghanistan Police Training Project, the New Zealand Police organized, in conjunction with the New Zealand Defence Force and the Ministry of Foreign Affairs and Trade, a reconnaissance mission to Afghanistan. This was undertaken between 5 and 13 August 2004 by the national manager of the Operations Group and the manager of Overseas Deployments. The managers were to address four points specified in the terms of reference that related to the possibility of a New Zealand Police deployment to Afghanistan (New Zealand Police, 2004a). These points were as follows:

1. To assess the potential role that the staff of the New Zealand Police staff would have as part of the Afghanistan Police Training Project.
2. To assess local security and environmental risks to New Zealand Police staff living and working in Afghanistan.
3. To assess management options for security and environmental risks.
4. To recommend the suitability of a New Zealand Police deployment with the Afghanistan Police Training Project (New Zealand Police, 2004a).

If the New Zealand Police were to deploy staff to Afghanistan, they would act as part of the American "International Police (Training) Program" (IPP). The program's objectives in 2004 were to perform the following:

- Train a cadre of police instructors for Afghanistan.
- Provide training in basic police skills, instructor development, and human rights to approximately 52,000 Afghanistan police officers by the end of 2005.
- Develop a series of police training centers throughout Afghanistan.
- Assist in the professionalization of the Afghanistan National Police (ANP) by creating a professional training organization (New Zealand Police, 2004a).

The International Police (Training) Program had a Central Training Centre in Kabul and seven Regional Training Centres that were based in the provinces throughout Afghanistan. The proposal was that the New Zealand Police would provide two officers who would act as a training team leader and a trainer in the Regional Training Centre at Bamiyan and would report to an American "Lead Police Training Advisor" based at Kabul (New Zealand Police, 2004a).

The reconnaissance mission noted that any officers deployed by the New Zealand Police would need to develop a number of formal and informal relationships with the Afghanistan Government, the New Zealand Defence Force, and the United States Department of State. During the mission, representatives from the International Police (Training) Program gave a verbal undertaking that they would provide accommodation, messing, and overhead support for the two New Zealand Police Officers deployed to undertake the training roles at the Bamiyan Regional Training Centre (New Zealand Police, 2004a). The officers from the New Zealand Police would be expected to reside with the other members of the International

Police (Training) Program at the Regional Training Centre rather than at the nearby New Zealand Defence Force camp (New Zealand Police, 2004a).

The stumbling block for deploying New Zealand Police Officers to Afghanistan, according to the reconnaissance mission, was the issue of security (New Zealand Police, 2004a). Staff from the German Police Project Office, which was located Kabul, told the reconnaissance mission members that Kabul was reasonably safe, but the situation had become more tense, with a number of rocket attacks that were probably in response to the forthcoming presidential elections that would be held in September/October (New Zealand Police, 2004a). Two weeks after the departure of the reconnaissance mission from Afghanistan, the building in which the mission was accommodated in was extensively damaged in a Taliban bomb attack, which killed 3 American police advisers and 5 Gurkha security staff and wounded more than 100 people (New Zealand Police, 2004a).

In parallel to the security threat in Afghanistan, the reconnaissance mission identified four more risks for the New Zealand Police if they were to deploy to Bamiyan:

1. The Afghanistan Police were corrupt and ineffective and were unlikely to be able to provide protection to the Regional Training Centre and the Afghanistan Police could become part of the risk.
2. The Taliban would not differentiate between New Zealand Police staff and staff from the International Police (Training) Program if it mounted an attack in Bamiyan. As a result, the staff from the New Zealand Police would be at risk while in Kabul.
3. The "hostage taking" tactic that was employed in Iraq may be replicated in Afghanistan, placing small groups of Western aid workers in remote locations at risk.
4. The security measures adopted by the International Police (Training) Program in Bamiyan may be sufficient for the existing security threat but may not be so if the threat increases (New Zealand Police, 2004a).

To mitigate these risks, the International Police (Training) Program proposed that the Bamiyan Regional Training Centre be supported by a five-person American Force Protection Team and a five-person Gurkha contingent, which would be tasked solely with providing security to the center and its international policing staff (New Zealand Police, 2004a). The reconnaissance mission did not consider that basing New Zealand Police staff at the New Zealand Defence Force camp would be a viable option, and while this would provide a better level of security while the police officers were in the camp, it could not provide security for officers when they were traveling outside the camp or while they were at the Regional Training Centre (New Zealand Police, 2004a). Furthermore, if the officers were to be accommodated at the camp, this would prevent them from contributing to the team dynamic at the Regional Training Centre.

The reconnaissance mission noted that apart from the British police who were stationed at Mazar-e-Sharif, all of the police advisers carried side arms and the majority of American United Nations CIVPOL advisers carried long arms (New Zealand Police, 2004a). At this time, staff from the New Zealand Police did not routinely carry firearms, especially long arms. Members of the mission highlighted that there was very little benefit in New Zealand Police Officers being armed with a side arm when the local militia and the Taliban were armed with AK47s and M16 derivatives or similar assault rifles (New Zealand Police, 2004a). The members did not believe that the security risk could be mitigated significantly by New Zealand Police Officers carrying side arms and did not support that suggestion (New Zealand Police, 2004a). The reconnaissance mission went on to state that "if the risk was such that NZPol had to be armed then the suggested deployment should be seriously questioned" (New Zealand Police, 2004a, p. 7).

The members of the reconnaissance mission concluded that the content and the delivery of training within the International Police (Training) Program were such that the New Zealand Police could play a meaningful part in delivering training to the Afghanistan Police at Bamiyan, and that while there were some significant security and environmental risks to consider, these could be managed and would be dependent upon the presence of the New Zealand Defence Force at Bamiyan (New Zealand Police, 2004a). The members also advised that it was not in favor of deploying retired New Zealand Police members as retired members would not be under the direction of the New Zealand Police Commissioner and their training and operational accreditation could not be certified by the New Zealand Police (New Zealand Police, 2004a). This would mean that any retired police staff who wanted to participate in the mission would effectively be employed as private contractors to the United States and the project.

The Mission – Operation Highland

The mission commenced on 31 March 2005 (Williams, 2013), but as a result of delays in negotiating amendments to the Military Technical Arrangement (MTA) to cover non-military personnel, the first two officers were not deployed to Afghanistan until 7 May 2005. The mission was to be called Operation Highland, and the objective of the New Zealand Police deployment was to strength the capacity of the Afghanistan National Police in the areas of training, management, and leadership. The tasks and responsibilities of the New Zealand Police were to.

1. Support the Bamiyan Regional Training Centre (RTC) to deliver training to the Afghanistan National Police (ANP)
2. Mentor the Bamiyan Provincial Police Chief and other senior managers in the Bamiyan province as required (Carswell, 2008)

The two officers, a Senior Sergeant (promoted to Inspector for the deployment) and a Sergeant (promoted to Senior Sergeant for the deployment), who were deployed on the mission, were trained and briefed by the New Zealand military. The officers attended 3 days of training at Linton Military Camp and 2 days of training at Trentham Military Camp. The training included the development of skills that would be fundamental to in-theater operations and topics that would be applicable to Provincial Reconstruction Team members (Headquarters Joint Forces New Zealand, 2005).

At the time that the United States made their request to the New Zealand Police, seven Regional Training Centres were being funded by the United States and centers were already operating in Kabul and in association with other Provincial Reconstruction Teams at Gardez and Mazar-e-Sharif and at a Provincial Reconstruction Team under construction in Kunduz. The United Kingdom were providing police officers to staff and operate the center in the Mazar-e-Sharif Provincial Reconstruction Team, and Germany was doing the same in the Kunduz Provincial Reconstruction Team.

The training curriculum that was developed by police officers from New Zealand for use in Afghanistan was adopted for use by Germany as the lead nation in Afghanistan for police reform and by the United States, who was funding the Regional Training Centres. To ensure that consistent training standards were being applied across the country, all seven Regional Training Centres were to use the curriculum, which would be delivered in two short courses, with 20 Afghanistan police students per course (Ministry of Foreign Affairs and Trade, 2004). The first course of 8 weeks was for illiterate officers, and the shorter, 2-week course was for literate officers (Ministry of Foreign Affairs and Trade, 2004).

It was intended that the Bamiyan Police Regional Training Centre would receive funding to operate until December 2005. The funding would also cover the cost of the two New Zealand Police Officers, six international personnel, and local Afghanistan personnel who would act as interpreters. When fully functional, each center was authorized to have an establishment of approximately 12 international police advisers and 50 Afghanistan National Police trainers and support staff (New Zealand Police, 2005). As well as being appointed the manager of the center, the New Zealand Police Inspector was appointed as a Senior Police Adviser and an adviser to the Bamiyan Police Chief.

The Bamiyan Police Training Centre was a temporary facility, pending the planned construction of a permanent training facility and was guarded by Gurkha soldiers with back up from the Provincial Reconstruction Team, if there was a need (Ministry of Foreign Affairs and Trade, 2004). The center was located at two sites; the main part of the training center being located adjacent to the Provincial Reconstruction Team. The second part was located approximately 1 km away from the Provincial Reconstruction Team and comprised two tents located adjacent to the Bamiyan Provincial Police Station (New Zealand Police, 2005). The capacity of the center was for less than 100 students, while the other six regional training centers were able to cater for about 1000 students each (New Zealand Police, 2005). Delays in constructing a similar facility at Bamiyan were owing to land disputes and ethnic tensions between the people from Bamiyan and the adjoining provinces, who had also contributed police staff to the center (New Zealand Police, 2005).

The American contractors advised in mid-2005 that in view of the difficulties encountered in expanding the Bamiyan Regional Training Centre and that initial training needed to be delivered to 52,000 Afghanistan National Police by the end of 2005, they would construct a smaller training center to meet the needs of Bamiyan and an adjoining province. Construction of this facility would not be completed until mid-2006, which would be after the winter period, as access to the province is difficult during this time and most building activity ceases owing to harsh weather conditions (New Zealand Police, 2005).

By September 2005, the role of the senior New Zealand Police Officer had changed to the "Lead International Training Adviser" and Adviser to the Afghanistan National Police Bamiyan Training Commander following the departure of an American contractor. At this time, officers from the New Zealand Police were performing the roles of training team leader and trainer in the center and their duties were to deliver training in the classroom and to mentor local police trainers. The New Zealand Police thought that by upgrading the role of the senior officer the New Zealand Police would be well placed to have a significant level of influence on the future development and character of the Afghanistan National Police within the Bamiyan province (New Zealand Police, 2005).

Security During the First Deployment

During the first deployment, Bamiyan province was considered to be secure and a relatively safe environment in comparison to other areas within Afghanistan. The regions where the southern and eastern borders meet Pakistan had experienced a higher level of insurgent violence, so, therefore, the international police advisers in Bamiyan and the other regional training centers were generally armed. New Zealand Police Officers carried both personal side arms and long weapons whenever they were away from the security of the Provincial Reconstruction Team compound.

During the deployment of the two officers, there were no security incidents. However, intelligence received during the deployment indicated that insurgents intended to target the police regional training centers in the lead up to the national elections in September 2005 (New Zealand Police, 2005). In late July, a United Kingdom Provincial Reconstruction Team and a police regional training center located north of Bamiyan, in Afghanistan's second largest city of Mazar-e-Sharif, were attacked by mortar, and fortunately no injuries resulted (New Zealand Police, 2005).

Proposed Changes to New Zealand Police Deployments

Following the completion of the training of the Afghanistan National Police Officers in December 2005, the United States proposed a continuing program of police reform that included the application and implementation of new policies and practices to break down ingrained past practices that were inconsistent with the principles of democratic policing (New Zealand Police, 2005). A mentoring program would be included in the proposed program, and this would be delivered to both the governing Ministry of Interior and senior officers of the Afghanistan National Police at the regional, provincial, and district levels. The goals of the mentoring program were to promote the professional growth of the Afghanistan National Police Service, inspire personal motivation at the command level, and enhance the effectiveness of command staff (New Zealand Police, 2005). The program contained three objectives that would support these goals:

1. Ensure proper application of approved policies, procedures, and regulations to enhance standardization of practices throughout the country and develop a stronger recognition of national authority.
2. Facilitate the delivery of community-based policing services that are effective, efficient, impartial, and accessible to the public.
3. Promote ethical behavior within the Afghanistan National Police, with a particular emphasis on removing corruption (New Zealand Police, 2005).

It was envisaged that the program would guide the Afghanistan National Police to shift from its current state toward one that was capable of self-sustainment prior to the withdrawal of international aid (New Zealand Police, 2005). To achieve the objectives and the goals of the program, the project would be implemented in four phases:

- Phase 1 – Pilot Program: From 1 July 2004 to 30 June 2005, the program was developed and trialed in a small number of "pilot" locations.
- Phase 2 – The "Hub and Spoke" Structure: From 1 July to 31 December 2005, a larger number of mentor teams would be deployed in the field. The ultimate goal was to have mentors in each of the police districts, but in the interim, each district would be served by mentors assigned to the region (hub) who would travel to outer districts (spokes). The objective was to deploy 34 teams consisting of two mentors each (68 personnel) to various locations, including Bamiyan province by the end of October 2005, where they would be based in the existing police Regional Training Centre.
- Phase 3 – Expansion: 1 January 2006 to 31 December 2008. This 3-year phase would comprise a full field of staffing for the mentoring program and a reduction in the reliance of the "hub and spoke" method of service delivery. Commanders and supervisors from the Afghanistan police who were working in the Ministry of Interior and in the districts would have mentoring services available to them, with over 400 new mentors deployed in the field.
- Phase 4 – The Exit Strategy: During this phase (post 1 January 2009), mentors would be withdrawn from the field and the mission would end (New Zealand Police, 2005).

September 2005, Review of New Zealand Police Deployment to Afghanistan

The initial agreement and the funding provided by Cabinet were for the New Zealand Police to deploy two officers to Afghanistan until the end of 2005. Cabinet also wanted the New Zealand Police to review their commitment of assisting the Afghanistan National Police during the deployment of New Zealand Police officers. Between 4 and 14 August 2005, the then Deputy Commissioner (Operations) and his staff officer visited Afghanistan as members of a party that comprised New Zealand and Australia Defence Force personnel (New Zealand Police, 2005).

Following the visit to Afghanistan, a number of options were proposed to assist the Afghanistan National Police. These options were as follows:

1. The withdrawal of the contribution made by the New Zealand Police in December 2005.
2. Maintain the deployment of two police officers until December 2008.
3. The participation of the New Zealand Police in the Afghanistan National Police Mentoring Program.
4. Maintain the role of trainers at Bamiyan Regional Training Centre and expand the role to include the mentoring program – the number of officers deployed would increase to three (New Zealand Police, 2005).

Option 4 was adopted by the New Zealand Police. Staff members would be deployed to Bamiyan and their roles would be as follows:

- A trainer at the Bamiyan province Regional Training Centre
- A principal mentor to assist the Bamiyan province Chief of Police
- A second mentor who would be available to support the trainer at the Regional Training Centre during periods of leave or other absences (New Zealand Police, 2005)

Early Training and Other Achievements

The first deployment of New Zealand Police Officers trained 193 Afghanistan police officers in a series of 5-week courses and 129 police officers in a series of 8-week courses during the period May–December 2005 (Ministry of Foreign Affairs and Trade, 2006). The approach taken to training by New Zealand was different from that provided by other nations. The training that New Zealand provided was more learner-centered and the training did not stop at the completion of the course (Ministry of Foreign Affairs and Trade, 2006).

The second deployment of officers developed a program that provided mobile training in parallel to the training that was delivered at the Regional Training Centre. The officer undertaking the mobile training was imbedded with the military patrols, which ventured into the Bamiyan province for a number of weeks at a time (Ministry of Foreign Affairs and Trade, 2006). The officer worked closely with district police chiefs to conduct training needs assessments and refresher training for Afghanistan police officers who had attended the course at the Regional Training Centre (Ministry of Foreign Affairs and Trade, 2006).

The New Zealand Police view of the training for the Afghanistan National Police Officers was that it was broad-based, covered the spectrum of policing, regardless of rank, expertise, or experience. In other words, they regarded training as being on a continuum (Ministry of Foreign Affairs and Trade, 2006). The New Zealand Police Officers, in addition to their efforts with new students, provided in-service training to the local managers of the Regional Training Centre and encouraged these managers to attend Central Training Centre (CTC) courses in Kabul.

As well as their training and mentoring roles, police officers from New Zealand also assisted with the building of police stations in five districts in the Bamiyan province (Ministry of Foreign Affairs and Trade, 2006). The New Zealand Provincial Reconstruction Team had also funded and built nine police checkpoints for the Afghanistan National Police in the Bamiyan province (Ministry of Foreign Affairs and Trade, 2006). Unfortunately, the Afghanistan National Police were almost entirely reliant on the New Zealand Provincial Reconstruction Team for weapons, ammunition, communications, vehicle repair, and uniforms (Ministry of Foreign Affairs and Trade, 2006). They were also reliant on the officers for assistance with basic criminal investigations. Criminal offending that required more developed investigation and crime scene assessment was beyond the skills of the local Bamiyan Police and required police experts from Kabul to conduct basic crime scene analysis, fingerprinting, and witness development (Ministry of Foreign Affairs and Trade, 2006).

Police officers from New Zealand also assisted with the construction of a number of new buildings at the Regional Training Centre. At the time, Afghanistan National Police Training Centre attendees slept on a dirt floor in a local mosque, 5 km from the training center, without heat and with barely any food to eat (Ministry of Foreign Affairs and Trade, 2006). The additions to be made to the training center included classrooms, living quarters, kitchen facilities, showers, and a toilet block. The completion of the additional classrooms would enable the New Zealand Police Officers to double the number of courses offered at the Regional Training Centre. The courses would be provided for both new and in-service students. More comprehensive courses were developed, including a 13-week basic training course that was based on the 8-week course coupled with a 5-week intensive literacy program. The larger compound and the second classroom meant that live firearm training could be conducted (Ministry of Foreign Affairs and Trade, 2006).

The Evolving Mission

In April 2006, the New Zealand Government extended the mandate for the deployment of New Zealand Police Officers until 30 September 2007, and in March 2007 this was extended again until 30 September 2008 and then again until 30 September 2009 (International Services Group, 2009).

In 2005, the New Zealand Police had initially deployed as part of the German-led Police Project, but by October 2007 their deployment changed to being a part of the European Police (EUPOL) Afghanistan Mission. The European Police Afghanistan Mission was then taken over by the German-led Afghanistan Police Reform Program (International Services Group, 2009). When the 5-year German-led police reform efforts came to an end, the European Union took over the German mission and launched EUPOL Afghanistan under the framework of the European Security and Defense Policy. This was a new mission that was based on the original mandate for the German Police Project Office mission (International Services Group, 2009).

EUPOL Afghanistan had incorporated the German-led program and had a focus on the field of policing but with linkages to the wider rule of law (International Services Group, 2009). The body responsible for the coordination of the EUPOL was the International Police Coordination Board. Their primary function was to coordinate the international community and their activities with the Afghanistan police reform strategy (International Services Group, 2009).

The transfer of the New Zealand Police Officers to EUPOL did not require any significant change to their roles or any additional funding. The New Zealand Police increased the number of officers deployed to Afghanistan to three in January 2005, and they were all attached to the Provincial Reconstruction Team in Bamiyan (International Services Group, 2009). The roles had changed slightly to one officer mentoring the provincial police chief and a senior Afghanistan police officer and two officers overseeing the training that was delivered in the Regional Training Centre in Bamiyan (International Services Group, 2009).

In 2005, there were eight Afghanistan National Police staff members at the Regional Training Centre, three of whom were in managerial positions. By 2008, there were 19 Afghanistan National Police Officers and 20 civilian support staff at the center (Carswell, 2008). The role of the New Zealand Police Officers was to strengthen the management of the Afghanistan National Police by mentoring senior officers and by establishing management and administrative systems (Carswell, 2008). The officers from the New Zealand Police also assisted with the planning for enrolments at the Regional Training Centre (Williams, 2013).

From March 2005 to May 2008, there were seven rotations of New Zealand Police Officers deployed to Operation Highland. The number of officers deployed on each rotation did not change significantly over that time and nor did the objectives of the rotations change. The objectives of the rotations during this period were as follows:

1. Support the delivery of training at the Regional Training Centre.
2. Mentor the management and instructors of the Regional Training Centre and provide advice on course delivery and administration.
3. Maintain basic training at the Regional Training Centre and explore the introduction of new courses to progress the development of the Afghanistan National Police.
4. Develop the investigative skills of the Afghanistan National Police.
5. Mentor the Provincial Chief of Police and senior managers (Carswell, 2009).

The police officers from New Zealand, along with the Afghanistan National Police Officers, trained 2504 officers between March 2005 and July 2008, and during this time introduced a criminal investigator course into the curriculum (Carswell, 2008). After the second rotation, the New Zealand Police Contingent Commander was assigned to mentoring the Provincial Chief of Police and his senior managers, including the District Chief of Police. The objectives of the mentoring program were to perform the following:

1. Apply the national promulgated policies procedures and systems
2. Facilitate the delivery of community-based policing services that are effective, efficient, impartial, and universally accessible to the public
3. Promote ethical behavior within the ANP with an emphasis on corruption (Carswell, 2008)

The New Zealand Police Contingent Commander spent the day at the Provincial Police Headquarters mentoring the Provincial Chief of Police, the District Chief of Police, and senior managers. The mentoring focused on building individual capacity; leadership development, strategy, and planning; and the management of personnel and resources and administration (Cremer, 2012). As a member of a number of provincial security committees, the Provincial Police Chief was supported by a New Zealand Police Officer when attending these meetings (Carswell, 2008).

During the 2005–2008 period, in addition to the training and mentoring commitments, the officers from the New Zealand Police sought to enhance the Provincial Police Headquarter facilities and the Afghanistan National Police's operational capability by securing funding to develop the following areas:

- Communications
- Fuel and vehicle management
- Building and compound security
- Building repair and additions (Carswell, 2008)

Carswell (2008) claimed that the strengths of the officers deployed by the New Zealand Police from 2005 to 2008 were as follows:

- Experienced in policing and able to provide mentoring advice to Afghanistan National Police in relation to management, administration, and strategic planning.
- Possessed the ability to engage with and build strong relationships with Afghanistan National Police Officers and with local and international key stakeholders.

- Possessed a strong work ethic and were motivated to develop staff from the Afghanistan National Police Regional Training Centre.
- Promoted women in policing.
- Promoted professionalism and integrity in policing.

The primary weakness encountered in the rotations during this period was that Operation Highland did not have a strategic project plan. This meant that the objectives of each rotation had been developed on an incremental basis with one contingent building on the achievements of the previous contingent (Carswell, 2009). A rotation would identify their objectives, and these would then be adopted by the following contingent. This was despite each rotation being required to submit a project plan to the New Zealand Police within the first 6 weeks of their mission. The project plan was to outline the rotation's objectives for the following 6 months (Carswell, 2008).

The planning framework was strengthened by officers that were part of the fifth rotation, Highland 5. These officers developed a discussion paper for the future direction of the rotation, which identified a number of strategic objectives (Carswell, 2008). These objectives were subsequently adopted by successive rotations and were expanded on by the Highland 7 rotation to incorporate the strategic goals of the New Zealand Police. These were incorporated to provide an understanding of the strategic direction of the rotation (Carswell, 2008).

The rotation planning process was also supported by the monitoring mechanisms that were required by the International Services Group at New Zealand Police National Headquarters. These mechanisms included the submission of weekly reports, a substantial mid-rotation report, and an end of mission report (Carswell, 2008).

By the end of 2008, the International Services Group (2009) noted that the Afghanistan National Police numbered approximately 79,000 of the target of 82,000 officers and that it was a developing institution that continued to experience capability problems. According to the group, the problems were caused by poor training, lack of infrastructure, extensive corruption, and weak leadership (International Services Group, 2009; New Zealand Police, 2009). These problems were further exacerbated by their role in fighting the insurgency, seeing personnel killed, and having police posts destroyed, and this diverted the police from their traditional policing roles (International Services Group, 2009; New Zealand Police, 2009). The police reform efforts were also hindered by a lack of coordination in developing an appropriate policing model for Afghanistan and the role that the Afghanistan National Police should undertake to suppress the insurgency (International Services Group, 2009; New Zealand Police, 2009).

The International Services Group (2009) claimed that as a result of these problems the reform of the Afghanistan National Police would take many years, and that while there had been a number of major achievements in terms of police structure, pay reform, training outputs, training facilities, and infrastructure development, the progress of the reform had not advanced as far as was hoped (International Services Group, 2009; New Zealand Police, 2009). The lack of progress was despite the assistance provided by several international contributors. Progress was not made on the Focused District Development (FDD) initiative led by the United States military either. This initiative was designed to improve the skills of police officers and the units at the district level and was supported by EUPOL's police development program (New Zealand Police, 2009).

Closure of Operation Highland

The New Zealand Police had initially planned for Operation Highland to be completed on 30 September 2012. However, the operation was extended for another 12 months. During this period, a joint Police/Defence/Ministry of Foreign Affairs and Trade Cabinet paper was submitted that sought agreement from the New Zealand Government to bring the withdrawal date of the Provincial Reconstruction Team in Bamiyan forward to sometime in early 2013 (Antoun, 2013). The New Zealand Police were included in the planning for the withdrawal, and it was agreed that the New Zealand Police would withdraw their contingent on the commencement of the final military deployment, which would be solely an extraction team. This meant that the exit of the New Zealand Police from Bamiyan would be 6 months earlier than the Defence withdrawal.

At the time of the planning and the submission of the Cabinet paper, the planning section of the military were working toward an October 2013 withdrawal from Bamiyan (Antoun, 2013). This meant that the New Zealand Police needed to plan for an April 2013 withdrawal of their officers. The final rotation was to deploy in October 2012, and its functions were to conclude the training and mentoring tasks, manage any relationship issues with key stakeholders, manage expectations, pack, and withdraw (Antoun, 2013).

Operation Highland closed formally on 4 January 2013 when the last remaining contingent members returned to New Zealand (Williams, 2013). The operation had been in effect for 2 months short of 8 years, with 53 officers being deployed on 16 rotations (Williams, 2013). The withdrawal of the last New Zealand Police Officers was on 24 December 2012 and was part of the overall New Zealand withdrawal from Afghanistan. Following the withdrawal of the New Zealand Police and the New Zealand Defence Force, the Provincial Reconstruction Team Base at Bamiyan was dismantled (Williams, 2013). At the same time, EUPOL withdrew their operation from Bamiyan and relocated their staff to other locations in Afghanistan (Williams, 2013).

There was some risk attached to the eventual departure date, in that New Zealand Police Officers may have been trapped by bad weather. It was important to the reputation of the New Zealand Police and EUPOL that all training commitments be concluded prior to their departure (Cremer, 2012).

The mentoring and training of the Afghanistan National Police had been the centerpiece of the engagement of the New Zealand Police, which had mainly consisted of mentoring the Governor of Bamiyan and the Provincial Chief of Police on security and policing matters (Cremer, 2012; Williams, 2013). The training of Afghanistan National Police Officers was also a principal component of the effort by the New Zealand Police in Bamiyan.

The training efforts of the New Zealand Police had a tangible impact and provided a visible benefit for the local population in that their police units were more effective and trusted (Williams, 2013). Other projects completed by the New Zealand Police were as follows:

- The equipping of mobile training teams – office equipment and education tools were provided by EUPOL to mobile training teams within the Afghanistan National Police in Bamiyan. This initiative enabled more effective training to be delivered to officers across the region.
- The establishment of an interagency crisis operations room at the Afghanistan National Police Headquarters in Bamiyan.
- The establishment of a trained Personal Close Protection Team for the Governor of Bamiyan and personal security and protection for the Provincial Chief of Police (Cremer, 2012; Williams, 2013).

The New Zealand operation remained constant despite the changes in partners. The German reform program was disestablished and handed over to NATO, who then handed the leadership role to the European Union (Williams, 2013). While these changes were taking place, the New Zealand Police Officers achieved as much as could be done (Williams, 2013).

Assessment of the Mission

The achievements and the effectiveness of the first 5 years (2005–2009) of the operation were difficult to document as the outcomes of the operation were not clearly articulated and there were no performance indicators stipulated for any of the contingents (Antoun, 2013). The objectives for the mission were developed on an incremental basis by each rotation and were based on a needs assessment of the Afghanistan National Police at the time. Some rotations developed a vision from the objectives of the previous mission.

There were several reasons for this. The first was that the New Zealand Police worked closely with international partners who defined many of the parameters for the activities undertaken and the resources that were required for each mission (Antoun, 2013). The New Zealand Police Officers who were based at the Regional Training Centre, for example, facilitated the implementation of the International Narcotics and Law Enforcement (INL) training curriculum and the EUPOL Operations manual in addition to their role of delivering training to the Afghanistan National Police. At the Police Provincial Headquarters, the police officers from New Zealand did have more autonomy, but were constrained by a lack of resources. This meant that the officers from the New Zealand Police had to be responsive to multiple stakeholders in a complex and dynamic environment (Antoun, 2013).

Objectives also changed because up until 2009 there was a lack of strategic direction for the Afghanistan National Police and a lack of coordination between the roles of the international community who were working with the Afghanistan National Police on their reform. Initiatives implemented by the International Police Coordination Board Secretariat in late 2009 led to a better alignment of the Afghanistan National Police and the direction of the international community (Antoun, 2013). The realignment was instrumental in determining the strategic direction of the New Zealand Police missions.

The missions were able to make advances in achieving many of their objectives and the tasks outlined in their specific Plans of Action (Antoun, 2013). While progress was made on several fronts overall, there were immense internal challenges – security, culture (corruption and political appointments being the biggest hindrances to progress and long-term sustainability of projects implemented), and limited resources (Antoun, 2013). According to Antoun (2013), the missions during this period were very efficient. The missions chose to spread themselves between the Provincial Police Headquarters and the Regional Training Centre and endeavored to place a third officer in a role to facilitate the training in the Afghanistan National Police districts. Changes in the location of the officers were made as it was recognized that follow-up training of the Afghanistan National Police in the districts was important to ensure that the Afghanistan National Police were implementing what they had been taught and that they continued to develop their policing skills that were appropriate for their rank.

Equally important to the capacity-building efforts by the New Zealand Police Officers was their ability to commit resources to the changing needs of each mission, for example, the establishment, training, and equipping of the Personal Close Protection team, who were responsible for the safety and security of Governor Sarabi and the Provincial Chief of Police. While the training course was not originally an objective of the mission, the implementation and the delivery of the course earned the New Zealand Police a reputation for being able to take the initiative and fill a void in existing capacity (Antoun, 2013). According to Antoun (2013), the delivery of training by New Zealand Police Officers at the Regional Training Centre was more effective after July 2011, following the development of the Transition Plan. Training had progressed significantly in the final 2 years of the operation in terms of growth and ability to provide courses to a wide range of members of the Afghanistan National Police at different ranks. The delivery of training by the Afghanistan National Police Officers at the Regional Training Centre was believed to be sustainable, but the management of the center was not thought to be sustainable without the assistance of the New Zealand Police (Antoun, 2013).

Increasing the ability of the Afghanistan National Police was not restricted to the courses delivered at the Regional Training Centre. There had been tangible gains made at the Police Provincial Headquarters in terms of enhancing operational capability through the mentoring of the Provincial Chief of Police and senior managers and through the upgrade of the facilities and the provision of new equipment (Antoun, 2013). The impact of the training delivered at both the Regional Training Centre and the Police Provincial Headquarters was evident in the increase in confidence and ability of the Afghanistan National Police to conduct investigations, albeit on a small scale (Antoun, 2013). This was after the New Zealand Police Officers demonstrated, coached, and mentored the staff of the Afghanistan National Police in the fundamentals of how modern criminal investigations should be conducted.

Another area that positively impacted on the organizational capability of the Afghanistan National Police was the "Train the Trainer" courses. This was demonstrated by the positive effect that the trained trainers were having on other staff members and the adoption of Community Policing by the Afghanistan National Police (Antoun, 2013). The long-term effects of the "Train the Trainers" course were not known as more time was required to assess whether the program had the ability to transform the Afghanistan National Police.

References

Antoun, F. (2013). *EUPOL End of Mission Activity Report – New Zealand Police (Operation Highland) Bamyan, Afghanistan.* 15 April. New Zealand Police, International Services Group.

Carswell, S. (2008). *Review of NZAID funded New Zealand Police activities in Bamyan, Afghanistan.* New Zealand AID.

Carswell, S. (2009). *Review of NZAID funded New Zealand Police activities in Bamyan, Afghanistan.* New Zealand AID.

Council of the European Union. (2007a). *Council Joint Action 369 (CJA 2007/369/CFSP).* Brussels, Belgium.

Council of the European Union. (2007b). *EU police mission in Afghanistan starts* (10939/07, Presse 140). Brussels, Belgium.

Cremer, G. (2012). *End of mission report.* New Zealand Police.

Greener, B. (2009). *The new international policing.* Palgrave Macmillan Publishers Limited.

Headquarters Joint Forces New Zealand (2005). *March 2005 pre-deployment training: Joining instruction.* February. New Zealand Defence Force.

International Services Group, New Zealand Police (2009). *Briefing: Afghanistan.* 9 April. New Zealand Police.

Jones, S., Wilson, J., Rathmell, A., & Riley, J. (2005). *Establishing law and order after conflict.* RAND.

Ministry of Foreign Affairs and Trade (2004). *Afghanistan: Bamian police assistance.* SPD/BSR/6/6, 29 March. Ministry of Foreign Affairs and Trade.

Ministry of Foreign Affairs and Trade (2006). *Unclassified Cable – Can Bamiyan Law Enforcement Reform?* New Zealand Embassy.

New Zealand Police (2004a). *Reconnaissance mission to Afghanistan: 5–13 August 2004.* New Zealand Police.

New Zealand Police (2004b). *Report to Minister of Police: Afghanistan – Bamian Police assistance.* Police National Headquarters.

New Zealand Police (2005). *Board of Commissioners: New Zealand Police deployments to Afghanistan.* 19 September, BO/05/129. New Zealand Police.

New Zealand Police (2009). *Afghanistan mission brief.* 27 July. New Zealand Police.

Williams, A. (2013). *Closure of Operation Highland.* Internal Memorandum, 7 January. New Zealand Police, International Services Group.

Chapter 5
New Zealand Police Peacekeeping Operations in Bougainville, Papua New Guinea

Garth den Heyer

Introduction

The civil war that occurred in Bougainville is often referred to as the Bougainville conflict, and it occurred on a number of different levels. The conflict took place between 1988 and 1998 in the North Solomons[1] province of Papua New Guinea and was between Papua New Guinea and the secessionist forces of the Bougainville Revolutionary Army and between the Bougainville Revolutionary Army and other armed groups on Bougainville. The conflict has been described as the largest civil war in Oceania since the end of World War II in 1945, with an estimated 15,000–20,000 Bougainvilleans killed.

The underlying reasons for the conflict began in the early 1970s with local landowners opposing the operation of a gold and copper mine at Panguna (May, 2005). This opposition led to a group of Bougainvillean nationalists declaring the unilateral independence of the North Solomons and blockading the airstrip at Arawa on the eve of Papua New Guinea's independence from Great Britain in September 1975 (May, 2005). To ease the tension, Papua New Guinea granted Bougainville a degree of autonomy, but by the 1980s there was further discontent by the landowners as to the environmental impact of the mine (May, 2005). The group of landowners evolved into the Bougainville Revolutionary Army, who eventually forced the closure of the mine.

In 1989, a state of emergency was declared, and the provincial government was suspended (May, 2005). In May 1990, the Independent Republic of Meekamui was declared and the Bougainville Interim Government was established (May, 2005).

[1] North Solomons and Bougainville have both been used at different times for the name of the province.

G. den Heyer (✉)
School of Social and Behavioral Science, Walden University, Minneapolis, MN, USA

G. den Heyer, J. F. Albrecht (eds.), *Police and International Peacekeeping Missions*, https://doi.org/10.1007/978-3-030-77900-9_5

Around this time, the Bougainville Revolutionary Army changed their name to the Bougainville Resistance Forces but continued fighting with the Papua New Guinea Defence Force and the Royal Papua New Guinea Constabulary. The fighting from the late 1980s continued until the end of 1990, despite a number of attempts to resolve the conflict. The conflict led to thousands of people relocating to "care centers" (May, 2005).

Between 1990 and 1996, tentative peace initiatives alternated with military operations that were implemented by the Papua New Guinea Defence Force. In late 1994, a group of Bougainville leaders and Bougainville Resistance Forces Commanders signed an agreement with the Papua New Guinea Government, committing themselves to a peaceful resolution to the conflict (May, 2005). The commitment by the Bougainvilleans led to a number of peace conferences being held in Australia and New Zealand. The factions committed to a peace agreement, and the Burnham Declaration was signed in September 1997. The signing of the Declaration led to the Burnham "Truce" (May, 2005).

Policing in Bougainville Following the Establishment of the "Truce"

Following the establishment of the truce, troops from the New Zealand Defence Force were deployed to Bougainville in late 1997 (Capie, 2012). A principal element of the post-conflict reconstruction process was the restoration of law and order to facilitate peace, security, and the protection of human rights (Sansom, 2009). Law and order had been maintained on most of mainland Bougainville during the conflict by a mix of members of the community and ex-fighter groups as only a few police personnel had remained at Buka (Bougainville Interim Provincial Government, 2003; Sansom, 2009).

It was in this context that the restoration of civil authority was made a priority, and in April 1998, the interim Bougainville Government made a request to the New Zealand and Australian governments to assist in establishing a new type of community policing, which would be based on a Bougainvillean identity (Sansom, 2009). The request formed the beginning of New Zealand's assistance for the establishment of community policing in Bougainville and the beginning of the Bougainville Community Auxiliary Police program (Bougainville Interim Provincial Government, 2003; Sansom, 2009).

Community policing was identified by the Bougainville Interim Provincial Government as the foundation for "a new Bougainville concept of policing" and thus was the guiding philosophy for the Bougainville Police Service (Bougainville Transitional Consultative Council, 2003). The Bougainvillean Government identified the role of Community Police as one that "deal[t] with problems in their communities in consultation with chiefs and other traditional leaders. They should only be involving the [regular] police in relation to serious criminal matters and matters that cannot be resolved through either chiefs or village courts." It was also recognized that there was a need for "a major reorientation of the roles of [regular] police to work more closely in supporting and supervising the work of [community police]" (Bougainville Transitional Consultative Council, 2003). These policing directions were compatible with the Papua New Guinea Government policy (2000), which had a focus on restorative justice and community policing.

The Bougainville Community Auxiliary Police would be part of the Bougainville Police Service, and members would be selected by the community in which they were to serve. Those selected were not to have had any previous policing experience (McGovern & Taga, 2009; Sansom, 2009). The Bougainville Police Service was, at this time, a part of the Royal Papua New Guinea Constabulary. The Bougainville Police Service was not formally established until 2005 when the Bougainville Constitution was ratified by the Papua New Guinea Government (McGovern & Taga, 2009; Sansom, 2009). Members of the Community Auxiliary Police would not be full-time police officers and would only serve on an "as-required" basis and would receive a modest monthly allowance (McGovern & Taga, 2009; Sansom, 2009). The main features of the relationships of the Community Auxiliary Police Officers, the regular Bougainville Police Service Officers, and the traditional leaders were as follows:

1. The focus of policing efforts under the transitional policing arrangements would be based on community policing, where both community police officers and full-time police officers work closely with communities and especially with chiefs and other traditional leaders.
2. The foundation of policing – especially in rural areas – would be community police officers, who would be supported and supervised by full-time police.
3. Community police officers would be trained to deal with problems in their communities in consultation with chiefs and other traditional leaders. Full-time police officers would only be involved in serious criminal matters that could not be resolved by chiefs or village courts (adapted from Dinnen & Peake, 2013, p. 14).

New Zealand Police Role in Bougainville

Since the first deployment in 1998, the New Zealand Police have assisted with the development of the Community Auxiliary Police. Assistance has been provided in a number of phases and has been delivered as a part of the Bougainville Community Policing Project. The initial deployment period of New Zealand Police Officers to Bougainville was not a part of the Bougainville Community Policing Project and only consisted of the delivery of one training course in mid-1998. The second deployment period (Phases 1 and 2: Bougainville Community Policing Project) was from February 2000 to early 2002, and the third deployment period (Phase 3:

Table 5.1 New Zealand Police assistance to the Community Auxiliary Police 1998–2006

Year	Project	Resources
Mid-1998	Training Course	Training of 30 Community Auxiliary Police Officers in Arawa
February 2000 – early 2001	Phase 1: Bougainville Community Policing Project	2 New Zealand Police advisers
Early 2001 – early 2002	Phase 2: Bougainville Community Policing Project	3 New Zealand Police advisers + Administration Manager
April 2004 – December 2006	Phase 3 Bougainville Community Policing Project	5 New Zealand Police advisers

Adapted from: New Zealand Agency for International Development (2006, p. 7)

Bougainville Community Policing Project) was from April 2004 to December 2006. The fourth deployment period (Phase 4: Bougainville Community Policing Project) was from January 2007 to December 2010, and Phase 5 was to follow upon completion of Phase 4. The project or phase of the deployments, the New Zealand resources committed to the phase, and the year of the phase are presented in Table 5.1.

The Bougainville Community Policing Project was managed and funded by the New Zealand Agency for International Development and was to achieve two objectives. The first objective was the development of a framework for implementing the Bougainville Community Policing Project. The project was designed to ensure that the Bougainville Police Service would be an effective Community Policing agency and that the Community Auxiliary Police program would be sustainable (New Zealand Agency for International Development, 2007; McGovern & Taga, 2009; Sansom, 2009). The second objective was to increase security for the people of Bougainville. It was proposed that an increase in security would stabilize the country, which would assist in improving the economy and lessen the population's vulnerability to poverty.

Bougainville Community Policing Project Phases 1–3

In 2001, the New Zealand Agency for International Development considered that the goal of Phase 2 had not been achieved. In 2006, another review was conducted and concluded that the goal had been achieved. The achievement was evidenced by the following:

- Community Auxiliary Police Officers had been deployed to all areas of mainland Bougainville.
- Community Auxiliary Police Officers had dealt with approximately 3200 crimes from July 2004 to July 2006, of which a significant percentage had been resolved at the community level.

- Village courts had resumed functioning – owing to Community Auxiliary Police Officers providing security to the village courts.
- Community Auxiliary Police Officers had been accepted by all factions and in some areas where Bougainville Police Service Officers could not operate (New Zealand Agency for International Development, 2006).

The focus of Phase 3 was to initially reduce the number of Community Auxiliary Police Officers, particularly those who had been trained in the 1990s under a different Community Policing ethos (New Zealand Agency for International Development, 2006). The retrenchment of 122 Community Auxiliary Police Officers enabled the training of 213 new Community Auxiliary Police Officers. The number of trained Community Auxiliary Police Officers and their location are presented in Table 5.2.

A number of other objectives and activities were achieved during Phase 3, which were as follows:

- Refresher training was delivered to Community Auxiliary Police Officers in northern and central Bougainville.
- A train-the-trainers workshop was delivered.
- A Community Auxiliary Police liaison officers' conference was held.
- 30 bicycles in 2005 and 300 uniforms in 2006 were purchased and distributed (New Zealand Agency for International Development, 2006).

The 2006 review also noted that Phase 3 had impacted positively on the lives and the security of the people of Bougainville. The project had provided the foundation for the Community Auxiliary Police to develop into a highly functional Community Policing system, which the New Zealand Agency for International Development (2006) claimed was a culturally and situationally appropriate system of law enforcement.

The Bougainville Community Policing Project had two main strengths. The first was the successful working relationship between the major agencies and the institutions involved in delivering the project, and the second was the establishment and the implementation of a monitoring and evaluation program (New Zealand Agency for International Development, 2006). As a result of the establishment of the

Table 5.2 Number of Bougainville Community Policing Project trained Community Auxiliary Police Officers and their location

Phase	Location	Number
Trained by Bougainville Community Policing Project Phases 1 and 2 – 2000–2002	Wakunai	40
	Buin	43
	Siwai	45
	Bana	40
Trained by Bougainville Community Policing Project Phase 3 – 2004–2006	Kieta	10
	Tinptz	16
	Torokina	19
	Total	213

Adapted from: New Zealand Agency for International Development (2006, p. 10)

monitoring and evaluation program, a number of project reviews were completed by government agencies and independent consultants. The first review was undertaken in October 2000, the second in October 2002, and a third in July 2006 (New Zealand Agency for International Development, 2006). Further reviews were completed in late 2009 and November 2012 (Dinnen & Peake, 2013).

All of the evaluations of the Bougainville Community Policing Project were positive, and conclusions were drawn that the project had "progressed toward" its goals and was highly regarded by a wide range of Bougainvillean stakeholders (Dinnen & Peake, 2013). Each evaluation identified a number of environmental challenges that had impacted on the success of the Community Policing Project, the most immediate was that the Bougainville Police Service was too institutionally weak to "resource and manage" the Community Auxiliary Police scheme effectively (Dinnen & Peake, 2013). The reviews also identified that the Bougainville Police Service had "insufficient capacity to respond to key law and order issues, such as juvenile drug use and domestic violence" (McGovern & Taga, 2009, p. 8; Dinnen & Peake, 2013).

The 2001 review recommended that the New Zealand Overseas Development Agency (now called New Zealand Agency for International Development) maintain its support for Community Policing on Bougainville for a further period of 18–24 months, which was during the transitional phase, to ensure the establishment of the Bougainville Police Service (New Zealand Agency for International Development, 2007). This recommendation led to the design and implementation of Phase 3 of the Bougainville Community Policing Project in April 2004, which was reviewed in July 2006 (New Zealand Agency for International Development, 2007). The 2006 review recommended that Phase 4 of the Bougainville Community Policing Project be established, and this commenced in 2007 (New Zealand Agency for International Development, 2007).

The review of Phase 3 determined that the project had achieved its goal of establishing Community-based Policing in Bougainville and establishing the Community Auxiliary Police in all parts of mainland Bougainville. The review identified, however, that there was a gap in the leadership and the command structure of the Bougainville Police Service (New Zealand Agency for International Development, 2006). At this time, the Bougainville Police Service had only one commissioned officer, while non-commissioned officers (Sergeants and Senior Sergeants) were acting above their rank and were managing and commanding major police stations (New Zealand Agency for International Development, 2007). The Sergeants and Senior Sergeants were also required to manage a large, inexperienced group of probationary Constables, as well as responding to incidents referred to them by the Community Auxiliary Police. In an attempt to address this gap, the New Zealand Agency for International Development financially supported the transfer of 30 experienced Bougainvillean Royal Papua New Guinea Constabulary members to Bougainville in 2004–2005 (New Zealand Agency for International Development, 2007).

The review noted that a number of objectives were achieved and Phase 3 was completed as planned. In addition to delivering training to the regular Bougainville

Table 5.3 Approximate numbers of regular Bougainville Police Service and Community Police 2003–2006

2003	Bougainville Police Service Regulars Officers	Community Auxiliary Police Officers	
Buka	41	264	Community Auxiliary Police – trained by Royal Papua New Guinea Constabulary in the 1990s
Districts	25	168	Community Auxiliary Police – trained by Bougainville Community Policing Project
Total	66	432	432 is the total number trained; approximately 396 were active Community Auxiliary Police Officers in 2003
2006	Bougainville Police Service Regulars	Community Auxiliary Police	
Buka	72	155	Many pre-Bougainville Community Policing Project Community Auxiliary Police retrenched
Districts	95	192	
Total	167	347	

Adapted from: New Zealand Agency for International Development (2007)

Police Service Officers and the Community Auxiliary Police, the mission achieved the following:

- An increase in the number of regular Bougainville Police Service Officers, with more than 100 officers graduating from Bomana Police College, who were deployed as probationary Constables
- A decrease in the number of Community Auxiliary Police Officers, as planned (New Zealand Agency for International Development, 2007)

The numbers of regular Bougainville Police Service and community police officers is presented in Table 5.3.

Bougainville Community Policing Project Phase 4

Those reviewing Phase 3 of the project made three observations. The first was in relation to the focus of the New Zealand Agency for International Development in establishing the Community Auxiliary Police. In 1998, the Community Auxiliary Police were established and were still operational in most parts of mainland Bougainville (New Zealand Agency for International Development, 2006, 2007).

The review noted that the events in Bougainville in the 1990s demonstrated that the collapse of law and order can lead to the collapse of economic and social conditions. The review also noted that the reform of the local policing sector can contribute to the following:

- Alleviating extreme poverty, where there is an inability to meet basic needs. This occurred widely in the 1990s after law and order collapsed.
- Alleviating poverty of opportunity, where opportunities to participate in economic, social, civil, and political life are limited by law and order issues.
- Alleviating vulnerability to poverty (adapted from New Zealand Agency for International Development, 2007).

The second observation was that the reform of the local police was particularly pertinent in Bougainville as pockets of resistance to the government remained. This meant that any future phases would need to consolidate the achievements made by past New Zealand Police Officers. The benefit that could be obtained by implementing a fourth phase was that the Bougainville Community Policing Project could be expanded to include support to the Bougainville Police Service Officers by the following:

- Enhancing the investment in the Community Auxiliary Police program. Weak support from the Bougainville Police Service was undermining the work of the Community Auxiliary Police.
- Enhancing the performance of the Bougainville Policing Authority and further reducing the incidence and fear of crime (adapted from New Zealand Agency for International Development, 2007).

The third observation was that there were a number of specific areas within the existing project, which, if strengthened, could improve the performance of the Bougainville Community Policing Project and the Community Auxiliary Police. These areas were as follows.

The Bougainville Community Policing Project:

- Improvement in the strategic management of the project, including the better preparation of staff, encouragement for an annual planning process, and better monitoring
- A greater focus on sustainability by providing support for the appropriate processes and analyzing the costs for sustaining the activities of the Bougainville Community Policing Project, which should include extending Community Policing to all atolls

The Community Auxiliary Police:

- Strengthening the systems that relate to performance management
- Providing training to a consistent level across all parts of Bougainville (including an extended period of refresher training for Bougainville Community Policing Project and extending the activities of the Bougainville Community Policing Project into southern districts)

- Supporting the Bougainville Police Service to increase their staff in the Community Policing Section and developing management capacities (New Zealand Agency for International Development, 2007)

The review also found that broader support for the Bougainville Police Service could be delivered by refocusing the project to concentrate more on strengthening the Community Policing system (New Zealand Agency for International Development, 2007; Sansom, 2009). The review recommended establishing a new phase, and it was determined that Phase 4 would be implemented with new goals and objectives (New Zealand Agency for International Development, 2007).

Phase 4 commenced on 1 May 2007 and ran for 3 years to 2010. One of the aims was that the Bougainville Police Service operate as an effective Community Policing agency and that it integrate and support a strong, sustainable Community Auxiliary Police program (New Zealand Agency for International Development, 2007; Sansom, 2009). The phase comprised three components, which were supported by a number of objectives. The three components and objectives are presented in Table 5.4.

The primary intention of Phase 4 was that the personnel of the Bougainville Community Policing Project would gradually divest themselves from direct involvement in the support activities of the Community Auxiliary Police as the capacity and capabilities of the local officers expanded. The plan was that as the expansion occurred the resources of the Bougainville Community Policing Project would then be redirected to the new Bougainville Community Policing Project Component 3,

Table 5.4 Bougainville Community Policing Project Phase 4 that pertained to the Bougainville Police Service

Component	Objective	Description
1: Project Management	2	To develop and support implementation of a sustainable strategy for the Bougainville Community Policing Project
2: Community Auxiliary Police	3	To build the capacity of the Bougainville Police Service to train and manage the Community Auxiliary Police
	4	To support further development of effective working relationships between Community Auxiliary Police and local stakeholders
	5	To develop further Community Policing competencies for current and new Community Auxiliary Police and achieve consistency in Community Auxiliary Police competencies throughout Bougainville
3: Bougainville Police Service	7	To build management practices and competencies with Bougainville Police Service
	8	To further develop operational policing competencies among regulars of Bougainville Police Service and support their active application of the Bougainville Police Service Community Policing philosophy
	9	To provide limited and appropriate logistical support to Bougainville Police Service

Adapted from: New Zealand Agency for International Development (2007)

which would provide operational policing support (New Zealand Agency for International Development, 2007; Sansom, 2009).

Prior to Phase 4, the Bougainville Community Policing Project was tasked primarily with delivering training and providing support to the Community Auxiliary Police across all areas of Bougainville. The introduction of the phase saw significant changes to the range of project activities that were undertaken and the composition of the New Zealand Police Project Team. Team members of the New Zealand Police were deployed for periods of 6 months, which was occasionally extended to 9 months, and successive team leaders were in place for periods of 1 year (Pokroy, 2008). The change in composition of the team and the length of deployment enabled the team to shift the focus of the project to strengthening the operational capability of the Community Auxiliary Police officers and to provide support for the Bougainville Police Service (Pokroy, 2008).

Phase 4: Management and Monitoring Strategies

The 2006 review made recommendations that Phase 4 be based on a comprehensive, but flexible, planning framework. The framework should include the following:

- That the Bougainville Community Policing Project team assume more responsibility for planning the project
- More focus on strategic planning
- Coordination of the local police planning processes with the planning processes of the Bougainville Community Policing Project (New Zealand Agency for International Development, 2007)

In order for the Bougainville Community Policing Project to achieve its goal of being able to operate as an effective Community Policing agency, the project needed to be led by the Bougainville Police Service (New Zealand Agency for International Development, 2007). This meant that the inputs of the New Zealand Police would be organized to address the areas of priority of the Bougainville Police Service and to meet its objectives. This also meant that the focus would be placed on the priorities of the Bougainville Police Service and that the management of Phase 4 would be transferred to the New Zealand Police Officers (New Zealand Agency for International Development (2007).

Arrangements to provide more operational support to the Bougainville Community Policing Project were requested by the International Services Group of New Zealand Police National Headquarters, and a project manager was appointed to assist and monitor the delivery of the project (New Zealand Agency for International Development, 2007). This meant that the day-to-day management of the Bougainville Community Policing Project and associated activities would be undertaken by a team leader with support from a project officer, who would be stationed in Bougainville and would work closely with their counterparts within the Bougainville Police Service (New Zealand Agency for International Development,

Table 5.5 Counterpart relationships for New Zealand Police and Bougainville Community Policing Project

New Zealand Police Role	Bougainville Police Service Role
Team Leader	Bougainville Police Service Commander
Operational Policing Adviser	Bougainville Police Service Commander and Station Commanders
Community Auxiliary Police Advisers	Senior staff of Bougainville Police Service Community Policing Section, Senior Community Auxiliary Police Officers

Adapted from: New Zealand Agency for International Development (2007)

2007). The roles of the New Zealand Police Officers and the Bougainville Community Policing Project are presented in Table 5.5.

The new planning framework was to comprise three documents that would be prepared by the Bougainville Community Policing Project team:

- A Sustainability Strategy – this provided an analysis of what was sustainable and provided a platform for the development of a program of activities to assist in the reform of the Bougainville Community Policing Project.
- A monitoring and evaluation plan that identified the following:
  - A baseline and project information that needed to be collected for the effective measurement of agreed indicators
  - A baseline and project information that needed to be collected for the effective measurement of the Bougainville Community Policing Project goals and objectives
- An Annual Plan that comprised the following:
  - An annual work plan, which itemized the activities to be undertaken to pursue the Bougainville Community Policing Project goals and objectives
  - An updated logical framework matrix that was designed to combine elements of the monitoring and evaluation plan and the risk management analysis as a single planning tool
  - Budget information (New Zealand Agency for International Development, 2007)

Bougainville Community Policing Project Phase 5

An evaluation in mid-2009 of the Bougainville Community Policing Project identified that the project was achieving its objectives (Averill et al., 2009). The report noted that progress had been made particularly in the development of infrastructure and capacity building within the provincial government. Higher-level changes, such as more access to justice, were also emerging (Averill et al., 2009). Insufficient policing and the lack of correctional services were, however, affecting communities and other law and justice agencies (Averill et al., 2009).

The need for an improved policing service in Bougainville was not highlighted in the design document of the Bougainville Community Policing Project Phase 5. The document did not define the objectives of Phase 5, although it did identify that the New Zealand Agency for International Development would continue its support for Community Policing into "a final phase" (Averill et al., 2009). The document also identified that while the New Zealand Police would provide the bulk of technical assistance to the Bougainville Police Service and the Community Auxiliary Police Officers, the Bougainville Community Policing Project could draw on the resources of other agencies in other Pacific Island countries (Averill et al., 2009). The technical assistance moved from being defined annually to being defined as short term projects. There were, as well, longer-term projects. The initial establishment of New Zealand Police Officers for Phase 5 was the following:

- One team leader (Buka)
- Two Community Auxiliary Police advisers (Buka)
- Two Community Auxiliary Police advisers (Arawa)
- Two Bougainville Police Service advisers (Arawa, Buka)
- One project officer (Buka) (Averill et al., 2009)

An internal review undertaken by the New Zealand Police of their commitment to the Bougainville Community Policing Project in mid-2012 noted that the program was working but was slowing down owing to a lack of leadership and mid-level management capability in the Bougainville Police Service (Hitchings, 2012). The project was also slowing because the number of New Zealand Police Officers deployed on each contingent had been reduced by half (Hitchings, 2012). Although the reduction in the number of New Zealand Police Officers was in line with the 2011 work plan, the number of advisers had been reduced from four to two, with two Community Auxiliary Police advisers being redeployed to Bougainville Police Service advisory roles in Buka and Arawa (Hitchings, 2012).

A review of the Bougainville Community Policing Project was undertaken by Dinnen and Peake (2013) at about the same time that a review was being undertaken by Hitchings (2012). According to Dinnen and Peake (2013), Phase 5 of the Bougainville Community Policing Project consisted of two components. The first component comprised managing the work of the 346 Community Auxiliary Police Officers that were delivering policing services at the village level throughout rural Bougainville (Dinnen & Peake, 2013). The second comprised developing the institutional capacity of the Bougainville Police Service (Dinnen & Peake, 2013). The review determined that the Bougainville Community Policing Project had some success in its work with the Community Auxiliary Police and the Bougainville Police Service (Dinnen & Peake, 2013).

The review by Dinnen and Peake (2013) highlighted that four aspects of the program had been achieved since the program was reviewed in 2009. The first was that the Bougainville Community Policing Project had expanded the geographical spread of Community Auxiliary Police significantly, which resulted in more Bougainvilleans having access to policing services than they did previously. It was noted that the Community Auxiliary Police Officers were responsible for investigating the majority of incidents reported to the Bougainville Police Service (Dinnen & Peake, 2013). The second noteworthy achievement was that the recruitment strategies of the Bougainville Community Policing Project had resulted in a significant increase in the number of women applying to become Community Auxiliary Police Officers. The report claimed that the number of women Community Auxiliary Police officers had increased from 5 percent of the total number officers to 21 percent during the period 2009–2012 (Dinnen & Peake, 2013). According to Dinnen and Peake (2013), the increase in woman officers provided Bougainvillean women with more opportunity to interact with female Community Auxiliary Police Officers in respect of potentially sensitive complaints. The third achievement was the establishment of a non-commissioned officer component within the program, which provided a leadership structure, a source of accountability, and a potential career incentive within the Community Auxiliary Police (Dinnen & Peake, 2013). The program had also introduced two performance measures that had improved the accountability and management in the Community Auxiliary Police structure (Dinnen & Peake, 2013).

The work of the Bougainville Community Policing Project with the Community Auxiliary Police was acknowledged as being highly relevant and well-regarded throughout Bougainville (Dinnen & Peake, 2013). Where the project had not been successful was, however, in relation to the transitioning of the day-to-day management of the program to the Bougainville Police Service and in developing the capabilities of the Bougainville Police Service (Dinnen & Peake, 2013). The dissatisfaction in the development of the capabilities of the Bougainville Police Service did not come as a surprise to Dinnen and Peake (2013), who noted that many of the problems confronting the New Zealand Police Officers in Bougainville were similar to those being experienced in other capability development projects elsewhere in the Asia-Pacific region (Dinnen & Peake, 2013).

The weakness in the capability program provided by the New Zealand Police to the Bougainville Police Service, according to Dinnen and Peake (2013), was that it "followed a well-worn and fairly unimaginative strategy of 'capacity development'" (p. 6). The development approach of the program focused primarily on strengthening the internal systems of the Bougainville Police Service with the intention that this would translate into an improved policing service in Bougainville, with tangible outcomes in terms of safety, security, and access to justice (Dinnen & Peake, 2013). The problem with the model and the approach was that, firstly, it was a Western approach, and secondly, it did not take into account the social or cultural appropriateness of the organizational and fiscal sustainability of the Bougainville Police Service. Although the program had generated a number of policies, procedures, and systems, they had been developed and implemented without input from or in reference to the Bougainville Police Service (Dinnen & Peake, 2013). Another problem with the development model was that New Zealand Police Officers had spent a large percentage of their time at the police station rather than engaging with community leaders (Dinnen & Peake, 2013). This meant that only a small percentage of the police officers' time was devoted to providing mentoring and policing advice to Bougainville Police Service Officers. The Bougainville Police Service organizational processes may have improved, but in terms of the functionality of the Bougainville Police Service and of it being able to solve practical policing problems, it had not improved (Dinnen & Peake, 2013).

Another problem that was encountered and that compounded the weaknesses in the development capability model was that the monitoring and evaluation record of the program had a number of deficiencies (Dinnen & Peake, 2013). The performance measurement framework of the project only recorded various types of outputs, for example, the number of training courses delivered and manuals produced, and there was no measurement in the framework for identifying the outcomes that the activities and outputs had produced (Dinnen & Peake, 2013).

Conclusion

The Bougainville Community Policing Project, according to Dinnen and Peake (2013), has provided "an unusual instance of qualified achievement" (p. 581). This was owing to the approach taken by the New Zealand Police Officers in delivering the programs, the innovativeness of the project, and the fact that it was "locally grounded" (Dinnen & Peake, 2013, p. 581). The implementation of the project also suggested that there was a much wider understanding of police reform than that presented in other policing development programs around the world. The principal strength of the project was that the reformers had taken the opportunity that was presented following the signing of the peace agreement to develop a policing solution that was primarily culturally based and appropriate for the Bougainville people. Furthermore, peace on Bougainville had been maintained owing to the project being based on community relationships and partnerships (Hayes, 2005), and the New Zealand Police taking a supporting rather than an operational role to assist the Bougainville Police Service.

References

Averill, K., Raka, S., Mokis, S., & Simpson-Edwards, M. (2009). *Provincial engagement evaluation report*. Papua New Guinea Law and Justice Sector.

Bougainville Interim Provincial Government. (2003). *Law and justice for Bougainville*. Bougainville Interim Provincial Government.

Bougainville Transitional Consultative Council. (2003). *Law and justice policy for Bougainville*. Interim Bougainville Provincial Government.

Capie, D. (2012). Peacekeeping – New Zealand's involvement in peacekeeping. *Te Ara: The Encyclopaedia of New Zealand*. Retrieved from http://www.TeAra.govt.nz/en/peacekeeping/

Dinnen, S., & Peake, G. (2013). *Bougainville Community Policing Project: Independent evaluation*. The Australian National University.

Hayes, J. (2005). Bringing peace to Bougainville. In J. Henderson & G. Watson (eds.), *Securing a Peaceful Pacific* (pp. 143–151). Christchurch: Canterbury University Press.

Hitchings, R. (2012). *PNG and Bougainville visit report*. Internal memorandum. New Zealand Police, International Services Group.
May, R. (2005). The Bougainville conflict and its resolution. In J. Henderson & G. Watson (Eds.), *Securing a peaceful pacific* (pp. 459–469). Canterbury University Press.
McGovern, J., & Taga, M. (2009). *Review of the Bougainville community police project (Phase 4)*. The New Zealand Agency for International Development.
New Zealand Agency for International Development. (2006). *Mid term: Bougainville Community Policing Project*. New Zealand Agency for International Development.
New Zealand Agency for International Development. (2007). *Bougainville Community Policing Project: Phase 4 project design document*. New Zealand Agency for International Development.
Pokroy, D. (2008). *Bougainville Community Policing Project: Phase 4 monitoring and evaluation framework*. New Zealand Agency for International Development.
Sansom, M. (2009). *Review of the Bougainville Community Policing Project (phase 4): Terms of reference*. New Zealand Police.

Chapter 6
New Zealand Police Rule of Law Reform Efforts in the Solomon Islands

Garth den Heyer

Introduction

The Solomon Islands are located northeast of Australia and consist of a double chain of more than 900 islands stretching from Bougainville Island in Papua New Guinea in the northwest to Vanuatu in the southeast.

The population in 2019 was estimated to be 680,806 (Solomon Islands National Statistics Office, 2019), and the capital, Honiara, the islands' only city, has an official estimated 2017 population of approximately 84,520. This number has increased significantly during the last few years from 60,000 (circa 2010) (Solomon Islands National Statistics Office, 2019). It is estimated by AusAid (2005) that by 2025 the population of Solomon Islands is likely to double to approximately 1000,000.

The Solomon Islands faces a challenge in generating sufficient employment, owing to the "fast growing labour force, small and narrow-based economy, a highly structured and rigid labour market, under-developed private and informal sectors and economic and political uncertainties that discourage investment" (United Nations Development Programme, 1999, p. 79). The islands' exports are exclusively commodities based and include timber, fish, cocoa, and copra, while most manufactured goods and petroleum products are imported.

The labor market is characterized by people who have low skills, have few vocational abilities, or an advanced level of education. A large number of high school graduates have difficulty in finding work, and as a result, there is a problem of matching their expectations with the opportunities that are available in the formal labor market (United Nations Development Programme, 1999).

The islands had little infrastructure, and what infrastructure did exist was extensively damaged by violence that occurred between 1998 and 2003. The violence caused extensive damage to personal property, transport and communication

G. den Heyer (✉)
School of Social and Behavioral Science, Walden University, Minneapolis, MN, USA

G. den Heyer, J. F. Albrecht (eds.), *Police and International Peacekeeping Missions*, https://doi.org/10.1007/978-3-030-77900-9_6

infrastructure, schools, water supply and sanitation systems, electrical supply, and government buildings. According to the Central Bank Solomon Islands (2003), the economy had contracted by approximately 25 percent from 2000 to 2002 or from US$1000 in 1996 to US$660 per person in 2002, and that it would take 10 years of an annual Gross Domestic Product (GDP) growth of 10 percent before the Solomon Islands would experience levels of income equivalent to those of the 4 years prior to 1999.

The Conflict and Its Origin

Between 1998 and 2003, the Solomon Islands experienced a conflict between ethnic-based militia groups that brought it closer to being a "failed state" than any other Pacific Island country (Watson, 2005). Ethnic opposition and greed were the reasons why the violent atrocities took place, and militia groups used rape, murder, theft, and destruction to intimidate and to seek retribution (Glenn, 2007). Militants also intimidated senior government officials. Ministers and members of the Parliament were involved in corruption and illegal practices, while many of the Solomon Island Police Officers were the perpetrators of violence (den Heyer, 2010).

The conflict continued to escalate, and on 5 June 2000, police officers aligned with members of the Malaita Eagle Force (MEF), raided a national armory, and deposed the prime minister in a de facto coup (Wainwright, 2005). The relationship between the police and the Malaita Eagle Force had developed because a high proportion of police officers, particularly those in the Police Field Force (armed tactical unit), were ethnically Malaitan (den Heyer, 2010). More than 100 people were killed and around 40,000 were displaced during the violence (Watson, 2005; Capie, 2012). This was the largest displacement of people experienced in the Pacific, with the majority of people taking refuge in Honiara or returning to Malaita (Watson, 2005). As a result of the number of refugees entering Honiara and the islands of Malaita, pressure was placed on local resources, and this became the catalyst for further violence (Watson, 2005).

According to Watson (2005), the origin of the conflict lies in the country's colonial history; the British colonial government, apart from clearing land for establishing farms and plantations, did not actively promote any infrastructure development or modernization of the country until well after World War II. The Solomon Islands gained self-governance from Great Britain in 1976, and independence was granted 2 years later, on 7 July 1978. Many former European colonies, especially in the Pacific, were "ill-prepared for the challenges of independent statehood that began to arrive in the second half of the 20th century" (Dinnen, 2007, p. 258). The lack of preparation or capability of the Pacific Islands for independent statehood was not helped by the abruptness of the act of independence being granted (Dinnen, 2007).

Honiara, the capital of the Solomon Islands, at the time of independence, had a population of approximately 15,000, who were of predominately Guadalcanal descent (Watson, 2005). Following independence, the population of Honiara increased and became dominated by people who were not of Guadalcanal descent, being primarily of Malaita descent. As the city increased in size, according to Watson (2005), the administration and the resources of the islands became concentrated in the capital, often at the expense of other islands. As a result of the movement of resources from the islands to the capital, a breakaway movement formed in the Western district, "which looked to ethnic affinities with Bougainville as the basis for a possible new state" (Watson, 2005, p. 401).

The granting of independence and the concentration of resources, together with weak accountability structures and leadership, created the foundation for the development of corrupt officials and the exploitation of the country's national resources (Watson, 2005). These factors were compounded by the unsuitability of the Westminster-style constitutional system that had been adopted by the islands. The culture of the Islands is based on wantokism[1] (Watson, 2005), and according to Kabutaulaka (2002, 2005), this led to the poor performance of successive governments and to the people not having any reason to believe in, or have faith in, the state.

Following the violence in 1998, the capacity of the Solomon Islands Government to manage the economy and provide basic services such as law and order was dramatically weakened (Kabutaulaka, 2005). The country's economy had deteriorated, undermining the government's ability to provide and maintain adequate social services (Kabutaulaka, 2005). Gross Domestic Product (GDP) had fallen by 14 percent in 2000 and 10 percent in 2001 (Central Bank Solomon Islands, 2003), and between 1996 and 2001 exports had declined by 60 percent and GDP per capita had halved in real terms since the islands' independence in 1978 (Australian Strategic Policy Institute, 2003). At the same time, public servants had not been paid, members of the Parliament feared physical attack, Cabinet had been subject to intimidation and extortion, and the police were identified as becoming increasingly corrupt (Greener-Barcham, 2005).

The situation led to the Solomon Islands being described as a failed state, and a report from the Australian Strategic Policy Institute advised that Australia should be proactive in order to stop the Solomon Islands from being used as a base for transnational crimes, such as money laundering, drug trafficking, people smuggling, and terrorism (Australian Strategic Policy Institute, 2003).

The First Steps in Resolving the Conflict

There had also been a number of attempts to reconcile the two main militias during the conflict, but these attempts were unsuccessful. The government then declared a 4-month state of emergency and requested assistance from Australia and New Zealand. These requests were initially rejected by both Australia and New Zealand.

[1] Wontok is derived from the Solomons Islands Pijin English term for "one talk," meaning from the same language, and implies giving preference to relatives or family members in the expectation of a series of reciprocal obligations being fulfilled.

The catalyst for granting the request for international assistance was the kidnapping of the prime minister of Solomon Islands by the Malaita Eagle Force in June 2000. The kidnapping led to the Australian-coordinated Townsville Peace Agreement in October 2000 and elections followed in the Solomon Islands in December 2001. The establishment of the agreement included the deployment of an unarmed 47-person International Peace Monitoring Team (IPMT) to observe the peace, monitor surrendered weapons, and work with the newly formed Peace Monitoring Council (Capie, 2012). The mission was Australian-led, with New Zealand providing the deputy commander and a number of defense, police, and civilian personnel (Capie, 2012).

The signing of the peace agreement did not bring order to the islands, and as Dinnen et al. (2006), claimed, but was the catalyst for further disorder. "Killings, assaults, forced displacement and looting continued," with support from the Royal Solomon Islands Police Force, who themselves "were implicated in extrajudicial executions, indiscriminate shootings, deliberate and arbitrary killings, torture, threats and harassment" (Dinnen et al., 2006, p. 96).

Things did not improve following the December 2001 elections, and law and order deteriorated further as the nature of the conflict shifted. Violence continued in the rural areas of Guadalcanal, but the militants in Honiara turned their attention to crime and extortion (Glenn, 2007). The offices of the Department of Finance in Honiara had been robbed a number of times, and the finance minister had been forced at gunpoint to sign a check made out to one of the militant groups (Glenn, 2007). Conflict also broke out in the Western province, and the elders of the province invited members of the Bougainville Revolutionary Army (BRA) to provide security for the villages.

In June 2002, the International Peace Monitoring Team withdrew from the islands as the incidence of violence had diminished, but the underlying causes of the conflict had not been resolved (Capie, 2012). According to Hagerty (2001), by April 2001, few weapons had been surrendered at the time of the withdrawal of the International Peace Monitoring Team, and it was estimated that about 500 high-powered guns remained in the community in the hands of former militants. Law and order problems continued with criminals continuing to operate with impunity and the conflict continued, not necessarily between the original parties of the conflict, but within Guadalcanal and Malaita communities, making the situation complex. The conflict could no longer be described as a conflict between two ethic or island groups (Kabutaulaka, 2005).

The unrest created a culture of violence that affected government institutions and former militants worked "with corrupt politicians, police officers, and public servants to commit crimes and extort millions of dollars from the government in the guise of the local custom of compensation" (Kabutaulaka, 2005, p. 284). By late 2002, the prevailing atmosphere of lawlessness, widespread extortion, and the ineffectiveness of the police force prompted the Solomon Islands Government to make a formal request for outside help.

The Royal Solomon Islands Police Force

At the time that the Solomon Islands was granted independence, the Royal Solomon Islands Police Force was widely regarded as an efficient and highly effective police force and a model for the newly emerging states of the South Pacific (den Heyer, 2010). However, from the beginning of the tensions in 1998 until the involvement of the Regional Assistance Mission to Solomon Islands (RAMSI) in 2003, there had been a decline in the effectiveness, capability, and the professional skills of the police. The police had been implicated in the tensions, and their knowledge and expertise across the range of police disciplines had eroded to the point where the organization was no longer able to effectively fulfill its law and order responsibilities.

The structures and the capability of the Royal Solomon Islands Police had also been weakened significantly during the conflict (Dinnen et al., 2006), and the organization had become corrupt and based on wantokism (Moore, 2007). The police did not have any guidelines for promotion, which was based on political and kin-based connections rather than on performance (Dinnen et al., 2006). As a result, the senior ranks were bloated, with a number of individual officers holding a senior rank but without an actual position or role (Dinnen et al., 2006). The organization did not maintain a roster, payroll system, or a procurement and budgeting process.

This decline occurred even though a small number of officers from the New Zealand and Australian Police Forces were providing assistance (den Heyer, 2010).

The Regional Assistance Mission to Solomon Islands (RAMSI)

As a response to the crises in the Solomon Islands, a formal request was made to Australia and New Zealand for assistance. On 24 July 2003, a joint, regional, inter-agency force landed in the Solomon Islands to "reinforce and uphold the legitimate institutions and authorities in the Solomon Islands, and to ensure respect for the country's constitution and implementation of its laws" (Glenn, 2007, p. III). The mission was under the "auspices of the Pacific Islands Forum and specifically the 2000 Biketawa Declaration on Mutual Assistance, which authorised forum leaders to consider collective action in response to a security crisis in a member state" (Dinnen et al., 2006 p. 97). The approach that the mission would take was agreed upon by the South Pacific Leaders Forum and was supported by the United Nations.

The Regional Assistance Mission to Solomon Islands would be an integrated, whole of government, multinational state-building initiative that would concentrate on providing security, economic governance, and improving the machinery of government (Wainwright, 2005). The intended model for the mission was comprehensive and unique and comprised eight key features: it was preventive, permissive, regional in nature, nationally led, supported by the United Nations, non-sovereign, police led, and had a light touch (Fullilove, 2006; den Heyer, 2010). The model also recognized that the establishment of security and the rule of law was an essential precondition for the success of the mission and the proposed reforms (Fullilove, 2006).

In contrast to other United Nations post-conflict intervention missions, the police, rather than the military, led the Regional Assistance Mission to the Solomon Islands. The mission was jointly led by Australia and New Zealand, but New Zealand was very much a minor leader. The force comprised Australian and New Zealand soldiers, police officers, and foreign affairs officials. According to Glenn (2007) and Capie (2012), more than 1800 military and 300 police officers were deployed initially. The police component of the mission, the Participating Police Force, was led by Australia (Dinnen et al., 2006).

Two of the strategic objectives of the Regional Assistance Mission to the Solomon Islands intervention were restoring law and order and the rebuilding of the nation (Kabutaulaka, 2005). The core objectives of this mission were, according to the New Zealand Ministry of Foreign Affairs and Trade (2003), to "re-empower the forces of law and order so that they are able to sustain law and order themselves, and [to] provide the Solomon Islands Government with the freedom to operate without the ongoing threat of intimidation and extortion at gunpoint" (p. 1).

The second objective of the mission was to provide a mechanism to reform the public sector in the Solomon Islands. The reform was perceived as being necessary because the machinery of the public service was not working (Kabutaulaka, 2005), owing to corruption. It needed to be reorganized if assistance were to be given to the government and services provided to the public.

The Regional Assistance Mission to Solomon Islands was to be a state-building operation that would comprise three phases and a number of separate elements and would involve both Australian and New Zealand agencies (Wainwright, 2005). The first phase of the mission, *commencement*, was to last approximately 6 months (Glenn, 2007). The objectives were to restore stability by disarming the militants, re-establish law and order, capture militant leaders and criminals, and strengthen the police force (Glenn, 2007). Phase 2, *consolidation*, was to begin in January 2004 and would end 12 months later. The phase would place an emphasis "on institutional reform: eliminating the corruption that ran rife through all aspects of the Solomon Islands Government and training officials so that they could provide the services to the citizens of the country" (Glenn, 2007, p. xii). The last phase, *sustainability and self-reliance*, was to start in January 2005 and would focus on the development of self-reliance and stabilizing the proposed governmental and social reforms (Glenn, 2007). To achieve the objectives and the phases of the mission, mission "personnel were to be placed in line positions and advisory roles in Solomon Islands agencies, and a civilian Special Coordinator was to oversee the operation" (Wainwright, 2005, p. 1).

The uniqueness of the mission was its organizational structure. The mission was led at a political level by an official from the Australian Department of Foreign Affairs and Trade, with the second in command being from the New Zealand Ministry of Foreign Affairs and Trade. At an operational level, it was the police who would be responsible and the military took a supporting role at the tactical, operational, and strategic levels (Glenn, 2007).

The mission was an initial success, and by November 2003, more than 3700 weapons had been handed in to the police as a part of the disarming program; and between 24 July and 24 December 2003, 733 people had been arrested on 1168 charges (Solomon Islands Broadcasting Corporation, 2003). A number of government officials and police officers had also been dismissed from their positions and had been charged with criminal offences (Kabutaulaka, 2005).

Regional Assistance Mission to Solomon Islands: Phase 1

The first task under Phase 1 of the mission was to restore law and order. This was a police task, with the role of the military being restricted to creating a secure environment and this would enable the police to operate effectively (Greener-Barcham, 2005; den Heyer, 2010). The restoration of law and order was quickly achieved by police officers from the Regional Assistance Mission to Solomon Islands, who were working alongside members of the Royal Solomon Islands Police Force (Greener-Barcham, 2005). How the operational delivery was structured initially created some difficulties in promoting a sense of local ownership of the new approach to policing (Greener-Barcham, 2005), but within a few months, the community were able to understand and appreciate the new form of policing, which was to restore order and security.

An evaluation of the mission that was completed by Winter et al. (2008), in late 2007, identified the following:

- The proportion of Solomon Islanders who believed that violence would return if the Regional Assistance Mission to Solomon Islands had left declined during the year (46%, down from 54% in 2006).
- The crime clearance rates were improving.
- There had been a significant reduction in the backlog of tension-related, criminal files and sexual assault files in the provinces.
- Thirty-two percent of Solomon Islanders believed that the Solomon Islands Police Force treated people with respect (down from 44% in 2006).

The Winter et al. (2008) evaluation, together with the results from the 2005, 2006, and 2007 People's Surveys, provided the basis for concluding that by late 2007 the Royal Solomon Islands Police Force had become an effective policing agency that was able to undertake general policing and conduct most investigations. However, the police acknowledged that it was unable, at that time, to undertake high-end policing or complex and technical investigations, such as investigating corruption, fraud, and computer crime (den Heyer, 2010). Research undertaken by den Heyer in 2008 supported the claim that the Royal Solomon Islands Police Force was capable of undertaking general policing. den Heyer (2010) claimed that since 2003 the Regional Assistance Mission to Solomon Islands had placed an emphasis on capacity development and there was little or no evidence of strengthened capacity development beyond the level of individual officers and staff members. This was viewed as being expected as it was understood that the sustainable development of the police would be a long-term process and that many of the conditions for success were not in place at the organizational or state level (den Heyer, 2010). Furthermore, political and security conditions since 2003 had not been conducive to capacity development of the police (den Heyer, 2010).

The results from the 2005, 2006, and 2007 People's Surveys led to the undertaking of a strategic review of the Royal Solomon Islands Police Force in 2006, which then led to the development of a plan for reforming the organization (den Heyer, 2010). The document directed that any future reform programs would be based on a sustainable capacity development framework. This would include the documenting of performance measures and a plan for improving the Royal Solomon Islands Police Force (den Heyer, 2010).

The Law and Justice program was seen by the local population as a positive face of the Regional Assistance Mission to Solomon Islands (ANU Enterprise Pty Limited and the Australian National University, 2007). Since 2003, the program accomplished two major successes: a reasonably functional and professional police force and a functional criminal and civil justice system. The result of this was a much-improved sense of security. However, when the riots, following the results of the election in April 2006, occurred, this demonstrated that security was far from perfect, and even though the damage to property was extensive, there was no loss of life and the number of injuries was minimal (den Heyer, 2010).

At the start of 2008, the Participating Police Force revised its work plan to align its support more explicitly with the corporate direction and organizational structure of the Royal Solomon Islands Police Force and to make it more outcome oriented. The partnership between the Royal Solomon Islands Police Force and the Participating Police Force was strengthened as a result of this. The support provided by the Participating Police Force shifted from focusing on operational policing to supporting senior and middle management in the Royal Solomon Islands Police Force and to providing administrative, system, and corporate support while still retaining the policing capability to respond to unrest and disorder should it arise.

Regional Assistance Mission to Solomon Islands: Phase 2

Phase 2 of the Regional Assistance Mission to Solomon Islands commenced in 2004 and continued to focus on law and justice (Wainwright, 2005). By mid-2004, approximately 25 percent (or approximately 400) of officers from the Royal Solomon Islands Police Force had been removed from office, with 88 of those being (including two deputy commissioners) arrested and charged with corruption, murder, or serious criminality (Wainwright, 2005; Moore, 2007). The majority of police officers that were removed were from the former paramilitary division or were Special Constables (Moore, 2007). A number of senior politicians and bureaucrats, including the former Minister of Police and the former Minister of Health, were also arrested (Wainwright, 2005). With court trials commencing and security stabilized with the aid of the Regional Assistance Mission to Solomon Islands, the country's economy was able to start to operate. The difficulty in removing such a large number of police officers, especially senior officers, was that it "weakened the knowledge and authority base of the Royal Solomon Islands Police Force" (Moore, 2007, p. 145).

Phase 2 was more robust than Phase 1 and contained two primary components. Deploying Participating Police Force Officers with the executive authority to restore law and order was the first, and the second was building the capacity of the Royal Solomon Islands Police Force (Dinnen et al., 2006). Dinnen et al. (2006) claimed that the capacity of the police to respond effectively to lawlessness was still limited and that the skill level of most officers was low. This meant that the police were not capable of undertaking routine criminal investigations or apprehending suspects. There were also concerns about the continual change in police leadership, the "politicisation of senior ranks, and growing levels of police corruption" (Dinnen et al., 2006, p.89).

The strategy for rebuilding the Royal Solomon Islands Police Force comprised two aspects. The first was that the Participating Police Force would take a lead role in implementing the reform of the Royal Solomon Islands Police Force, which was to begin with "vetting, recertification and internal investigation of their personnel" (Dinnen et al., 2006, p. 99). The reason that vetting was undertaken was because it was thought that the public would have more confidence in the force if the compromised officers were identified and removed. The implementation of the vetting policy proved to be effective and by "February 2004, over 50 police officers (including two deputy commissioners) had been arrested and charged with 285 offences" (Dinnen et al., 2006, p. 99). Following the completion of the vetting and recertification program, the Participating Police Force reviewed the processes and systems of the Royal Solomon Islands Police Force. The second aspect was that Participating Police Force officers would be embedded as role models in the Royal Solomon Islands Police Force and would set an example as to how policing should be undertaken (Dinnen et al., 2006).

The main weakness at the time of the implementation of Phase 2 was that the Royal Solomon Islands Police Force were not fully engaged in the reform process and a number of strategies that were designed to increase participation met with disappointing results (Dinnen et al., 2006). According to Dinnen et al. (2006), there were two reasons for the weak engagement by the police. The first reason was because the police had not been included in the management structure of the Regional Assistance Mission to Solomon Islands, and the second was that there was a difference in the cultures of the police forces that made up the Participating Police Force and the Royal Solomon Islands Police Force (Dinnen et al., 2006). There were also a number of other possible reasons for the weak engagement. The majority of officers from the Royal Solomon Islands Police Force were not educated to the same level as the leaders and planners of the Participating Police Force and often appeared not to have the same level of understanding of the reform concepts. Another possibility was that the Royal Solomon Islands Police Force had lost the majority of its more senior officers, and as a result, a number of executive and senior officers of the Royal Solomon Islands Police Force were new in their roles and were still learning how to balance their roles with the reforms and the wishes of the Solomon Islands Government.

Regional Assistance Mission to Solomon Islands: Phase 3

In 2007–2008, the Solomon Islands had experienced two distinct periods in their political environment (AusAid, 2008). Prior to December 2007, the Regional Assistance Mission to Solomon Islands had operated in a challenging political context, experiencing numerous events that destabilized the implementation of Phase 3 of the program, and this negatively impacted on the effectiveness of their service delivery. However, in mid-December 2007, a new government came to power and they established a more positive environment that enabled the Regional Assistance Mission to Solomon Islands to operate more effectively (AusAid, 2008).

Phase 3 of the Regional Assistance Mission to Solomon Islands focused on emphasizing development and capacity building as a part of the reform of the Royal Solomon Islands Police Force (Wainwright, 2005). The Royal Solomon Islands Police Force were now capable of undertaking more general policing, which enabled the Participating Police Force to step back from an operational role to concentrate on providing training and mentoring, especially in relation to more serious criminal investigations (Wainwright, 2005).

The Participating Police Force

The Participating Police Force comprised members from police agencies from 15 South Pacific Forum states,[2] who were deployed to the Solomon Islands as part of Regional Assistance Mission to Solomon Islands under Operation Helpem Fren in July 2003 (Nautilus Institute for Security and Sustainability, n.d.-b). The force was led by a senior officer from the Australian Federal Police, at the rank of Commander and was also sworn in as a Deputy Commissioner with the Royal Solomon Islands Police Force (Nautilus Institute Security and Sustainability, n.d.-b).

The Participating Police Force was deployed to every province in the Solomon Islands, and its initial role was to stabilize security in the islands by disarming the militia and restoring law and order (Nautilus Institute for Security and Sustainability, n.d.-a). Following the implementation phase in 2003–2004, the force assisted in strengthening and reforming the Royal Solomon Islands Police Force (Nautilus Institute for Security and Sustainability, n.d.-b).

---

[2]Australia, Cook Islands, Federated States of Micronesia, Fiji, Kiribati, Marshall Islands, Nauru, New Zealand, Niue, Palau, Papua New Guinea, Samoa, Tonga, Tuvalu, and Vanuatu.

By July 2007, the Participating Police Force included 308 police officers, of which 215 (approximately 70 percent) were Australian (Nautilus Institute for Security and Sustainability, n.d.-b) and 35 were from New Zealand. The rest were from other South Pacific nations. By 1 July 2008, the number of officers of the Participating Police Force had decreased to 297 (Winter et al., 2008).

The Strategy of the Participating Police Force

The role of the Participating Police Force component of Regional Assistance Mission to Solomon Islands initially consisted of three phases. These were establishing law and order, consolidating law and order, and capacity development and sustainment. The elements of the three phases are described in Table 6.1.

During Phases 1 and 2 of the Regional Assistance Mission to Solomon Islands, a strategic review of the Royal Solomon Islands Police Force was undertaken, and as a result of this review and taking the lessons learnt from the implementation of Phases 1 and 2, Phase 3 of the mission strategy was expanded to ten phases (Planning and Development, 2006). The review resulted in the development of a planning document that focused on the design of future programs that would provide for a sustained capacity development. The document also included a framework for measuring the success of the reform of the Royal Solomon Islands Police Force. Owing to a range of factors, such as differing skills and the size and scope of capacity

Table 6.1 Initial three phases of the Participating Police Force

RAMSI phase	Description	Elements
1.	Establish Law and Order July 2003 to December 2003 (originally named Commencement)	Initial deployment and force establishment Restoration of basic law, order, and security Removal of illegally held weapons from the community Disarmament and neutralization of key militants
2.	Consolidate Law and Order January 2004 to December 2004 (originally named Consolidation)	Consolidation of the rule of law Institutional reform Building community trust and confidence Creating the environment for economic reconstruction and commerce
3.	Capacity Development and Sustainment January 2005 to June 2008 and beyond (originally named Sustainability and Self-Reliance)	Transition to self-reliance by Royal Solomon Islands Police Force Training and capacity building Entrenching reform and the systems enabling long-term sustainability Draw down and eventual exit of Participating Police Force

Adapted from: Planning and Development (2006)

Table 6.2 Principles for the application of the ten -phase model

1. The delivery of sustainable capacity development to the Solomon Islands Police Force will be driven by "circumstances or events" rather than time.
2. Each component of the capacity development and sustainment program will progress to the next phase along staggered time lines.
3. Phase 10 – Sustainment will be reached at different times by each work area. It is acknowledged that sections within each work area will reach Phase 10 while other areas continue to work through Phases 3–9.

Adapted from Planning and Development (2006)

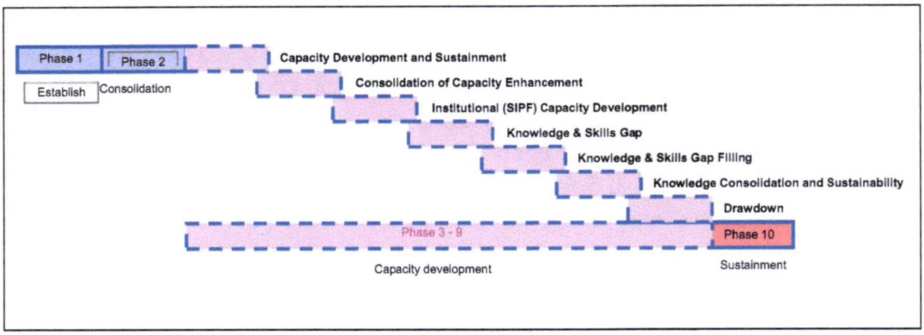

Adapted from Planning and Development (2006)

Fig. 6.1 The PPF ten-phase model. (Adapted from: Planning and Development (2006))

development projects, three "over-arching" principles were developed to guide the application of the additional phases. These principles are presented in Table 6.2.

The ten phases of the model are presented in Fig. 6.1. The figure presents the strategic direction and the associated phases that the Participating Police Force adopted to assist the Royal Solomon Islands Police Force achieve self-reliance and self-sustainability. The expansion of the number of phases had implications for both the Royal Solomon Islands Police Force and the Participating Police Force. In relation to the Royal Solomon Islands Police Force, the review identified that there was a need to develop the capacity of both the institution and its personnel. In relation to the Participating Police Force, the review highlighted challenges for the organization as the shift was made from an operational focus to one of capacity development. Professionalizing the approach by adopting a standardized project management methodology across the entire Regional Assistance Mission to Solomon Islands was another challenge.

In late 2006, a review of the strategic plan of the Participating Police Force commenced to ensure that it remained relevant in achieving the Regional Assistance Mission to Solomon Islands's goal of providing a safer and more secure Solomon Islands (Participating Police Force, 2008). The review was also initiated as a response to developments in the Regional Assistance Mission to Solomon Islands Performance Framework and increasing demands made by the Solomon Island Government for the Regional Assistance Mission to Solomon Islands to

Table 6.3 Capacity development and sustainment working group five objectives

Identify and manage the delivery of the Participating Police Force's Capacity Development objectives consistent with the annual Royal Solomon Islands Police Force Business Plan
Identify and manage the integration of related projects and programs
Manage the reporting to relevant bodies on arising issues
Identify and manage the "events" required to occur during each stage of the Royal Solomon Islands Police Force Capacity development and Sustainment Strategic Project Plan life cycle
Identify and manage the performance measurement procedures of the Royal Solomon Islands Police Force Capacity Development and Sustainment Program.

Source: Participating Police Force (2006)

demonstrate where its capacity development efforts were being directed and the progress being made. At the same time, a number of independent reviews had commenced, which determined that the Strategic Plan of the Participating Police Force had not met all of the needs or demands of the stakeholders and contributors and that a different style of document was required (Participating Police Force, 2008).

To ensure that a coordinated approach would be taken to sustaining the capacity development of the Royal Solomon Islands Police Force, the Capacity Development and Sustainment Working Group (CD&SWG) was established (Participating Police Force, 2006). This group comprised managers from both the Participating Police Force and the Royal Solomon Islands Police Force and developed five objectives (which are presented in Table 6.3) to deliver a consistent and culturally relevant capacity development that would sustain the reform of the Royal Solomon Islands Police Force.

To ensure that the Participating Police Force was able to instill capacity development at both the individual and organization levels, the original scope of the project was modified to include taking responsibility for providing sustainable capacity development of Royal Solomon Islands Police Force skills in the following areas:

- Human resources
- Finance
- Logistics
- Planning and policy

This change resulted in an emphasis in the planning for and the implementation of a sustainable capacity development program for the Royal Solomon Islands Police Force. It was intended that once the level of capacity development had been achieved the Participating Police Force would reduce the number of personnel and resources to a level that would provide ongoing sustainment assistance. The Participating Police Force implemented three projects that directed the delivery of the sustainable capacity development project for the Royal Solomon Islands Police Force in 2006. The three projects were as follows:

1. Learning and Development – enhance the professional skills, knowledge, and expertise of all ranks in the Royal Solomon Islands Police Force by delivering

effective on-the-job-training and sustainable formal training, and from an educational program.
2. Force Structure Review – implement an effective, ethical, sustainable structure for the Royal Solomon Islands Police Force, which is able to meet government-directed law enforcement and security outcomes and priorities.
3. Legislation and Corporate Governance – update legislation affecting the structure, management, and operation of the Royal Solomon Islands Police Force (Planning and Development, 2006).

Each project was of long-term duration and had not been established with any timeframe in mind as these were fundamental to each of the ten phases and, therefore, allowed for the different areas within the Royal Solomon Islands Police Force to be at different capacity and sustainability levels within the phases.

By the end of 2007, the Participating Police Force had transitioned from the two earlier phases (Restore Law and Order and Consolidate the Rule of Law) to a third phase known as Capacity Building and Sustainment. The refocused strategic project plan of the Participating Police Force had two objectives: (1) normalizing the law and order and security and (2) rebuilding the Royal Solomon Islands Police Force. The implementation of the policing program was to be undertaken by the way of 17 activities that were defined in project (work area) plans and had been mapped to and were consistent with the eight goals of the Royal Solomon Islands Police Force Strategic Directions 2005–2010 and the Royal Solomon Islands Police Force Annual Business Plans (Winter & Schofield, 2007). It was also at this stage that the Participating Police Force seconded a New Zealand Police Officer, who was a specialist in strategic management, to design an end state and an exit plan for the mission. This officer was instrumental in developing the processes that the Participating Police Force would adopt to downsize the mission and withdraw staff leading to the finalization of the Regional Assistance Mission to Solomon Islands in 2017.

The project that the police officer from New Zealand designed was called the Future Directions Program and was a result of an evaluation of the direction and delivery of the mission and the need to change the focus of the mission not only by resolving a number of outstanding issues but also by resolving a number of historical concerns (Strategic Projects, 2008). These changes placed an emphasis on the Participating Police Force building the capacity of the Royal Solomon Islands Police Force at the mid and senior management levels and their systems and processes (Strategic Projects, 2008). To undertake the proposed change, the Participating Police Force needed to review their structures, governance, and accountability systems and processes.

The goals of the Future Direction Program were to perform the following:

- Refocus the mission to one dedicated to the provision of sustainable capacity development of the Royal Solomon Islands Police Force staff, organization, and systems and processes
- Gradual withdrawal of the operational deployment

- Gradual reduction in Participating Police Force personnel and resources to a level that would be suitable for maintaining the long-term sustainable capacity development of the Royal Solomon Islands Police Force (Strategic Projects, 2008)

The Future Directions Program comprised one master project plan (Future Directions Project Management Plan) and the following subproject plans:

1. Rationalization of Participating Police Force Outposts Project – this project included
   (a) Audit/Evaluation/Review Program
   (b) Establishment of Provincial Capital Posts
   (c) Rationalization of Participating Police Force support assets
2. Combined Task Force (military) Involvement in Provincial Capital Posts Project
3. Re-Structuring of the Participating Police Force Project
4. "Unfinished Business" Project
5. Rearming of the Royal Solomon Islands Police Force Project (Strategic Projects, 2008).

To achieve the implementation of the Future Directions program, a Participating Police Force Strategic Plan 2009–2011 was developed and implemented. The strategic plan had two objectives and are presented in Table 6.4.

The Success of the Regional Assistance Mission to Solomon Islands

The Regional Assistance Mission to Solomon Islands had an immediate effect on law and order and stabilizing security in Honiara and the wider Solomon Islands (Capie, 2012; Glenn, 2007). The primary reason for the success of the mission was

Table 6.4 Participating Police Force Program objectives and long-term outcomes

Program objective	Long-term outcome
Capacity development of Solomon Islands national and provincial government individuals and institutions	The Solomon Islands public service has the capacity to identify its own directions, to lead and manage sustainable change, to reflect on its strengths and weaknesses and to continuously improve its own performance
Law and Justice	
To contribute to a safer and more secure Solomon Islands	Safe and stable communities created through collaborative equitable crime prevention, community safety, and security initiatives
	Professional effective and accountable law enforcement agencies
	Improved justice sector capacity in areas of coordination, strategy, planning, policy, and reform.

Source: Strategic Projects (2008)

that it planned for a whole-of-government (foreign affairs, police and military, and aid agencies) approach, prior to the mission arriving in the Solomon Islands and in the execution of the mission plan (Glenn, 2007). According to Glenn (2007), a second reason for the initial success of the mission was the cooperation between the three lead Australian representatives from the Department of Foreign Affairs and Trade, police, and military. Their example set the level of dedication to the mission, and this filtered across to members at all levels of the Regional Assistance Mission to Solomon Islands (Glenn, 2007).

Cooperation between the three lead Australian representatives was a "unity of message and effort" (Glenn, 2007). This unity encouraged the Regional Assistance Mission to Solomon Islands to consistently communicate the objectives of the mission and the common cause of the 15 participating nations.

Another reason for the success of the mission, according to Fullilove (2006), was that it was led by the police, but supported by the military. The support and force protection provided by the military enabled the Participating Police Force to undertake their policing duties effectively and enabled them to begin the second phase of the mission, which was to investigate corruption and reform the Royal Solomon Islands Police Force.

Following the arrival of the mission in Honiara in July 2003, a number of arrests were made of high-profile and violent offenders and more than 3700 illegal weapons were collected and destroyed. Law and order were restored, but sustaining the peace in the Solomon Islands proved to be challenging (Capie, 2012). After 9 months of the mission commencing, a number of civilians arrived to assist with implementing the Regional Assistance Mission to Solomon Islands, and this made it possible for the military to reduce the number of soldiers deployed from 1800 to 700. By the end of 2004, the military had reduced their personnel in the Solomon Islands to 60 personnel (Glenn, 2007).

Conclusion of the RAMSI

In 2016, the Ministry of Foreign Affairs and Trade and the New Zealand Police, in consultation with the Royal Solomon Islands Police Force, the Solomon Islands Government, and the Australian Federal Police, designed a new program that would support the Royal Solomon Islands Police Force. The program was designed so that the New Zealand Police would continue to provide assistance to the Royal Solomon Islands Police Force through the Solomon Islands Policing Support Program, which was a bilateral policing assistance program that provided advice and support to the Royal Solomon Islands Police Force.

The Solomon Islands Police Support Program provided funding for eight advisers from the New Zealand Police to be based in Honiara and whose role it would be is to focus on the areas of expertise of the New Zealand Police: community policing, family violence, and crime prevention (Hames, 2017). The new program commenced on 1 July 2017 and was designed to ensure a smooth transition from the Regional Assistance Mission to Solomon Islands, which finished on 30 June 2017.

References

ANU Enterprise Pty Limited and the Australian National University. (2007). *RAMSI peoples pilot survey: Final report*. Regional Assistance Mission to Solomon Islands.

AusAid. (2005). *Australian aid: Promoting growth and stability*. AusAid.

AusAid. (2008). *Annual program performance report for Solomon Islands 2007–08*. Australian Agency for International Development (AusAID).

Australian Strategic Policy Institute. (2003). *Our failing neighbour: Australia and the future. of Solomon Islands*. ASPI Publications.

Capie, D. (2012). *Peacekeeping – New Zealand's involvement in peacekeeping*. The Encyclopaedia of New Zealand. Retrieved from http://www.TeAra.govt.nz/en/peacekeeping/

Central Bank Solomon Islands. (2003). *Annual report*. Solomon Islands.

den Heyer, G. (2010). Measuring capacity development and reform in the Royal Solomon Islands Police Force. *Policing and Society, 20*(3), 298–315.

Dinnen, S. (2007). A comment on state-building in Solomon Islands. *The Journal of Pacific History, 42*(2), 255–263.

Dinnen, S., McLeod, A., & Peake, G. (2006). Police-building in weak states: Australian approaches in Papua New Guinea and Solomon Islands. *Civil Wars, 8*(2), 87–108.

Fullilove, M. (2006). *The testament of Solomons: RAMSI and international state-building*. Lowy Institute for International Policy.

Glenn, R. (2007). *Counterinsurgency in a test tube: Analysing the success of the Regional Assistance Mission to Solomon Islands (RAMSI)*. Rand Corporation.

Greener-Barcham, B. (2005). The New Zealand experience. In J. Henderson & G. Watson (Eds.), *Securing a peaceful pacific* (pp. 215–218). Canterbury University Press. (p. 215).

Hagerty, D. (2001). *Small arms in post-conflict situation: Solomon Islands*. Paper presented at the Pacific Islands Forum Small Arms Workshop, 9–11 May. International Peace Monitoring Team, Solomon Islands. Retrieved from http://rspas.anu.edu.au/papers/melanesia/working_papers/workingpaperhegarty.01_5.htm

Hames, S. (2017). *Briefing on RAMSI drawdown celebrations*. International Services Group.

Kabutaulaka, T. (2002). *A weak state and the Solomon Islands peace process*. Pacific Islands Development Series, Working Paper No. 14,

Kabutaulaka, T. (2005). Australian foreign policy and the RAMSI intervention in Solomon Islands. *Contemporary Pacific, 17*(2), 283–308.

Ministry of Foreign Affairs and Trade. (2003). *Solomon Islands: Strengthened assistance*. Memorandum to Ministry of Defence. Ministry of Foreign Affairs and Trade.

Moore, C. (2007). Helpem Fren: The Solomon Islands, 2003-2007. *The Journal of Pacific History, 42*(2), 141–164.

Nautilus Institute for Security and Sustainability. (n.d.-a). *International force east Timor (INTERFET)*. Retrieved from: https://nautilus.org/publications/books/australian-forces-abroad/east-timor/international-force-east-timor-interfet/

Nautilus Institute for Security and Sustainability. (n.d.-b). *Participating police force (PPF)*. Retrieved from https://nautilus.org/publications/books/australian-forces-abroad/solomon-islands/participating-police-force-ppf/

Participating Police Force. (2006). *Capacity development and sustainment working group: Terms of reference*. Internal Memorandum.

Participating Police Force. (2008). *Solomon Islands police force capacity development program: November 2007 to November 2008*. Participating Police Force.

Planning and Development (2006) Capacity Development and Sustainment Strategic Project Plan. Participating Police Force, Regional Assistance Mission Solomon Islands.

Solomon Islands Broadcasting Corporation. (2003). *Online News: RAMSI success*. Retrieved from http://www.sibconline.com.sb

Solomon Islands National Statistics Office. (2019). *Population*. Retrieved from: https://www.statistics.gov.sb/statistics/social-statistics/population

Strategic Projects. (2008). *Future directions programme*. Participating Police Force.
United Nations Development Programme. (1999). *Report on the Solomon Islands*. UNDP.
Wainwright, E. (2005). *Australia's Solomon Islands commitment: How is it progressing?* Australian Strategic Policy Institute Speech to the Sydney Institute.
Watson, G. (2005). Conflict overview. In J. Henderson & G. Watson (Eds.), *Securing a peaceful pacific* (pp. 401–407). Canterbury University Press.
Winter, J., & Schofield, K. (2007). *Annual performance report 2006/2007: A report on the performance of the regional assistance mission to Solomon Islands*. Regional Assistance Mission to Solomon Islands.
Winter, J., Schofield, K., & Duituturaga. (2008). *A report on the performance of the regional assistance mission to Solomon Islands*. Regional Assistance Mission to Solomon Islands.

Chapter 7
The New Zealand Police Peacekeeping Deployment in Timor-Leste

Garth den Heyer

Introduction

Timor-Leste, formally East Timor, shares an archipelago that is situated to the northwest of Australia, with the Indonesian West Timor. For more than 400 years, the island was colonized by the Portuguese, who used the island as a trading post (Howard, 2008). In 1974, Portugal withdrew from East Timor, and this resulted in civil war (New Zealand Police, 2018). East Timor was granted independence from Portugal on 25 April 1974, but owing to the fractured nature of the government and the civil war, the country was invaded by Indonesia 9 days later.

For more than 24 years, Timor-Leste was the 27th province of Indonesia (Howard, 2008). The Timorese mounted resistance to the Indonesian occupation (New Zealand Police, 2018), with between one-quarter and one-third of the population, approximately 200,000 people were killed in the fighting and from famine during the occupation (Kiernan, 2003). The Indonesian military committed "unspeakable crimes … bombings, execution, torture, and disappearances, which left no family untouched" (Jolliffe, 2000). Thousands also fled the country (Howard, 2008).

According to Howard (2008), by the late 1990s, a number of international events occurred that would support East Timor in gaining independence from Indonesia. The first event was the 1997 Asian economic crisis, which lead to the second event, the downfall of the Indonesian Government led by President Suharto in May 1998 (Howard, 2008). The third event was the election of B. J. Habbie as President of Indonesia, who "abruptly announced in late January 1999 that the East Timorese could decide for themselves whether they wanted independence or autonomy within Indonesia" (Howard, 2008, p. 264).

The declaration by President Habbie led to a United Nations-assisted independence referendum in September 1999. Violence erupted in East Timor after the

G. den Heyer (✉)
School of Social and Behavioral Science, Walden University, Havelock North, New Zealand

G. den Heyer, J. F. Albrecht (eds.), *Police and International Peacekeeping Missions*, https://doi.org/10.1007/978-3-030-77900-9_7

results of the vote were declared as being overwhelmingly in favour of independence from Indonesia (Capie, 2012). The violence was caused entirely by the Indonesian Government (Howard, 2008). The pro-Indonesian militias within East Timor wreaked havoc once the results became known and more than 1000 people were killed (Capie, 2012).

The violence perpetrated by the militias, who were sponsored by the Indonesian Government, caused international consternation, which resulted in the United Nations calling for a multinational force to restore order and to provide humanitarian assistance until a United Nations peacekeeping force could be organized (Capie, 2012). Under pressure from a number of countries, including Australia, the United States of America and the World Bank, the Indonesian Government conceded to the deployment of a United Nations-mandated peacekeeping force to East Timor (Greener, 2009). The Australian-led International Force East Timor (INTERFET) entered Timor-Leste on 12 September 1999, with more than 5000 Australian defence personnel (Capie, 2012; Greener, 2009; Nautilus Institute for Security and Sustainability, n.d.). New Zealand was the second largest contributor to INTERFET, deploying a battalion of light infantry troops, transport aircraft, helicopters and three navy ships (Capie, 2012). By October 1999, the New Zealand contingent comprised of more than 1100 soldiers and support staff, making it the country's largest military deployment since the Korean War (Capie, 2012).

The mandate of INTERFET was to create a secure environment within the territory and to restore order (Greener, 2009). INTERFET was a force capable of combat, but it also contained humanitarian and civil law and order elements (Greener, 2009).

Missions to East Timor/Timor-Leste

There were six United Nations-mandated missions to East Timor/Timor-Leste that took place from June 1999 to 31 December 2012. The six missions and their purposes were the following:

1. The United Nations Mission in East Timor (UNAMET) (June–October 1999) was mandated to organize and conduct a popular consultation to ascertain whether the East Timorese people accepted a special autonomy within Indonesia or rejected the proposed special autonomy, leading to East Timor's separation from Indonesia. UNAMET was a political mission.
2. The International Force East Timor (INTERFET) (September 1999–March 2000) was an international force formed to address the deteriorating humanitarian and security environment in East Timor.
3. The United Nations Transitional Administration in East Timor (UNTAET) (25 October 1999–20 May 2002) was a peacekeeping operation. The Security Council established UNTAET following the rejection by the East Timorese of

special autonomy. UNTAET exercised administrative authority over East Timor during the transition to independence.
4. The United Nations Mission of Support in East Timor (UNMISET) (May 2002–May 2005), also a peacekeeping mission, was mandated to provide assistance to the newly independent East Timor until all operational responsibilities were fully devolved to the East Timor authorities and to permit the new nation, now called Timor-Leste, to attain self-sufficiency.
5. On the withdrawal of the peacekeeping mission a new political mission, the United Nations Office in Timor-Leste (UNOTIL) (May 2005–20 August 2006), provided support for the development of critical state institutions and the police and provided training in the observance of democratic governance and human rights.
6. United Nations Integrated Mission in Timor-Leste (UNMIT) (25 August 2006–31 December 2012) was established by United Nations police force in Timor-Leste to maintain law and order until the national police could undergo reorganization and restructuring (Nautilus Institute for Security and Sustainability, n.d.; UNMIT, n.d.; UNTAET, n.d.).

The United Nations Mission in East Timor (UNAMET): June to October 1999

To ensure that the environment was reasonably secure for holding an independence referendum, the Security Council, by resolution 1246 (1999), authorized the establishment of the United Nations Mission in East Timor (UNAMET) on 11 June 1999. It was planned that the mission would operate until 31 August 1999 (United Nations Mission of Support in East Timor, n.d.). The mission was not a peacekeeping mission, but a referendum monitoring mission (Howard, 2008). The mandate specified that after the referendum, UNAMET would manage a transition period pending the implementation of the decision made by the East Timorese people (United Nations Mission of Support in East Timor, n.d.).

The referendum was held on 30 August 1999, with more than 98% of registered East Timorese voters voting, with approximately 78.5% rejecting the proposed autonomy (to remain part of Indonesia) and to begin a process of transition towards independence (Howard, 2008; United Nations Mission of Support in East Timor, n.d.). Following the announcement of the result of the referendum, the pro-integration militias, with support from the Indonesian security forces, launched a campaign of violence, looting and perpetrating arson throughout the country (Howard, 2008; United Nations Mission of Support in East Timor, n.d.). The violence followed a "scorched earth" approach, with more than 70% of the physical infrastructure and nearly all of the residential homes destroyed in 3 weeks (Howard, 2008). Following the outbreak of violence, the Indonesian Armed Forces, the police and government administrators left the country (United Nations Mission of Support in East Timor, n.d.).

On 12 September 1999, as a result of deteriorating security and the collapse of law and order in East Timor, the Indonesian Government accepted an offer of assistance from the international community (United Nations Mission of Support in East Timor, n.d.). Following the acceptance, on 20 September 1999, the United Nations authorized the establishment and deployment of the multinational force (INTERFET) under a unified command structure but led by Australia, to restore peace and security (Howard, 2008; United Nations Mission of Support in East Timor, n.d.). The force stopped the violence and destruction quickly, stabilized the country and established a foundation so that UNTAET could be deployed (Howard, 2008).

Timor-Leste (1999–2002): United Nations Transitional Administration in East Timor (UNTAET)

On 25 October 1999, UNAMET was replaced by the United Nations Transitional Administration in East Timor (UNTAET), which was established under United Nations Security Council Resolution 1272 (Howard, 2008; Greener, 2009; United Nations Transitional Administration in East Timor, n.d.). The mission was mandated to provide security and maintain law and order throughout the territory of East Timor; to establish an effective administration; to assist in the development of civil and social services; to ensure the coordination and delivery of humanitarian assistance to support capacity building for self-governance; and assist in establishing the conditions for sustainable development (Greener, 2009; United Nations Transitional Administration in East Timor, n.d.).

Never before had a mandate for a peacekeeping mission focused so much on administrative responsibilities of the state and economic development (Howard, 2008). According to the United Nations Secretary General Kofi Annan, the mandate of UNTAET was "unprecedented" as the mission was to "establish a national civil administration, assist in the development of civil social services and support capacity building for self-government" (United Nations, 2001). The view that UNTAET was unique was also noted by Howard (2008), who claimed that the mission "was the most ambitious UN peacekeeping operation of its time" (p. 260). Howard (2008), also held this perspective, owing to that fact that not only was the mission mandated under Chapter VII peacekeeping, but it also included elements of civilian policing, humanitarian assistance and government administration.

The implementation of the mandate did, however, give rise to tensions, which were centred on the requirement to deliver the services of the state as quickly as possible while building the capability of the local population to administer the state (Howard, 2008). The two tasks were not easy to integrate with one another and they required two different skill sets; having the capacity to administer government services and having the ability to teach the administration of government services (Howard, 2008).

The structure of UNTAET included three main pillars: governance and public administration; the peacekeeping force and humanitarian assistance and emergency rehabilitation (Howard, 2008). UNTAET consisted of governance and public administration components, a civilian police component of up to 1640 civilian police (including five Formed Police Units) and an armed United Nations peacekeeping force, of equivalent size to INTERFET, which took over command of the operations of the military in February 2000 (Greener, 2009; Howard, 2008; United Nations Transitional Administration in East Timor, n.d.). Also, in February 2000, UNTAET began a process of reorganizing itself to resemble more closely the future government of East Timor and to increase the direct participation of the East Timorese (United Nations Mission of Support in East Timor, n.d.).

One of the mandated goals of UNTAET was to prepare East Timor for independence and to achieve this goal, the mission was to provide security and establish and maintain law and order throughout the country. The United Nations Police (UNPOL) had a broad mandate (Howard, 2008) and were originally given executive policing powers as the law enforcement capabilities of East Timor had not been established (Greener, 2009). In addition to an interim policing mandate, the United Nations were also tasked with reforming and building the capacity of the East Timor Police as it was recognized by the United Nations Secretary General that an important part of establishing law and order included the rapid development of a credible, professional and impartial police service (Greener, 2009).

The United Nations Police was organized as a separate division from the military component of the mission and began with very few resources and staff (Howard, 2008). The physical, logistical, and political separation of the police from the military "was designed to be a model for the future East Timorese governing institutions, where civilians, rather than the military, would be connected with policing activity" (Howard, 2008, pp. 281–282). While serving a symbolic function, the separation caused a number of problems. The first, was that the separation resulted in poor coordination between the military and the police, which subsequently resulted in a lack of joint doctrine or concept of operations (Howard, 2008). The result was "that there was no permanent coordination in the event of riots, internal unrest, or even electoral-monitoring duties" (Howard, 2008, p. 282). Another problem that was encountered in relation to the separation was that the separation made the police invisible to the leadership of the military and the mission (Howard, 2008).

The problems caused by the separation of the police from the military were compounded by internal coordination problems in the organization of the United Nations Police (Howard, 2008). These problems arose because police officers from contributing countries were not deployed as units of officers, but instead, were deployed as individual police officers (Howard, 2008). This form of deployment meant that there was very little understanding across the various national police contingents as to how policing was to be delivered. The second problem was in the quality of some of the officers who had been deployed. Contributing countries kept their highly skilled and well performing officers at home, which meant that not only were the number of officers deployed insufficient, but also the calibre of some of them was left wanting (Howard, 2008). Another dimension to these problems was that of language, as many police "did not have the language skills necessary to communicate well with each other much less with the East Timorese, and good interpreters were difficult to find" (Howard, 2008, p. 282). The fourth problem encountered was that contributing countries were slow in deploying their police officers, which meant that the police component of the mission was slow to start. By the end of February 2000, 6 months after the mission had commenced, there were less than 500 United Nations Police Officers deployed, even though the force was mandated at 1640 officers (Howard, 2008). These problems, as noted by Howard (2008), were exacerbated by the police not communicating well with either the military or with the local people and it was therefore not surprising that it took some time before the United Nations Police were able to perform competently in their role.

An early success for the United Nations Police, even though they were not fully staffed, was the opening of a police training academy in Dili in March 2000 and the first tranche of officers who were trained there, graduated in July 2000 (Howard, 2008). The academy was established to build the capability of the East Timor Police Service to ensure that they were able to undertake the responsibilities that were required of a national policing agency.

By mid-2000, the United Nations Police had started to undertake their role within the mission mandate and assist in achieving the three pillars specified in the mandate. The first stage of the reform was to formally establish the East Timor Police Service and this commenced on 10 August 2001 (Greener, 2009). Unfortunately, the new police force had three name changes during 2002: East Timor Police Service, Timor Lorosa'e Police Service and finally Policia Nacional de Timor-Leste (PNTL).

On 20 May 2002, East Timor, which is now called Timor-Leste, became an independent country (Greener, 2009). The establishment of an independent Timor-Leste also signaled the completion of the UNTAET mandate and the transformation of the mission to a new mission, which was called the United Nations Mission in Support of East Timor (UNMISET). The new mission was established to provide assistance to the new Timor-Leste Government and the mandate was to have this completed by 20 May 2005 (Greener, 2009).

New Zealand Police and UNTAET

In early 1999, the United Nations made a request to the New Zealand Police to make their officers available for the United Nations Transitional Authority in East Timor (UNTAET). The New Zealand Police initially contributed eight personnel for a six-month period, which was followed by the deployment of two further contingents of eight officers each (New Zealand Police, 2018).

Timor-Leste (2002–2005): United Nations Mission of Support in East Timor (UNMISET)

UNMISET was established by United Nations Security Council resolution 1410 (2002), on 17 May 2002, 3 days before the Timor-Leste became an independent nation. The role of the mission was to provide assistance to the government to ensure the viability and political stability of East Timor and to provide interim law enforcement and public security (Greener, 2009; Howard, 2008; United Nations Mission of Support in East Timor, n.d.). The intention was that the mission would, over a period of 2 years, devolve its responsibilities to the East Timorese Government (United Nations Mission of Support in East Timor, n.d.). The mandate for the mission was initially approved by the Security Council for 1 year, but it was renewed for 3 years, owing to the difficulty in overcoming the Indonesian and colonial legacies of misrule (Howard, 2008).

The mission initially comprised of 1250 civilian police and 5000 military troops (Greener, 2009; Howard, 2008; United Nations Mission of Support in East Timor, n.d.) and was responsible for continuing to provide executive policing while assisting with developing the Timor-Leste Police (Greener, 2009). The mission enabled the United Nations Police to concentrate on developing the skills and knowledge of local police officers and ensuring that the responsibilities of maintaining law and order were exercised (United Nations Mission of Support in East Timor, n.d.).

Timor-Leste (May 2005–August 2006): United Nations Office in Timor-Leste (UNOTIL)

In April 2005, another mission, called the United Nations Office in Timor-Leste (UNOTIL) was established for 1 year, following the end of UNMISET. The mission was not to include any peacekeeping troops, but was to comprise of only 45 civilian advisors, 75 police advisors and 10 human rights officers (Howard, 2008). The mission was successful in implementing its mandate, but when the mission was scheduled to end in May 2006, a series of events in Timor-Leste culminated in a political, humanitarian and security crisis, which led to the United Nations Security Council extending the mission until 20 August 2006 and strengthening its presence (United Nations Mission in Timor-Leste, n.d.).

On April 24, 2006, a large number of former Timorese soldiers and their supporters marched in the capital claiming that they had been discriminated against while being re-employed by the new military of Timor-Leste (F-FDTL) (Kelly & Walters, 2006). The march was initially peaceful but became violent when the former soldiers attacked a market run by people from the east of Timor (ABC, 2006a). The protests continued and on 28 April, the former soldiers clashed with the newly formed Timor-Leste military, who fired on the crowd, killing five people (ABC, 2006b). Two days later, members from the military attacked the police headquarters in Dili, killing nine police officers (New Zealand Police, 2018). This led to further violence and destruction with more than 100 buildings being destroyed and an estimated 21,000 Dili residents fleeing the city (ABC, 2006b; New Zealand Police, 2018).

Against this backdrop, on 24 May 2006, the Timor-Leste Government requested police and military assistance from Australia, New Zealand, Malaysia and Portugal, and on 26 May, international forces began securing key installations around the country (New Zealand Police, 2018; United Nations Mission in Timor-Leste, n.d.). By August 2006, the violence had abated significantly, but in the interim, the Timor-Leste Government requested that the United Nations establish a United Nations police force in Timor-Leste to maintain law and order until the national police could undergo reorganization and restructuring (United Nations Mission in Timor-Leste, n.d.). The request led to the establishment of a United Nations multidimensional, integrated mission, with a mandate to support the Government of Timor-Leste and to ensure, through the deployment of the United Nations Police, the restoration and maintenance of public security (United Nations Mission in Timor-Leste, n.d.).

Timor-Leste (2006–2012): United Nations Mission in Timor-Leste (UNMIT)

The United Nations Mission in Timor-Leste (UNMIT) was established on 25 August 2006, by resolution 1704 (2006), and comprised of 1608 police personnel and had an initial component of 34 military liaison and staff officers (United Nations Mission in Timor-Leste, n.d.). The mission had a far-reaching mandate, which was to assist the Timor-Leste Government to overcome the consequences and the underlying causes of the April to June 2006 crisis (United Nations Mission in Timor-Leste, n.d.). The role of the United Nations Mission in Timor Leste was to assist with rebuilding democratic institutions, foster good governance, support the process for elections, review defence and security needs and coordinate economic development assistance to Timor-Leste (Emmott et al., 2010).

The role of the United Nations in Timor Leste was to restore and maintain public security, develop institutions and review the security sector. The mandate took the role of the United Nations beyond capacity building to reforming, restructuring and the rebuilding of the Timor-Leste Police. The United Nations also assisted the government in undertaking a review of their police, military, the Ministry of Interior and the Ministry of Defence (Greener, 2009). Screening new recruits, registering existing and newly recruited personnel, delivering a basic five-day training course and mentoring recruits after they had completed their six-month basic recruit course (Greener, 2009) were the main areas that were undertaken to rebuild the Timor-Leste Police.

The police component of United Nations in Timor Leste comprised of approximately 1500 police personnel from 40 contributing countries (United Nations Mission to Timor-Leste, n.d.). Its mandate included capacity development, interim law enforcement and public security until the Timor-Leste Police was reconstituted. In May 2009, United Nations in Timor Leste and the Timor-Leste Government agreed upon a process for the Timor-Leste Police to gradually resume the responsibility of delivering policing services (Emmott et al., 2010; United Nations Mission to Timor-Leste, n.d.). The United Nations in Timor Leste was to progressively hand over responsibility, district by district. Responsibility would be handed over based on joint assessments of the preparedness of the Timor-Leste Police in each district and unit, in accordance with mutually agreed upon criteria. The United Nations Police were to maintain their presence in the districts where the Timor-Leste Police had resumed responsibilities and would provide support and advice and would monitor the police, especially in protecting human rights. It was proposed that the presence of the United Nations Police would slowly diminish across Timor-Leste and would be in line with the transfer of responsibility (Emmott et al., 2010).

Following the deployment of the United Nations in Timor Leste, the overall situation in Timor-Leste improved, although security remained volatile and the political climate, fluid (United Nations Mission in Timor-Leste, n.d.). The volatility of Timor-Leste was revealed on 11 February 2008, when an armed group, led by a former Military Police Commander carried out armed attacks against the President and the Prime Minister (United Nations Mission in Timor-Leste, n.d.).

These incidents presented an unexpected and serious challenge to the state institutions of Timor-Leste, but in contrast to the events of 2006, the situation did not precipitate a crisis that destabilized the country (United Nations Mission in Timor-Leste, n.d.). The situation was quickly brought under control and there were no further breakdowns in law and order between February 2008 and when the United Nations in Timor Leste completed its mandate on 31 December 2012 and withdrew its staff.

New Zealand Police: Operation TUITUIA (2006–2012)

On 20 June 2006, on the release of the United Nations Security Council Resolution 1690 (2006), the United Nations Security Council expressed its appreciation and full support for the international security forces that would be provided by the governments of Portugal, Australia, New Zealand and Malaysia. The security forces would be deployed to restore and maintain security as requested by the Government of Timor-Leste.

The mandate for the new mission was for the United Nations Police to assist with the restoration of rule of law and public security in Timor-Leste. The United Nations Police would be supported by the Timor-Leste Police and the United Nations Police would provide training and develop the Timor-Leste Police (New Zealand Police, 2006). The United Nations Police would also assist in the planning and preparation of security arrangements for the elections (New Zealand Police, 2006).

The main role of the mission was in the area of restoring public safety and would be twofold. Phase I, the immediate interim phase, would be to assist in maintaining law and order in Dili and to reconstitute the Timor-Leste Police (New Zealand Police, 2006). Phase II would involve advising and supporting the Timorese Government in the reform, restructuring and rebuilding of its police force and the Ministry of the Interior (New Zealand Police, 2006).

On 26 June 2006, the New Zealand Government authorized the deployment of 20 to 25 New Zealand Police personnel to Timor-Leste for a term of 3 months, subject to the Minister of Police being satisfied that the level of risk was acceptable. The minister also needed to be satisfied that the timing of the deployment was acceptable to the Timor-Leste Government and that outstanding issues relating to legal, operating, command and control and logistical arrangements would be resolved (New Zealand Police, 2006). Operation "TUITUIA", a New Zealand Police contingent of 25 personnel, deployed to Timor-Leste on 11 July 2006 (New Zealand Police, 2006), as a part of the Australian-led international force. In September 2006, the New Zealand Government agreed that the 25 New Zealand Police Officers would participate in United Nations in Timor Leste for 12 months. This was extended in 2007, and then again in 2008, by the Cabinet External Relations and Defence Committee (Emmott et al., 2010).

Staff from the New Zealand Police were deployed to Timor-Leste as a part of the United Nations Police component of UNMIT. They joined police personnel from 39 other countries (New Zealand Police, 2018). The New Zealand Police Officers quickly became frustrated with the inertia of UNMIT and the disconnect between the United Nations Police and the Timor-Leste Police (New Zealand Police, 2018). The situation was exacerbated by their lack of confidence in the United Nations Police and this eventually came to the attention of the New Zealander Ambassador in Dili (New Zealand Police, 2018). The Ambassador wrote to the Special Representative of the Secretary General of the United Nations, who agreed that New Zealand should manage a Community Policing Project (to be called the Community Policing Pilot Program – CPPP) in two distinct areas of Timor-Leste, as a part of UNMIT (New Zealand Police, 2018).

The Community Policing Pilot Program commenced in October 2008 and was completed in June 2010. It was funded as a part of the overall New Zealand Police deployment in UNMIT, which consisted of approximately NZ$4m of the NZ$10m annual (2009/10) budget of the New Zealand Agency for International Development (Emmott et al., 2010). The goal of the Community Policing Pilot Program was to support the Timor-Leste Police in developing a sustainable Community Policing model and philosophy, assist in restoring community trust and confidence in the police and create an environment, which would be conducive to all aspects of community development (Emmott et al., 2010). The four components of the program were the following:

1. Implementation of the community policing pilots in Becora and Suai;
2. Capacity development of the Timor-Leste Police Community Policing Unit;
3. Support to the Timor-Leste Police Academy for training on using community policing methodologies; and

4. Establishment of a measurement and evaluation framework to assess and measure community policing management and the performance of the Community Policing Pilot Program (Emmott et al., 2010, p. i).

The program commenced as a mandated United Nations Police Community Policing model and was later included in the induction training of the United Nations Police (United Nations Integrated Mission in Timor-Leste, 2012). The program attracted a significant amount of positive publicity from both local and international media groups as it represented a strategic advancement for post-conflict reform policing. It had been based on the methodologies of the host country, which had never been adopted within a peacekeeping framework before (United Nations Integrated Mission in Timor-Leste, 2012).

Four members advised the supervisors and officers of the Timor-Leste Police in Community Policing as a part of the New Zealand Police Community Policing Project (Spence, 2012). An independent review of the project found that the program contributed to the establishment of Community Policing in Timor-Leste (New Zealand Police, 2018), but problems were encountered. The Timor-Leste Police lacked resources and the new recruits were being trained in paramilitary policing (Spence, 2012).

Following the completion of the Community Policing Project in October 2010, the contribution of the New Zealand Police to UNMIT reduced to 10, from 25 personnel, and in June 2011 this was reduced further to 5 police officers (New Zealand Police, 2018). The contribution remained at this level until the end of the UNMIT mandate in 2012, when all New Zealand staff returned to New Zealand (New Zealand Police, 2018).

Post 2012: The New Zealand Police Timor-Leste Community Policing Program

The Timor-Leste Community Policing Program (TLCPP) commenced in July 2011 after an initial request and the completion of a pilot study in 2008. It was originally developed as a four-year bilateral program between the New Zealand Police and the Policia Nacionale de Timor-Leste to support the long-term professional development of the police (Timor-Leste Community Policing Program, 2012; Sustineo, 2013). The program was designed in response to requests made by the Timor-Leste Secretary of State for Security and the Timor-Leste Police (Sustineo, 2013). The Timor-Leste Community Policing Program built on earlier assistance that was provided by the New Zealand Police. The earlier assistance included the Community Policing Pilot Program (CPPP), which was implemented between September 2008 and March 2010.

The Timor-Leste Community Policing Program comprised of three components:

1. A strategic component that provided support for the Timor-Leste Police to further develop and institutionalize its Community Policing policy that would enable the police to engage with community stakeholders and develop special program on key Community Policing issues, in consultation with their districts.
2. A training component to support effective recruitment and in-service training of Community Policing that would develop the knowledge and skills of the Timor-Leste Police and would provide the motivation, confidence and commitment to implement Community Policing.
3. An operational component that focused on providing support for the Timor-Leste Police District Commanders and staff to institutionalize Community Policing and to deliver the program at the district, sub-district and village levels. This was to be achieved by strengthening partnerships and consultative mechanisms (Sustineo, 2013).

The Timor-Leste Community Policing Program was funded by New Zealand Agency for International Development and had a budget of $14.9 million. As a part of the program, police officers from New Zealand mentored the Timor-Leste Police in Community Policing (Timor-Leste Community Policing Program, 2012). The initial New Zealand Police contingent comprised of three sworn members; a team leader at the rank of Assistant Commissioner and two Inspectors, who were responsible for logistics and training and were supported by two language assistants (Timor-Leste Community Policing Program, 2012).

The Timor-Leste Community Policing Program consisted of an implementation phase that was to be undertaken in early 2012. This phase, however, was delayed by parliamentary and ministerial elections, but was finally completed in 5 weeks, during July and August 2012 (Timor-Leste Community Policing Program, 2012). The phase comprised of nine police officers from New Zealand Police being deployed as mentors to work alongside Timor-Leste Police District Commanders in allocated districts to advise on Community Policing. It was intended that the relationship between the New Zealand Police Officers and their counterparts would be strengthened when the mentors returned to Timor-Leste later in 2012 and again in 2013 (Timor-Leste Community Policing Program, 2012). The program also included the deployment of technical advisers from the New Zealand Police for up to 12 weeks at a time, who would assist with a range of administrative and service delivery areas that had been identified by the Timor-Leste Community Policing Program. The assistance that was provided by the advisers was in areas such as Information Technology, the policing of youth, domestic violence, station management, road policing and the establishment of a police band.

In 2014, a number of significant changes were made to the delivery of the Timor-Leste Community Policing Program to ensure that effective collaboration with the Timor-Leste Police and other stakeholders was maintained and to assist with achieving sustainable program outcomes (New Zealand Police, 2014). The changes included the following:

- The phasing out of the "fly in, fly out" model for a more New Zealand Police permanent stationed presence. This change in delivery was designed to enhance the capability and capacity of the Timor-Leste Community Policing Program and to provide more appropriate support to the Timor-Leste Police;

- A commitment to the selection of advisors with skills and knowledge appropriate to the local context with special consideration given to language skills; and
- A renewed commitment to a robust monitoring and evaluation framework through the SUSTENIO intervention (New Zealand Police, 2014).

In was noted that during this period, Community Policing in the Timor-Leste Police had improved. The Timor-Leste Police realized that they could not work in a vacuum and that they needed to develop relationships with the community in order to find out what was happening in the community (New Zealand Police, 2014). However, progress remained hampered by a lack of logistical support and the reliance of the Timor-Leste Police on "things" they needed to be able to do to undertake their role (New Zealand Police, 2014). The 2014 Annual Report note that Timor-Leste Community Policing Program had played an active role in contributing to improvements in community safety and security to the extent that they were able to motivate, inspire and facilitate the Timor-Leste Police to take more proactive, preventative policing steps (New Zealand Police, 2014).

Assessment of the Missions to Timor-Leste and the New Zealand Police's Role

There have been five separate United Nations missions to Timor-Leste since June 1999. The first two missions occurred before the Timor-Leste Declaration of Independence in May 2002 and the other three were subsequent to the country's independence. The last role for the New Zealand Police was the Timor-Leste Community Policing Program, which was completed in 2015.

The first mission, UNTAET was praised for its swift deployment (Greener, 2009), and was organized into three main pillars: (1) governance and public administration, (2) the United Nations peacekeeping force and (3) humanitarian assistance and emergency rehabilitation (Howard, 2008). UNTAET made progress in achieving its mandate, and after experiencing some significant first-level organizational dysfunction, it gradually moved into a learning mode, which enabled it to implement most of the goals of the mission (Howard, 2008). The success was achieved mainly because it heeded the lessons learned from earlier United Nations post-conflict peacekeeping missions (den Heyer, 2012), despite it being an ambitious operation.

To ensure success, the police component was given executive authority and disarmament, demobilization and re-integration were implemented early in the mission. Unfortunately, at first, the focus on tight and centralized control in the field was not accompanied by an adequate devolution of power within the field operations, especially by the district offices. Nor was there adequate integration with local leaders and nor was the community involved in the decision-making of the mission (Howard, 2008).

There were, however, a number of familiar shortcomings in the performance of the mission (den Heyer, 2012). The mission was slow in deploying the police component and failed to prepare for an outbreak of violence, which followed the autonomy referendum. A procedure for dealing with criminals was also slow to develop. A lack of institutional infrastructure together "with untrained CIVPOL personnel and bureaucratic divisions within UNTAET hampered criminal investigations" (Greener, 2009, pp. 48–49).

The civilian police component of the mission was the less successful component of UNTAET and resulted in the policing component of the mission being carried over to UNMISET (Howard, 2008). This was despite the fact that "police development" was intended to be a major part of UNTAET and UNMISET (Greener, 2009). The primary weakness of the police component of UNTAET, as noted by Greener (2009), was that "none of the 1,270 officers were recruited to be trainers or institution building experts, whilst within UNMISET none of the 150 police advisors had development or capacity building expertise" (p. 49).

The police component completed its mandated tasks during UNMISET. However, it was UNOTIL that assumed responsibility for any outstanding tasks (Howard, 2008). According to Howard (2008), the United Nations missions assisted with forming new governing institutions; rebuilding the physical infrastructure; maintaining security; training people in the tasks of governing, policing, law-making and the holding of elections. They also educated the population in non-corrupt governance and electoral politics.

According to Durch (2006) and Greener (2009), much of the criticism that UNTAET received could be directly attributed to a lack of pre-deployment planning and mission preparation. Although the lack of planning was attributed to inadequate resources within the United Nations Department of Peacekeeping Operations, the United Nations did not prepare an appropriate concept of operations at the time and failed to identify how the police component would cooperate with other components of the mission. The deficiency in the planning was carried through to the mission itself. The mission did not develop any performance benchmarks, had no clear understanding of an "end state", and did not develop a strategic plan to prepare the nation for independence (Durch, 2006).

The United Nations has been criticized for not taking a strategic perspective in building a viable security sector, particularly with regard to establishing democratic control of the security sector (Greener, 2009). Overall, the planning for the missions by the United Nations was described as "cursory" and the policing effort has been criticized as constituting a story of slipshod planning, squandered opportunities and unimaginative leadership (Martin & Mayer-Rieckh, 2005; Hood, 2006).

By 2005, UNMISET had successfully concluded its mandate in Timor-Leste (den Heyer, 2012). It was succeeded by a small political mission—UNOTIL. This mission was established by the United Nations Security Council to ensure that the underpinnings of a viable state were firmly in place (United Nations, 2010). Internally, the Timor-Leste Police had a lack of respect for discipline and human rights, while operationally, they lacked professional skills and values and policing experience. Nor did they have the necessary equipment and infrastructure and lacked management and co-ordination capabilities (United Nations, 2004).

Conclusion

The early UNAMET mission was lauded for its success in competently undertaking difficult electoral tasks, and later missions that included more interactive forms of policing were also praised (Greener, 2009). However, it is not known as to whether the missions met the needs of the local community. Overall, the New Zealand Police contribution to the United Nations missions was commended by the Timorese Government and the Timor-Leste Community Policing Program brought extensive New Zealand experience to the implementation of Community Policing in Timor-Leste.

The earlier Community Policing Program was effective in that it had achieved much of what it set out to do and laid the groundwork for the Timor-Leste Community Policing Program. In so doing, it contributed to the effectiveness of the Timor-Leste Police by demonstrating that Community Policing was an appropriate and implementable concept (Emmott et al., 2010). Working within the UNMIT was a challenge for members of the New Zealand Police and led to some misunderstandings, but the earlier Community Policing achievements would not have been possible without the support of the United Nations Police (Emmott et al., 2010). A considerable amount of capacity has been developed in the Timor-Leste Police by the United Nations mission and the New Zealand Police Community Policing Program. The factors that limited the effectiveness of the capacity development and the implementation of Community Policing were the short duration of the New Zealand Police deployments and the lack of strategic direction. The short duration of the deployments resulted in a loss of momentum with each change (Emmott et al., 2010).

The Community Policing Program and the Timor-Leste Community Policing Program have made a strong contribution to Community Policing in Timor-Leste (Emmott et al., 2010). The New Zealand Police had an advantage over the other international police agencies in Timor-Leste and that was their ability to introduce Community Policing ("the New Zealand way") in a practical, operational way, rather than introducing solely a theoretical model of policing.

References

ABC. (2006a, April 24). *Former soldiers protest turns violent in Dili*. Retrieved from: https://web.archive.org/web/20080418070345/http://www.abc.net.au/news/newsitems/200604/s1622612.htm

ABC. (2006b, July 25). *Defence force dispute puts East Timor in crisis*. Retrieved from: https://web.archive.org/web/20080725164631/http://www.abc.net.au/news/indepth/featureitems/s1647295.htm

Capie, D. (2012). Peacekeeping – New Zealand's involvement in peacekeeping. *Te Ara: The Encyclopaedia of New Zealand*. Retrieved from http://www.TeAra.govt.nz/en/peacekeeping/

den Heyer, G. (2012). *The role of civilian police in peacekeeping 1999–2007*. Police Foundation.

Durch, W. (2006). *Twenty-first-century peace operations*. United States Institute of Peace.

Emmott, S., Barcham, M., Ali Khan, T., & Soares, E. (2010). *Community policing programme, Timor Leste: Independent review report*. New Zealand: NZAID.

Greener, B. (2009). *The new international policing*. Palgrave Macmillan Publishers Limited.

Hood, L. (2006). Security sector reform in East Timor: 1999–2004. *International Peacekeeping, 13*(1), 60–77.

Howard, L. M. (2008). *UN peacekeeping in civil wars*. Cambridge University Press.

Jolliffe, J. (2000). Foreword. In L. Cardoso (Ed.), *The crossing: A story of East Tmor* (pp. vii–xviii). Granta Books.

Kelly, P., & Walters, P. (2006, May 27). Back for good. *The Australian*. Retrieved from: https://web.archive.org/web/20080201045833/http://www.theaustralian.news.com.au/story/0%2C20867%2C19267564-28737%2C00.html

Kiernan, B. (2003). The demography of genocide in Southeast Asia: The death tolls in Cambodia, 1975–79, and East Timor, 1975–80. *Critical Asian Studies, 35*(4), 585–597.

Martin, I., & Mayer-Rieckh, A. (2005). The United Nations and East Timor: From self-determination to state-building. *International Peacekeeping, 12*(1), 125–145.

Nautilus Institute for Security and Sustainability. (n.d.). *International Force East Timor (INTERFET)*. Retrieved from: https://nautilus.org/publications/books/australian-forces-abroad/east-timor/international-force-east-timor-interfet/

New Zealand Police. (2006, August 7). *Police executive meeting: United Nations mission in Timor-Leste*. New Zealand Police.

New Zealand Police. (2014). Timor Leste community policing programme: 2014 annual report . New Zealand.

New Zealand Police. (2018). *Past ISG deployments*. Retrieved from http://www.police.govt.nz/about-us/programmes-initiatives/isg/past-deployments

Spence, J. (2012). *Weekly report Tui Tuia 14*. Dili, Timor Leste.

Sustineo. (2013). *Timor Leste community policing programme: Monitoring and evaluation services – Milestone 2: Inception report*. Australia.

Timor-Leste Community Policing Programme. (2012, September). *Briefing note: Timor Leste community policing project*. Dili, Timor Leste.

United Nations. (2001, October 18). *Report of the Secretary General on the United Nations Transitional Administration in East Timor*. S/2001/983. United Nations.

United Nations. (2004, November 9). *Progress report of the secretary-general on the United Nations mission of support in East Timor (for the period from 14 August to 9 November 2004) (S/2004/888)*. Retrieved from http://www.un.org/Docs/sc/sgrep04.html

United Nations. (2010). *East Timor: UNMISET—Mandate*. Retrieved from http://www.un.org/en/peacekeeping/missions/past/unmiset/mandate.html

United Nations Integrated Mission in Timor Leste. (2012). *New Zealand's contribution to the United Nations Police in Timor Leste*. Dili, Timor Leste.

United Nations Mission in Timor Leste. (n.d.). *Background*. Retrieved from https://unmit.unmissions.org/background

United Nations Mission of Support in East Timor. (n.d.). *East Timor – UNMISET – Background*. Retrieved from https://peacekeeping.un.org/mission/past/unmiset/background.html

United Nations Transitional Administration in East Timor. (n.d.). *East Timor – UNTAET: Mandate*. Retrieved from: https://peacekeeping.un.org/en/mission/past/etimor/UntaetM.htm

Part III
The Role of the Canadian Police in Post-conflict Peacekeeping Missions

Chapter 8
Contributions of the Canadian Police in International Peacekeeping Missions

Benoit J. S. Maure

Introduction

In 1956, Egypt nationalized the Suez Canal, a critical shipping route for petroleum from the Persian Gulf going to Europe, which had been administrated and controlled by French and British interests. Shortly after that and despite much opposition from the United States, Great Britain and France, along with Israel, launched attacks on Egypt (Suez Crisis, 2020). Egypt then appealed to the Soviet Union for help, which the latter threatened to intervene if the countries did not withdraw from Egypt. The world was on the brink of World War III (CBC Learning, 2001; Tunzelmann, 2016).

Thanks to the actions of former Canadian Prime Minister Lester B. Pearson, who spearheaded the dispatch of a large international peacekeeping force to the Suez Canal, the war was averted. Since then, Canada has earned the reputation of being a peacekeeping country (Granastein, 2019; Lester B. Pearson, 2020). The fact that Canadian Armed Force personnel have taken part in many overseas peacekeeping operations since then is well-known. What may be less notable is Canadian police officers' role in overseas peace operations (Veterans Affairs Canada, 2020a).

Since their first involvement in Namibia in 1989, Canadian police officers have been a continuous presence in many international peacekeeping missions. In over 30 years, more than 4000 Canadian police officers have participated in over 33 missions, including those in the Former Yugoslavia, Guatemala, East Timor, Sudan, Afghanistan, and Haiti (RCMP, 2020a). Canadian officers have helped shaped human security in fledgling democracies or in countries torn by conflicts by promoting human rights, reinforcing their economies, and contributing to the strengthening or rebuilding of their police services. These initiatives fall within one of Canada's overarching goals to help build a more secure world (Maure, 2020).

B. J. S. Maure (✉)
Royal Canadian Mounted Police, Surrey, BC, Canada

G. den Heyer, J. F. Albrecht (eds.), *Police and International Peacekeeping Missions*, https://doi.org/10.1007/978-3-030-77900-9_8

In Canada, the Royal Canadian Mounted Police (RCMP) is the authority that manages Canadian police deployment on behalf of the Government through what is called the Canadian Police Arrangement (CPA). This arrangement consists of a partnership between Global Affairs Canada, Public Safety Canada, and the RCMP. It is the CPA that ultimately decides if Canadian police will participate in a given mission. The RCMP will take the lead in planning and evaluating missions, selecting and training personnel, and providing support throughout the deployment (RCMP, 2020a). Individuals participating in United Nations missions will come from the RCMP or from other Canadian police agencies invited to participate in peace operations. These men and women will come from a wide diversity of experience and ranks depending on the particular mission's needs. For example, some of the duties attached to the Canadian police peacekeeper will include the following:

- training, mentoring, and monitoring local police engaged in an investigation, public order issues, or other duties;
- supporting free and fair elections;
- investigating human rights violations; and
- responding to humanitarian crises.

Canadian police can also be deployed to work in select units that are assigned to capacity-building in community policing, management, development, and serious and organized crime (RCMP, 2020a). Moreover, in recent years, Canada has been closely working with the United Nations and other Member States to identify effective ways to increase uniformed women's participation in peace operations (Canada, 2020). Currently, only 7% of the approximately 83,000 military and police personnel deployed in peace operations have been women. Through the Elsie Initiative, Canada is working towards creating a better gender balance whereby women will have a 20% representation in international police missions by the year 2028. This goal will also reflect the crucial need for diversity and the creation of peacekeeping missions that better reflect the population they serve (Canada, 2020).

Canadian police officers bring a vast amount of experience to peace operations and learn a great deal from them, often coming back home as more complete and experienced officers. However, the experience they have gained abroad has come at times with a hefty price tag, including separation from a spouse, divorce, or even posttraumatic stress syndrome (PTSD) (Buis, 2020; Maure, 2020). For instance, one officer coming back from an international mission after a one-year absence from home had difficulty reconnecting with his spouse and children. Even his faithful dog ignored him for some time (Maure, 2020).

For this chapter and to illustrate the diverse roles Canadian police officers have played on international deployments, the author has selected five United Nations-mandated peace operations that have supported Canadian police presence over the last 30 years. These missions are the following:

- The 1989–1990 United Nations Transition Assistance Group (UNTAG), in Namibia;
- The 1994–2004 United Nations Verification Mission in Guatemala (MINUGUA);

- The 1999–2002 United Nations Transitional Authority for East Timor (UNTAET);
- The 2001–2013 International Security Assistance Force (ISAF), in Afghanistan; and
- The 2004–2017 United Nations Stabilization Mission in Haiti (MINUSTAH).

The challenges associated to working on an international peace operation are numerous and may require a generous dose of leadership, diplomacy, and courage. Consider, for example, the RCMP's participation in its first peacekeeping mission, UNTAG. At the time, Namibia, also known as South West Africa, was a former German colony that had been under the control of South Africa (British Crown) since the end of World War I (United Nations, 2001).

As a result of a fledgling market for diamonds and livestock after World War II, the prosperity of Namibia increased. Alas, this new wealth was almost exclusively reserved for European settlers in the south. Distress further increased among the indigenous population as a result of the introduction of segregation laws by South Africa (Gascoine, 2001). From the late 1940s on, South Africa's interest in Namibia started to clash against those of the United Nations, which saw the latter coming to the defense of indigenous people in disputing South African rule over them (Gascoine, 2001). However, it is not before 1989 that South Africa agreed to a series of conditions with the United Nations, amongst them, supervised elections to decide for Namibia's Independence, the establishment of UNTAG to oversee the electoral process and the subsequent withdrawal of South African forces from Namibia (United Nations, 2001).

United Nations Transition Assistance Group (UNTAG)

In essence, UNTAG was a political operation mandated to ensure the first free and fair elections for that country after more than a hundred years of colonialism (Maure, 2020). For that mission, Canada would supply a police contingent of 100 (96 men and 4 women). Their mission, with other Civilian Police (CIVPOL) contingents from 26 nations would be to provide safety for the country's first parliamentary elections ever and also ensure that the South West Africa Police, the local police force at the time, fulfilled its duty of maintaining law and order in an efficient, professional, and non-partisan manner (United Nations, 2001).

From the beginning, participation in that mission promised unprecedented challenges, starting with the troop's 22-hour journey from Canada to Namibia. After a series of flight connections that took the troop through London, England, and Lagos, Nigeria, the contingent overnighted in Lagos to get ready for the last leg of the trip. The next day, as they boarded an older, chartered Boeing 707 passenger plane, peacekeepers noted something inside the plane that was not entirely up to the aviation standards they had been used to in North America. They observed that two emergency doors at the back of the plane had been sealed off with metal rails welded onto the fuselage. In the event of an emergency, those exits would be unavailable.

Concerns soon rose amongst the Canadians as to what else might have been altered on the aircraft and all hastily deboarded. After much reassurance from a United Nations official that the plane was airworthy, the Canadians hesitantly re-boarded it. Then, as the plane thundered down the runway, bouncing up and down to gain speed to take-off, some alarmed peacekeepers made another troubling observation: a wing on the aircraft appeared to flap like that of a bird while rivets holding it together were so loose that they were spinning. Suddenly, overhead bins abruptly opened, and carry-on luggage tumbled out onto horrified peacekeepers. While everyone gasped for air as it were their last breath on Earth, a resounding roar indicated that the jet was airborne. Though far from graceful, the plane eventually reached its cruising speed and altitude. With this emotionally charged take-off, many peacekeepers could not help but wonder what else awaited them once in-theatre (Maure, 2020). They would soon find out!

The date was October 20, 1989, and this was the Canadian contingent's first day in-theatre. With only 3 weeks to go before Election Day, apprehension was high amongst the troop, which was the last to arrive in-country. Officers were soon divided and were assigned to one of the 18 different areas of the country. A high-ranking Canadian peacekeeper was assigned the function of Chief of Staff. He would be the 3rd officer in importance within the United Nations Civilian Police (CIVPOL) organization after the Deputy Commissioner and Police Commissioner's positions. As Chief of Staff, the officer worked within the United Nations headquarters building located in the Capital City of Windhoek. He also oversaw the functioning of the 1500 police officers that made up CIVPOL. As per the United Nations Organizational chart, he reported directly to the United Nations Police Commissioner.

On his first day as Chief of Staff, the officer got a taste of the challenges related to his functions and the high level of diplomacy it required. Following an overnight gunfight in one of the regions, the Police Commissioner gave him orders to assign an investigator to look thoroughly into the matter. As per the Organizational chart, he approached a police Superintendent from a Commonwealth country who was in charge of directing all investigations. The Chief of Staff passed along the pertinent details of the incident to the Superintendent and asked him that whomever he assigned should report on their findings as soon as possible. The Superintendent acknowledged and left (Maure, 2020).

Five minutes had barely gone by when the Chief of Staff heard hurried footsteps coming down the hall towards his office. In a matter of seconds, he found himself face-to-face with the imposing figure of the Deputy Commissioner. As the second in command, the Deputy Commissioner bluntly demanded answers as to why the Chief of Staff had not asked a Black CIVPOL officer to carry out the assignment mandated by the Police Commissioner. He continued by questioning the Chief of Staff's decision and reluctance to put faith into the investigative capabilities of people of color (Maure, 2020).

Calmly, the Chief of Staff replied that, as per the organogram, he had assigned the matter to the Superintendent because all investigations fell under his purview. The Deputy Commissioner, himself a man of color, reminded the Chief of Staff that this was the United Nations. Just like that, without saying much more, he disappeared from the Chief's office. This unexpected visit from the Deputy Commissioner within the first half-hour of the Chief of Staff's Namibian duties exposed him to a harsh reality; that even though officers from many nations worked together as equals, racial tensions were ever-present, even amongst the rank of the United Nations. In moving forward, the Chief of Staff ensured that all tasks were divided amongst all police contingents, albeit still under the purview of the Superintendent (Maure, 2020). As a former peacekeeper and diplomat, the author truly appreciates how difficult and sensitive the above situation was. Rightfully and to avoid favoritism, the Chief of Staff opted to share the tasks equally. However, the reality of some missions was that even if police officers of all nations were equals in status, not all displayed the same investigative capabilities. Assigning work to the less "capable" police contingents without offending them became a balancing act of tact and diplomacy, which the Chief of Staff in this example handled admirably.

One of the main objectives of the presence of CIVPOL and, to a measure, to the Canadian contingent's presence was to help with security and to ensure safe elections. As Election Day neared attempts were on the rise to destabilize the country and prevent the elections by burning polling stations and stealing ballots. Some of the undermining efforts came from both neighboring Angola's communist regime and South Africa (a country losing its grip with apartheid) (Green, 2019; Maure, 2020). Neither country wanted to see their control of Namibia vanish due to the country gaining its independence. Election Day, November 7, 1989, finally arrived. On that day, an army of international peacekeepers took positions in critical areas at the various polling stations around the country. Some of those stations were mere huts, made of mats, poles, and tanned skins (Wapenyi, 1990). A Canadian peacekeeper observed that it was amazing to see such a high voters' turnout at the polling stations. Despite some mishaps, Election Day (which lasted 5 days) was considered a success. Once all the votes counted, it became clear that Namibians wished their independence from South Africa.

The role of many peacekeepers changed after Election Day, including that of the Canadian Chief of Staff. From then on, his duties encompassed the additional task of monitoring the creation and recruitment of staff for the new Namibian police service. It was a daunting and monumental task to accomplish, with only 4 months to recruit and train new officers. All had to be ready for March 21, 1990, the date set for Namibian independence. However, the Chief of Staff would rely on Scotland Yard and other United Kingdom law enforcement institutions' great expertise to set up the training and the curriculum.

Interestingly, despite the many dangers lurking, including people cavalcading with weapons and incursions from Angola insurgency fighters, the Canadian peacekeepers were instructed by the United Nations not to carry weapons on the mission. Although they had received permission to bring their weapons, the now-retired Smith and Wesson .38 revolver, they were locked away as the United Nations did not want CIVPOL monitors to carry weapons (Maure, 2020).

As alluded earlier, every mission has its dangers, and the Namibian mission was no different. While no Canadian police peacekeepers died during that mission, a total of four CIVPOL, 11 military and three civilian peacekeepers perished, acting as a reminder that United Nations missions can be very perilous (United Nations, n.d.). Amongst the mission's challenges, one Canadian observer noted that those related to incidents involving criminality committed by peers from other police contingents were the most challenging. These required a considerable amount of tact and diplomacy. Take, for example, the suspension of a United Nations CIVPOL monitor who sexually abused village women. It started when the officer was assigned to a small rural community where the United Nations had established a post to oversee the voting process. The officer's duty was to provide security for the village's water supply. When some of the village women came to get some water to bring back home, the officer would only allow them access to the water in return for sexual favors. Sadly, the officer was able to carry on his depravity for some time until one victim spoke out. However, trying to get the officer's Contingent Commander to take disciplinary or criminal action against his officer became a nearly impossible endeavor. The Commander's unwillingness to act infuriated other peacekeepers as well as the victimized villagers. Outraged by the inaction of the Commander, a Canadian observer appealed to the mission's Police Commissioner explaining the reason the offender had to be removed from the area. Eventually, the officer was redeployed to another zone until scheduled to leave the mission. Although he should have been immediately expelled from the mission and disciplined upon his acts being discovered, the best that one could do at the time was to transfer him. Thankfully, incidents like the this are addressed much faster nowadays; still, the issue of sexual exploitation and abuse of a position of vulnerability committed by peacekeepers (uniformed and civilian personnel) remains a hot topic that deserves more attention and more accountability (Wheeler, 2020).

At last, came the big day: Independence Day, March 21, 1990. At midnight that day, all of the South African police and South African military personnel still in Namibia departed. The only ones who stayed behind were South African law enforcement officers who supported Namibia's independence and who had agreed to stay to help with the new police transition. In Windhoek, hundreds of thousands of people had gathered on the street to witness the take-down of the South African flag and the rising of the new Namibian flag. All were finally rejoicing a country of their own! Representatives and dignitaries from all of the Commonwealth countries were also present: their security details all fell within the purview of the Canadian CIVPOL Chief of Staff. Thanks to the international military and months of preparation, all went well!

The moment the Namibian flag went up, all United Nations observers present witnessed Namibian indigenous population embrace their Caucasian countrymen. Forgiveness was in order after decades of fighting. Black, White, young, and old, all were rejoicing with tears in their eyes! And just like that, a new country was born!

For the Canadian contingent, being part of the birth of a country was something they would never forget. From a cross-cultural perspective, the experience that members of the Canadian contingent experienced in dealing with others was second to none. All came out of the mission as better people and as better police officers. But this experience was not just a one-way street. Members from other CIVPOL units whose countries may have had little knowledge or respect for human rights learned a great deal on high ethics in policing. Being able to pass that on to police officers from other countries was something very dignifying (Maure, 2020). The Canadian contingent in Namibia was, in a sense, a pioneering Canadian police unit. Its success and accomplishments within the realm of Canadian police peacekeeping remains very inspirational to this date.

United Nations Verification Mission in Guatemala (MINUGUA)

Canada's contributions to international missions have not been as considerable in size as the one in Namibia. Take the case of MINUGUA, for which Canada contributed a handful of officers (five officers on a one-year rotation). Candidates for that mission had to be fluent in Spanish, the official language of the mission. Particular to that mission was the fact that all Canadian peacekeepers were spread throughout the various regions and did not work together. Instead, they would work closely with police colleagues from Italy, El Salvador, Spain, and other nations. Working in parallel with officers from other countries required a language aptitude and an acculturation ability to participate in the mission. Established in 1994 after a cease-fire agreement between the Guatemala government and the Guatemalan National Revolutionary Unit (URNG), MINUGUA sought to end 36 years of civil war and promoted the rebuilding of the country (Government of Canada, 2018; Rauch, 2020). To accomplish its goal, MINUGUA counted on the signing of the Peace Accords, which included a series of 12 agreements towards a firm and lasting peace. For example, these accords included: an Agreement on the Resettlement of the Population; the Return of Refugees; the Establishment of a Commission to Clarify Past Human Rights Abuses; the Indigenous Identity and Rights; and Human Rights and a Police Reform . The role of the Canadian police peacekeepers in Guatemala was both diverse and extremely challenging and required adapting quickly to the environment. Unlike the previous mission discussed in this chapter, in Guatemala, Canadian peacekeepers had to make their way independently, often arriving one-at-a-time when a rotation ended. The Canadians were well-prepared for this mission as all had undergone a Spanish language ability test in addition to having an average of at least 10 years of operational policing. The mission in Guatemala was a mission unlike others at the time as it was a verification mission. It meant that officers participating in the assignment were there to report on the advances of specific Peace Accords. For example, a Canadian observer posted in the region of Quetzaltenango (located at nearly 9000 feet altitude) reported that he often traveled down to sea level and back during an 8-hour day to monitor the living conditions of ex-URNG combatants. Without electricity, running water, sanitation, with children roaming around in the mud, and with only a cheap tin roof over their heads, these ex-combatants' living conditions were heart breaking. The peacekeeper's role was to build rapport with them and report to United Nations Headquarters on how to help them. The United Nations Headquarters would then turn around and report its findings to the Government of Guatemala, which oversaw the development and improvement of the community. This process was a slow one, which was at times, was difficult and frustrating to witness for Canadian observers used to a more rapid government intervention at home. Since this mission focused on Peace Accords' verification, the dangers faced by peacekeepers were different from those of other missions where, for example, the peace was maintained between two rival armies. In the case of MINUGUA, the perils were not always obvious; still, they could sneak in many forms, from traffic accidents on narrow stretches of winding roads to being caught in the middle of a summary execution in rural Guatemala. In all, four peacekeepers perished in accidents during the length of the mission, but the tally could have been much higher (United Nations, n.d.). Take the case of a Canadian observer in the mountainous region of Polugua, in February of 1999. At that time, four suspects allegedly involved in a vehicle theft were captured by an angry mob. The suspects were then beaten, tied up, and their leader turned over to the police with the implied condition that the police would accompany the gang leader to the location where the vehicle was. This strategy from the crowd was in an attempt to return the vehicle to its lawful owner. However, the crowd refused to turn over the remaining three suspects and threatened to immolate them on the spot. Thanks to the town's mayor's quick intervention, the mob agreed to turn the suspect over to the mayor's office, pending the return of the stolen vehicle.

The next day, local authorities contacted MINUGUA to seek help and monitor the volatile situation. A team of two MINUGUA peacekeepers, a lawyer and a Canadian police observer were dispatched to the scene. Arriving at the village, the two peacekeepers found no sign of danger or commotion. Both met with the local police and local Justice Department representatives who addressed the crowd, which latter agreed to give the police enough time to recover the stolen vehicle. The police then left and a crowd of a few hundred dispersed. The MINUGUA team then attended the mayor's office and confirmed that the three suspects would be safe so long as they remained in his office, out of sight of the village's population. However, the mayor confessed that he feared he may not be able to ensure the suspects safety for long. The MINUGUA team then return to their vehicle. On their way through the town's central square, a citizen on a loudspeaker asked them to explain the presence of the United Nations in the village. In an attempt to illustrate to the few curious onlookers that the United Nations wanted a peaceful resolution to the matter, the MINUGUA attorney took the microphone. Alas, this action sealed the fate of the team. Within a few minutes, hundreds of villagers gathered to listen, surrounding the peacekeepers in the process. Then, out of the blue, a drunken man shouted that the United Nations should remain in the village until the police and the Justice Department came back with the stolen vehicle. The crowd cheered to the remark and from that moment on, the MINUGUA team found itself with no escape. The euphoria that ensued was hard to describe: more villagers encircled the peacekeepers, who in short time found themselves surrounded by thousands. Individuals in the crowd kept on shouting that the United Nations was only there to protect the criminal. With this statement came more menaces towards the team, including the wavering of machetes near their faces and decapitation threats. All the team could do was radio to its headquarters that the situation was dire. When a short time later the village's mayor attended the central square to help the peacekeepers, he was threatened with harm if he intervened. The apogee was reached a few hours into the ordeal when the peacekeepers noticed the crowd cheer at the sight of a vehicle carrying gasoline canisters and tires. In this region of Guatemala, where many citizens did not understand or trust the judicial system, summary executions would, at times, take place. First tires would be placed around a suspected criminal's waist and torso to prevent the individual from moving. Then the person would be doused with gasoline and set on fire for everyone to watch.

Despite the horrifying smell of gasoline and the sight of the tires, the crowd took no other action and the atmosphere around the peacekeepers calmed down. More than 2 hours into the ordeal, it was still impossible for the MINUGUA crew to go anywhere. Suddenly, the MINUGUA team saw the mayor appear with a handful of assistants who pushed their way through the crowd and joined the peacekeepers. He then informed the crowd that the peacekeepers needed to make an important call for an update. This stratagem worked and the mayor, out-of-sight of the crowd, led the team to a small building, hundreds of meters away. From there, an escape route was identified, and the peacekeepers were able to leave town. It is important to note that this entire situation could have been avoided if the peacekeepers had received an in-depth briefing at the beginning of the mission on local customs and the near-total distrust that some villages displayed towards authorities, including the United Nations. Having such a cross-cultural training at the beginning of the mission would have undoubtedly convinced the peacekeepers not to stay around, even if the general atmosphere was calm. On the positive side, in-depth cross-cultural training is now provided for peacekeepers joining new missions. Still, it does not deviate peacekeepers from getting hurt or killed.

The Guatemala mission also brought peacekeepers some other unique challenges. Take for example the role of a Canadian police observer who investigated a Human Rights complaint of an individual who alleged he was wrongfully arrested, beaten, tortured, and thrown in jail by the local police. What made the situation somewhat of a challenge was the polar, multidimensional role of the peacekeeper. On the one hand, they wore the hat of a police liaison officer focused on monitoring the transition of the local Guatemalan police's transition into democratic policing, while on the other hand, they investigated the same police for human rights abuse complaints. This dual role brought on complex circumstances that made it very difficult for the peacekeeper to be fully trusted by its host.

For the Canadian police, tact and diplomacy were two critical attributes to possess in order to be a successful peacekeeper in Guatemala. Adapting to the local culture of the mission and adapting to the multicultural aspect of the mission was something that Canadian peacekeepers did well given Canada's multicultural environment.

United Nations Transitional Authority for East-Timor (UNTAET)

Officially launched on October 25, 1999, to hold democratic elections on the territory of East Timor, the United Nations Transitional Authority for East-Timor (UNTAET) had the overall responsibility for the administration of East Timor and the administration of its justice. These institutions had been completely demolished earlier that year by a campaign of violence by pro-Indonesian militia (Ishizuka, 2010; Public Safety Canada, 2001).

Canada's participation to the mission was in the form of a deployment of 20 police officers whose main task, along with CIVPOL officers from around the world, was to maintain law and order and establish the East Timor Police Services (Public Safety Canada, 2001). However, Canada's contribution to that mission would prove at times, somewhat challenging. For example, take the role of a senior RCMP executive who arrived in Dili, the capital city of East Timor, ready to undertake the functions of Canadian Contingent Commander and that of Chief of National Investigations. The moment he landed, the senior officer found out to his dismay that a unilateral decision had been made by the mission's Police Commissioner to demote him to the role of local commander in a difficult-to-access, malaria-infested area of the country (Maure, 2020). The officer, a proven leader and someone with an extensive background in major crime investigations, had been aware that his skillset might be put to other ends once in-theatre. However, the one-sided Police Commissioner's decision to isolate him from leading his troop was questionable, at best. This situation was particularly alarming since the Canadian Senior Executive had been identified by Canada, with the support of the United Nations Department of Peacekeeping Operations (DPKO) in New York, to be the Chief of National Investigations. Furthermore, this impromptu assignment neither called for the officer's expertise in major crimes, nor acknowledged his need, as the Canadian Contingent Commander, to be centralized in Dili. Being stationed in a remote area with limited communications did not suit one of his primary roles, Contingent Commander, for the Canadian deployment. As it turned out, the Police Commissioner's decision had the appearance of having everything to do with the strained relationship he entertained with the outgoing Canadian Contingent Commander, the new arriving Senior Executive being the unwitting beneficiary of that tense relationship. It was also evident to the Senior Executive that the Police Commissioner had another candidate in mind for the job of National Chief of Investigation: a senior police officer from his own country. Standing his ground and asserting to the Police Commissioner that he would be informing his superiors in Canada, who would, in turn, engage the DPKO, the Senior Officer prepared for his next move: diplomacy. Recognizing this situation as an opportunity to redefine the relationship with the Police Commissioner, the Senior Executive convinced his counterpart that as the Contingent Commander for Canada, it was imperative that he be posted in Dili. From there, he could direct his full energy into supporting the Police Commissioner's Leadership Team while ensuring a vital contribution from the Canadian Contingent. The approach worked. Seeing an opportunity to improve relations and avoid a showdown with Canada, the Police Commissioner relented and assigned the Canadian officer to a newly created Border Liaison Officer position (Maure, 2020). Being the Border Liaison Officer meant that the officer would liaise between the United Nations Civilian Police Headquarters in Dili and the Border Services Agency of the Timorese government. Over the next few months, the officer took every opportunity to prove to the Police Commissioner that the latter had made the right choice.

At the time of the Canadian officer's arrival in May 2001, UNTAET was in full swing and was getting ready for Parliamentary Elections, set for August 31, 2001. In East Timor, Canadian police officers were involved on many fronts to help the Timorese people. For instance, some were involved in a program which brought local youths and police together in a non-confrontational environment. Once their working day was completed, officers would spend time listening and talking to youths, providing them with sports equipment and clothing. During the mission, a group of Canadian police officers partnered with the Ontario Federation of Teachers to acquire school supplies for 50 learning establishments. In another instance, a school liaison pilot project was initiated whereby Canadian officers and their Timorese police counterparts would attend local schools and speak with students (Public Safety Canada, 2001). Actions and projects led by Canadian peacekeepers were outside of the box initiatives to promote democratic policing and build rapport with communities. This savoir-faire has been a trait of Canadian peacekeeping, seen in many other United Nations missions. One Canadian observer who worked in the Former Yugoslavia in the mid-1990s recalled that he partnered with Spalding Canada, makers of basketballs, before his departure on the mission. Being an avid basketball player and coach, he brought several basketballs and used them to play with youths and get closer to the community. His initiative helped him develop trust and better relations with the children and their parents (Maure, 2020).

A Canadian who was assigned the duty of Chief of Strategic Planning recalled that the role placed him in charge of a team of 12 staff whose duties were to support the upcoming elections. In that function, the officer worked closely with military units from other nations and with whom he set up a Joint National Operations Centre. The duties enabled the leader to travel to the various districts of East Timor, attend security briefings, coach the regions on how to get ready for the election process, and instruct the regions how to report instances of violence so that police and military units could be dispatched in a flash. At stake was the safety of the elections, along with a grim reminder that, 2 years earlier, the pro-Indonesia militia had ravaged the country after the elections and caused a violent riot and massacre (Saul, 2001).

As Election Day came, 8000 armed peacekeepers from all nations ensured that the streets and polling stations throughout the country were safe and that no violence occurred. A Canadian observer assigned to foot patrols in the capital Dili remembered the day as one with a sense of excitement and euphoria displayed by the Timorese people. Although feelings of apprehension existed amongst some peacekeepers, this election thankfully went without any major incidents. The victory for the Revolutionary Front for an Independent East Timor was later announced after the party secured 55 out of 88 seats. The elections over, they were followed by a period of transition where the focus shifted to ensuring the support and the training of a new police force, the National Police of East Timor. A Canadian observer shared that from that time on, his duties transitioned to the oversight of firearm training for the new Police force, general police investigation techniques, and the formation of specialized police units, such as a Family Violence Unit and a Professional Standards Unit (Maure, 2020). As discussed earlier, the importance of professional standards within the United Nations ranks cannot be stressed enough. A Canadian observer once described the conduct of a particular officer in his unit as both unacceptable and disgraceful. The officer's contribution to the mission was to prey on young and impoverished Timorese women whom he reportedly paid to have sex with him. What was even more troubling was that some of the women with him appeared to be underage. While off-duty and at times, while on-duty, the officer would wear ethnic garments that made him look like royalty. Understandably, Timorese women were drawn by the officer's apparent high status. When the Canadian observer reported the behavior to the officer's supervisor, accusations of harassment were levelled back at him. Eventually, the individual was held accountable and transferred to another unit. Sadly, as previously noted in this chapter, efforts to promptly remove individuals from a mission who displayed poor ethics or even criminal behaviors were not always met with strong support. Often, these officers' own command supported or condoned the behaviors, which they might have viewed as an acceptable norm in their country of origin. When denounced or targeted by other peacekeepers, they, in turn, complained to mission management that racially motivated co-workers targeted them (Maure, 2020). Unless a crime as such could be proven forthwith, an internal investigation would need to be conducted. In many instances, it would take several months to amass the necessary evidence of crime or misconduct. By that time, many culprits would have completed their tour of duty or were near the end of it. More than a decade after the Namibia mission example of misconduct, peacekeeper accountability, ethics, and wrongdoing remained a challenge for the United Nations. For example, a 2012 study published by the Government Accountability Project (GAP): a non-profit organization promoting corporate and government accountability, identified severe issues within the United Nations system (Spielmann, 2012). These controversies addressed peacekeepers misconduct that often went unpunished. The report underscored the many difficulties encountered to prosecute culprits, citing cases such as: seeking sexual favors from United Nations applicants; sexual exploitation of civilians; storing pornography on United Nations computers; making derogatory sexual comments on fellow workers; beating a spouse who was a United Nations Volunteer and causing injuries requiring hospitalization; threats to kill a supervisor; theft and sale of United Nations properties (i.e. cameras, radios, computers). In 2 years, the report identified a 68% complaint dismissal rate. In the writer's opinion, as a former peacekeeper, United Nations employees accountability should be at the highest standard, especially in cases where the evidence supports misconduct or criminality. However, it seems that sexual misconduct has been a prominent part of an ongoing problem, the total size of which appearing much more significant than first thought. Any occurrence of sexual exploitation or abuse by a peacekeeper impairs the United Nation's credibility in the very communities it is trying to help (Maure, 2020). For the great majority of devoted and committed peacekeepers, it is very distressful to observe unethical officers or civilians tarnish the United Nation's reputation with their unacceptable behaviors. However, with this issue having posed a constant challenge to a succession of Secretaries-General, more must be done to keep peacekeepers and the member states sending them at a much higher accountability (Leeuwen, 2019).

One of the most challenging experiences a Canadian peacekeeper shared was that of being away from his family. At the time of the mission, the peacekeeper had two teenage children, which the task of raising had suddenly befallen onto his spouse, who was thousands of miles away and by herself. While that peacekeeper was missing his spouse, other Canadian contingent members were trying to cope with their own family drama at home. At least one of those members who experienced problems at home, later confessed that he had left for the mission without his spouse's full consent. Over time, the distance became a further impediment, and the relationship worsened. Despite some of these disparaging tales, there is some good news stories. Nowadays, almost 20 years after this mission, means of communications have improved drastically. The Internet and software applications like SKYPE, ZOOM and FaceTime have enhanced the way peacekeepers contact distant loved ones. In conclusion, despite some initial hiccups, the mission in East Timor helped many Canadian participant grow into better persons and become better police officers. Many who participated to the mission eventually received promotions, some even reaching upper management ranks (Maure, 2020).

International Security Assistance Force (ISAF) in Afghanistan

Without a doubt, one of the most perilous and dangerous missions that Canadian Police participated in has been that of the United Nations-mandated and NATO-led International Security Assistance Force (ISAF) in Afghanistan. The mission, which lasted from 2001 to 2013, claimed 158 Canadian military lives and many more from other NATO countries. Canada's involvement in Afghanistan was like no other (Veterans Affairs Canada, 2019a). For one, this was Canada's most extended and most significant combat engagement since the Korean War of the 1950s (Azzi & Foot, 2009). Throughout the mission, approximately 300 Canadian police officers served along with military units from Canada and the United States (Maure, 2020; Veterans Affairs Canada, 2020a). One of the many functions of the police officers was to train and mentor their Afghanistan police counterparts and, through those efforts, help to rebuild the fragile institution of the Afghanistan National Police (ANP). However, building a country still at war was no easy task (Maloney, 2006). Mission pre-deployment: compared to the average two-week pre-deployment training for other international missions, the 6 weeks training for the police officers looked more than adequate. Topics like the use-of-force, war crime investigations, child soldiers, along with some cross-cultural training about Afghanistan were part of the academic segment that lasted 4 weeks. A two-week C-7 assault rifle coaching followed. However, by all account, this training was insufficient for those police officers without previous military experience. With the Canadian Forces soldiers undergoing a six-month preparation training before leaving for the Afghanistan campaign, the police candidates were at a disadvantage. This absence of in-depth practice became obvious later in-theatre when some police officers handling the C-7 carbine were facetiously referred to as more dangerous than the Taliban insurgents (Maure, 2020). On the positive side, many police candidates identified for this mission had previous military background, thus helping the adaptation. Moreover, the C-7 training shortcoming was quickly identified from candidate feedback, and subsequent rotations of police officers benefitted from a more thorough military preparation (Maure, 2020). One officer who departed for a tour of duty in 2009 admitted that for him, leaving the safety of home, a spouse and a young child to go to a war zone was no easy task. However, he added that one of the driving forces behind his decision had been his desire to make a positive difference in the world. A proud father of a one-year old baby girl, he was well aware that women in Afghanistan were poorly treated and considered second-class citizens. He believed that his contribution would aid paving the road for bettering women's rights and conditions in that far-away land.

Arriving in Afghanistan via a Hercules military transport plane and spending the first day at the Kandahar Airfield revealed the scope of what this Canadian police officer had gotten himself into:

- dust blowing;
- dark and grim perimeter fences;
- bunkers and anti-blast walls;
- the deafening drone of helicopters coming and going; and
- the roars of turbine jets taking off.

There was no mistake about it; this was a war zone! Despite the initial negative impression, the Kandahar Airfield turned out to be a fascinating place to be: over 30,000 people lived on the base, including military, police, and other civilians support staff, all hailing from over 30 countries. The Kandahar Airfield would be called home until some of the Canadian police observers assigned to the southern region would transition to Camp Nathan Smith (CNS). CNS was a former food factory damaged during the Afghanistan civil war and turned into an American military base. The arrival at Kandahar Airfield also brought a perspective that remained throughout the mission: that death lurked around unannounced. As a case in point, in March 2009, a day before the rotational arrival of a Canadian police officer, an Improvised Explosive Device (IED) blast killed two Canadian soldiers while on patrol in their 17-ton Light Armored Vehicle (LAV). The force of the blast was such that the vehicle flipped into a ditch (Afghanistan: A Canadian Story 2001–2014, 2012). As if this news was not horrific enough, the newly arrived police officer learned that the LAV that transported the two deceased soldiers was also supposed to carry a Canadian police officer. It was only by a pure twist of faith that the

Canadian police officer escaped grievous injuries or death: at the last minute, for strategic reasons, the officer boarded the LAV that rode behind. The bravery, emotional stress, and survivor guilt this officer went through as he and his military platoon recovered the body of their deceased comrades and loaded them into a responding helicopter is hard to imagine (Maure, 2020). Sadly, this would not be the only instance where a Canadian police officer would be hurt. In August 2009, a Canadian police officer stationed in Kabul as part of the same mission survived a suicide car bombing that killed seven people and wounded 91 others (CTV News, 2009).

Canadian police officers were carrying a multitude of different tasks during the Afghanistan assignment. Functions such as Policy Director or Intelligence Analysts had a degree of danger to them merely due to the environment. Many were part of what was called the Provincial Reconstruction Team (PRT). Canada led a 250-man PRT based in Kandahar City, which conducted various activities throughout the region. These activities consisted of Patrol Company and that of Other Government Departments (ODGs) (Maloney, 2006). The Patrol Company was a light infantry unit that provided support, such as security and transport, for some of the ODGs. These ODGs included organizations such as USAID, Foreign Affairs Canada, The Canadian International Development Agency (CIDA), The British Department of Foreign and International Development and the Royal Canadian Mounted Police (RCMP). Without the Patrol Company and its professionals, ODG elements, such as the RCMP in its training of the Afghanistan police, would not possibly operate effectively, especially in areas frequented by insurgents (Maloney, 2006).

Thus, in its training of the ANP, one could argue that one of the most unpredictable and dangerous aspects of the Canadian police mission was that involving what it called "presence patrol." These operations were conducted in the sand-and-dust filled streets and alleys of Kandahar and were quite nerve-racking. For instance, the assignment consisted of going out on foot patrols with a Canadian military platoon of approximately 30 soldiers, along with translators and ANP officers. As police mentors, the Canadians had to overview how the ANP officers reacted to certain situations in order to elevate ANP policing skills. Thus, ANP officers would be supervised to assess how they conducted themselves with the public, how they interviewed witnesses or suspects, and how they made notes. The latter could turn out to be a task of a sizeable challenge, given that many ANP officers did not know how to read and write. On one of his initial patrols, a Canadian officer recounted that he and his company had been walking for less than 10 minutes when they heard an engine rev up and noted a rider on a dilapidated motorcycle race towards them. Alarmed at the idea that this could be a suicide bomber, all raised their weapons and aimed at the oncoming rider. Realizing that his life was in danger, the rider applied his brakes and came to a stop in a cloud of dust. Cautiously and nervously, the officer and a few of his military comrades approached the rider, watching his hands and ensuring they were well above his head. As it turned out, the individual was a former security guard working for an allied troop training center. Satisfied that the individual was no threat, the company moved on and continued its foot patrol. Then, within a few minutes, a farmer frantically waved at the troop in an effort to get noticed. When asked what was wrong, the famer pointed to a wall ahead of the troop where a live IED had been concealed by insurgents. Faced with the possibility of grievous harm or death, the Canadian officer's heartbeat revved up again! The troop then set a safety perimeter around the wall and a few intrepid soldiers approached it. With many of the military officers on their last patrol before completing their mission, approaching the wall and assessing the situation was not a popular endeavor. However, this is a task that had to be done to make the area safe. Suddenly, a loud explosion rocked the ground and sent the troop for cover. As a column of smoke rose in the backdrop, the police officer thought his brave colleagues had surely perished. The sound of a nearby gun battle abruptly broke the deathly silence that had followed the explosion. However, as far as the patrol platoon was concerned, no member seemed to be injured, including the audacious soldiers who had approached the wall. Soon, all learned that two suicide bombers on motorcycles had blown themselves up near the entrance of the headquarters of the Afghanistan security agency, the National Directorate of Security (DNS), which was located less than 1 kilometer away from where the foot patrol was.

In the chaos that followed, the troop attempted to respond to the attack but was called back to the base while an American unit military responded to the incident. As the foot patrol hurried back with heavy gear in the scorching Afghanistan heat, it paused for a brief moment. Suddenly, another threat surged: an unknown civilian vehicle loudly raced towards them. Fearing that the vehicle was another suicide bomber part of a broader coordinated attack, a soldier fired a few rounds at the vehicle which caused it to crash into a ditch. Scared but unharmed, the driver apologized for his erratic driving as he turned out not to be an insurgent. Later, in the safety and comfort of the base, the Canadian police could not help but wonder what he had got himself into (Maure, 2020). Thankfully, not all situations were as emotionally charged and dangerous as those described above for the police officers. During patrols with the Afghanistan Counter-Narcotic Police, a Canadian police observer remarked that he and his team had decommissioned several hundred kilograms of raw opium and heroin, likely destined to European and North American markets. The seizure and destruction of the drugs was indeed an accomplishment that gave the Canadian police, however ephemeral, a more positive outlook on the mission.

In another case, a Canadian peacekeeper recalled the challenges in dealing with the cultural gap between the Afghanistan hosts and their Canadian trainers. During an attack at a checkpoint, an Afghanistan police trainee was killed after he was hit in the chest by a grenade fragment. ISAF investigators discovered that not only the deceased was not wearing his issued body armor, but that all of the brand-new body armors issued to that police team had been thrown in a garbage bin. To make matters worse, when the Canadian peacekeeper questioned the checkpoint commander about the deceased not wearing his body armor, the commander replied that the death had been "god's will". Whether or not the death of the subordinate had been a twist of fate did not matter. The lack of empathy displayed by the checkpoint commander incensed the Canadian trainer who, along with ISAF investigators, believed the injuries might not have been fatal had the subordinate been wearing his bulletproof vest. After much effort to bridge cultural gaps and make the checkpoint commander more accountable to his troop, the checkpoint commander became one of the most vigilant and well-turned out Afghan officers the mission had seen. Sadly, the commander was killed months later in an IED incident (Maure, 2020).

This very brief snapshot of the Afghan campaign recognized only a handful of all of Canadian police's work and duties during the assignment. Still, it depicted a stressful, dangerous and hostile environment. Despite this, Canadian police officers rose to the challenge and contributed to the best of their abilities to the mission and set a wheel in motion to modernize and professionalize the ANP.

United Nations Stabilization Mission in Haiti (MINUSTAH)

The last mission to be discussed in this chapter is that of the United Nations Stabilization Mission in Haiti (MINUSTAH), which took place from 2004 to 2017. In 2004, the mission established its goal of providing a secure and stable environment to a new transitional government. It was not the first time the United Nations was in Haiti. In fact, it had been there on and off since 1994, after it took over from the United States military which oversaw a transition from a military government into a civil one (BBC News, 2019; Veterans Affairs Canada, 2020b). With a series of United Nations engagements in Haiti starting with UNMIH—United Nations Support in Haiti, followed with UNTMIH—United Nations Transition Mission in Haiti and MIPONUH—United Nations Civilian Police Mission in Haiti, Canada would be engaged in Haiti's reconstruction for a number of years (Maure, 2020; United Nations, 2003; Veterans Affairs Canada, 2019b). Throughout the period that preceded the New Millennium, positive developments were made in Haiti, including creating a national police force that came with the return to some democratic rules. Unfortunately, by the early 2000s, Haiti's political climate deteriorated with the United Nation's departure, and the situation reverted to lawlessness and violence. In 2004, amongst rising political and gang violence, the United Nations established a stabilization mission, this time under the name of MINUSTAH (Boileau, 2019; Security Council Report, 2020). From the monitoring of the Haitian National Police reform, the fostering of the rule of law, supporting the Haitian Constitutional process, MINUSTAH would prove to be a mission capable of adapting to Haiti's continuously changing needs. However, on January 12, 2010, MINUSTAH would face one of its most daunting challenges, following a destructive earthquake that reportedly killed an estimated 220,000 Haitians, many buried alive (Pallardy, 2020).

MINUSTAH was not spared: 102 serving UN employees, including two Canadian Police officers, lost their lives, making it the most extensive single loss of United Nations personnel in the entire history of the organization (United Nations, 2020). For this segment's purpose and to provide the reader with a preview of some of the unforeseen dangers lurking, the Canadian police experience in Haiti will focus on the time of the earthquake, as recounted by a surviving Canadian peacekeeper. Canadians who signed up for that mission might have expected facing some civil unrest, flood, hurricane, but no one was prepared to deal with such a devastating earthquake. January 12, 2010, started as a beautiful day in a hot and warm and sunny Port-au-Prince, the capital city of Haiti, where many United Nations peacekeepers were stationed. At 12 minutes to 5 in the afternoon, a Canadian peacekeeper emerged from the United Nations Headquarters located in the former Christopher Hotel building. After a long 10-hour day, the officer recalled that he felt relieved to be off shift and was looking forward to enjoying the warm evening with his comrades. Then, without any warning, the ground started to shake violently. It took the officer a few seconds to realize that this was an earthquake and that he had better brace himself. As the shaking intensified, he observed the roofs of nearby homes located on a hill collapse under a massive cloud of dust. Closer to him, in the parking lot, white United Nations-marked Toyota vehicles started to bounce up and down like rubber balls, some vehicles crushing others in their path.

The ground's shaking and waving motion was so intense that the officer was forced onto his knees, dropping one hand on the ground to keep his balance. Fear sank in and the officer could imagine a crater opening under him and swallowing him into the abyss. He closed his eyes for a moment as he braced for more shocks. Then, he heard a loud, thunderous roar in the background, which was immediately followed by a cloud of dust engulfing him. When he wiped the dust off his face and opened his eyes, an unbelievable spectacle unfolded in front of him. There, meters away, the once proud five-storey United Nations Headquarter building had been rendered into a giant ski slope. An entire wing of the building had collapsed onto itself, making the stacked-up floors look like pancakes. Amongst the echoes of moans and cries coming from colleagues trapped in the collapsed building, the officer's years of police training kicked in. Putting his altruistic values first, he, along with a small team of United Nations military soldiers who had escaped the building's collapse, bravely reentered the crumbled wing. Inside, they managed to locate a few survivors, including the Canadian Contingent commander (Maure, 2020). Throughout the evening, aftershocks continued to hamper rescue efforts. With the collapse of its headquarters and the death of many of its staff, including the Chief of Mission, MINUSTAH was devastated. By midnight on January 12, most surviving peacekeepers had regrouped with their contingents and had contacted their embassies. Using a United Nations vehicle that had not been destroyed, the Canadian officer regrouped with other Canadian peacekeepers and started to look for missing contingent members in the various areas of Port-au-Prince. High on adrenaline and with victims in all parts of the city, the officer would not sleep for another 72 hours. The stress and intensity of the second day, were, in many ways, worse than that of the first day. During the second day, the officer would be facing situations that no training could ever have prepared him enough.

He would later admit that those events would shake his ethics and value system for the rest of his career. While driving through the ruined city, he and two colleagues came across a frantic husband who sought his help to free his wife. The woman, who had miraculously survived the collapse of her home, was pinned inside the structure. To reach her, the husband had crawled in a small hole no larger than 2 feet by 2 feet. That hole narrowly extended a few feet inside the collapsed home, making it extremely dangerous to go in. Only equipped with an improvised rope (a thick electrical cord), the peacekeepers soon realized they had a colossal task ahead: remove several thousand pounds of concrete to clear a passage and free the woman. After much effort to clean up some of the rubbles, they discovered that one of the woman's legs rested under a large piece of concrete. To make matters worse, the block of concrete supported the entire roof's load: itself weighing several tons. Her only saving grace would have been to have access to hydraulic equipment to lift the concrete or having a medical crew perform amputation. Unfortunately, none of those were available in the immediate aftermath of the quake and the Canadian peacekeepers, after radioing their position, moved on. Being powerless and having to abandon someone in need of help shook the peacekeepers to their core. However, without the proper tools that Search and Rescue teams possess, they could do little. Then, only a few hundred feet away, another woman could be heard crying for help. Amongst the rubbles of what used to be a middle-class home, an arm came out of a small hole and waved. Because the house was located on a slope, it had caved in under the strength of the tremors. At first sight, the structure appeared very unstable and risked crushing anyone coming close. Again, heartbroken, the only thing the peacekeepers could do was try to reassure the woman that help would be on its way. Having to leave people behind who desperately needed their help had a devastating effect on the peacekeepers. But for a particular officer, the situation would get worse. With so many people injured and in need of medical attention, one of the United Nations bases that had not been damaged in the quake instantly became an emergency care clinic. Thus, on this second day, some Canadian peacekeepers were summoned by the United Nations medical staff to provide security at the clinic. The officers' duties at the clinic were awful. They would engage them in making some of the most heart-wrenching decisions of their careers: decide who lives or who dies. For example, in a desperate attempt to get medical care, many surviving civilians had made their way to the clinic. However, it was not long before the constant influx of critically hurt civilians overwhelmed the small medical facility which soon faced a grave dilemma: there was simply not enough space for new patients (Maure, 2020). To make matters worse, the small back-up of medical supplies was quickly running out.

Acting on doctors' instructions not to let more patients in, the peacekeepers had no other choice but to turn newcomers away. These actions were not without any consequences: One Canadian police recalled that he was well aware that some of the people he turned away would not survive another day. Conditioned to serve and protect and to save lives, this police officer never thought that he would have to face such predicament one day. The necessity to turn people away who needed his help deeply troubled him. However, it was with a little consolation that doctors at the emergency room reminded him that his actions had helped save the lives of patients who were already at the clinic and in need of urgent care (Maure, 2020). On the evening of the second day, the Canadian officers were called to attend their embassy in Port-au-Prince to provide security at the compound. This action was needed until the Canadian military arrived in-country to provide additional help and support. It is only then, roughly after being awake for 60 hours and surviving on raw peanut butter, that one of the peacekeepers could finally take a shower: using a 1-liter bottle of water. As military units and Search and Rescue teams from around the world arrived in Haiti, some of the Canadian police peacekeepers returned to their MINUSTAH duties.

One of them recounted that one of the new duties he was assigned was to ensure the safe arrival and deployment of Search and Rescue teams. Roughly 2 weeks after the initial quake, an estimated 80 to 90 international Search and Rescue teams had arrived in Haiti. With many Port-au-Prince neighbors crippled with crime before the earthquake, going to those areas to save people was no easy endeavor. With food and water shortage and a jailbreak of approximately 4000 prisoners who escaped when the national penitentiary walls crumbled, Port-au-Prince almost instantly became forbidden ground (Doyle, 2010). At nights, echoes of gunshots could be heard through the city. This situation made rescue teams' efforts even more challenging (Maure, 2020). For instance, a peacekeeper recalled that a rescue team leader would approach him in the late afternoon to inform that survivors had been located. They would then ask the officer to provide them with a security detail of United Nations Police so that they could go out immediately and start the rescue. However, the officer had to deliver the difficult news that it would be too dangerous to head out as darkness fell over the city. These decisions did not go well with some of the rescue team commanders, who, more often than not, did not seem to understand the potential risk to their teams if relief efforts were undertaken at night. With the safety of the United Nations security details and the rescue teams as a top priority, the Canadian officer would often make the decision to postpone a rescue operation till daybreak. Again, these were tough decisions to make knowing that a trapped survivor may not make it through the night if not rescued immediately.

Even though the officer was fully supported by United Nations management, the hard decisions he had to make deeply affected his morale and sense of values. He was aware that his pronouncement could lead to another civilian not surviving. Weeks after the quake, and as the city very slowly started to recover, some of the Canadian peacekeepers found comfort helping small congregations rebuild and find support from non-governmental organizations that were pouring into the country to assist. Providing people with food, water and shelter was crucial to these communities to help them move ahead. Continuing support, capacitation training and help the Haitian National Police get back on its feet also became a priority for MINUSTAH.

Although strewn with daunting challenges, there is no doubt that the Haitian mission showed the altruistic nature of Canadian peacekeepers in the face of immeasurable adversity. Their actions throughout the ordeal and in the aftermath of the earthquake is a testimony to the commitment they had to contribute to helping the people of Haiti and help them rebuild their destroyed country.

Conclusion

Even though Canada's police participation in peacekeeping operations has dwindled in the last decade, Canada remains very much entrenched to its commitment to build a more secure world (Government of Canada, 2017; Maure, 2020; Pocuch, 2019).

This philosophy has been evidenced by Canada's recent participation in a bilateral engagement with the Ukrainian government to support police reform. Canada has also been deploying officers to the West Bank to mentor senior leaders of the Palestinian police. It is also participating in multidimensional integrated stabilization missions, like the one in Mali, by sending police facilitators (RCMP, 2020b).

With demand for Canadian police officers in other parts of the world, there is a need to revitalize Canada's contribution to peacekeeping by sending more police officers and military personnel to fledgling and neophyte democracies. Such commitment would also be in-line with the Government's 2019 Mandate Letter to expand Canada's support for United Nations peacekeeping operations, including promoting conflict prevention, investment in women, peace, security, and peacebuilding (Dorn, 2020; Office of the Prime Minister, 2019). Canadian participation in peacekeeping operations is an area that will need to be closely monitored in the months and years ahead.

NOTE: The views and opinions expressed in this chapter are those of the author and do not necessarily reflect the official policy or position of the Royal Canadian Mounted Police (RCMP).

References

Afghanistan: A Canadian Story. (2012). *Canadian Afghan Mission 2001–2014*. Retrieved from http://www.afghanistanacanadianstory.ca/whats-new/casualties/

Azzi, S., & Foot, R. (2009). *War in Afghanistan*. The Canadian Encyclopaedia.

BBC News. (2019). *Haiti Profile-Timeline*. Retrieved from https://www.bbc.com/news/world-latin-america-19548814

Boileau, J. (2019). *Canadian peacekeepers in Haiti*. The Canadian Encyclopaedia.

Buis, J. A. (2020, September 19). *Back on the beat/interviewer: J. Daly*. Talk Show, CKNW Radio.

Canada. (2020, September 3). *Elsie initiative for women in peace operations*. Retrieved from https://www.international.gc.ca/world-monde/issues_development-enjeux_developpement/gender_equality-egalite_des_genres/elsie_initiative-initiative_elsie.aspx?lang=eng

CBC Learning. (2001). *Suez Canal crisis: Lester B. Pearson pulls the world back from the brink of war and wins the Nobel Peace Prize*. Retrieved from https://www.cbc.ca/history/EPISCONTENTSE1EP15CH1PA3LE.html

CTV News. (2009). *Ottawa-based Mountie injured in Kabul attack*. Retrieved from https://ottawa.ctvnews.ca/ottawa-based-mountie-injured-in-kabul-attack-1.425984

Dorn, W. (2020). *Tracking the promises: Canada's contributions to UN peacekeeping*. Retrieved from https://www.walterdorn.net/256

Doyle, M. (2010, March 17). *Haiti jail reveals chaos behind quake breakout*. Retrieved from http://news.bbc.co.uk/2/hi/americas/8572049.stm

Gascoine, B. (2001). *History of Namibia*. HistoryWorld. Retrieved from http://www.historyworld.net/wrldhis/plaintexthistories.asp?historyid=ad32
Government of Canada. (2017). *Evaluation of the Canadian Police arrangement and the International Police Peacekeeping and Peace Operations Program*. Retrieved from https://www.international.gc.ca/gac-amc/publications/evaluation/2018/cpaipp_apcpip18.aspx?lang=eng
Government of Canada. (2018). *United Nations Verification Mission in Guatemala (MINUGUA) – VISION*. Retrieved from https://www.canada.ca/en/department-national-defence/services/military-history/history-heritage/past-operations/central-america/vision.html
Granastein, J. (2019). *Canada and peacekeeping*. The Canadian Encyclopaedia.
Green, R. (2019). *Namibia*. Encyclopaedia Britannica Inc.
Ishizuka, K. (2010). *The history of peace-building in East Timor: The issues of international intervention*. Foundation Books.
Leeuwen, J. V. (2019). *Addressing the gap: Accountability mechanisms for peacekeepers accused of sexual exploitation and abuse*. Retrieved from: http://www.nzlii.org/nz/journals/VUWLawRw/2019/6.pdf
Lester B. Pearson. (2020). Encyclopaedia Britannica.
Maloney, S. (2006, March). *Canada's new and dangerous mission in Afghanistan. Policy options*. Retrieved from http://policyoptions.irpp.org/wp-content/uploads/sites/2/assets/po/the-prime-minister/maloney.pdf
Maure, B. (2020). *Leading at the edge—True tales from Canadian police in peacebuilding and peacekeeping missions around the world.*
Office of the Prime Minister. (2019). *Minister of National Defence Mandate Letter*. Retrieved from https://pm.gc.ca/en/mandate-letters/2019/12/13/minister-national-defence-mandate-letter
Pallardy, R. (2020). *2010 Haiti earthquake*. Encyclopaedia Britannica.
Pocuch, S. (2019). *The fall of Canadian peacekeeping: Should it be revived?* Retrieved from http://natoassociation.ca/the-fall-of-canadian-peacekeeping-should-it-be-revived/
Public Safety Canada. (2001). *Peacekeeping 2000–2001 annual review*. Retrieved from https://www.publicsafety.gc.ca/lbrr/archives/rcmp-par-2000-2001-eng.pdf
Rauch, R. (2020). *Alvaro Arzu*. Encyclopaedia Britannica.
RCMP. (2020a). *Peace operations*. Retrieved from https://www.rcmp-grc.gc.ca/en/peace-operations
RCMP. (2020b). *Current operations*. Retrieved from https://www.rcmp-grc.gc.ca/en/current-operations
Saul, B. (2001). Was the conflict in East Timor "genocide" and why does it matters? *Melbourne Journal of International Law, 2*. Retrieved from https://law.unimelb.edu.au/__data/assets/pdf_file/0003/1680222/Saul.pdf
Security Council Report. (2020). *Chronology of events*. Retrieved from https://www.securitycouncilreport.org/chronology/haiti.php
Spielmann, P. J. (2012). *Associated press: Study—UN misconduct goes unpunished*. Retrieved from https://whistleblower.org/in-the-news/associated-press-study-un-misconduct-goes-unpunished/
Suez Crisis. (2020). Encyclopaedia Britannica.
Tunzelmann, A. (2016). *Blood and sand: Suez, Hungary, and Eisenhower's campaign for peace*. Harper Collins.
United Nations (n.d.). *Peacekeeper Fatalities*. Retrieved from United Nations Peacekeeping https://peacekeeping.un.org/en/peacekeeper-fatalities
United Nations. (2001). UNTAG. Retrieved from https://peacekeeping.un.org/sites/default/files/past/untagFT.htm
United Nations. (2003). *United Nations Mission in Haiti*. Retrieved from https://peacekeeping.un.org/mission/past/unmih.htm
United Nations. (2020). *Remember the fallen: Haiti earthquake memorial*. Retrieved from https://www.un.org/en/memorial/haiti/

Veterans Affairs Canada. (2019a). *Canada in Afghanistan – Fallen Canadian Armed Forces Members.* Retrieved from https://www.veterans.gc.ca/eng/remembrance/history/canadian-armed-forces/afghanistan-remembered/fallen?filterYr=2009

Veterans Affairs Canada. (2019b). *The Canadian Armed Forces in Haiti.* Retrieved from https://www.veterans.gc.ca/eng/remembrance/classroom/haiti

Veterans Affairs Canada. (2020a). *They too served: Five places overseas where RCMP members deployed.* Retrieved from https://www.veterans.gc.ca/eng/art-hub/they-too-served

Veterans Affairs Canada. (2020b). *UN Mission in Haiti (UNMIH).* Retrieved from https://www.veterans.gc.ca/eng/remembrance/medals-decorations/details/156

Wapenyi, F. (1990). *Elections in Damaraland.* UNTAG Journal, 3. UNTAG Windhoek, Namibia.

Wheeler, S. (2020). *UN peacekeeping has a sexual abuse problem.* Retrieved from https://www.hrw.org/news/2020/01/11/un-peacekeeping-has-sexual-abuse-problem

Part IV
Europe

Chapter 9
The Role of Police Reform in Conflict Resolution in Ukraine's Donbas Region

Robert Peacock

Introduction

This chapter seeks to highlight the potential for police reform to support conflict resolution even where combatants continue to die on both sides of the conflict within Ukraine. Specifically, the conflict in Ukraine's Donbas (short for Donets Coal Basin) may appear a protracted stalemate from the outside, but casualties are a daily occurrence on the frontline and the OSCE has recorded more than one million ceasefire violations since the peace process began in 2014 (Atland, 2020). The focus of stakeholders for the last several years has been on implementing the 2015 Minsk II peace agreement to gain a permanent solution to the conflict. The likelihood that Ukraine achieves a negotiated peace in the Donbas depends considerably on how well the country has reduced the potential for conflict in the half of the Donbas controlled by the Kyiv government. Specifically, the chapter examines how, in the aftermath of the 2013–2014 Maidan protests, Ukrainian police reform impacts community trust and cooperation with the Ukrainian National Police in the Kyiv-controlled half of the Donbas region.

Conflict Resolution in Ukraine

Since the start of conflict between combined Russian/separatist forces and the Ukrainian government in 2014, ceasefires have been short lived and casualties continue between the Ukrainian military and those of the self-proclaimed "Peoples Republics" of Donetsk and Lugansk (hereinafter, DNR and LNR). The mostly

R. Peacock (✉)
Florida International University, Weston, FL, USA
e-mail: rpeacock@flu.edu

G. den Heyer, J. F. Albrecht (eds.), *Police and International Peacekeeping Missions*, https://doi.org/10.1007/978-3-030-77900-9_9

mortar and sniper fire is largely limited to a 500 km-long ribbon of territory that separates the DNR/LNR-controlled territory from the rest of Ukraine (Zimmerman, 2020).

The disjointed peace process in Ukraine has led to some incremental progress notably around the exchange of prisoners and the withdrawal of heavy artillery from the zone of separation (Palermo, 2020). In the years since the current road map (2015 Minsk II peace agreement), a stalemate has formed without a successful first step in fulfilling the negotiated path to peace. Most notably, Ukraine has yet to regain control of their external border and externally recognized elections have not taken place in the DNR/LNR.

This study acknowledges Brik's (2019) categorization of the Donbas conflict as not just an intra-state struggle but also an "internationalized conflict." Specifically, Russia has not only provided thousands of tanks, BM-21 multiple rocket launchers, and other armaments for the DNR/LNR separatists but also has committed its own forces to the conflict (Kramer & Gordon, 2014; Mitrokhin, 2015; Walker, 2019). Most notably, Russian regular units took part in the 2014 Battle of Ilovaisk that reversed Ukrainian success in splitting Donetsk from the rest of the DNR and the destruction of Ukrainian offensive capacities at Debalsteve in early 2015 (Sanders & Tuck, 2020). This makes for what Malyarenko and Wolff (2019, p. 3) describe as a "blended conflict" in which an internal dispute is simultaneously an international war. Nevertheless, this study focuses narrowly on the internal dispute and how police reform has served to reduce the potential for conflict in the territory of the Donbas region controlled by the Kyiv government.

Internal Conflict

While not likely to have broken in to armed conflict without Russian state intervention (Bowen, 2017), the Donbas region has been a source of regional distrust for most of independent Ukraine's history. A basin in Ukraine roughly the size of the state of Kentucky (40,000 km^2) and rich with natural resources, the sparsely populated Donbas at the turn of the twentieth century drew in waves of transplant labor to stand up the coal and later steel industry that is now synonymous with the word Donbas (Kuromiya, 1998). The USSR's largest coal mining and heavy industry center in the 1920, the coal mine production fell and Donbas already was a rustbelt dependent on government subsidies even prior to the fall of the Soviet Union (Stebelsky, 2018). Soon after the 1991 independence of Ukraine, the industrial region began to vote as a bloc and its parties allied with other regions that viewed themselves as outsiders antagonistic to the centralized government based in Kyiv.

The conflict is often described in the media as a conflict between ethnic Russian and Russian-speaking separatists in Eastern Ukraine seeking to break away from Ukrainian hegemony. The empirical evidence suggests this description may greatly exaggerate the differences in language-use and ethnicity across the country. Aliyev (2019) points out that prior to the conflict that 60% of Russian-speakers in Ukraine identified themselves as ethnically Ukrainian. With the exception of Lviv, the Russian language is the dominant language on the street across the largest cities in Ukraine. Nevertheless, Ukrainian political parties spent decades seeking to politicize the language issue for their own advantage and certainly the topic is sensitive to some Donbas residents that following the breakup of the Soviet Union suddenly needed to fill out state forms or college applications in a Ukrainian language that was not taught in their schools.

The first year of fighting in the Donbas conflict effectively split the region into two nearly equal-sized territories (the half controlled by the DNR/LNR breakaway republics and the Ukrainian-controlled half organized in to the Donetsk and Luhansk oblasts). Recent polling across the Donbas region suggests that even the DNR/LNR remains a heterogenous mix of ethnicities and languages. Sasse and Lackner (2020) reported that approximately two-thirds of the population of DNR/LNR identified themselves as Russian speakers, while half of the residents in government-controlled Donbas reported Russian as their first language.

In terms of ethnicity across the Donbas, a survey by the Centre for East European and International Studies found the ethnic divide also is far from simple (Sasse & Lackner, 2019). Most notably, a slightly larger portion of surveyed DNR/LNR inhabitants self-identified as ethnic Ukrainian (13%) when compared to those who identified as ethnic Russian (12%). The largest portion in the DNR/LNR identified themselves as mixed Russian and Ukrainian (21%) or simply a person from the Donbas (18%). Across the separation line, the population was similarly splintered with 29% identifying as ethnic Ukrainian, 26% gave as their first choice to be identified as a Ukrainian citizen, while nearly 25% chose either to identify as a person from the Donbas or viewing themselves as mixed Russian and Ukrainian (Sasse & Lackner, 2019).

Language-use and ethnicity are complicated and independent phenomenon across the whole of post-Soviet Ukraine, but may be less important to conflict resolution in the East than the longstanding perception by residents of the Donbas region that they are overlooked and not respected in Kyiv (See Giuliano, 2018). The political parties that succeeded in the Donbas were most often those that portrayed themselves as champions of the outsiders seeking more influence in the capital (Stebelsky, 2018). This perception also serves as a lever through which police reform that counters this perception may reduce the potential for conflict. Most notably, those reform steps that raise the perception among Donbas residents that their police force represents the community and can be trusted as unbiased enforcers of the law.

Police Reform Process

Since the ongoing conflict in 2015 first stabilized into the present stalemate, the Government of Ukraine has supported some institutional reforms in terms of local budgets, state procurement, and government service centers in the Kyiv-controlled half of the Donbas. This study is specifically focused on the role that national police reform has helped to lessen conflict in the Ukrainian-controlled half of Donbas. In the aftermath of the 2014 Maidan protests, Ukraine stood up a new National Police (NPU) largely with former militia employees but also stood up entirely new branches of the NPU for the police functions that have the most interaction with the public. Most notably, an entirely new National Patrol Police for the 30 largest cities and Territorial Community Officers in the rural parts of the country.

Pre-reform Militia

The extent of police reform in Ukraine has to be evaluated in terms of the pre-2014 centralized national militia (Peacock & Cordner, 2016). Reviewing Ukrainian policing since the collapse of the Soviet Union, Beck (2005) found that the word *continuity* best described the post-Soviet history of the Ukrainian militia. A patrol officer or investigator from 1980s Soviet Ukraine surveying the 2013 Ukrainian militia would be struck by how little had changed. Most notably, the militia had retained a culture and structure formed over nearly a century of protecting the state as its primary mission (Beck et al., 2002).

The primary route into the militia was to enter as a teenager either through five-year universities or vocational police school. The majority of sworn officers went through a university system and began their careers as lieutenants, typically serving their entire career in a precinct office as investigators or staff (Lyashenko, 2002). Less than 15% entered through vocational police schools to become non-sworn officers in either the traffic police or the relatively small contingent of preventive patrol.

As a practical matter, the public viewed policing by the militia as corrupt, inefficient, and untrustworthy (Sohryu, 2015). During the 2015 polygraph sessions associated with the transition from the militia to the National Police, the criminal police have admitted to a culture in their units of actively participating in crimes that ranged from stealing property from crime scenes to selling the drugs seized in raids. Moreover, civil service rules were ignored as applicants to the militia generally paid bribes from the moment they enrolled to each step in their testing including a negotiated fee to pass the entrance physical (Peacock & Cordner, 2016).

On the streets of pre-conflict Ukraine, roadside traffic police regularly waved batons to pull over vehicles and demand small bribes. Drivers understood the system and usually preferred the bribe rather than enduring a purposely onerous process required to pay or contest a citation over several days of effort. Across Europe, according to citizen surveys, police bribe-taking was highest in Ukraine, and trust in police fairness was characterized as “catastrophically low” (Hough et al., 2014).

Reform Focuses on Police–Public Interaction

In February 2014, 3 months of street demonstrations around Kyiv's main square (Maidan) led to a caretaker government and new Ukrainian presidential and parliamentarian elections. The violent dispersal of protestors over the course of the Maidan protests not only influenced public attitudes opposing the previous regime but also would sway the newly elected government to prioritize police reform. Given the militia's role in the violence on the Maidan, the new government's first law enforcement reform step was to dissolve the militia's special forces (Berkut) units. Civil activists and the media further advocated for sweeping reform of the Soviet model militia (Goncharova, 2014; McLaughlin, 2015).

The new government brought in Georgian reformer Ekaterine Zguladze to serve as the Deputy Minister of Internal Affairs and invited European Union and North American experts to assist in the first phase of police reform. An entirely new patrol police would be stood up to replace the former militia's traffic enforcement and preventive patrol units across Ukraine's largest cities (Goncharova, 2014; BBC, 2015). In less than 18 months, new police-civil society hiring commissions and ad hoc training sites produced nearly 18,000 newly recruited patrol officers to form 31 urban patrol departments. The new patrol police operated in urban centers representing half the country's population, including six Patrol Police Departments functioning in the Donbas (Kramatorsk, Sloviansk, and Mariupol in Donetsk oblast; Sievierodonetsk, Lysychansk, and Rubizhne in Lugansk oblast). Moreover, the country's first emergency response call centers and computer-aided dispatch systems were stood up in each city to allow the patrol police to function as the country's first service-oriented law enforcement agency.

Most outside observers of the new Ukrainian patrol police focus on how the officers appear to differ in their attitudes toward police service than the former militia patrol or GAI officers they replaced (BBC, 2015). This certainly was partly a function of the hiring commissions for the National Patrol Department operated outside of the existing MIA HR and university structures in which personal connections or bribes had long been the primary entry route into the police (Peacock & Cordner, 2016). Applications were taken online or at independent municipal facilities outside MIA control (Peacock & Cordner, 2016). The interview commissions included activists and civil society representatives. Active duty United States and Canadian police conducted train-the-trainer sessions to prepare hundreds of Ukrainian police trainers that provided the new police agency's tactical and scenario-based training. Much of the classroom training for the newly hired patrol police was provided by Ukrainian lawyers, human rights workers, and similar non-police instructors supported by a range of international NGOs, such as OSCE and La Strada Platform for Countering Human Trafficking (Peacock & Cordner, 2016).

The new urban patrol police dramatically increased the public perception that Ukraine now had a preventive patrol. Besides the visible presence of foot and road patrol in the daytime, the patrol vehicles partially flash their lights at night to heighten the public's awareness of the first 24-hour, city-wide patrols. After the introduction of the patrol police, the average response time on emergency calls fell from more than 30 minutes to less than 10 minutes (Focus, 2015). Moreover, the street units of the militia, that represented the bulk of corrupt interactions with the militia for the average Ukrainian, were replaced by a police force that has had far fewer incidences of corruption or misconduct (Lough & Dubrovskiy, 2018).

The introduction of the patrol police led to the tripling of public satisfaction, as well as public calls for service, across the cities that patrol police operated in over the first year of service (Peacock & Cordner, 2016). Over the next few years, political corruption in the Ministry of Internal Affairs and the largely unreformed investigative arm of the police have limited public enthusiasm for the National Police. Most surveys over the last 2 years continue to show that just under half of urban residents trust the National Police.

The recruitment and selection of the new police by local public commissions may explain the higher judgment of the police in the Donbas where residents have limited trust in institutions under national government control. For example, the Center for Insights in Survey Research (IRI, 2019) found that the city with the highest approval rating for the police was Mariupol on the frontline with the DNR, while Sievierodonetsk on the frontline with the LNR was tied for the fourth highest approval rating. In a conflict zone, where outside national security and police units dominate the local law enforcement, the patrol police appear to be viewed by residents as their indigenous police force.

The NPU also appear to recognize the public's differentiation between the patrol police and the majority of their officers. After a recent scandal over the National Police handling of a protest in East Ukraine, the public trust in the patrol police was a factor in the NPU's decision to stand up half dozen new crowd control units composed of patrol police. In interviews with the author, US Department of Justice advisors in Ukraine stated that in dealing with the most sensitive or political protests, the NPU now keeps their full-time crowd control units in reserve and prefers to use the numerically much smaller, United States-trained crowd control units in the patrol police. The patrol police units are trained to initially operate without shields or helmets as they pursue de-escalation tactics before escalating their response based on observed threats.

Impact of Police Reform on Conflict Resolution

The patrol police are normally the branch of government that has the most frequent contact with the public and are most intimately involved with the public's well-being (Travis, 1998; Moore & Poethig, 1999). In developing countries struggling with corruption, the police's role as the government's street-level bureaucrat often leads to them being the most publically visible and distrusted face of the government (Beck et al., 2002). This is the primary reason, reformers in Ukraine prioritized standing up an entirely new patrol police to quickly reshape the views of the public on police performance (Peacock & Cordner, 2016). The disproportionate support for the new police developed in the Donbas suggests that another key element in gaining trust is for a national police agency to integrate outside local representatives on the commissions to choose the future police for that community.

The ad hoc selection panels integrating outside members may also have served to break up the corrupt human resource and academy networks that undermined merit-based hiring in Ukraine for decades. Throughout the post-Soviet sphere, corruption in law enforcement institutions has led to wide spread distrust and underuse of the police (Beck & Robertson, 2009a, b). The patrol police may still represent a small fraction of the NPU (still less than 25% of the NPU's total of officers), but by replacing the traffic police and untrained patrol officers that symbolized police corruption, the new patrol police has reduced the public's experience with officer requests for bribes (BBC, 2015).

Territorial Community Police Officers

The most recent law enforcement innovation with the potential to impact the resolution of conflict in the Donbas is the development of local Territorial Community Police Officers (TCPO) in the rural portions of the Donbas. These units represent the rural counterpart of the patrol police in Ukraine's cities, but also are a product of the ongoing decentralization of municipal governance in the country. The 50% of the population that lives in suburban or rural communities in Ukraine have received greater budgetary and regulatory functions and many of them have jointly invested in having district police officers located in municipally funded facilities. United States and Canadian police instructors have developed an independent training program for existing officers selected to become a TCPO in a rural community. The officers are often referred to in the press as Ukraine's sheriffs because they work in rural villages and sometimes operate from a home provided for their family as well (2 + 2 Nightly News, 2019).

The TCPO program began late in 2018 in the neighboring oblasts of Dnipro and Kharkiv, but in 2020 the first TCPOs selected began a United States-led training program prior to being assigned to their host Donbas village councils. The NPU have agreed that each TCPO has the incentives and autonomy to implement community policing solutions to their district's concerns. The officers also will take the lead in facilitating NPU investigation of the rare cases of serious crime in the villages where they work, but their primary focus is on ensuring that victims and others in the community understand the process. As with the urban patrol police, the new rural community policing officers are likely to raise community acceptance of the NPU based on this further transition toward Donbas officers viewed as part of the communities in which they serve.

Conclusion

Police reform can serve as a critical prerequisite for Ukraine's success in gaining the regional trust necessary for a negotiated settlement to work in the Donbas region of Ukraine. A critical step required of Kyiv government officials in the Minsk II Peace Agreement is to trust the residents of the Donbas to choose their local governments through elections and to further decentralize power in Ukraine. How Ukraine succeeds in gaining the trust and cooperation of those living in government-controlled Donbas and further decentralizing budget and policy decisions to the local leadership will demonstrate their means to do the same across the whole of the Donbas region.

Kyiv is confident that a free and fair election in the DNR and LNR would allow for reintegrating the whole of the Donbas region in Ukraine (Brik, 2019). Sasse and Lackner (2020) found in 2016 and 2019 surveys that 55% of those living in the DNR/LNR expressed a preference for belonging to the Ukrainian state. A key influence on DNR and LNR residents is how Kyiv has followed through on decentralization in urban and rural Donbas. The NPU is not likely to break up into regional police entities anytime soon, but integrating local concerns in the selection and deployment of urban and rural police can change local perspectives over whether the police are representative of their communities. Moreover, as the larger decentralization movement leads to more villages and settlements in rural Donbas merging in to enlarged rural units with larger financial and administration roles in their own governance (Palermo, 2020), the patrol police and TCPOs must continue to be integrated into the local regulation of crime and disorder in the Donbas.

Once foreign assistance and guidance became focused on a defined strategy, the new patrol police were recruited, trained, and deployed at a torrid pace. In 2016, a still largely ad hoc police training structure was standing up a new police force the size of the department in Richmond, Virginia (a relatively large American city), every week. The lack of experience meant mistakes were made, but they won the most important battle in winning the hearts and minds in the cities they worked. Ukraine must also look at urban patrol police and the rural community policing officers as critical interlocutors with the public in the Donbas region of Ukraine. Moreover, police reform must continue to the next and most difficult step left in the NPU, reforming the cadre of criminal investigators across the country. In the Donbas, as well as throughout Ukraine, satisfaction with the police is unlikely to increase while the largest portion of officers and criminal investigators remain largely unreformed from the 2013 Militia, which was not highly trusted by the public. Ukraine's search for a negotiated peace in the Donbas will depend in part on how well key reforms, such as the continued reform of the police, are conducted in the government-controlled territories in Donbas and throughout the remainder of Ukraine.

References

2 + 2 Nightly News. (2019, September 5). *У дніпровському селі громадян почали охороняти шерифи* [In Dnipro oblast villages sheriffs will begin to protect citizens]. Retrieved at: https://www.youtube.com/watch?v=yB-p27isc8k&feature=youtu.be

Aliyev, H. (2019). The logic of ethnic responsibility and progovernment mobilization in East Ukraine conflict. *Comparative Political Studies, 52*(8), 200–231.

Atland, K. (2020). Destined for deadlock? Russia, Ukraine, and the unfulfilled Minsk agreements. *Post-Soviet Affairs, 36*(2), 122–139.

BBC Ukraine. (2015, February 25). Eka Zguladze on the police: Fewer bosses, more officers (Russian language). *BBC Ukraine.*

Beck, A. (2005). Reflections on policing in post-Soviet Ukraine: A case-study of continuity. *The Journal of Power Institutions in Post-Soviet Societies, 2*. Retrieved at: http://pipss.revues.org/294

Beck, A., & Robertson, A. (2009a). The challenges to developing democratic policing in post-Soviet societies: The Russian experience. *Police Practice and Research, 10*(4), 285–293.

Beck, A., & Robertson, A. (2009b). Policing in the "new" Russia. In M. Hinton & T. Newburn (Eds.), *Policing developing democracies*. Routledge Publishing.

Beck, A., Barko, V., & Tatarenko, A. (2002). Developing police management training in post-Soviet societies: Understanding the context and setting the agenda. *Police Quarterly, 5*(4), 447–469.

Bowen, A. S. (2017). Coercive diplomacy and the Donbas: Explaining Russian strategy in Eastern Ukraine. *Journal of Strategic Studies, 42*(3–4), 312–343.

Brik, T. (2019). Ukraine's Type 4 conflict: Why is it important to study terminology before changing it. *Ponars Eurasia Policy Memo, No. 575*. George Washington University.

Focus. (2015, September 18). Nachalo Reformi pravooxranitelnoy systemi [The start of reform in the law enforcement system]. *Focus Weekly Magazine.*

Giuliano, E. (2018). Who supported separatism in Donbas? Ethnicity and popular opinion at the start of the Ukraine crisis. *Post-Soviet Affairs, 34*(2–3), 158–178.

Goncharova, O. (2014, December 25). Zguladze says she is working to transform Ukraine's militia into model police force. *Kyiv Post*. Retrieved at: http://www.kyivpost.com/content/kyiv-post-plus/zguladge-says-she-is-working-to-transform-ukraines-militia-into-modern-police-force-376114.html

Hough, M., Jackson, J., & Bradford, B. (2014). Trust in justice and the legitimacy of legal authorities: Topline findings from a European comparative study. In S. Body-Gendrot, M. Hough, K. Kerezsi, R. Levy, & S. Snacken (Eds.), *The Routledge handbook of European criminology* (pp. 243–264). Routledge.

IRI. (2019). *Annual survey of center for insights in survey research*. Retrieved at: https://www.iri.org/sites/default/files/fifth_municipal_survey_ukraine_septoct2019_final_12-5-2019.pdf

Kramer, A. E., & Gordon, M. R. (2014, June 13). Russia sent tanks to separatists in Ukraine. *New York Times*. Retrieved at: https://www.nytimes.com/2014/06/14/world/europe/ukraine-claims-full-control-of-port-city-of-mariupol.html

Kuromiya, H. (1998). *Freedom and terror in the Donbas: A Ukrainian-Russian borderland.* Cambridge University.

Lough, J., & Dubrovskiy, V. (2018). *Are Ukraine's anti-corruption reforms working*. Chatham House. Retrieved at: https://www.chathamhouse.org/publication/are-ukraines-anti-corruption-reforms-working/2018-11-19-ukraine-anti-corruption-reforms-lough-dubrovskiy.pdf

Lyashenko, N. (2002). Career growth in the bodies of internal affairs. *Vistnyk of the National University of Internal Affairs*, 446–452.

Malyarenko, T., & Wolff, S. (2019). *The dynamics of emerging de facto states: Eastern Ukraine in the post-Soviet space*. Routledge.

McLaughlin, D. (2015, May 22). New Kiev patrol: The beginning of police reform. *Irish Times*. Retrieved at: http://www.irishtimes.com/news/world/europe/new-kiev-patrol-force-the-beginning-of-police-reform-1.2221493

Mitrokhin, N. (2015). Infiltration, instruction, invasion: Russia's war in the Donbas. *Journal of Soviet and Post-Soviet Politics and Society, 1*(1).

Moore, M., & Poethig, M. (1999). The police as an agency of municipal government: Implications for measuring police effectiveness. In *Measuring What Matters: Proceedings from the Policing Research Institute Meetings*. Washington, DC: NIJ COPS Office. Retrieved from: http://gse.buffalo.edu/fas/yerrick/ubscience/UB_Science_Education_Goes_to_School/21C_Literature_files/Klockars,%201999.pdf#page=149

Palermo, F. (2020). The elephant in the room: Ukraine between decentralization and conflict. *Ethnopolitics, 19*(4), 369–382.

Peacock, R., & Cordner, G. (2016). "Shock therapy" in Ukraine: A radical approach to post-Soviet police reform. *Public Administration and Development, 36*(2), 80–92.

Sanders, D., & Tuck, C. (2020). The Ukraine conflict and the problems of war termination. *Journal of Slavic Military Studies, 33*(1), 22–43.

Sasse, G., & Lackner, A. (2019). *Attitudes and identities across the Donbas front line.* ZOIS August report. Retrieved at: https://www.zois-berlin.de/fileadmin/media/Dateien/ZOiS_Reports/ZOiS_Report_3_2019.pdf

Sasse, G. & Lackner, A. (2020). The displaced as 'ordinary citizens': Exploring variation in the political attitudes of the displaced from Donbas. *Europe-Asia Studies, 72*(3), 354–382.

Sohryu, L. (2015, June 24). *Spell our name with a 'mi': Ukrainian law enforcement and the new patrol police*. EuroMaidan Press. Retrieved at http://euromaidanpress.com/2015/06/24/spell-our-name-with-a-mi-ukrainian-law-enforcement/

Stebelsky, I. (2018). A tale of two regions: Geopolitics, identities, narratives, and conflict in Kharkiv and the Donbas. *Eurasian Geography and Economics, 59*(1), 28–50.

Travis, J. (1998). Policing in transition. *Security Journal, 11*(2–3), 151–154.

Walker, S. (2019, August 18). New evidence emerges of Russian role in Ukraine conflict. *The Guardian*. Retrieved at: https://www.theguardian.com/world/2019/aug/18/new-video-evidence-of-russian-tanks-in-ukraine-european-court-human-rights

Zimmerman, V. (2020, February 25). The role of snipers in the Donbas trench war. *Eurasia Daily Monitor, 17*(26).

Chapter 10
Enhancing Law Enforcement and Criminal Justice within Kosovo: Evaluating the Challenges in Rule of Law Reform in a Post-conflict Developing Democracy

James F. Albrecht

History of Kosovo

Kosovo is a region that is located in the southernmost area of the Republic of Serbia that had previously been under the political control of the former Federal Republic of Yugoslavia. It encompasses around 4200 square miles (or 11,000 square kilometers) with a population of approximately 2 million, which presently consists of a majority (90+ %) ethnic Albanian population who had moved into the region during the 500-year Ottoman occupation. Kosovo originally was designated an autonomous province in 1945, but did not gain actual political autonomy until 1946 (Mertus, 1999). After the fall of Yugoslavia, autonomy came to an end under the direction of Serbian President Slobodan Milosevic in 1989. Milosevic ordered that all government positions could only be filled by ethnic Serbians. The ethnic Albanian population formed a parallel society and declared their independence in 1990. This was not recognized by Serbia, nor by other countries, and Milosevic flooded Kosovo with Serbian paramilitary and law enforcement officials. The Albanian population countered by forming the Kosovo Liberation Army (KLA) and engaging in guerilla conflict with Serbian authorities. Originally the KLA was designated a terrorist organization by the international community, but the widespread ethnic cleansing perpetrated under Milosevic's guidance later resulted in repeated efforts by the international community to end the armed conflict. Milosevic and Serbian officials repeatedly participated in peace negotiations, but refused to sign any treaties. As such, the North Atlantic Treaty Organization (NATO) in March 1999 engaged in an 11-week bombing campaign that crippled Serbia's infrastructure and military operations in Kosovo (Hagan, 1999; Solana, 1999).

J. F. Albrecht (✉)
Department of Criminal Justice and Homeland Security, Pace University, New York, NY, USA

G. den Heyer, J. F. Albrecht (eds.), *Police and International Peacekeeping Missions*, https://doi.org/10.1007/978-3-030-77900-9_10

In June 1999, NATO and Serbia signed a technical agreement that led to the withdrawal of Serbian troops from Kosovo. The United Nations Security Council in 1999 also ratified resolution 1244 that designated the region of Kosovo as a United Nations administered territory. As such, the United Nations took over political control of this area. More than 700,000 ethnic Albanians, who had mainly fled to neighboring Albania and Macedonia during the NATO conflict, quickly returned, but many found their homes, businesses, and neighborhood mosques had been destroyed by Serbian forces or their ethnic Serbian neighbors (Sklias & Roukanas, 2007). With a power and security vacuum in existence, the leadership of the KLA took control and advantage, reportedly engaging in organized crime to gain financial resources, and also often taking revenge by killing ethnic Serbs and destroying their homes, and by killing other Albanians that either were accused of collaboration with Serbian authorities or were not considered to be in line with KLA endeavors.

The United Nations-Administered Kosovo

Once Serbia capitulated at the conclusion of the NATO bombing raids, the United Nations Security Council adopted Resolution 1244 on June 10, 1999, which established the United Nations Interim Administration in Kosovo (UNMIK). The first UN officials arrived three days later to observe a devastated and destroyed region with a limited population. However, by July 1999, it is estimated that more than 650,000 refugees, predominantly ethnic Albanians, had returned. Initial criminality commonly involved the looting and destruction of Serbian residences and intimidation against the Serbian population. The previous law enforcement and judicial system had collapsed and the majority population took advantage of the crime control vacuum. Criminal gangs, mainly headed by former Kosovo Liberation Army leaders, engaged in rampant organized crime that included smuggling and drug and human trafficking among other illicit activities (Strohmeyer, 2001). The suppression of violence, interethnic criminality, and organized crime became the responsibility of the Kosovo Force (KFOR), which was an international military mission, staffed by United Nations member nations. However, their responsibilities ended after apprehension and detention. The overwhelming challenge involved the creation of a justice system, specifically the hiring and training of prosecutors and judges to move the cases along. However, the task proved to be difficult as the quest to develop a pool of prosecutors and judges from the different ethnic groups often led to intimidation and violence. Quite quickly a prosecutorial and judicial backlog developed that still exists to this day.

One of the daunting tasks was the development of a legal framework. The majority ethnic Albanian population refused to accept legislation that had been imposed by the oppressive Serbian regime, so former Yugoslavian law was instituted. On December 12, 1999, UNMIK promulgated a regulation that provided that the legal framework in place prior to March 22, 1989 would serve as the provisional legislation within Kosovo. However, this proved to cause difficulties as some of the provisions were in violation of accepted human rights practices (Strohmeyer, 2001). In May 2001, UNMIK implemented the Constitutional Framework for Provisional Self Government in Kosovo, which resulted in the subsequent elections in November 2001 and later the development of provisional legislation for criminal justice administration (Yannis, 2004). Thereafter, local political, government, and criminal justice actors have remained under the supervision and guidance of United Nations personnel.

As for law enforcement, the primary responsibility fell upon the international community under the supervision and coordination of the United Nations (i.e. CIVPOL program[1]). The 1800 international police officers in 1999 rapidly increased to 4450 in 2000. All were professional law enforcement practitioners from United Nations member countries. Their two primary tasks were to immediately establish law and order and to develop law enforcement capabilities at the local level. While CIVPOL rapidly deployed throughout Kosovo, the responsibility of developing, training, and deploying a new Kosovo Police Service (KPS) was predominantly accomplished through the United States Department of Justice ICITAP (International Criminal Investigative Training Assistance Program)[2] program and through the support of the Organization for Security and Cooperation in Europe (OSCE).[3] The Kosovo Police Service commenced recruitment in June 1999 and the KPS School in Vushtri became fully operational in March 2000. In 2000, there were 2516 KPS officers working across Kosovo, and this increased to 5704 in 2004 (Wilson, 2006) and finally to the present level that exceeds 7000.

In addition to the establishment of rule of law and the development of the criminal justice agencies (i.e. police, prosecutors, judges and correctional system), the United Nations has also been responsible for the administration and coordination of humanitarian assistance; civil administration; democratization and institution building; and reconstruction and economic development (Wilson, 2006). What this resulted in was the distribution of funds from many donor nations and organizations, which eventually supported the corruption-prone atmosphere endemic in Kosovo.

[1] CIVPOL is the designation granted to civilian law enforcement, in contrast to the military police, that are deployed to post-conflict regions by the United Nations. The complement is composed of police personnel from contributing United Nations member states.

[2] The United States Department of Justice International Criminal Investigative Training Assistance Program is utilized by the United States government to provide criminal justice, law enforcement, and organized crime investigation assistance to foreign governments.

[3] The Organization for Security and Cooperation in Europe is an international assistance organization in which the United States, European Union member states, Russia, and other nations provide assistance to developing nations across Europe and other eastern countries.

The Ahtisaari Proposal

The Secretary General of the United Nations, Ban Ki-moon, in 2007 requested special envoy Martti Ahtisaari to prepare the report *Comprehensive Proposal for the Kosovo Status Settlement*, often called the Ahtisaari Proposal or the Ahtisaari Plan, which outlined the requirements for the region of Kosovo to declare her independence under international supervision and eventually to gain its total independence once the provisions outlined within the document have been achieved. Included within these requirements are: elimination of interethnic tension; decentralization of government; a professional and impartial justice system; protection of religious and cultural heritage; protection of property and investigation of missing persons; sustainable economic development; a professional, multiethnic, and democratic security sector comprised of the Kosovo Police and the Kosovo Security Force; and the continuation of an international supervisory mechanism that will include NATO, the European Union, and the OSCE. A new constitution, legislation, and general and local elections were to follow within a nine-month time period (Ki-moon, 2007).

European Union Involvement

As part of the Ahtisaari Plan, there was to be a 120-day transition period allowing transfer from United Nations administration to supervision under the European Security and Defense Policy (ESDP) Program. In April 2006, the European Union in conjunction with the United States of America[4] and Norway deployed the European Union Planning Team (EUPT) in Pristina, Kosovo to prepare for this development. The ESDP initiative was called the European Union Rule of Law Mission in Kosovo (or EULEX – Kosovo). EULEX would be primarily deployed to support the Kosovo institutions responsible for law enforcement, customs, and justice and act in a monitoring, mentoring, and advisory (MMA). The EULEX mission would also retain limited executive authority[5] and would be responsible for conducting criminal investigations involving war crimes, corruption, organized crime, and financial crimes. The total complement of EULEX was planned for approximately 1950 international staff with more than 75% of this cadre dealing with policing and customs control.

[4] The author was the sole American representative on the European Union Planning Team from 2007 through 2008.

[5] The author was the EULEX police chief with executive authority to conduct criminal investigations involving war crimes, corruption, terrorism, organized crime, and other politically sensitive cases from 2008 through 2010.

The "Russian Roadblock"

The 120-day transition from United Nations administration to supervised independence under the guidance of the European Union was to commence on February 17, 2008, with the United Nations-supported declaration of independence and formation of the new Republic of Kosovo. The plan called for the end of United Nations administration on April 9, 2008. Only days prior to the declaration of independence and the implementation of that stage of the Ahtisaari Plan, Russia, as a permanent member of the United Nations Security Council, in mid-February 2008 obstructed the initiation of the process. This created chaos and an atmosphere of indecision. In February 2008, the Republic of Kosovo declared her independence, but there was no coinciding transition from UN to European Union control. In reality, the last hour ploy by the Russian government, consistently a Serbian ally, created overwhelming confusion and the abrupt end to international rule of law participation across Kosovo. Many United Nations member states had commenced the withdrawal of personnel and those involved in criminal justice functions that had remained undertook a "wait and see" position, leaving arrests and case prosecutions in limbo. Since the European Union and the EULEX mission had not been granted executive authority, the staff maintained their planning mode. In the interim, this uncertainty ultimately hampered many United Nations member states from recognizing Kosovo as an independent country.[6]

The European Union Rule of Law Mission in Kosovo

Even given the ambiguity, the European Union and other cooperating nations commenced the large-scale deployment of justice, customs, and law enforcement personnel to Kosovo in the spring of 2008. Eventually in November 2008, the United Nations Security Council, with overwhelming pressure from the United States, Germany, the United Kingdom, France, and other key nations, approved a resolution that called for the one-day transition of authority from the United Nations to the European Union. The date designated for the application of executive authority to the EULEX mission was December 9, 2008.

Two things compounded the initial ineffectiveness. Although the EULEX mission had sufficient rule of law personnel to undertake their designated responsibilities, the mission headquarters had not arranged for logistical support and office accommodation for these resources.[7] As such, EULEX police personnel and staff

[6] To date, not all United Nations member states recognize an independent Kosovo, which does not allow for general United Nations participation and representation.

[7] Since the commencement date of the EULEX mission was uncertain and since the United Nations suspended the transition stage until direction was provided by the United Nations Security Council, the transfer of work accommodations, vehicles, and equipment did not occur in a planned and timely fashion, and the European Union Planning Team had not requisitioned any supplies.

did not have adequately assigned office space, lacked sufficient transportation means to get to and from work and to carry out their assigned responsibilities, and had only limited office and professional equipment. The December commencement had another interesting effect. As soon as the Christmas and New Year holiday season commenced, which was around December 15, 2008, the vast majority of European Union personnel went on vacation, with most not returning until mid-January 2009 after the date of Orthodox Christmas. In plainer English, even with the confusion of mission commencement, the European Union opted to unofficially suspend overall operation for more than one month so that European Union managers and personnel could go home for the holiday season.

Sensing the disarray, Serbian radicals in the northern ethnic Serbian enclave of North Mitrovica engaged in routine attacks on ethnic Albanian residents and businesses. Gunfire, arson, and serious assaults were common throughout December 2008[8] and were only deterred by the eventual presence of NATO forces. In addition, due to the confusion caused by the recent United Nations Security Council resolution, which reported that concessions had been made to Serbia in order to commence the EULEX mission, ethnic Albanian radicals reportedly planned an attack likely using explosives at one of the EULEX facilities. The response by EULEX was to close all of their sites. The preemptive action appeared to have prevented the attack, but left key personnel without the ability to continue mission planning and deployment for a brief period. As a result, the first two months of the EULEX mission did not result in notable progress or achievement.

On April 6, 2009, the Head of the EULEX mission announced full operational capability. Of course, without functional work accommodations, sufficient vehicles to get to work, and lacking key investigative equipment, the mission was functional only in theory, but not in practice.

The European Union Institute for Security Studies Evaluation of EULEX

One year after the EULEX mission commenced, the European Union Institute for Security Studies (EU-ISS) conducted a comprehensive evaluation (EU-ISS, 2009) of this endeavor. The EU-ISS noted that the EULEX mission is the largest of all ESDP deployments and is the only mission with integrated justice, police, and customs mechanisms that are further divided into advisory and executive responsibilities. Although late in implementation, the mission had been recognized for its programmatic approach in which performance indicators with attainable time tables were delineated for the mission and for local criminal justice actors.

On the other hand, the mission has also been noted for its overwhelming lack of efficiency and effectiveness. Over the course of the first few years, i.e. from 2008

[8] The author and a number of other American EULEX mission personnel responded to the site of all of the attacks since most international police officers from EU states were on leave.

through 2011, rule of law reform and institution building can best be described as negligible to minor. Mission personnel did not deploy across all of Kosovo, most specifically into and throughout the ethnic Serbian enclave of North Mitrovica.[9] EULEX justice personnel stood idle as ethnic Serbian enclaves continued to acknowledge and honor only UNMIK and Yugoslavian laws, even after the Kosovo government implemented its own national legislation for the entire country. In addition, EULEX made no effort to recognize Kosovo border and customs laws at the northern borders with Serbia and did not sufficiently support the local Kosovo Police Border Department and the Kosovo Customs Authority in undertaking their new responsibilities. An unexpected decision was made at EULEX headquarters to permit the Kosovo Police working in ethnic Serbian enclaves to report directly to the Head of the EULEX Police, rather through the Kosovo Police chain of command. As previously reported above, EULEX failed to provide functional work sites and equipment to mission personnel. And EULEX rule of law staffing levels regularly fluctuated between 50% and around 80%. Most importantly, the failure of all 27 European Union member states[10] to recognize an independent Kosovo has caused the EULEX mission to operate with the dictum that they are "status neutral," but at the same time supporting "local ownership." Politically this situation has caused confusion and misunderstanding among both EULEX mission personnel and their local counterparts and has proven to be counterproductive in gaining cooperation with regional governments, authorities, and organizations[11] (EU-ISS, 2009). The transfer of both police and prosecution cases from UNMIK to EULEX was slow and has led to most cases being dismissed due to legal temporal constraints.[12] New cases at the local level that were to be monitored by EULEX prosecutor and police advisors have not received the mandated attention within the courts, which had led to a backlog in excess of 100,000 criminal cases that failed to receive investigative or prosecutorial action as most cases were dismissed due to legislated deadlines requiring mandatory prosecutorial and judicial action. Of interesting note is that similar failures and shortcomings were reported within the European Union Police Mission in Bosnia and Herzegovina (Howorth, 2007), and as a result, the European Union had been reportedly forced to conclude its law enforcement advisory capacity endeavors there.

---

[9] The EULEX mission had deployed a significant complement of rule of law personnel, mainly international police officers, with the intent to mobilize them throughout North Mitrovica, but these resources were reassigned to other responsibilities. It is highly likely that EULEX could have easily flooded the North Mitrovica region to ensure security and constrict smuggling and organized crime activity.

[10] Spain, Greece, Slovakia, Romania, and Cyprus have yet to recognize the independence and statehood of Kosovo.

[11] Interpol, Europol, and SECI (Southeast European Cooperative Initiative) would not cooperate in criminal investigation and intelligence sharing with similarly tasked EULEX personnel, even though most police personnel were from the United States or European Union member states.

[12] In order to continue investigating and prosecuting criminal cases, judicial approval must be obtained within legally designated time frames (e.g. six months). Failure to "renew" the investigation or prosecution before a judge has led to the dismissal of almost all inherited cases.

Rand Corporation Analysis of European Union Post-Conflict Involvement

The US Office for the Secretary of Defense in 2009 requested Rand Corporation to conduct a thorough assessment of the European Union's capabilities to participate in post-conflict environments. As a result, the EULEX mission in Kosovo was examined to determine to which extent the United States should support or directly participate in future ESDP endeavors. The Rand study concluded that the non-military institution building capacity of the European Union was limited and faced with a number of challenges. The most notable shortcomings were: the failure of the European Union to properly staff mission positions, the inability to maintain designated staffing levels, and the need to improve training capabilities for the Kosovo Police (Chivvis, 2010). This analysis reported that the EULEX mission in Kosovo could be considered a success when compared to the inadequacy and ineffectiveness of the European Union police training mission in Afghanistan. Ultimately, Rand supported future European Union involvement in civilian capacity building in post-conflict regions and proposed that the United States government consider providing logistical support and personnel resources to those initiatives (Chivvis, 2010). However, the budgetary restraints placed on the United States government over recent years have caused the United States to dramatically reconsider, reduce, or withdraw prior commitments, specifically those for the EULEX mission in Kosovo.[13]

Criminality and Safety within Kosovo

The development of a relatively professional and effective Kosovo Police agency supported by international advisors and colleagues has resulted in continuing crime reductions since the conflict officially concluded in 1999. While the rates for most crime categories are relatively low when compared to European Union and United States averages, the most accurate measure of violence affecting the estimated population of two million could be assessed through the analysis of murder incidents. The reported murder rate in Kosovo for 2000 was 12 per 100,000 residents; for 2005 was 3 per capita (United Nations Office on Drugs and Crime, 2008); and for 2010 was 2.5 per capita (International Crisis Group, 2010). Murder statistics continue to reveal a downward trend that reflects the reduction in overall crime recorded within Kosovo Police annual reports from 2000 through 2010,[14] and these impressive declines have fortunately continued.

[13] The CIVPOL staffing by the USA has declined from 220 in 2008 to 80 in 2009 to 30 in 2012 to around 10 in 2019.

[14] The author personally reviewed daily, monthly, and annual Kosovo Police statistics and reports while deployed to Kosovo from 2007 through 2010.

Kosovo is not noted for overwhelming danger and violence, and most murders and assaults can be said to be the result of property, family, or personal disputes. On the other hand, the United Nations and other international organizations estimate that there are more than 350,000 unaccounted for small arms present throughout Kosovo (United Nations Development Program, 2010). Given this potential threat, it is quite surprising that firearm-related incidents are limited. However, the greatest safety hazard within Kosovo involves the general lack of traffic safety. In 2007, there were 127 vehicle fatalities and 17,006 vehicle accidents; in 2008, 114 fatalities and 15,939 accidents; in 2009, 176 fatalities and 19,212 accidents; and in 2010, 175 fatalities and 18,030 accidents (Bislimi, 2011). Recent data revealed that the traffic fatality rate in Kosovo is 50% higher than in other European Union nations on average[15] and that the vehicle fatality rate has declined since 2016 (Haziri, 2019).

In general, police traffic enforcement, other than speed control, is negligible. The vast majority of drivers within Kosovo operate defective vehicles,[16] do not wear seat belts,[17] and drive in a reckless and haphazard fashion. Thorough traffic accident statistical evaluations were not conducted by the Kosovo Police with the goal of increasing traffic safety, and traffic intersection engineering assessments were clearly not supervised by international experts. Quite amazingly, the command staff of the Kosovo Police was repeatedly unresponsive to proposals by international law enforcement experts to enhance vehicular, pedestrian, and traffic safety.[18]

Organized Crime Activity within Kosovo

While crime in general is relatively low, Kosovo is a notorious smuggling hub between Asia, Africa, South America, North America, and Europe. Two main smuggling routes are used for smuggling drugs, humans, contraband, and other goods from Asia to the European Union. Goods from the east enter Turkey and exit either into Bulgaria continuing through Romania into Hungary; or exit Turkey into Greece, traveling through Macedonia and ending up in Kosovo. Afghanistan heroin is smuggled in this fashion. Although farmers in Kosovo have been known to grow marijuana,[19] both cocaine and marijuana normally arrive in Kosovo after arriving at

[15] The per capita rate (per million) for vehicle fatalities in Kosovo is approximately 100, while the European Union average rate is 63.

[16] Most vehicles are purchased from car dealers in European Union countries after the cars can no longer pass safety and inspection standards.

[17] The author repeatedly surveyed drivers in Kosovo and noted that more than 95% of all drivers failed to wear a seat belt nor utilize child safety seats.

[18] The author lived in Kosovo for three years and discontinued walking outdoors due to the lack of vehicular-related safety and since most areas had no pedestrian sidewalks; even when sidewalks existed they were used for residential and business parking, thereby forcing pedestrians to walk on the street.

[19] Kosovo does not have a large consumer drug population.

Albanian and Montenegrin ports from South America or Africa. Ethnic Albanian crime groups then repackage the material into small parcels for transit to European nations, normally in private vehicles, tour buses, and commercial trucks.

Due to the large number of illegal small arms and explosives still remaining from the conflict, the smuggling of weapons between ethnic Albanian groups in Kosovo to ethnic Albanian communities in southern Serbia and Macedonia has been routine. Most of the illegal weapons are under the control of former KLA fighters (or Serbian radicals in North Mitrovica).

Human smuggling mainly takes three forms. There are a very small number of females smuggled from Ukraine or Moldova into Kosovo for sex trade purposes, but prostitution routinely involves ethnic Albanian females to avoid the attention of the international community or United Nations/European Union law enforcement. Organized crime groups are active in offering stolen, counterfeit, or duplicate[20] travel documents (i.e., passports and visas) to the local population in order for them to gain entry into the European Union. And finally, due to the presence of the United Nations and other human rights organizations and due to lax passport and border control, Kosovo has become a location where persons from China, Afghanistan, Iraq, Somalia, Pakistan, Algeria, and other countries enter, often illegally by crossing mountain borders, request asylum, and then continue their illegal journey to Europe.[21]

Both ethnic Serbian and ethnic Albanian organized crime groups are known to engage in regular fuel smuggling in order to avoid paying related customs fees and taxes. Coffee, tobacco, and other goods routinely enter Kosovo in similar illegal fashion, normally through unguarded mountainous border areas. In addition, Kosovo is recognized for the open sale of pirated and counterfeit products (United States Department of State, 2011). Finally, due to the lack of cooperation and information exchange with other law enforcement agencies, it is common to observe vehicles stolen from the United States and European Union nations being operated on the streets of Kosovo with their original license plates.[22]

Corruption within Kosovo

Corruption within southeast Europe has normally taken three general forms. Government employees routinely demand bribes from the citizens and business persons in order to engage in official misconduct, thereafter either performing or

[20] Duplicate travel documents include actual passports and visas that are resold to similar looking individuals in an effort to allow them to travel to the United States or European Union.

[21] The author noted numerous cases in which these illegal migrants requested asylum, received financial assistance, then in less than 24 hours entered Serbia illegally through unguarded forest border regions to continue on to a European Union nation.

[22] Neither the Kosovo Police nor the EULEX Police have access to European Union or United States vehicle identification databases.

failing to perform the responsibilities of their job. The second type of corruption involves direct political interference into criminal justice processes. The third version of corruption involves the participation of government representatives reportedly overseeing or taking part in organized crime activity. Because these factors are common within Kosovo, Kosovo is often referred to as "Europe's mafia state" (Filiminova, 2010), since it has been alleged that government leaders consistently have engaged in all three activities with little to no reaction from the United Nations, European Union, American, and other international supporters. And many of the local criminal justice actors within Kosovo are under the control and influence of key political leaders or those with relatives involved in politics or public office, so no comprehensive, if any, investigative, or enforcement action from their side usually occurs.

A survey of the residents of Kosovo has revealed that corruption is a highly perceived occurrence among government actors. Findings revealed that corruption was present in all government sectors, including political party leaders (33.7%), municipal government (28.2%), the judiciary (27.7%), prosecutors (25.2%), the Kosovo President (16.4%), Parliament (15.6%), and Kosovo government (14.3%), but was viewed as being limited within the Kosovo Police (9.4%). Almost 39% of Kosovo residents rated corruption as the second most relevant problem facing Kosovo (following unemployment), and 40% of the public believed that all government officials are involved in corrupt practices. Over 16% of all residents report being asked for unofficial cash by a municipal employee to deal with an official issue, as compared to 10% who were coerced to pay a bribe to a federal government official over the last 12 months (Spector et al., 2003). A more recent survey that has measured the perception of corruption across the globe reported that Kosovo presently ranks at 101 out of the 179 countries and received a score of 3.6 out of 10[23] in corruption perception by Kosovo citizens. Transparency International ratings over the course of the last decade reveal that this low score has remained consistent over the last decade (Transparency International, 2020).

The political leadership of Kosovo, at the request of the international community, has developed a number of official mechanisms to address the issue of corruption. The Kosovo Anti-Corruption Agency was introduced in 2007 and the Prime Minister established the Task Force against Corruption in 2010. However, both have proven to be ineffective. Investigation has revealed that both have been routinely staffed by relatives of or members from the most prominent government parties, who clearly have been appointed to provide warnings to corrupt politicians and other government employees and to obstruct investigations. The head of the Task Force against Corruption was arrested himself in April 2012 for engaging in bribery and for covering up corruption involving prominent government leaders (Karadaku, 2012).

What is likely most disturbing is that the most corrupt officials in Kosovo have reportedly included the present and former prime ministers, presidents, and numerous parliamentary and ministerial officials, many of whom continue in office. It has

[23] With 10 being perceived as the most legitimate and 0 as the most corrupt.

been reported by European Union investigators that current Kosovo President Hashim Thaci, the leader of the ruling PDK political party, has been identified as the leader of the Drenica organized crime group (Marty, 2010). Although Thaci cannot account for his questionable financial resources in any credible fashion, the international community has permitted him to remain in power across a number of government positions. In addition, it has been alleged that a former Prime Minister, Ramush Haradinaj, the leader of the AAK party, the ruling party in western Kosovo, is recognized as the leader of the Haradinaj organized crime group functioning throughout the western Province of Peja. Haradinaj has repeatedly been detained at the Hague and has undergone a number of war crimes investigations and trials. Former Minister of Transport and Telecommunications Fatmir Limaj, a top member of the PDK party, stepped down from office due to recurrent allegations that he accepted bribes in return for major government contracts. Former Prime Minister Agim Ceku, a former Minister of Security Forces and member of the PDK party, has been reported to be a key coordinator of narcotics trading that has and continues to occur within Kosovo's borders. In addition, and extremely noteworthy is that the above four former KLA members and "national heroes" are all suspects in serious allegations and incidents involving genocide and war crimes that targeted both ethnic Serbian and Albanian populations during and after the Yugoslavian conflict.[24] War crime cases involving a long list of current and former government officials continue to be investigated to this day.

Corruption will remain endemic among the political elites of Kosovo until the international community ensures that corrupt officials are removed or barred from their positions and guarantees that their illicit actions are properly addressed through the criminal justice system. In addition, beyond their involvement in organized crime activities, it is imperative that they be held accountable in a court of law, be it at the Hague, in Serbia, or in Kosovo, or whether by local, regional, or international prosecutors, for the war crime atrocities that they have been associated with. There is presently sufficient evidence to, at the least advocate, that they many government officials be removed from their present positions and be barred from active involvement in Kosovo government and politics. Unfortunately, these apparent criminals have moved from one critical government position to the next without much of any criticism or input from key international players. As such, Kosovo has sincerely earned the title of "Europe's mafia state."

[24] These are the four most notable corrupt national officials. The list of all other reportedly identified federal or municipal corrupt officials would be overwhelming.

Recommendations for Kosovo to Move Forward

A number of recommendations could be proposed to improve the distressing situation in Kosovo and permit the nation and her citizens to move forward. The most critical step is for the international community, most notably the European Union, which has had supervisory authority over Kosovo, with the support of the United States, a key supporter of Kosovo, to direct the immediate removal of suspects of serious war crime allegations and those with noted affiliations with organized crime groups and bar those individuals from government employment. A "fresh start" would permit Kosovo to integrate more rapidly into the European Union and to earn the cooperation of her regional neighbors. This may sound severe, but until this occurs, Kosovo could continue to be viewed as a state associated with organized crime and an illegitimate regional presence, ruled by war criminals and supported financially by rampant organized crime activity and corruption.

In addition, effort should be made to revise Kosovo legislation so as to permit the criminal justice system to evolve into a functional institution. Political influence into the appointment of police commanders and the assignment of Kosovo Police personnel should be eliminated, and more importantly police criminal investigations must remain free of political interference. Overall justice effectiveness could be instantly and dramatically improved by enacting legislation to switch to a common law system, which would permit independent police investigations and arrests.[25] This would eliminate the present legal requirement for personal direction by prosecutors and judges in order to commence and continue criminal investigations. It is also crucial that the legislated mandate to "renew" a criminal investigation before a judge every 60 days be immediately removed. Since the law presently delineates the statute of limitations for each crime, this suffices to ensure cases are not excessively drawn out. Mandatory court renewal of criminal investigations merely delays the investigatory process and allows corrupt and politically influenced prosecutors and judges the opportunity to bring an end to major cases, particularly those involving government officials or members of their families or clans.

Quite frankly, other than a small number of former ranking police chiefs, the Kosovo Police have not been noted for being overly corrupt and impressively have been recognized as the least corrupt law enforcement agency in southeastern Europe. It is imperative that the upper stratum of the Kosovo Police hierarchy, which includes police directors (i.e. department chiefs) and regional commanders, be re-vetted to ensure that they have no connection with the present political parties, no war crime associations, and no allegations involving affiliations with organized crime or other criminal groups. The process should be conducted under the direct

[25] This is strongly recommended since the Kosovo Police are likely the most professional and least corrupt of the criminal justice actors; however, the bigger concern deals with political interference into serious police investigations. The present civil law system relies heavily on the approval and quick actions of the prosecutors and judiciary, which often does not take place. This allows for many criminal investigations to be closed, possibly as the result of political interference.

supervision of the international community to ensure legitimacy. The European Union and the EULEX mission failed to take this critical step before or after the declaration of independence of Kosovo. The Kosovo Police should also be trained and equipped to engage in crime and traffic safety computer analysis and "hot spot" deployment to further reduce crime rates and the number of traffic accidents and vehicular fatalities.

A workload analysis should be conducted to rectify the overwhelming backlog of criminal cases and eliminate direct political interference or corruption into court cases. Efforts must be made to recruit, properly screen, hire, and train a sufficient number of prosecutors and judges with similar vetting instructions that are outlined above, as recommended for the Kosovo Police to ensure the highest levels of integrity and commitment.

All personnel working in the Kosovo Anti-Corruption Agency and the Task Force against Corruption should be immediately terminated and international actors should implement a revised vetting and training process to hire new staff in order to root out political control, influence, and interference.

In lieu of reducing agency staffing levels, as has continued since 2012, EULEX should have planned on increasing the number of prosecutors within the EULEX Special Prosecutors Office in an effort to deal with the overwhelming criminal caseloads, particularly with an emphasis on cases reportedly involving government officials, and just as importantly, those offenders operating within the Serbian enclave of North Mitrovica who have repeatedly coordinated and been involved in attacks on international officials, NATO troops, and the Kosovo Police. In particular, war crime, terrorism, corruption, and organized crime cases that have exhibited and possessed sufficient evidence for arrest should have been moved forward and promptly and effectively prosecuted. As one option, the Hague or other European Union court venue could be used to maintain impartiality, legitimacy, and professional decorum. In many cases, offenders involved in serious offences had been identified by the UNMIK police and prosecutors, yet EULEX did not promptly move many of the cases forward. Judicial inaction generally creates an atmosphere of empowerment and a sense of impunity among criminal actors and networks. This could have been avoided had effective reform and prosecutorial action taken place in a timely fashion.

The predominant international actors present within Kosovo must take or support these and other necessary measures in order to bring enhanced legitimacy to Kosovo. Unfortunately, many countries appear to be more concerned with their own national interests within and across the region, rather than with the welfare of the people living within Kosovo. Uncomfortable decisions have to be made and all recommendations to improve the current state of affairs and eliminate corruption and organized criminal activity must be made with a "stick and carrot" position, i.e. international funding and aid would only continue if obvious and effective measures are being taken to better legitimize government operations and improve the effectiveness and integrity of the criminal justice system. There is hope for Kosovo, but not when the international community, most notably the European Union and the

United States, appears to exhibit indifference to clear and unacceptable misbehavior, corruption, ineffectual government, and political mismanagement.

Summary and Conclusion

The Kosovo Liberation Army was a guerilla organization that took up arms against Milosevic's Serbia in order to obtain self-governance for the former Yugoslavian province of Kosovo. At stake were the freedom and liberty of the predominantly ethnic Albanian population that had lost the possibility of employment and education following the directive of Milosevic to "Serbianize" the entire Kosovo region. Small scale guerilla warfare turned into a full-scale conflict, with most of the regional population fleeing into neighboring countries. Genocide and atrocious war crimes committed by both sides of the conflict led to the involvement of NATO forces, eventually bringing an end to the military struggle in 1999. As part of the peace agreement, the United Nations took over administration of the Kosovo region. By the start of the new millennium, a locally elected government and generally functional criminal justice mechanism had been put in place under the supervision of the United Nations. The Ahtisaari Plan called for the transfer of international supervision and management from the United Nations to the European Union. This was to take place in 2008 and coincide with the declaration of independence of Kosovo. Unfortunately, due to the objections of Serbia and the interference of Russia, the time table and objectives outlined within the Ahtisaari Plan were sent into disarray. Eventually the European Union did take over supervision of Kosovo, but the deployment of European Union and partner nation staff did not occur smoothly.

After the unilateral declaration of independence in 2008, Kosovo had the unique opportunity to enact new legislation and elect and appoint new government officials that would move the country forward into a functional democracy with effective and legitimate rule of law practices. Unfortunately, even with the presence and guidance of the international community, nothing has since dramatically changed. The government hierarchy continues to be loaded with former KLA commanders who are suspected of involvement not only in serious and horrific war crimes but also for their reported connection to organized crime groups involved in illicit drug, human, weapons trafficking, and acts of political corruption. Global leaders, most notably those from the United States and European Union, have missed a significant opportunity to properly guide the people of Kosovo in a more positive direction. It would appear that many have looked in the opposite direction, failing to admit that "the king has no clothes," likely in an effort to further national agendas and personal aspirations. There is hope for the people of Kosovo, but until key global actors initiate steps to "clean house," support the replacement of corrupt officials, and assist in developing a legitimate and effective rule of law mechanism, Kosovo will sadly continue to be viewed as Europe's dysfunctional "mafia state." These limitations and the lack of effectual democratic reform, as the European Union shifts support and resources away from Kosovo, have likely curtailed the potential recognition of Kosovo as an independent nation by many United Nations member states. It had originally been foreseen that Kosovo could be acknowledged as a model of democracy for other eastern European countries, but this unfortunately has not been the case. The potential for constructive reform for Kosovo in the future remains high, but pragmatic and visionary leadership at the national and local levels will be needed.

References

Bislimi, M. (2011). *An assessment of road traffic safety in Kosova*. American University of Kosovo.

Chivvis, C. S. (2010). *EU civilian crisis management: The record so far*. Rand Corporation.

European Union Institute for Security Studies. (2009). *European security and defence policy: The first 10 years (1999–2009)*. EU-ISS.

Filiminova, A. (2010). *Kosovo: Europe's mafia state and the rule of law*. Centre for Research on Globalization.

Hagan, W. H. (1999). The Balkans' lethal nationalisms. *Foreign Affairs, 78*, 52–64.

Haziri, F. (2019). *Traffic accidents in the republic of Kosovo for the period 2014–2018*. University for Business and Technology.

Howorth, J. (2007). *Security and defence policy in the European Union*. Palgrave Macmillan Publishers.

International Crisis Group. (2010). *The rule of law in independent Kosovo: Executive summary and recommendations*. International Crisis Group.

Ki-moon, B. (2007). *Letter dated 26 March 2007 from the United States Secretary General to the United Nations Security Council*.

Karadaku, L. (2012). Head of anti-corruption task force arrested for corruption. *Southeast European Times*, April 4.

Marty, D. (2010). *Inhumane treatment of people and illicit trafficking in human organs in Kosovo*. Report to the Parliamentary Assembly of the Council of Europe in Brussels on 12 December 2010.

Mertus, A. J. (1999). *Kosovo: How myths and truths started a war*. University of California Press.

Sklias, P., & Roukanas, S. (2007). Development in post-conflict Kosovo. *South-Eastern Europe Journal of Economics, 2*, 267–287.

Solana, J. (1999). NATO's success in Kosovo. *Foreign Affairs, 78*, 114–120.

Spector, B., Winbourne, S., & Beck, L. (2003). *Corruption in Kosovo: Observations and implications for USAID*. Management Systems International.

Strohmeyer, H. (2001). Collapse and reconstruction of a judicial system: The United Nations mission in Kosovo and East Timor. *The American Journal of International Law, 95*(1), 46–63.

Transparency International. (2020). *Corruption perceptions index 2019*. Transparency International.

United States Department of State. (2011). *Money laundering and financial crimes country database*. US DOS Bureau for International Narcotics and Law Enforcement Affairs.

United Nations Development Programme. (2010). *Dogs join fight against weapons in Kosovo*. United Nations.

United Nations Office on Drugs and Crime. (2008). *Crime and its impact on the Balkans and affected countries*. United Nations.

Wilson, J. (2006). Law and order in an emerging democracy: Lessons from the reconstruction of Kosovo's police and justice systems. *Annals of the American Academy of Political and Social Science, 605*(1), 152–177.

Yannis, A. (2004). The UN as government in Kosovo. *Global Governance, 10*(1), 67–81.

Part V
The Americas

Chapter 11
Challenges and Lessons Learned in United Nations Mentoring of Local Police in Haiti 2009–2010

Michael Raymond Sanchez

Introduction

Successfully performing the task of a United Nations Police (UNPOL) officer mentor requires considerable flexibility, patience, and interpersonal skills. During my one-year deployment to Haiti, I saw the mentoring program in the Les Cayes region from the perspective of the *new guy* trying to learn the job, as a police mentor, as a Zone Commander, as the Deputy Regional Commander, and ultimately as the Regional Commander for the Les Cayes region. I had a full-spectrum view of the challenges faced by UNPOL mentors, supervisors, and commanders in Haiti, as well as the failures and lessons learned.

When I arrived in Les Cayes Haiti in May of 2009, there was no real mentorship program at work in the Les Cayes region per se. Although the colocation of UNPOL officers with the Police Nationale d'Haïti (PNH) was considered by the United Nations to be important to the success of the mission, UNPOL officers were regionally centralized. Although the Les Cayes region had 23 *commissariats* (precinct houses), spread throughout a 1000 square mile region, all UNPOL officers were centralized in Les Cayes proper for safety reasons. Frequent unrest and violence in Haiti could put isolated UNPOL officers at risk. The lessons learned in this book chapter are based on my personal experiences as an UNPOL Mentor, Zone Commander, Deputy Regional Commander, and ultimately as a Regional Commander in the Les Cayes Region of Haiti from May 2009 to May 2010.

M. R. Sanchez (✉)
University of Texas Rio Grande Valley, Los Fresnos, TX, USA
e-mail: michael.sanchex@untrgv.edu

G. den Heyer, J. F. Albrecht (eds.), *Police and International Peacekeeping Missions*, https://doi.org/10.1007/978-3-030-77900-9_11

A Brief History of Haiti

The country of Haiti occupies the western third of the island of Hispaniola in the Caribbean. Haiti borders the Dominican Republic to the east, and the sea to the north, south, and west. In area, Haiti is slightly smaller than the US State of Maryland and has an estimated population of 11 million people and is both tropical and mountainous (CIA, 2020).

Haiti was originally a French colony, after Spain ceded that portion of Hispaniola to the French in 1697. Haiti became a very valuable French colony as a center for sugar and exotic hardwood. Much of the success and wealth in Haiti was due in large part to its reliance on the cheap labor provided by slavery (CIA, 2020). Much of the cultural roots of Haiti can be traced back to its time as a French colony. In order to maximize the productivity of their slaves, the French maintained a brutal authoritarian rule over the slaves of Haiti. The slaves of Haiti were conditioned to respect only the brutal *strongman* (Fatton, 2007).

At the very end of the eighteenth century, a large rebellion spread throughout the colony. Led by Toussaint L'ouverture, 500,000 slaves revolted and overthrew French rule. Slavery was abolished in 1804 and Haiti become the first country in the world to be born as a result of servile insurrection (CIA, 2020). The Western world was very hesitant to recognize Haiti as an independent republic. Slavery was still the backbone of many economies in the Western Hemisphere. As a Black independent nation that was the product of a slave revolt, there were fears that legitimizing Haiti through national recognition could imperil other slave holdings throughout the Caribbean and the Western Hemisphere (Ceïde, 2008).

From the outset of its independence, Haiti was subject to continuous power struggles as competing strongmen battled for both political and military control of Haiti. A lack of an institutional history forced the Haitian people to support, obey, and ultimately admire only the strong. With an ever-present and continuous struggle for power, Haiti never seems to have stabilized politically, developed institutions, and followed a political trajectory toward the development of democratic ideals. In Haiti, only the strong lead.

The involvement of the Western Hemisphere in trying to bring stability to Haiti has been going on for at least the last century. In 1915, United States Marines landed in Haiti following the assassination of Haitian dictator Vilbrun Guillaume Sam. Sam was executed in response to his heavy-handed tactics in murdering his political enemies. The general point of view toward Haiti at that time was that the United States needed to intervene because the Haitian people were innately incapable of governing themselves. This perception was bred of both colonialism and a racist view. The United States occupied Haiti until 1934, when power was handed over to the Haitian military (Castor & Garafola, 1974).

In 1957, Francois "Papa Doc" Duvalier came to power and ruled Haiti with a heavy and brutal hand. Duvalier ruled Haiti until his death in 1971, when he was succeeded by his son, Jean-Claude "Baby Doc" Duvalier. As with every strongman ruler of Haiti since its inception, the Duvaliers ruled with repressive, brutal, and corrupt regimes. Corruption and incompetence led to a significant drop in Haiti's gross domestic product between 1980 and 1986 (CIA, 2020; Heine & Manigat, 1988).

In 1986, the shooting of four school children during a demonstration in Gonaives was the last straw. A revolt, born of economic frustration, political unrest, and anti-Duvalier activists, drove Jean-Claude Duvalier out of Haiti in a self-imposed exile. After the ouster of Duvalier, Haiti was rocked by political instability and widespread violence. Violence and instability are recurrent themes that consistently mark the periods of time between strongmen leaders in Haiti (Heine & Manigat, 1988). The wrangling for power is best exemplified by the fact that in the first 4 years after the ouster of Jean-Claude Duvalier, no fewer than *five* different military and civilian governments seized and attempted to hold on to power in Haiti (Heine & Thompson, 2011).

In an internationally acclaimed election on December 16, 1990, Jean Bertrand Aristide rose to power in Haiti. The elections that brought Aristide to power were conducted with the assistance of the United Nations (UN) and the Organization of American States (OAS) (Fatton, 2002). Aristide's election generated hope in the Western Hemisphere that Haiti had turned a corner and was ready to embrace democratic norms. As with previous leaders in Haiti, Aristide quickly became heavy-handed, corrupt, and unpredictable. In October of 1991, General Raoul Cédras overthrew Aristide in a coup d'état. As with Duvalier, Aristide was forced into exile (Heine & Thompson, 2011).

Believing in the sanctity of the democratic process, and with hopes that the democratization of Haiti would not die in its crib, the Organization of American States (OAS) and the United Nations (UN) intervened. The continued instability in Haiti had deteriorated to the extent that Haiti's situation was seen as a threat to international peace and security. The UN and the OAS exerted a coordinated campaign to restore Aristide as the legitimately elected leader of Haiti. The measures undertaken included diplomatic pressure, economic pressure, and the threat of military force. On October 15, 1994, Aristide was returned to power, but lost the presidency to Rene Preval in a 1996 election (Heine & Thompson, 2011).

Preval became the first elected leader of Haiti to serve a full five-year term in office. In 2001, Aristide was again elected as the president of Haiti. Starting immediately in 2001, right-wing anti-Aristide movements took hold and strengthened in Haiti. In 2004, Aristide was once again removed from power by a military coup. Aristide was exiled to South Africa where he took up residence (Dupuy, 2005). After 2 years of the presence of international peacekeepers, Preval was again elected as the President of Haiti in 2006.

Enter the United Nations

The United Nations charter was ratified by the United States, China, France, Russia, and the United Kingdom on October 24, 1945. October 24th is still celebrated as *United Nations Day* around the world (United Nations, 2000). The United Nations is dedicated to the idea of collective security as a mechanism for the maintaining of international peace, in that United Nations member states would come to the aid of any member nation that was attacked. The United Nations Charter grants the responsibility and authority to carryout intervention activities to the United Nations Security Council (Ram, 2006).

Throughout its history, the United Nations has become increasingly more involved in peacekeeping operations around the world. The United Nations' role in peacekeeping operations has evolved over time to address increasingly more complex peacekeeping issues. The United Nations now engages in peacekeeping operations of all types all over the world. The rate of peacekeeping missions has increased to the extent that fully 70 percent of all peacekeeping missions engaged in by the United Nations have been initiated after 1990 (Bayley, 2006). One particularly important component of modern peacekeeping is bringing democratic reform to post-conflict or unstable regions (Rotmann, 2011).

The composition of a United Nations peacekeeping mission is a mixture of civilian administration, military, police, and formed police unit components. Each peacekeeping mission has a unique mixture of these components. Each mission's staffing levels, and proportionality of components, is dependent on the security situation, social situation, political situation, and the nature of the conflict or unrest that led to the deployment of a United Nations Peacekeeping mission. The exact composition of a peacekeeping mission is also dependent on the *mission mandate* as defined by the United Nations Security Council (Hårleman, 2003).

The first United Nations peacekeeping mission that utilized a police component was when a police component was added to the United Nations Mission in Congo in the 1960s (Mobekk, 2005). The general mandate for United Nations Police (UNPOL) missions is to bring democratic reform, modernization, capacity building, and an adherence to human rights to the police forces of post-conflict or unstable regions. Increasingly more robust police components have become a critical part of modern United Nations peacekeeping missions (de Saint-Claire, 2007).

The importance of the addition of police reform to United Nations peacekeeping missions stemmed from the realization that real and meaningful democratic reform and stabilization cannot occur until the police have been reformed. In repressive regimes or unstable societies, the oppression of the population, or of a particular minority, occurs frequently at the hands of the police. Since the police are under the control of the repressive regime, and extend to all areas of a society, the police frequently become a most effective agent of oppression. No effort to democratize a region can be effective if the police are still oppressing the society, or a subset of the society (Bayley, 2006; Durch & England, 2010).

UNPOL Monitoring and Executive Mission

In the early UNPOL missions, UNPOL officers were tasked with monitoring duties. The concept of the police monitor was that UNPOL officers would monitor the behavior of the local police forces. Should the local police forces engage in any oppressive behavior, or behavior that violated human rights, the UNPOL monitor would report the observed activity. The theory behind the monitoring mission would be that if the police forces knew they were being watched, they would not commit excesses or abuses (Levine, 2008).

The reporting of oppression had the effect of curtailing such behaviors on the part of the local police forces; however, fundamental changes to police training, behavior, ethics, or concepts of democracy were not changed. The local police forces only refrained from committing excesses in the presence of the UNPOL monitors. Once the UNPOL monitors left the mission, there was nothing to prevent the local police from reverting to their previous behavior. The monitoring mission did not have any effect on the training, mentality, or overall quality of the local police (Sanchez, 2018).

The nature and mission of a police component in United Nations peacekeeping missions passed through several growth stages until 1999, when the United Nations fielded the United Nations Mission in Kosovo (UNMIK) and the United Nations Transitional Administration in Timor-Leste (UNTAET). Both UNMIK and UNTAET were large well-staffed police missions. Both missions were fielded with *executive police authority*. The UNMIK and UNTAET missions marked the beginning of what is known as the *fourth generation* of peacekeeping missions (Silander, 2009). As with the composition of a peacekeeping mission, the exact manpower, duties, authority, and tasking of an UNPOL mission were dependent on the mission mandate as articulated by the United Nations Security Council (Sanchez, 2015).

The inclusion of executive authority changed the very nature of an UNPOL officer. An UNPOL officer in a monitoring mission has no *real* authority to enforce the law, or even to intervene if excesses are witnessed. The UNPOL monitor could only observe and report. With executive authority, an UNPOL officer had the authority of a police officer in the host nation and had the authority to enforce the law. UNPOL officers in an executive mission could arrest offenders, conduct criminal investigations, and file criminal charges (Silander, 2009). UNPOL officers in an executive mission had much more power to create change.

The fourth generation of peacekeeping missions marks the start of the *modern era* of peacekeeping in general, and of the modern era of UNPOL missions specifically. In early peacekeeping missions, an UNPOL officer's duties were to *observe and report.* Nothing more. The modern UNPOL mission now saw UNPOL officers empowered to engage more actively in promoting and even enforcing democratic reform. The new generation of UNPOL officers are tasked with duties that gave the UNPOL mission a real opportunity to promote lasting change. The larger role played by UNPOL officers in modern peacekeeping missions includes the tasks of training, mentoring, and capacity building of local police forces. The UNPOL component of a peacekeeping mission is now considered to be a crucial element in bringing about *real* democratic reform (Smith et al., 2007).

The modern UNPOL mission also undertakes additional tasks such as protecting civilians from human rights abuses. UNPOL missions now take an active role in promoting democratic police reform through operational support and mentoring. An unstable region, with a corrupt police force, is an attractive home or way-stop for narcotics trafficking, the trafficking of human beings, and the perpetuation and support of violent extremism (Heine & Thakur, 2010). Modern UNPOL missions also focus on developing the local police capacity to address these transnational crimes (United Nations Security Council, 2016).

UNPOL Mission Mandates

The guiding force behind the operation of a peacekeeping mission is the *mission mandate,* which is determined and defined by the United Nations Security Council. Like all peacekeeping missions, the UNPOL component of a peacekeeping mission is established through the passage of a *resolution* by the United Nations Security Council. The Security Council resolution defines the nature, scope, responsibilities, and limitations of the peacekeeping mission, including the UNPOL component. Every peacekeeping mission and every UNPOL mission has a unique and different mandate from all other missions. The mandate of the mission is based on many factors including the security situation, the nature of the conflict or unrest giving rise to the mission, the political and cultural climate, and the needs of the mission area (Hårleman, 2003).

The exact wording of a mission mandate, as articulated in a United Nations Security Council Resolution, can be remarkably broad and succinct. The interpretation of the precise methods required to achieve the mission mandate is left to the United Nations Department of Peacekeeping Operations. A good example of the breadth of a mission mandate would be the mandate that created and guided the United Nations Mission in Kosovo (UNMIK) International Police mandate. The goals of the UNMIK police were broad, challenging, and lofty. The UNMIK police was an executive mission, so UNPOLs had executive authority. The UNMIK Police engaged in police patrol, responding to calls for service, conducting criminal investigations, conducting war crimes investigations, providing border patrol and border check point services, recruitment and training of the Kosovo Police Service from scratch, the establishment of policies and procedures, the mentoring of mid- and upper-level managers, and many other such duties. The entirety of the mission mandate that authorized the UNMIK police was contained in a single sentence in United Nations Security Council Resolution 1244, which authorized the UNMIK mission. According to Resolution 1244, the UNMIK Police were responsible for "…maintaining civil law and order, including establishing local police forces and meanwhile through the deployment of international police personnel to serve in Kosovo" (UNSCR 1244, 1999, p. 4). The details of how this mandate would be accomplished was left to the discretion of the Police Division of the Department of Peacekeeping Operations and mission management.

MINUSTAH Mission

In February 2004, an anti-Aristide insurrection based in Gonaives once again plunged Haiti into instability. The presence of a rebel militia descending on Port-au-Prince caused President Jean Bertrand Aristide to once again flee Haiti and enter self-imposed exile (Dupuy, 2005). The destabilization of Haiti, once again, became an extreme concern of the OAS, the United Nations, and of the Western Hemisphere in general. Much of what was gained by previous interventions by the United Nations and the OAS evaporated. Once again, Haiti plunged into instability. The international community had to come up with a plan to do better.

The early interventions into Haiti had been primarily concerned with restoring stability and some form of democratic governance. The problem with these early missions, was that these missions did not address issues that are at the core of Haiti's intrinsic political and social fragility. Without addressing the core issues, there can be no lasting change. Once the international presence that had restored order leaves, society would revert to its previous condition. In 2004, the United Nations took a broader view of intervention in an attempt to address the root causes of Haiti's stability issues (Heine & Thompson, 2011).

In June of 2004, the United Nations Stabilization Mission in Haiti (MINUSTAH) was established by the United Nations Security Council through United Nations Security Council Resolution 1529. While the conceptualization of international intervention in Haiti was broader, the MINSTAH UNPOL mandate was characteristically succinct. Item #2, paragraph *c* of UNSCR 1529 requires the MINSTAH UNPOL to "... facilitate the provision of international assistance to the Haitian police and the Haitian Coast Guard in order to establish and maintain public safety and law and order and to promote and protect human rights;" (UNSCR 1529, 2004, p. 2).

The breadth of the mission mandate, specifically the inclusion of a component to promote and protect human rights, tasks that the mission provides lasting democratic police reform. The MINISTUAH UNPOL mandate is indicative of the evolution of the role UNPOL officers perform from a mere monitor to the transformational role of a democratic reformer, mentor, and capacity builder (Durch & England, 2010). Peacekeepers and UNPOL officers in the MINUSTAH mission were now expected to operate on a multidimensional and transformational level. The establishment and maintenance of peace and security were still key responsibilities; however, the additional mandate of mentoring and building the police capacity of the *Police Nationale d'Haïti* (PNH), also called the Haitian National Police, added to the UNPOL component of the MINUSTAH mission the responsibility of implementing lasting democratic and human rights reforms (Decaens, 2014).

The instability and security situation in Haiti took precedence at the outset of the MINUSTAH mission. In a confluence of security sector reform and democratic reform, one of the first orders of business for the MINUSTAH mission was to plan, secure, and assist in the execution of safe, fair, and free elections in 2006. It is notable that the MINSTAH mission was complicated by the fact that Haiti was not a post-conflict society per se. Rather, Haiti was an unstable society with the roots of that instability going back for hundreds of years. This made the implementation of security sector reform, and the establishment of social stability all the more challenging (Lemay-Hébert & Koops, 2015).

UNPOL Mentoring

Perhaps the most important role in the modern UNPOL mission is that of mentoring the local police force at all levels. Democratic reform and improvement can be conceptualized in fine detail; however, if those ideas are not instilled in the local police, and the concepts operationalized, there will be no change. Working closely with counterparts in the local police forces, the UNPOL officer is expected to train, guide, support, and assist the local police in moving toward democratic reform. The importance of mentoring was noted in the MINUSTAH UNPOL SOP (2004), stating that the role of UNPOL is to:

- Conduct decentralized, standardized mentorship program at the main HNP territorial units to complement the basic training delivered at the HNP Academy and continuously monitor the learning progress of the new recruits;
- Oversee the compliance of locals to international criminal justice, human rights, and policing standards;
- Proactively assist the local police in their daily operational policing functions and in their effort to deliver democratic police services; and,
- Issue report and recommendations to the Trainers on the enhancement of basic and advance training program as well as provide inputs to certification program (p. 42).

The MINUSTAH SOP conceptualized an ever-expanding mentorship program where UNPOL mentors train PNH mentors to continue the work. When I arrived in Haiti in 2009, this lofty goal had not even been started in my region. Much of these duties can only be accomplished through direct interpersonal contact and exchange of information between the UNPOL officer and the PNH officer.

In 2017, the United Nations Department of Peacekeeping Operations published a comprehensive manual entitled *Police Monitoring, Mentoring and Advising in Peace Operations.* While this manual was not in existence during my 2009–2010 MINUSTAH mission, it is nevertheless an excellent source to understand the United Nations' conceptualization of the role of the UNPOL Mentor.

Perhaps the first critical element of UNPOL mentoring that new UNPOL officers face is the reality that mentoring in an UNPOL mission is completely different from mentoring in one's home domestic police force. An UNPOL mentor will have to teach the local police concepts and operations that may not be the norm in the UNPOL mentor's home country. The problem with this idea is that the policing operational concepts and guiding principles, as well as the community's response to those principles, are different from country to country. This issue is compounded by the cross-cultural dissonance between the UNPOL officer and the local police (UN-DPKO, 2017)

Mentoring Challenges and Lessons Learned in Les Cayes

Because of the centralization of the UNPOL force in Les Cayes, teams of UNPOLs took day trips to different commissariats throughout the region. The UNPOL team would show up at the commissariat, take down the staffing history of the commissariat from the operations logbook, hang around for a few hours, and then go back to Les Cayes. There were several commissariats in Les Cayes proper and the surrounding area that were visited more than the outlying commissariats. Some of the outlying commissariats took several hours to reach by road, and several hours back. The first thing I noticed when I was taken around on the daily commissariat inspections was that the UNPOL officers spoke to the PNH officers as if they were children, not colleagues. The PNH officers returned this attitude with a begrudging and minimal cooperation.

The approach of most of the UNPOLs I saw when I arrived in Les Cayes is understandable, if nevertheless wrongheaded. I had experienced pre-deployment training in Washington DC twice. Once before deploying to the UNMIK mission, and once before deploying to the MINSUTAH mission. When a police officer is undergoing UNPOL pre-deployment training from their national police force, the future UNPOL officers are told that they represent the *best of the best.* That they have been selected to *show them how it is done.* While such exhortations are meant to build the morale of the future UNPOL, it tends to give them a sense of superiority over the local police they are to mentor. The PNH officers reacted as any police officer would react if an interloper arrived saying *I am here to teach you how to do your job.* I took note of this problem. Later in my mission, I was able to put this observation to good use.

MINUSTAH accomplished a great deal in Port-au-Prince with the PNH. New PNH officers were vetted and selected, and MINUSTAH was very instrumental in modernizing the PNH police academy. However, at the regional and local level, MINUSTAH efforts at mentoring and capacity building represented little more than monitoring.

Broad-Spectrum Mentoring

While a concerted effort was made to bring considerable capacity building to the PNH, this effort was attempted in a vacuum. The situation in Haiti was such that all of Haiti's criminal justice institutions required significant reform, refocusing, mentoring, and capacity building. The entire criminal justice system in Haiti was corrupt, extraordinarily out of date, and ineffective. Haiti had never modernized its criminal codes, which dated back to the Napoleonic era. For any change to take hold, and to represent a long-term shift in institutional methodology, reform must occur concurrently at every level and across the entire criminal justice spectrum. The various elements of the criminal justice system did not work effectively together and inter-departmental relations were very strained (Crane et al., 2010).

The fact that Haiti's penal system and judicial system remained much as they were before reform came to the PNH, severely restricted lasting change in the PNH (Mobekk, 2005). For example, at the time I was in Les Cayes, the local justice of the peace wielded considerable power and he was shown much deference by the PNH and the Haitian people. Over the 1 year I was in Haiti, the justice of the peace for Les Cayes only heard criminal cases 1 or 2 days per month. There were significant and egregious administrative shortcomings in the judicial system. There were cases of prisoners who had been arrested for something as minor as stealing a cell phone, who were held for 2 years before their case was heard. Other prisoners had their case files lost. In fact, in 2008, 83 percent of the people incarcerated in Haiti were in pre-trial detention. Indeed, Haiti lacked the basic administrative and operational ability to investigate, detain, arrest, prosecute, sentence, and incarcerate criminals; even those guilty of serious crimes (International Crisis Group, 2008).

The reform operation in Haiti should have been organized and delivered in a coordinated manner, across a broad-spectrum encompassing police, civil administration, judicial, and penal institutions. Moreover, such a broad-spectrum approach should have been a coordinated one. If mentorship of the PNH makes them much more effective in their investigations, so they arrest more suspects, it only exacerbates the existing overloads in the judicial and penal systems. The Les Cayes UNPOL had two corrections monitor/mentors attached to our region, but there was no nationwide effort at penal reform and capacity building in the regions to any meaningful extent, so these corrections personnel made monitoring site visits much like the UNPOL officers.

The MINUSTAH UNPOL SOP (2004) did articulate the intent of following a *top-down and bottom-up approach* to the mentoring, development, and capacity building of the PNH. The idea was that the development of police executives, main headquarters personnel, and regional command staff should be coordinated with mentorship and development at the regional and commissariat level. The mission envisioned the development of the PNH at all command levels; however, this was certainly not the case in 2009–2010. Such an approach would have been highly effective to the accomplishment of the mission mandate in Haiti; however, this approach would have required much more manpower than was available.

The Les Cayes Region alone had 23 commissariats. The region would have needed, at a very minimum, one UNPOL mentor as a counterpart and mentor to the *Chef du Poste* (Precinct Commander) and one or two UNPOL mentors to work with the officers of each commissariat. At a bare minimum, the top-down/bottom-up approach would have required 46–69 officers just to deal with the commissariats effectively. Additional personnel would have been needed for regional command staff, regional and administrative counterparts to the PNH at the regional level, and liaisons to the MINUSTAH military and FPU components. To pursue the top-down/bottom-up approach in the Les Cayes region would have required at least 60 UNPOL officers. In 2009, the Les Cayes region fielded less than 30.

Aside from needing a large number of UNPOL officers, the United Nations requires that a prospective UNPOL officer have a minimum of 5 years of experience (DPKO, 2007). Five years of experience may be an acceptable level of experience for a line-level mentor; however, officers with only five years of service do know have the experience or the knowledge base to mentor supervisors, mid-level managers, regional commanders, or police executives. A persistent problem in almost all UNPOL missions was the inability to obtain enough UNPOL officers with higher levels of experience and managerial skill sets (Hansford, 2006; Monk, 2008). In order to administer the top-down/bottom-up program, MINUSTAH UNPOL would have required a considerable number of UNPOL officers with first-line supervisor, second-line supervisor, command, and executive experience.

In addition to the manpower requirement, for the top-down/bottom-up approach to have worked, UNPOL officers would have to have been collocated in their respective commissariats. The security situation was such that the UNPOL officers were restricted to living accommodations in the Les Cayes area. The risk of having officers strewn throughout the region was considered to be too great.

Lack of Consistency in Doctrine

In addition to the fact that Haiti's criminal code was severely outdated, reform efforts were inhibited by the fact that there had been no mission-wide doctrine from which to mentor the local PNH. Without *first* revising the operational conceptualization and tactical doctrine for the PNH, what should a regional level UNPOL monitor try to teach the PNH? For the most part, any UNPOL who undertook to try and mentor the PNH, myself included, drew from their own experience and tactical doctrine (Belo et al., 2011).

This lack of consistency in doctrine was not unique to the MINSTAH mission. In his final report to the United Nations Department of Peacekeeping Operations, Richard Monk, the seventh Police Commissioner for the UNMIK mission, commented on this very issue. Commissioner Monk relayed a situation where after *8* years of UNMIK mentorship and capacity building, the regional support units for the Kosovo Police (called ROSU Units) had all been trained in different crowd control methodologies. This meant that in the event of a large-scale riot, these regional teams did not have the ability to work together (Monk, 2008).

The UNPOL officers in the MINUSTAH mission cannot be faulted for trying to teach the PNH their own national tactics. At least they wanted to teach the PNH *something*. Nevertheless, it seems that UNPOL missions, while of necessity are thrown together ad hoc, should at some point appoint a commission to establish a universal tactical and operational doctrine that *fits* the local police force *and the culture of the society* (Mobekk, 2005).

In addition to a lack of coherent planning or of a mentoring doctrine, pre-deployment training of new UNPOL officers entering the MINUSTAH mission was completely devoid of any training on any aspect of mentoring. Even though there was not a codified mission doctrine on mentoring, operations, and tactics, training could have been conducted on cross-cultural relations, building partnerships, cross-cultural communications, and cultural sensitivity. If the air of superiority affected by many UNPOL officers could have been softened or turned into a desire for good communication, many UNPOL mentors might have been more successful even if doctrinally left to their own devices.

Without an articulated and codified mission development doctrine, UNPOL officers have no idea precisely *what procedures and methods* to teach the local police. An UNPOL officer thrust into a mentoring role, without a clearly defined doctrine, will fall back on his or her own knowledge and experience base. Ultimately, the UNPOL officer simply tries to duplicate their own strategies, procedures, tactics, and policing models (Call, 2003).

Understanding Reform in the Local Cultural Context

There were considerable attempts to bring some sort of democratic reform to the police in Haiti, and in Les Cayes specifically. When I arrived in the mission, there was an effort to bring *Community Policing* to Haiti. While the concept of community policing would be a benefit to the PNH institution in Haiti, a critical mistake was made in the implementation of this program. The community police program in Les Cayes fell flat on its face because the program was *not* developed with any understanding of the geography, staffing, history, or culture of Haiti.

Police reforms brought by the United Nations are always rooted in the knowledge and experience of foreign policing experts. While all police systems have some basis in foreign models, UNPOL reforms need to be designed and conceptualized with the deep involvement of the local police and population. Reforms must be culturally appropriate and acceptable to both the police culture and the societal culture, in order for those reforms to take hold (Call, 2003).

The commissariats in the Les Cayes region, with the exception of the commissariat at Les Cayes PNH Regional Headquarters, in Les Cayes proper, were very sparsely staffed. For example, the commissariat in Torbek was generally staffed by two or three PNH officers per shift. Because of the limited staff available, standard procedure was for the PNH officers to stay at the commissariat. The people of Torbek *knew* that if they needed the police, they would have to go to the Torbek commissariat. While this is not an efficient arrangement, it was nevertheless the norm.

One of my first site visits to Torbek occurred 1 week after I have arrived in Les Cayes. My team arrived at the Torbek commissariat... and it was closed. No one was there. I found out at this time that the PNH in the Les Cayes Region (with the exception of Les Cayes proper) had no radios in their police cars and no reliable form of communication. There was no way to contact the PNH officers, so we camped out at the commissariat to wait for them. Approximately 4 hours later, the two PNH officers pulled up in their PNH pick-up truck. They told me that they had been ordered to engage in *community policing*. They were told that community policing meant patrolling amongst the populace.

The problem is that the model of community policing they were experimenting with was completely wrong for Torbek, and most of the other commissariats in the Les Cayes Region. Geographically, Torbek was a large precinct with rough, mountainous areas. There was no reliable cell phone signal throughout two-thirds of the Torbek area. So, when the PNH officers went off to patrol, as far as the populace was concerned, they may as well have dropped off the face of the earth. There were several occasions were citizens of Torbek were in dire need of the PNH, so they came to the commissariat only to find it locked... and the officers out *somewhere* on patrol.

The lesson learned here is that one cannot try to transplant a policing philosophy, tactics, or operations into another nation without *first* adjusting that program to fit the conditions and culture in the local population of the mission. The community policing model, that died shortly after my arrival in Les Cayes, was not crafted to *fit* the requirements of the people and police in the Les Cayes Region. The development of tactical or operational reforms must be developed *in conjunction with the community*. A new policing paradigm must be crafted to fit the needs of the community, or it will fail (Baranyi, 2019; Meharg & Arnusch, 2010).

Now increased patrol *was* a positive thing in the Les Cayes main commissariat, in the heart of Les Cayes proper, a city of approximately 50,000 people. But this was because each shift in Les Cayes had 8–10 PNH officers, so several officers could patrol, but there were still officers at the commissariat to address walk-in complaints and emergencies (Call, 2003; Caparini, 2014).

Failure to Understand Needs

Along the same lines as understanding reforms in the local context, is the failure to understand the reform needs of the population and policing institution before acting. Donor states and Non-Governmental organizations have difficulty in conceptualizing the needs of a local police force within the cultural framework, capabilities, and culture of the recipient local police force. One tends to see police needs in the context of what one knows (Chance, 2007; Ceïde, 2008).

One organization, with the absolute best of intentions, decided that since computers are considered a force multiplier in first world police departments, providing computers to the PNH would make the PNH more efficient. Computers allow officers to type reports more quickly and legibly, transmit, receive, and review reports more effectively, and track local crime statistics to provide more accurate police patrols.

So, each commissariat in the Les Cayes Region of Haiti received a brand-new desk-top computer. The problem with this gesture was that no one had apparently conducted a needs analysis to see if computers were what the PNH in Les Cayes *needed.* As it turned out, almost half of the commissariats in the Les Cayes Region at the time did not have electricity. None had internet. There was no training provided for those officers with electricity on *how* to use the computer in a policing context. In addition, no printers were provided. The few computers that worked were universally used to play solitaire.

At the same time each commissariat was getting a new computer, by my own observation, approximately 20–25 percent of the PNH in the region did not have a holster for their side arm. At the time, almost all PNH carried 0.38 revolvers. I met quite a few PNH officers who would carry their sidearm in their hip pocket, because they did not have a holster. In addition, I checked the PNH officers' revolvers at random and found that most PNH officers had two or three bullets in their guns, and those were very old.

A simple needs analysis would have revealed that the PNH needed holsters and ammunition far more than they needed a platform to play solitaire. When contemplating a new program, or an element of capacity building, in addition to the culture and the conditions, the mission must understand the *needs* of the local police force. Unfortunately, many times UNPOLs or non-governmental organizations would provide what they thought the PNH need, based on their knowledge of their own first-world police force, rather than in the context of the culture and needs of the local police force (MINUSAH, 2004).

Assignment as the Les Cayes Deputy Regional Commander

In September of 2009, I was promoted to Deputy Regional Commander for the Les Cayes Region (also called *Regional Coordinator).* Because of this extensive experience, my Regional Commander, who was in his first mission, gave me considerable autonomy in my duties. Immediately upon being promoted, my Regional Commander assigned me two critical and challenging tasks.

First, my Regional Commander wanted me to rebuild and refocus the mentoring program in the Les Cayes Region. Since there was little coordination or guidance from MINUSTAH headquarters on mentoring, I was tasked with improving the program to the extent that some positive change could be made possible. The current monitoring focus of UNPOL mentors in the Les Cayes Region was not accomplishing any reform or capacity building.

Second, I was tasked with finding a way to improve UNPOL relations with the police officers in the main commissariat in Les Cayes proper. UNPOL officers were assigned to patrol with PNH officers from the Les Cayes commissariat every night. PNH cooperation in this venture was begrudging at best but got significantly worse. One night in August of 2009, a PNH officer was shot and killed in the presence of two UNPOL officers, one officer was directly next to the PNH officer when he was shot. The suspect escaped the scene. The failure of the UNPOL officer to shoot the suspect, after he had shot the PNH officer, caused a complete collapse of the relationship between the PNH officers in the Les Cayes commissariat and the Les Cayes UNPOL. The PNH officers were angry that UNPOL officers, where *supposed* to be showing them how it is done, could not stop a suspect from killing their officer, or *at the very least,* take that suspect out rather than to allow him to escape. PNH officers in Les Cayes refused to patrol with UNPOL officers after that incident. They were nonconfrontational about this refusal, making lame excuses like they do not have enough people or enough gas, every day, but they refused to patrol with UNPOL officers every night.

The Importance of Creating Relationships in Mentoring

By its very nature, mentoring is an interpersonal process. Effective mentoring requires the ability to build strong cross-cultural relationships. UNPOL mentors must have a strong sense of cultural awareness, strong cultural intelligence, cross-cultural communication skills, and diplomatic skills. These cross-cultural interpersonal skills are just as important to an effective mentor as technical knowledge (UN-DPKO, 2017). It does not matter how much knowledge an UNPOL mentor has, if he or she cannot form a cooperative relationship with their local mentee, the knowledge is useless.

The complexity of the UNPOL mentoring task transcends the ability to communicate and build relationships. The UNPOL mentoring function is complicated by the necessity for the UNPOL officer to maintain objectivity and impartiality. In a post-conflict mission, UNPOLs could not take sides in any intercultural or societal tensions, but must maintain professional objectivity. The UNPOL mentor's ability to create relationships must be tempered with objectivity and the discipline to avoid becoming biased (UN-DPKO, 2017).

A common mistake in leadership and management is the assumption that an employee who is an outstanding worker at the line-level will automatically make an excellent supervisor. Supervision requires skills above and beyond just being a hard worker. Gerspacher (2012) made the observation that the selection process for UNPOL officers frequently follows the same flawed logic. Because a domestic police officer is an outstanding officer, with exceptional technical knowledge, does not necessarily mean that officer is going to make a good UNPOL mentor (Caparini,

2017; Monk, 2008). Effective mentoring, particularly in a cross-cultural environment, requires developing trust and engaging in effective communication. These skills are every bit as important as technical knowledge.

Make Them Want What You Want to Give Them

In contemplating how to revise the Les Cayes approach to mentoring, I realized that the first step was that a few changes within UNPOL must occur. First, I would have to train the UNPOL officers on some basic police strategies and tactics, so that everyone is teaching the same thing. Second, and much more importantly, I had to change the approach and attitude of the UNPOLs in my region. In a training session, I posed the question *"If you are hard at work in your police agency in your home country, and someone from another country comes waltzing into your station telling you 'I am here to teach you how to do your job'... what would your reaction be?"*

Most officers, including myself, admitted that they would react very negatively to this situation, wondering *who the hell are YOU to tell me how to do MY job?* I posited that this is precisely how the PNH officers must feel when we waltz into their commissariat with that air of superiority. Continuing the hypothetical, if my command structure gave me a direct order that I *will cooperate...* I would do so begrudgingly and with as little effort as possible. After this discussion, it was easy to see that the reaction of the PNH officers to our presence and attitude was not only understandable... it was predictable and reasonable.

Before we could apply this newfound approach, we had to get the PNH on board with the *new UNPOL approach.* Perhaps the most challenging aspect of UNPOL mentoring of local police is that the UNPOL mentor's job is to change the behaviors, attitudes, policing philosophies, and perceptions of the local police force. Such characteristics of any local police force have been calcified in the local policing culture through decades or centuries. Changing minds in an UNPOL mentoring context is exceptionally challenging (UN-DPKO, 2009).

The UNPOL attitude of superiority had created a resistance to any UNPOL assistance that would have to be overcome before any real mentoring could happen. This required a personal touch. I spent several weeks visiting every commissariat in the region several times per week. Each commissariat has a commanding officer known as a *Chef de Poste*. Upon visiting each commissariat, I would meet with the *Chef de Poste*. For my initial meeting with each *Chef de Poste*, I said basically the same thing:

> Please forget how the UNPOL officers have approached you in the past. I am in command now and the truth is that I know policing in America. I do not know policing in Haiti. I cannot POSSIBLY know your job, your community, or your people as well as you do. We are NOT here to tell you HOW to do your job... you know that better than I ever could. What I am here for, is to try to help you do your job better. What can I do to help you do your job better?

Every *Chef du Poste* listened politely and seemed to appreciate the respectful tone of the conversation; however, when asked *What can I do to help you do your job better?* The answer was always *Nothing.* I accepted that answer and then spent an hour or two engaging in *cop talk* with the *Chef* and the officers of the commissariat. The reason for this was to start building a bridge. Mentoring take a relationship and the building of a relationship takes patience. The PNH had a lot of resentment to get through before they would be interested in my assistance. This is where patience and timing are extremely important assets to a good mentor.

This pattern went on for several weeks. Each week the *Chef du Poste* would say that he did not need our assistance. Finally, the patience paid off. I was meeting with the *Chef du Post* in Arniquet and he refused our assistance as usual. Afterward, during the *cop talk* session with the officers in the commissariat, one of the officers assigned to Arniquet told me about another officer (I assume it was him) who had someone that put a gun to the back of his neck. The officer asked me: "W*hat could we do when that happens?"* This was the moment I had been waiting for.

I demonstrated a few very basic takeaway and defense techniques. I went through these basic tactics, all of the officers in Arniquet watched with rapt attention. After I demonstrated a few techniques, I said that it was time to leave, but the officers were clamoring for more. I told them that, if their *Chef du Poste* approves, I would be happy to come back in a few days and take a few hours to *teach* them the techniques. The officers excitedly sought and received the *Chef du Poste's* approval. So, I started weekly training sessions in Arniquet.

One week, when the training was done, the PNH officers said that they had some *mandates* (arrest warrants) to serve. I asked if they wanted help. The *Chef du Poste* now said *Sure!* So, I accompanied them on their mandate service. I gave a few suggestions on their technique, which they accepted.

One week later, I received a phone call from the *Chef du Poste* for the St. Jean du Sud commissariat, which was adjacent to Arniquet. The *Chef du Poste* told me *I hear you have been training the officers in Arniquet. Can you come teach my officers too?* Of course! I willingly agreed. During all of my meetings and visits, I was brining different UNPOL teams with me each visit. This gave them all a firsthand view of the approach and how to develop a cooperative relationship.

The mentoring program in Les Cayes improved considerably, and the PNH officers were not only willing to accept development... they sought it out. The key lesson learned here was that we developed a *respectful relationship* with the PNH where we ultimately made them *want* what we wanted to give them. On this topic, Call and Stanley (2001) assert that "...no amount of training or institutional development will produce positive results where domestic actors are not really interested in changing the status quo" (p. 170). In other words, an UNPOL mentor must find a way to make the local police *want* what you want to give them. This approach proved much more effective than trying to jam development down their throats. Our program was so successful that regional commanders from several other regions in Haiti were sent to Les Cayes to observe our program. The fate of this program will be discussed later.

Demonstrate Basic Tactics in the Field to Build Credibility

My second task, to find a way to restore a positive relationship with the PNH officers and leaders in the Les Cayes commissariat, proved to be just as challenging. I spoke with a few of the Les Cayes PNH officers who had been more candid with me in the past. Aside from their absolute fury at UNPOL for (in their view) allowing their officer to get shot, the PNH were angry about the hypocrisy of the UNPOL air of superiority, when the UNPOL officers could not even take out the suspect. Had the UNPOL officers present at the shooting have shot the suspect, it would have made a huge difference. In addition, the PNH officers told me that they did not like that fact that when UNPOL officers patrolled with them, when answering a call, the UNPOL would sit in the car and would not assist, observe, or participate.

In addition to the negative reaction to the shooting, I was hearing that the UNPOL officers lacked credibility in the eyes of the PNH, because they never *demonstrated* anything, they just talked. Just like with the PNH reaction to the initial approach of the UNPOL officers, this reaction is understandable. The problem was that the PNH officers were still making lame excuses to not patrol with UNPOLs.

I determined to work night shift myself for a few days. I was hoping that they would find it much harder to blow me off, because of my position. I was correct. Albeit in a surly and begrudging manner at the start, the nightshift officers in the Les Cayes commissariat went out on several patrols with me.

As luck would have it, our first night was a particularly busy night. There were several *burglary in progress* calls, an assault call, and a domestic violence call in one night. On each call, the PNH officers were shocked that when they arrived at the door, I was there with them. On one burglary call, the homeowner thought the suspects were still in the house. This gave me the opportunity to demonstrate and teach the PNH officers how to clear a house. They learned basics like how to pie a corner and much of it was done with hand signals. The suspect had already fled because the house was clear. We caught up with the suspect shortly thereafter by shutting off the police car and listening to where the dogs were barking.

In each call, I demonstrated a little something to improve their knowledge base. One must resist the urge to do everything, and to try to teach everything all at once. It was enough that they were patrolling with me and it was enough that they were receptive to the few things I showed them. Even though UNPOL officers in the MINUSTAH mission were non-executive, we were able to *assist* the PNH in their duties. I took full advantage of this language and tried to participate in patrolling and mandate service whenever possible.

The lesson learned here was that in order to establish credibility, not by merely telling stories about how good you are at home, an UNPOL mentor must be out there with the officers. Moreover, some skills must be demonstrated in the real world. Both to make the technique more understandable in the context of an actual incident, and to establish the credibility of the UNPOL mentor.

We had an excellent group of UNPOL officers in Les Cayes. I was very pleased to see that the UNPOL officers in Les Cayes bought in to these new programs enthusiastically. Their enthusiasm contributed to the creation of an excellent working relationship between UNPOL and PNH. With a little guidance, the UNPOLs in our region got very good at developing positive relationship with their PNH counterparts. Our cooperation and collaboration with the PNH in the entire region continued to improve.

Lack of Executive Authority

The UNPOL officers in the MINUSTAH mission did not carry executive authority. This means that an UNPOL officer did not have a legal right to make an arrest or intervene in a criminal act, unless public safety was immediately imperiled. In order to palpably improve the PNH's operational effectiveness, there were times when police operations must be demonstrated in the real world. In addition, reforms also require policing the police. Non-executive UNPOL officers have very limited tools at their disposal to address corruption and criminality within the ranks of the PNH (Donais, 2011).

Without the definitive authority to intervene and take charge of a situation where there is criminality or corruption, the MINUSTAH UNPOL had no real teeth to enforce a new set of ethical paradigms. The MINUSTAH Standard Operating Procedure (2004) explains that one of an UNPOL officer's primary responsibilities is to:

> Advise the local police on the appropriate means to handle the situation, be persuasive and attempt to explain, demonstrate and encourage the appropriate response. If necessary, verbally intercede and strongly recommend appropriate action" (p.16).

The MINUSTAH SOP (2004) goes on to say that if the unacceptable behavior of the organic police continues, the UNPOL should "*…complete an incident report*" (p.16).

Such limitations are reminiscent of the limitation of being an UNPOL monitor, where an UNPOL's only recourse is to *tell* on the offending local officer. The UNPOL officer does not have the authority to assume control when a situation gets out of hand. In an executive mission, the UNPOL would have the authority to arrest a local officer who is engaging in illegal or corrupt activities. In MINUSTAH, the UNPOL is limited to *recommending* and *reporting.*

By being limited to recommending and reporting, there were disastrous actions taken on the part of the PNH that could have been avoided had the MINISTUAH UNPOL officers been given executive authority. During the week after the January 12, 2010 earthquake in Haiti, many inmates in Haitian prisons took advantage of the instability and staged breakouts. Prison breaks with 100% of the prisoners escaping were reported from all corners of Haiti. In the first few weeks following the earthquake, MINUSTAH headquarters was in adject chaos, so the regions were left to manage their affairs as best they could, with whatever resources were on hand.

One week after the earthquake in Haiti, a large-scale riot at the Les Cayes Prison, which was located directly behind the PNH regional headquarters in Les Cayes, was reported. At the time, I was the Deputy Regional Commander for the MINUSTAH UNPOL in Les Cayes. When the UNPOL Regional Commander and I arrived at the Les Cayes prison, the situation was dire. The prisoners had overpowered the *Direction de l'Administration Pénitentiaire* (Directorate of Prison Administration) or DAP officers and had taken control of the Les Cayes Prison. The DAP officers had escaped and left the prison in the hands of 467 inmates. The inmates were all over the prison facility trying to find avenues of escape.

At the time, there were 11 PNH officers present. We had 15 UNPOL officers, 40 Senegalese Military Police (as a formed-police-unit), and 40 Uruguayan soldiers who were part of our regional United Nations military presence. The Senegalese Military Police were directed to establish a perimeter around the prison. Should any prisoners escape, they would present a direct risk to public safety, allowing the FPU officers to detain them. This is consistent with the promotion of human rights and public safety.

The Regional Commander for the PNH asked the UNPOL Regional Commander and I to order the Senegalese and the Uruguayans to enter the prison and restore order. This is where a non-executive UNPOL's mandate and responsibilities get complicated. The United Nations could not send non-executive officers into a facility to enforce Haitian law. That would constitute a violation of Haitian sovereignty. We could detain escapees as a public safety measure, but we could not enforce Haitian law directly. This would exceed the MINUSTAH UNPOL mandate. These legal hairs were split in the moment and the request was denied.

We further explained to the PNH Regional Commander that we could *assist* him in restoring order, but we could not restore order *for him.* We convinced the PNH Regional Commander that we could develop a coordinated tactical plan to restore order in the prison, with UNPOL, FPU, and Uruguayan solders assisting, but the operation must be led by PNH officers.

We were making some progress in developing a plan that would restore order in the prison, but that would also be consistent with the restrictions of the MINUSTAH mandate. At this point in time, several hours after we had arrived, a Haitian VIP arrived and met privately with the PNH Regional Commander. We were told that this VIP was the *Department Delegate,* somewhat equivalent of a congressman.

After the Department Delegate left, the PNH Regional Commander advised the UNPOL Regional Commander and I that the PNH Deputy Regional Commander and 10 PNH officers were going to make entry into the prison and restore order. The UNPOL Regional Commander and I thought this plan was nothing short of insane and recommended against it and suggested that we continue working on our tactical plan. The PNH Regional Commander told us that he was ordered by the Department Delegate to restore order immediately and restore order he shall.

At this point in time, the UNPOL Regional Commander and I are limited in our ability to intervene in this monumentally bad idea by the language of the MINUSTAH SOP. According to the MINUSTAH SOP (2004), we could only "...be persuasive and attempt to explain demonstrate and encourage the appropriate response. If necessary, verbally intercede and strongly recommend appropriate action" (p.14). We protested and *strongly recommended* in the strongest manner possible against this operation. For 11 police officers to enter a prison during a full-blow riot, outnumbered more than 10–1, this operation could only end in disaster. As the PNH Regional Commander was absolutely determined to execute this plan, the UNPOL Regional Commander and I refused to participate in it and pulled our personnel back.

We watched as the PNH officers made entry into the prison yard through a side door. After a delay of a few seconds, a fusillade of shots lasting several seconds rang out. The PNH officers had made entry into the prison and had shot 11 prisoners dead. It worked. However, the shooting of unarmed prisoners was a human rights violation of epic proportions. There were only two possible outcomes of the PNH entry into the prison. The officers would get severely wounded or killed or they would shoot prisoners. Ultimately, all of the officers who entered the prison, including the PNH Deputy Regional Commander, would go to prison in Haiti for murder. The Department Delegate did not.

The UNPOL Regional Commander and I knew full well that the PNH making entry into the Les Cayes Prison could only end in disaster. However, without the executive authority to *lead* a tactical operation to restore order, or to forcibly stop the PNH from executing such an ill-advised operation, we were unable to prevent a completely foreseeable disaster. We were restricted by the language of the SOP, which was consistent with a non-executive mission, from preventing a human rights catastrophe.

If future UNPOL missions are not granted executive authority, there must at least be language in the mandate that empowers UNPOL officers to act under exigent circumstances. While situations such as the Les Cayes Prison riot are rare, they do occur. UNPOL officers should either have executive authority or some codified emergency authority that would empower them to act in such situations.

Length of Mission

Perhaps the most critical variable in the failure of mentoring programs is the limited deployment time of UNPOL officers. An UNPOL officer's tour of duty with the United Nations is *1-year*. While an UNPOL may extend his or her mission beyond 1 year, only 2 6-month extensions are granted. Then an UNPOL officer must return home (DPKO, 2007). Many nations do not allow for extensions and all. Moreover, there are some nations that only allow UNPOL deployments of 6 or 9 months (Sanchez, 2011).

Mentoring of foreign police forces in an international context is exponentially more difficult and challenging than mentoring police officers at home. Working in a foreign environment requires extensive adjustment on the part of the UNPOL officer. It takes several months for an UNPOL officer to adjust to the mission, the society, the structure and culture of the mission, the culture and structure of the local police forces, and to fully internalize the mission goals and mandate. This period of adjustment is incrementally more complex for UNPOL officers in command positions. UNPOL officers on a one-year mission are truly productive for approximately 6 months of that 1 year (Sanchez, 2011).

Strategic Vision

At the command and executive level, the one-year deployment is not conducive to a consistent strategic vision for the mission, which is incredibly important to creating lasting change. UNPOL officers in command and executive positions tend to have a strategic vision that does not extend beyond 365 days. An UNPOL commander will tend to implement a policy that will look good in 1 year, rather than take the long view of the mission.

If a command level officer in an UNPOL mission implements a 5-year plan, that officer's successor will scrap the program and install his own. Each person in a command or executive position wants to put their own footprint on the mission. This occurred in the Les Cayes region. I was refused an extension of my mission and left MINUSTAH in May of 2010. Les Cayes UNPOL officers contacted me a few weeks after I had left the mission. They told me that the new Regional Commander had scrapped my mentoring plan because he wanted to do things *his way*. Even if the new regional commander's program yielded results, his successor would scrap *that* program anyway.

While the mission mandate, and even the overarching strategic vision articulated in the MINUSTAH SOP, may present a particular vision for the mission, how is that vision implemented in a constant state of change? As headquarters coordinators, executives, and regional commanders in the field come and go, the strategic goals and methods of achieving those goals change constantly. If command-level officers and policymakers had longer tours of duty, there would be more consistency in strategic vision and strategic methodology not only in MINUSTAH but also in all UNPOL missions.

Institutional Knowledge and Relationships

A new UNPOL officer must do a considerable amount of learning and adjustment at the beginning of their mission. Each new UNPOL arrives in mission with little to no intuitional knowledge of the mission. It takes time to understand the nature of the mission, the cultural context of the local police and society, and even adjust to fellow UNPOLs from different nations. This all takes time, generally several months (Sanchez, 2011).

With personnel leaving the mission at one-year intervals, there is no accumulation of institutional knowledge. Everyone only has 1 year of institutional knowledge at the most. In his final report to the United Nations Department of Peacekeeping Operations, Richard Monk, who was the seventh Police Commissioner in the

UNMIK mission, made particular note of the problems caused by the dearth of institutional knowledge. Commissioner Monk gave an example of complex investigations where a new investigator is assigned every year. It takes months of a new investigator to digest what has been accomplished up to that point, before the investigator can be productive. Each subsequent investigator is productive for shorter periods of time as the case become ever more voluminous (Monk, 2008).

By its very nature, mentoring is relationship centric. A mentor must develop a strong and trusting relationship with the mentee before any real learning can take place (UN-DPKO, 2017). The development of a trusting relationship takes time and patience to become productive. The United Nations Police Monitoring, Mentoring and Advising in Peace Operations Manual (2017) recognizes the important of the need for extended personal relationships, stating "...mentoring presupposes a long-term, intense caring relationship while personnel rotations in a peacekeeping mission are a natural hurdle in developing such long-term relationship of confidence and trust" (p. 14).

As mentoring progresses, the mentor will have to have developed a deep understanding of the local police *and* the local culture. Specialized knowledge provided by the UNPOL mentor must be in the context of his or her understanding of the police and societal cultures present (Caparini, 2014). Cross-cultural understanding can only be developed through exposure and over time. Each new UNPOL must learn the same things as his or her predecessor in order to be effective. As Deputy Regional Commander, and ultimately Regional Commander for Les Cayes, I found the rotation of people to be frustrating. Those UNPOL officers who were the top performers were generally the officers with the most mission experience. They inevitably left and were replaced with a new officer. This new officer would then have to try to develop new relationships.

Additionally, there is the very distinct possibility that PNH officers and commanders will become frustrated with an endless chain of new mentors, each telling them something different. Several *Chefs du Poste* in the Les Cayes region expressed to me that they found the endless parade of different UNPOL officers to be frustrating, as there was little in the way of consistency. Unfortunately, I became simply one more UNPOL in the parade, and most of my success was unraveled. Bayley (2001) discussed the issue of length of mission, "Foreigners assigned to produce change abroad must reside in country for substantial periods of time to provide programmatic continuity, expeditious advice, and informed midcourse corrections..." (p. 42).

Conclusion

As an organization, and in a strategic sense, the United Nation understands what it takes to mentor local police forces in an UNPOL mission effectively. The United Nations Police Monitoring, Mentoring and Advising in Peace Operations Manual (2017) is an excellent resource. Much of the ideas and concepts of mentoring contained in the 2017 manual were contained in the 2004 Standard Operating Procedures for the MINUSTAH UNPOL mission. Based on my experiences, the strategic vision at the highest levels is very good. But there is a serious disconnect that prevents the translation of that strategic vision into effective applications at the local level. There needs to be stronger and more consistent middle management to ensure that the mission strategies are operationalized at the region and station levels.

References

Baranyi, S. (2019). Second-generation SSR or unending violence in Haiti? *Stability: International Journal of Security & Development, 8*(1), 1–19.

Bayley, D. (2001). *Democratizing the police abroad: What to do and how to do it.* US Department of Justice, Office of Justice Programs.

Bayley, D. (2006). *Changing of the guard: Developing democratic police abroad.* Oxford University Press.

Belo, N., Koenig, M., & Everett, S. (2011). *Institutionalizing community policing in Timor-Leste: Exploring the politics of police reform.* The Asia Foundation.

Call, C. (2003). *Challenges in police reform: Promoting effectiveness and accountability.* International Peace Academy.

Call, C., & Stanley, W. (2001). Protecting the people: Public security choices after civil wars. *Global Governance: A Review of Multilateralism and International Organizations, 7*(2), 152–172.

Caparini, M. (2014). *Capacity-building and development of host state police: The role of international police.* International Forum for the Challenges of Peace Operations.

Caparini, M. (2017). *Challenges in deploying effective police to international peace operations.* Norwegian Institute of International Affairs.

Castor, S., & Garafola, L. (1974). The American occupation of Haiti (1915–34) and the Dominican Republic (1916–24). *The Massachusetts Review, 15*(1/2), 253–275.

Ceïde, E. L. (2008). *Securing Peace in Haiti: An assessment of the United Nations Stabilization Mission in Haiti (MINUSTAH).* University of Tromsø.

Central Intelligence Agency. (2020, July 21). *Central intelligence agency – world fact book: Haiti.* Retrieved from Central Intelligence Agency: https://www.cia.gov/library/publications/the-world-factbook/geos/ha.html

Chance, L. (2007). *Haiti: risk, conflict and sustainable change.* Retrieved from Alterpress.com: https://www.alterpresse.org/spip.php?rubrique35

Crane, K., Dobbins, J., Miller, L., Ries, C., Chivvis, C., & Haims, M. (2010). *Building a more resilient Haitian State.* Rand Corporation National Security Research Division.

de Saint-Claire, S. (2007). The significance, role and impact of UN police in peace operation: Regarding transnational crime, peacebuilding and normalization. .

Decaens, S. (2014). *Policing, peacekeeping and development: United Nations peacekeeping in Haiti* (Master's Thesis). Nova Scotia: Saint Mary's University.

Donais, T. (2011). Reforming the Haitian National Police: From stabilization to consolidation. In J. Heine & A. Thompson (Eds.), *Fixing Haiti: MINUSTAH and beyond* (pp. 97–114). United Nations University Press.

Dupuy, A. (2005). From Jean-Bertrand Aristide to Gerard Latortue: The unending crisis of democratization in Haiti. *Journal of Latin American Anthropology, 10*(1), 186–205.

Durch, W., & England, M. (2010). *Enhancing United Nations capacity to support post-conflict policing and rule of law* (revised). The Stimson Center.

Fatton, R. (2002). *Haiti's Predatory Republic: The unending transition to democracy*. Lynne Rienner Publishers.

Fatton, R. (2007). The fall of Aristide and Haiti's current predicament. In S. Shamsie & A. Thompson (Eds.), *Haiti: Hope for a Fragile State* (pp. 15–24). Wilfrid Laurier University Press.

Gerspacher, N. (2012). *Special report 312: Preparing advisers for capacity-building missions*. The United States Institute of Peace.

Hansford, B. (2006). UN police strive for quality over quantity as role changes. *UN Police Magazine*, 8–9.

Hårleman, C. (2003). *An introduction to the UN system: Orientation for serving on a UN field mission*. United Nations Institute for Training and Research, Programme of Correspondence Instruction..

Heine, J., & Manigat, L. (1988). *The Caribbean and world politics: Cross currents and cleavages*. Holmes and Meier.

Heine, J., & Thakur, R. (2010). *The dark side of globalization*. United Nations University Press.

Heine, J., & Thompson, A. (2011). Introduction: Haiti's governance challenges and the international. In J. Heine & A. Thompson (Eds.), *Fixing Haiti: MINUSTAH and beyond* (pp. 1–24). United Nations University Press.

International Crisis Group. (2008). *Reforming Haiti's Security Sector, Latin America/Caribbean Report 28*. International Crisis Group. Retrieved from https://d2071andvip0wj.cloudfront.net/28-reforming-haiti-s-security-sector.pdf

Lemay-Hébert, N., & Koops, J. (2015). United Nations Stabilization Mission in Haiti (MINUSTAH). In J. Koops, J. A. Koops, N. MacQueen, T. Tardy, & P. Williams (Eds.), *The Oxford handbook of United Nations peacekeeping operations* (pp. 720–731). Oxford University Press.

Levine, D. (2008). *African civilian police capacity for international peacekeeping operations*. Henry L. Stimson Center.

Meharg, S., & Arnusch, A. (2010). *Security sector reform: A case study approach to transition and capacity building*. Strategic Studies Institute.

Mobekk, E. (2005). *Identifying lessons in United Nations international policing missions*. Geneva Centre for the Democratic Control of Armed Forces.

Monk, R. (2008). *End of mission report of the seventh police commissioner of the United Nations international police in Kosovo*. This is an unpublished report and was obtained from the author.

Ram, S. (2006). *The history of United Nations peacekeeping operations during the cold war: 1945 to 1987*. United Nations Institute for Training and Research, UNITAR POCI Dag Hammarskjöld Centre.

Rotmann, P. (2011). First steps towards a police doctrine for UN peace operations (2001–2006). *Policing and Society: An International Journal of Research and Policy, 21*(1), 84–95.

Sanchez, M. (2011). *An analysis of administrative policies and procedures of the United Nations Mission in Kosovo International Police* (Master's Capstone Project). Utica College.

Sanchez, M. (2015). Coordinating police responses to critical events in United Nations Mission Areas. In J. Albrecht, M. Dow, & D. D. Plecas (Eds.), *Policing major events: USA perspectives from around the world* (pp. 151–177). CRC Press.

Sanchez, M. (2018). *United Nations international police officers in peacekeeping missions: A phenomenological exploration of complex acculturation*. Routledge.

Silander, D. (2009). The United Nations and peace building: Lessons from the UN transitional administrations in East Timor and Kosovo. *Social Alternatives, 28*(2), 23–28.

Smith, J., Holt, V., & Durch, W. (2007). *From Timor-Leste to Darfur: New initiatives for enhancing UN civilian policing capacity*. The Stimson Center.

United Nations. (2000). *About the United Nations*. Retrieved from United Nations: http://www.un.org/aboutun/history.htm

United Nations Department of Peacekeeping Operations. (2007). *Guidelines for United Nations police officer on assignment with peacekeeping operations*. United Nations Department of Peacekeeping Operations.

United Nations Department of Peacekeeping Operations. (2009). *UN Peacekeeping PDT standards, specialized training material for police: Mentoring and advising*. United Nations Department of Peacekeeping Operations.

United Nations Department of Peacekeeping Operations. (2017). *Police monitoring, mentoring and advising in peace operations*. United Nations Department of Peacekeeping Operations.

United Nations Security Council. (1999). *United Nations Security Council Resolution 1244*. United Nations Security Council.

United Nations Security Council. (2004). *United Nations Security Council Resolution 1529*. United Nations Security Council.

United Nations Security Council. (2016). *United Nations Security Council Resolution 2282*. United Nations Security Council.

United Nations Stabilization Mission in Haiti. (2004). *Standard operating procedures for MINUSTAH civilian police officers*. United Nations Department of Peacekeeping Operations.

Part VI
International Police Peacekeeper Perspectives from the Field

Chapter 12
Complex Acculturation – The Hidden Cultural Challenge in United Nations Police Missions

Michael Raymond Sanchez

Introduction

Serving as an international police officer for the United Nations (UN) in a UN peacekeeping mission is a very challenging assignment. The United Nations Police (UNPOL) officer is a domestic police officer in his or her home country, who is temporarily assigned to the United Nations to assist in peacekeeping operations. The UNPOL officer is deployed by the UN to a foreign country to assist the United Nations in bringing stability and democratic police reform to a post-conflict nation, or to bring peace and stability to unstable regions. The challenges of working to bring peace and order out of chaos are innumerable.

UNPOL missions consist of UNPOL officers from every inhabited continent on the earth. UNPOL officers represent every conceivable culture, ethnicity, region, religion, governmental system, and level of economic attainment. Each UNPOL organization is a melting pot comprised of police officers from dozens of different nations.

The United Nations provides extensive training to new UNPOL officers regarding the societal, cultural, and religious norms of the population and society of the host nation, where the peacekeeping mission is working. However, it is interesting to note that the United Nations has never seemed to address the fact that UNPOL missions are hyper-diverse organizations with police officers from all over the world who are required to work together. UNPOL officers never receive cross-cultural training on how to ***work together*** effectively.

The cross-cultural challenges of dealing with perhaps two competing cultures in a post-conflict region would seem to pale in comparison to having to work in a unit with police officers with dozens of different cultures, religious, communication

M. R. Sanchez (✉)
University of Texas Rio Grande Valley, Los Fresnos, TX, USA
e-mail: michael.sanchex@untrgv.edu

G. den Heyer, J. F. Albrecht (eds.), *Police and International Peacekeeping Missions*, https://doi.org/10.1007/978-3-030-77900-9_12

paradigms, policing philosophies, national leadership philosophies, and levels of police training. This chapter explores the idea that perhaps the most challenging factor of an UNPOL mission is the diversity of the UNPOL organization itself. UNPOL officers must navigate a kaleidoscope of swirling and competing cultural norms while finding a way to achieve the UNPOL mission's mandate. All without the benefit of training on how to work effectively in such a diverse organization. Could this be the hidden cultural challenge of serving as an UNPOL officer that has heretofore been overlooked? Could the amount of cross-cultural dissonance that attends such hyper-diversity inhibit the efficiency and effectiveness of an UNPOL mission?

Overview of United Nations Police

The United Nations was founded on 24 October 1945, when the United Nations Charter was ratified by the United States, China, France, Russia, and the United Kingdom (United Nations, 2000). The United Nations was founded on the principle of assuring world peace through the concept of collective security. If any United Nations member state is invaded or attacked by another state, the collective power of United Nations member states will be brought to bear on the aggressor. Occasions in which the United Nations intercedes in an intrastate or interstate conflict are known as *peacekeeping missions*. The element of the United Nations that is charged with guarding international peace and security is the United Nations Security Council. Peacekeeping missions are launched under the authorization of the United Nations Security Council through a Security Council Resolution (UNSCR) (Ram, 2006).

The first United Nations Peacekeeping mission was deployed to Palestine in 1948. A peacekeeping mission can take many different forms. A peacekeeping mission can involve military intervention, the placing of United Nations troops between warring parties as a buffer, and in post-conflict security, stabilization, democratization, and development. The exact nature of each United Nations Peacekeeping mission is entirely dependent on the nature of the conflict, unrest, or instability that brought about the need for international intervention. From 1948 to 2020, the United Nations has engaged in at least 70 peacekeeping missions around the world (DPKO, 2020).

In 1960, the United Nations began including a police component as a part of the United Nations Operation in the Congo (Mobekk, 2005). Initial police components to peacekeeping missions were tasked with *monitoring* local police. The concept behind a monitoring mission was that the United Nations would deploy experienced police officers to monitor and observe the organic police forces in the mission area.

The presence of United Nations Police Officers (UNPOL)[1] served two purposes. It was believed that organic police forces would refrain from engaging in human rights abuses in the presence of an international observer force. Second, the UNPOL component could report any observed violations to the United Nations (Levine, 2008).

The concept of the UNPOL monitoring missions was a failure. In almost all cases, any organic police force would simply refrain from violating human rights in the presence of the UNPOL monitors. Once the monitors left, the organic police officers would revert to their previous behaviors. UNPOL monitoring of organic police did not create a fundamental change in the organic police behavior (Sanchez, 2018).

Creating some change and reform in organic police in a post-conflict or unstable region is extremely important to the ultimate success of a peacekeeping mission. In many oppressed, undemocratic, and unstable societies, the police are a primary agent of oppression. It is well-nigh impossible to stabilize or democratize a post-conflict, unstable, or oppressed region without accomplishing democratic reform of the organic police (Bayley, 2006; Durch & England, 2010).

The Modern Era of Peacekeeping

The role of the UNPOL officer evolved significantly in 1999 with the creation of the United Nations Transitional Administration in East Timor (UNTAET) and the United Nations Interim Administration Mission in Kosovo (UNMIK). These two missions represent the start of the fourth generation, or the *modern era* of peacekeeping missions for the United Nations (Silander, 2009). Modern UNPOL missions engage in activities such as training, mentoring, and capacity building of the organic police forces in the mission area. In other words, the modern UNPOL missions are not only focused on protecting civilians from human rights abuses through monitoring but also tasked with overseeing and instilling democratic reform into the organic police forces. Additionally, UNPOL missions can engage in training, organizing, assisting, vetting, and even mentoring organic police officers at all levels. The UNPOL component of modern peacekeeping mission is now recognized as a critical element in providing lasting democratic reform to an unstable region (Smith et al., 2007).

Along with the expanded tasking and responsibilities came increased manpower. Modern UNPOL missions are far more robust than previous generations of peacekeeping missions (Hårleman, 2003). The UNMIK mission had an authorized strength of 4718 UNPOL officers and the UNTAET mission had 1640 authorized UNPOL officers. In 1998 there was approximately 3000 UNPOL officers deployed in various peacekeeping missions around the world. By 2010, the number of

[1] United Nations Police Officers were initially called CIVPOLs for Civilian Police. This designation was changed to UNPOL in 2005. For the sake of clarity, I will use the current term UNPOL throughout.

deployed UNPOL officers had increased exponentially to more than 13,500 UNPOLs, representing 87 different nations serving in 13 different peacekeeping missions around the world (Rotmann, 2011).

In addition to the inclusion of democratic reform and capacity building duties, UNPOL officers serving in the UNTAET and UNMIK missions were granted executive authority, the authority to actually enforce the law within the mission country. The addition of executive authority was a huge undertaking in giving UNPOL officers the authority to create real change (de Saint-Claire, 2007). In monitoring missions, UNPOL officers had absolutely no authority. If an UNPOL monitor were to observe two police officers raping a civilian, the UNPOL officer's only recourse would be to report the incident. Such situations create extreme frustration for UNPOL officers and embolden organic police to commit further abuses. Additionally, the public who is supposed to be safer with the presence of the United Nations condemns the UNPOL officer who can only stand and watch a human rights abuse take place. With executive authority, an UNPOL officer has the legal standing to intervene and take the offending officers into custody.

The inclusion of executive authority in an UNPOL mission changed the very nature of the UNPOL officer. The UNPOL was no longer a security guard who would *observe and report.* The UNPOL was able to function as a police officer. UNPOL officers with executive authority have the ability to conduct criminal investigations, file criminal charges, and arrest offenders (Silander, 2009). The UNPOL officer now had the authority and the standing to create real change.

In addition to local crime, UNPOL missions also assisted organic police forces in setting up mechanisms to detect, track, and fight transnational crime. A post-conflict nation or unstable region of the world is an attractive home or way station for transnational criminals. A region that is in political chaos rarely has the resources to fight transnational crime. Countries and regions that are frequently the target for United Nations Peacekeeping missions are also attractive targets for transnational crime. Crimes such as narcotics trafficking, the trafficking of human beings, and violent extremist groups gravitate toward unstable regions (Heine & Thakur, 2010). The modern UNPOL mission focuses on assisting the organic police forces in developing police capacity to address and fight transnational crime (United Nations Security Council, 2016).

UNPOL Mission Mandates

United Nations Peacekeeping missions are authorized by United Nations Security Council Resolutions (UNSCR). A UNSCR lays out the structure and scope of a peacekeeping mission, including the goals (called a mandate) for the police component. The mandate of an UNPOL mission can be remarkably broad and succinct. The overarching goals are contained in the mandate. The method and manner of precisely *how* that mandate will be achieved is left to the Department of Peacekeeping Operations and the mission's management officers. For example, the mission mandate for the UNMIK Police was comprised of a single sentence. According to UNSCR 1244, which authorized the UNMIK mission and the UNMIK Police, the UNMIK Police were responsible for "...maintaining civil law and order, including establishing local police forces and meanwhile through the deployment of international police personnel to serve in Kosovo" (UNSCR 1244, 1999, p. 4).

The mandate for UNMIK included serving as the de-facto police for Kosovo enforcing laws, conducting investigations, manning the borders, and every other function of a full-service police agency. The UNMIK Police was also tasked with organizing, planning, recruiting, vetting, training, supporting, and mentoring an organic police force, quite literally from the ashes of the former Yugoslavia. In the pursuit of this mandate, the UNMIK Police worked first as trainers, then as mentors, then as partners, and ultimately as advisors to the Kosovo Police. These duties were very challenging and required considerable and constant interaction between UNPOL officers and the Kosovo Police.

Each UNPOL mission has a completely different mandate, as the goals of a peacekeeping operation are entirely dependent on the situation in the target country or region. For example, the mission mandate for the *Mission des Nations Unies pour la stabilisation en Haïti* (MINUSTAH) police component was not charged with creating a police force from scratch, as in Kosovo. When the MINUSTAH mission was authorized, Haiti was and had been a sovereign nation with an existent police force. While Haiti was experiencing political and social instability, the MINUSTAH police's mandate was geared more toward mentoring, supporting, training, and assisting the MINUSTAH police. The MINUSTAH mission was authorized by UNSCR #1529 in 2004. Item #2, paragraph *c* of UNSCR 1529 requires the MINSTAH UNPOL to "... facilitate the provision of international assistance to the Haitian police and the Haitian Coast Guard in order to establish and maintain public safety and law and order and to promote and protect human rights"; (UNSCR 1529, 2004, p. 2). MINUSTAH is what is known as a *development and capacity building mission.* While each mission has a unique set of circumstances, and is unique in its precise composition, much of an UNPOL officer's duties are similar, and all of an UNPOL officer's duties require communication and interaction with others.

Staffing of UNPOL Missions

A United Nations Police force is not an organic police force as one might think. Rather, an UNPOL force is comprised of police officers from many different nations. UNPOL organizations are unusual in that they are highly diverse. An UNPOL police force consists of police officers from United Nations member states known as *Police Contributing Countries.* In a process known as *secondment,* police officers are placed on temporary duty with the United Nations, to serve in an UNPOL mission. The police officers are paid by their home police organization, but are provided with a per diem called a *Mission Subsistence Allowance* by the United Nations (Sanchez, 2011).

UNMIK			MINUSTAH			UNAMID (Darfur, Sudan)		
Argentina	Hungary	Portugal	Bangladesh	Guinea	Romania	Bangladesh	Jordan	Senegal
Austria	India	Romania	Benin	India	Russian	Brazil	Kyrgyzstan	Sierra Leone
Bangladesh	Italy	Russia	Brazil	Indonesia	Federation	Burkina	Madagascar	Tajikistan
Brazil	Jordan	Slovenia	Burkina	Jordan	Rwanda	Faso	Malawi	Thailand
Bulgaria	Kenya	Spain	Faso	Madagascar	Senegal	Cameroon	Mongolia	Togo
China	Kyrgyzstan	Switzerland	Cameroon	Mali	Slovakia	Djibouti	Namibia	Tunisia
Croatia	Lithuania	Sweden	Canada	Nepal	Spain	Egypt	Nepal	Turkey
Czech	Malawi	East Timor	Chad	Niger	Sri Lanka	Ethiopia	Nigeria	Tanzania
Republic	Nepal	Turkey	Colombia	Nigeria	Sweden	Fiji	Pakistan	Zambia
Denmark	Netherlands	Uganda	Djibouti	Norway	Togo	Gambia	Rwanda	Zimbabwe
Egypt	Nigeria	UK	El Salvador	Pakistan	Tunisia	Ghana	Samoa	
Finland	Norway	Ukraine	Ethiopia	Philippines	Turkey	Indonesia		
France	Pakistan	United	France	Portugal	USA			
Germany	Philippines	States	Germany		Uruguay			
Ghana	Poland	Zambia						
Greece		Zimbabwe						
Adapted from UNMIK Police personnel report (June 2008).			*Source: United Nations Peacekeeping, 2017.*			*(United Nations Police, 2019)*		

Fig. 12.1 Police Contributing Countries for the UNMIK, MINUSTAH, and UNAMID police missions

As of 30 June 2020, there are 72 Police Contributing Countries seconding their police officers to the United Nations for UNPOL missions (United Nations Police, 2019). Not all Police Contributing Countries second police officers to every UNPOL mission. Rather, Police Contributing Countries generally only send police to UNPOL missions in which the contributing country has a particular political or human interest (Sanchez, 2011).

The composition of each UNPOL mission, as pertains not only to duties and mandate but also to national composition, is unique. The uniqueness of the national composition of each UNPOL mission can be observed by comparing the nations providing police officers to different UNPOL missions in Fig. 12.1. While the overarching goals of all UNPOL missions are similar, each mission is also unique in its staffing, national balance, contributing countries, mandate, and individual duties.

UNPOL Officer Duties

Depending on the mission, UNPOL officers can engage is a wide variety of duties from administrative support to police patrol, from investigations to border check points, from police academy instructor to police mentor in the field. There is a broad array of duties, both direct and in support, that help an UNPOL mission pursue the completion of its mandate. Perhaps the most common UNPOL duty would be the mentoring and capacity building of organic police forces in the mission area. This mentoring can be accomplished through training at the police academy, meetings and guidance for mid-level managers, or actually patrolling with the organic police officers providing them with guidance and mentorship.

In 2017, the United Nations published the Police Monitoring, Mentoring and Advising in Peace Operations manual. This manual outlines the duties and expectations of UNPOL Monitors, Mentors, Advisors, and Mission Leadership in peacekeeping missions. The main duties of UNPOL officers around the world will be synopsized to provide an understanding of the challenges of the role of an UNPOL officer (UN-DPKO, 2017).

Monitoring

While the modern era of peacekeeping is geared more toward democratic police reform, there are still some monitoring duties in peacekeeping missions. UNPOL officers can be engaged in human rights monitoring, the watching of an organic police force in order to identify and report human rights violations. Monitors can also be tasked as *performance monitors.* A performance monitor observes the host state's organic police to ascertain their performance in key areas. Performance monitors may evaluate internal processes, policies and procedures, training and administration, budgeting and procurement, or any other critical process as identified in the mission mandate. The goal of the performance monitor is to ascertain the amount of progress made by the organic police force and to prepare recommendations for adjustment to be made to further progress and achievement (UN-DPKO, 2017).

Human rights monitoring and performance monitoring are labor-intensive as they both require that UNPOL officers spend a lot of time in the host nation's organic police force's operational area. Monitoring is most effective when it is accomplished over time and with broad coverage. Monitoring missions, regardless of the type, rely on *teams* of UNPOL monitors who coordinate, collaborate, and compare their observations. In addition, in order to get an accurate view of either the security situation or the performance of a particular organic police force, the UNPOL monitors must be very engaged with the organic police components that are being assessed. The United Nations strongly recommends that UNPOL monitors do everything possible to engage stakeholders during a monitoring mission (UN-DPKO, 2017).

Mentoring

An UNPOL mentor is defined as an "...experienced and competent professional from a police-contributing country who supports his/her host-State counterpart(s) ('mentees') in their professional and personal development (UN-DPKO, 2017, p. 12)." The mentoring relationship is one where the UNPOL mentor works with and shadows his or her mentee in the organic police force. The UNPOL mentor is expected to use his or her experience and expertise to guide and develop the mentee. The main goals of this mentoring process would be: (1) to provide development and professional growth for the mentee, (2) to motivate the mentee to accept the guidance and to *want* to operationalize the democratic reform process, and (3) to have the mentee contribute to an overall improvement of the delivery of police services in the host country organic police force (UN-DPKO, 2017). This broad-based reform when collectivized is called *capacity building.*

The UNPOL mentor must be an outstanding communicator, because the mentoring relationship depends on being able to cooperate, collaborate, and communicate effectively with the host country mentees assigned to the UNPOL mentor. UNPOL mentors must be able to motivate their mentees to change, which can be difficult. This process requires not only excellent communication skills but also excellent cultural intelligence. The cross-cultural nature of the UNPOL mentoring relationship can be particularly challenging.

As with the UNPOL monitor, UNPOL mentors do not work in a vacuum. Generally, UNPOL mentors work in teams. These teams either work with different officers, in different divisions (according to the UNPOL's particular area of expertise), on different shifts, or in different stations. However, since the ultimate goal is capacity building, the mentoring process must be a *collective* process (UN-DPKO, 2017). UNPOL mentors must share notes, communicate, identify common areas of strength or weakness in their mentees, and then develop remedies to provide a systemic approach to individual mentoring that provides a collectivist approach that is necessary to achieve organizational capacity building. In short, UNPOL monitors and mentors must work well together toward their common goal.

Advisors

UNPOL advisors work at the strategic level of the host country organic police force. Advisors work toward providing democratic police reform in an overarching and strategic manner, rather than the on-the-ground guidance provided by the UNPOL mentor. The role of the UNPOL advisor is critical to the success of the mission. All of the line-level capacity building accomplished will not be lasting if the host country's organic police hierarchy has not adjusted its mentality, approach, policy, and strategic vision concurrent with the changes taking place on the ground (UN-DPKO, 2017). Lasting change requires input from all of the major stakeholders and policy makers in a police organization.

The role of the UNPOL advisor is all the more challenging because there are overarching political, cultural, and national concerns that must be addressed. The effective UNPOL advisor is not only a police expert, an excellent communicator, with strong cultural intelligence, he or she must also be a diplomat and a pragmatist. As with all UNPOL functions that interface with the host country's police forces, UNPOL advisors work in teams. Effective communication, coordination, and collaboration at the UNPOL advisor level is particularly essential to effective capacity building. As UNPOL advisors encourage the adjustment of strategic vision, police, and approach, their efforts must be coordinated so as to provide consistent conceptualization of the strategic changes across the board. If every UNPOL advisor did their own thing, there would be dozens of different approaches that would create extreme operational dissonance.

One of the key elements of democratic police reform is to help the police culture of the host country's organic police force to evolve into a policing concept and culture that is in line with democratic policing norms. This type of change is an intangible change that cannot be made at the ground level. A force-wide evolution of policing culture must necessarily come from the top down (Monk, 2008). The UNPOL advisor is a key element in creating this evolutionary process.

Mission Support and Leadership

In addition to the UNPOL officers who interface with the host country's police forces, UNPOL missions also have mission leadership and support personnel, whose duties are to keep the UNPOL mission itself functioning smoothly. UNPOL missions must have a training center, administrative center, information technology services, logistics and supply, inspection and audit, and a multitude of other services required to operate and organization. While UNPOL support officers do not work directly with the host country's police, they do work with each other and must be effective in collaboration and cooperation.

Cultural Training in UNPOL Missions

In the training course entitled *United Nations Civilian Police: Restoring Civil Order Following Hostilities,* the subject of cultural awareness for UNPOL officers is addressed by the following: "UN Civilian Police Officers must display a thorough understanding of the differences between their own national culture and economic background and those of the host nation" (Heepen & Freisleben, 2005, p. 34). Indeed, the ability to work and communicate effectively is an integral part of being an effective UNPOL officer. However, there is a cultural element to being an UNPOL officer that has a much greater effect on the overall effectiveness and efficiency of an UNPOL mission.

Pre-deployment training courses each have blocks of training on the respective cultures of the local people in the deployment area. Upon arrival in mission, all UNPOL officers attend approximately 7 days (it varies from mission to mission) of induction training, which is designed to prepare the new UNPOL officer for the realities of participating in an UNPOL mission. Subjects in induction training vary from mission to mission; however, there are some training topics that are universal. A training block on the culture of the host nation is one such block of training that all UNPOL induction courses contain. The ability to understand, adapt, and work well with the host country organic police in the cross-cultural sense is very important.

UNPOL Mission Effectiveness

In the 19 months that I served as the Director of Personnel and Administration,[2] I came to see that there was an inherent inefficiency to the UNMIK Police. For the most part, most countries sent good qualified police officers to the UNMIK Police, yet there seemed to be a consistent pattern of slow performance. Positive changes and beneficial programs marked progress in the UNMIK mission, but implementation and progress always seemed sluggish.

I left the UNMIK Police in December of 2008, when the police mission was handed over to the European Union. In addition, I served 1 year in the MINUSTAH mission in Haiti, ultimately as the Regional Commander for the MINUSTAH Police in Les Cayes. I noted the same lack of efficiency and slow performance that I had noted in the UNMIK mission.

Thorough research has revealed that since the 1990s, and the advent of the modern era of peacekeeping, UNPOL missions have consistently been described as ineffective, inefficient, or demonstrative of overall poor performance in the pursuit of their mandate (Greener, 2012; Kearney et al., 2011; Monk, 2008; Scheye, 2008). These observations were made by both researchers and UNPOL mission executives. Moreover, one study of UNPOL missions determined that 57 percent of UNPOL missions could be classified as having failed to achieve their mandate in full or in part (Çelik & Çetin, 2013).

Expatriate Acculturation

There has been considerable research into expatriate worker acculturation (also called cross-cultural adjustment, expatriate adjustment, and intercultural adaptation). Expatriate workers are employees who are sent overseas to work in foreign offices for their company or organization (Firth et al., 2014).

Existing research indicated that expatriate workers have considerable difficulties adjusting to the cultural differences in their assignment country (Okpara & Kabongo, 2011). Take as a hypothetical example, an American worker who is sent to Tokyo to work in a satellite office must adjust to Japanese societal culture and norms, Japanese work culture, and Japanese office culture. Depending on the country of assignment, the differences from the expatriate's heritage culture could be considerable.

There is an extensive body of research exploring the difficulties of expatriate acculturation. The success or failure of an expatriate worker in an international assignment is clearly tied to the expatriate's ability to adjust to the societal, work,

---

[2] I was deployed as an UNPOL officer to the UNMIK mission in Kosovo in December of 2005. In May of 2007, after having served as an investigator on a counter-terrorism task force, an international police instructor in the police training center, and deputy chief of the police training center, I was promoted to the Director of Personnel and Administration.

and office cultures of their assignment country (Firth et al., 2014; Koveshnikov et al., 2013). Research into quantifying the failure rates of expatriate workers is somewhat inconsistent. This is primarily because there are many different interpretations of what constitutes the *failure* of an expatriate worker's assignment. Josien (2012) estimated that between 25 and 40 percent of expatriate workers failed in their assignments due to an inability to adjust.

UNPOL Adjustment

The idea that an expatriate worker will experience difficulty with an international assignment due to an inability to adjust culturally to the host nation is both intuitive and borne out by research. Could the concept of expatriate acculturation apply to UNPOL officers? Could this be the problem behind the chronic inefficiency of UNPOL missions? This seemed possible, but there are a few critical differences between an expatriate assignment and an UNPOL mission. A careful analysis of expatriate assignment and an UNPOL mission revealed both similarities and distinct differences between them.

UNPOL Officers Are in Fact Expatriate Workers

The classification of expatriate workers includes both private sector *and* public sector employees. Foreign service employees working in embassies around the world would be an example of public sector expatriate workers. As domestic police officers temporarily assigned to the United Nations for peacekeeping duties, UNPOL officers would fit the definition of public sector expatriate workers.

Training Both private and public sector expatriate workers receive training pertaining to the cultural norms of their assignment country. Much of the research into expatriate acculturation in the private sector pertained to identifying training methods to prepare expatriate workers for the cultural dissonance of their assignment. UNPOL officers also receive cultural and historical training, to understand the intercultural dynamics of the country to which they are going to be assigned.

Societal culture Public and private expatriate workers, including UNPOL officers, must adjust to a new societal culture. Like other expatriate workers, UNPOL officers live in the host nation *on the economy,* meaning they must rent residential accommodation, obtain utilities, shop for food, patronize restaurants, etc. In this regard, an UNPOL officer must learn to adjust to the host nation's societal culture in much the same way as other expatriate workers (Black, 1988).

Workplace culture Exploring the dimension of workplace culture was where the true root of the differences between an UNPOL mission and other expatriate assignments was identified. The hypothetical American expatriate worker who is assigned to Tokyo must be able to adapt to Japanese workplace and office culture. In other words, an expatriate worker must adjust to *a single* new culture.

A United Nations police force is a fully homogenous and integrated organization. National groups, known as *contingents,* deploy to an UNPOL mission en masse and attend induction training together, or in combination with one or two other contingents. After induction training, the UNPOL officers are assigned to a job and a location where the mission needs their particular skill set. Any unit in an UNPOL mission will contain UNPOL officers from dozens of different countries.

A new UNPOL officer deploying to a United Nations peacekeeping mission does not have to adjust to a single new workplace culture like the expatriate worker. The UNPOL officer must adjust to literally *dozens* of conflicting and competing cultures. For example, looking back to Fig. 12.1, it is clear to see that the cultural mixture of an UNPOL mission covers the entire spectrum of religions, societal culture, governmental systems, and policing philosophy, as well as every conceivable level of economic attainment. An UNPOL mission is truly a *hyper-diverse* environment.

An UNPOL officer assigned to his or her first mission is confronted with a cacophonous kaleidoscope of cultural dissonance. Simple interactions between UNPOL officers can be a minefield of cultural communication norms (Sanchez, 2016). For example, when I was first deployed to the UNMIK Police, I was talking with a British UNPOL. As it was getting close to end of duty, I told the officer "…I will fill you in tomorrow for sure," meaning I would finish telling him tomorrow. The officer suddenly jumped up in my face and got very aggressive. I was shocked.

I tried to de-escalate, but he was suddenly violently angry at me. I got out of the situation with some difficulty and later found that in British vernacular, "…fill you in…" means "beat you up." So, what I was saying was "…I will finish giving you the details tomorrow. What the British officer heard was "I am going to kick your butt tomorrow," which explained his sudden demeanor. I quickly realized that the simple act of communication with my colleagues was going to be a major intercultural challenge.

A new United Nations police officer conveyed an interesting explanation of one's first experience in an UNPOL environment:

> First of all… when I landed, I didn't know what damn planet I was on. Not only my first time out of the country, but my first time in that kind of environment. You know, being around strange people who I never was around before. So, the whole thing was not traumatic, but it certainly was… difficult. (Sanchez, 2016, p. 94)

The Missing Link

It now seems as though the problems in UNPOL missions might be rooted in *culture.* UNPOL officers receive training on how to deal with the societal culture of their assignment country. This makes sense. But the missing element of pre-deployment preparation is that prospective UNPOL officers *never* receive training on how to communicate, collaborate, and function effectively *with each other.*

If the requirement of adjusting to a single new culture is so challenging that 25–40 percent of expatriate workers fail at their assignment, due to an inability to acculturate to *one* culture, then having to adjust to *dozens* of different cultures *simultaneously* would seem to be exponentially more difficult. It might very well be possible that the cultural dissonance generated by all of these broadly different cultures trying to work in unison in an UNPOL mission could absorb so much time and effort, that the UNPOL officers would have considerably less time or energy for operational matters.

The idea that there is a considerable difference in difficulty between the expatriate worker and the UNPOL officer, as pertains to their respective intercultural challenges, has never been explored, or even identified. To this end, I have defined the standard expatriate paradigm of having to adjust to a single new culture as *simple acculturation.* I then defined the UNPOL paradigm of having to adjust to multiple cultures simultaneously as *complex acculturation* (Sanchez, 2016). I advanced to a phenomenological analysis designed to define and describe the phenomenon of complex acculturation. One cannot very well research complex acculturation if it has never been defined as a phenomenon through scholarly research.

The UNPOL Experience and Complex Acculturation

It was therefore critical to conduct a phenomenological exploration of complex acculturation in the context of an UNPOL officer on his or her first mission. The goal was to explore an UNPOL officer's first mission experience with an eye toward describing, defining, and modeling complex acculturation as a phenomenon. Once described, the complex acculturation paradigm was compared against the simple acculturation paradigm to ascertain if complex acculturation was a unique and individual phenomenon in its own right, as opposed to merely being a variation of simple acculturation.

The UNPOL Experience – First Mission

This research focused on UNPOL officers who had completed at least one complete mission. As quoted by one of the participants, a new UNPOL officer's sudden immersion into a hyper-diverse environment can be a shocking and disorienting experience. Communicational paradigms unique to each culture, expectations of others, policing philosophy and approach, concepts of leadership and followership all vary from culture to culture (Sanchez, 2016). When cultural paradigms clash, this is known as cultural dissonance. Cultural dissonance can occur as a result of any interaction. For example, at the UNMIK Police Training Center in Kosovo, where new UNPOL officers would undergo induction training, two contingents had deployed at the same time. When this occurred, the two national contingents would attend induction training together.

On one occasion, it was the dead of winter in Kosovo and snowing. We had one contingent from an equatorial region and the other contingent was from a Nordic region. These two groups experienced considerable cultural dissonance over something as simple as environmental conditions. The equatorial contingent was not used to the cold, so they were suffering. These officers cranked all the heaters in the classroom to maximum, which made them more comfortable. Now the Nordic officers were suffering. At the first break, the Nordic officers turned off the heaters and threw open the windows for some "fresh air. Now the equatorial contingent was suffering. So, it went back and forth. By the second day, there was considerable tension between the groups. A compromise as to the room temperature had to be imposed, which did not please either group.

Four stages of the complex acculturation process have been identified. These stages are the initial stage, the decision stage, the cultural engagement stage, and the refinement stage. These stages vary when an UNPOL officer is unsuccessful in negotiating a particular stage (Sanchez, 2016). Each stage, and sub-stage, will be described briefly below.

The Initial Stage As with an expatriate worker, a new UNPOL officer finds themselves in a foreign land with a different societal culture. At the workplace, the UNPOL experience diverges from that of the expatriate worker. Once induction training is completed, UNPOL officers are assigned a specific role and duty station in accordance with their particular skill sets and the needs of the mission. Since UNPOL missions are fully integrated, national groups are not deployed in a group, but are deployed to individual positions throughout the mission. The first unit to which a new UNPOL officer is deployed will generally have from 5 to 15 different nationalities in the unit (Sanchez, 2016).

Whereas the expatriate worker is faced with a single new culture, the new UNPOL officer is suddenly immersed in an environment with many different cultures. The UNPOL environment is all the more complex because there is no overarching or dominant culture. All of the cultures in an UNPOL mission combine to make an institutional culture that is transcultural, or an organizational culture that is an amalgamation of all the cultures present, called *hyper-diversity*. The participants in my research found their initial exposure to a hyper-diverse environment to be disorienting and stressful (Sanchez, 2016).

One participant described the experience as "You will be dealing with different nationalities, some of them you even didn't know they existed..." (Sanchez, 2016, p. 97). The participants were unanimous that their initial immersion into the hyper-diversity of the UNPOL mission was culturally disorienting and confusing. As noted earlier, intercultural communication with others whose cultural paradigms are unknown to you can be a minefield of misunderstanding and misinterpretation.

The Decision Stage Once the shock of the sudden immersion into hyper-diversity wears off, the UNPOL officer must decide how he or she is going to handle the stress of this new environment. The decision appears to be binary, and many times, the decision is subconscious. Either the officer is going to commit him or herself to engaging in the next stage, cultural engagement, or the UNPOL officer will decide to compartmentalize (Sanchez, 2016).

If an UNPOL officer compartmentalizes, they either seek out closed groups of other UNPOLs of similar cultural backgrounds, or they isolate themselves. If the UNPOL officer selects closed groups, the officer avoids contact with UNPOLs from other cultures and makes every effort to work with and socialize only with other UNPOLs from the same or very similar culture as compared to the UNPOL officer's heritage culture. An UNPOL officer who seeks out closed groups will be marginally functional in the mission, but only in a limited sense and only with duties that can be undertaken in concert with other members of the closed group (Sanchez, 2016).

If the UNPOL officer is unable to function even in closed groups, the UNPOL officer will isolate him or herself from every other UNPOL. When an UNPOL officer resorts to isolation, the officer becomes nonfunctional in the mission. The officer may still attempt to perform his or her duties, but by isolating him or herself; the isolated UNPOL is not effective. The UNPOL who self-isolates usually wound up ending mission and going home or was sent home by his or her contingent (Sanchez, 2016).

The Cultural Engagement Stage UNPOL officers who make the conscious effort to culturally engage with the hyper-diverse environment do so to learn and grow. Many UNPOL officers have described hyper-diverse social events such as going for coffee, dinner, or merely socializing with a mixed group at a colleague's accommodation. The cultural engagement stage starts out tentative, but as trusting interpersonal relationships with people from other cultures are formed, discussions evolve into deeper discussions (Sanchez, 2016).

As an example, when I was first re-deployed to the Police Training Center in Kosovo, I had the good fortune to share an office with an Egyptian police officer. We tentatively felt each other out, as is normal. After we got to know each other, we had some of the best conversations I ever experienced. We would have wide ranging discussions about religion, Islam, Christianity, Muslim culture, Western culture, etc.

In short, we were sharing and learning about each other's culture, which created ever-increasing cultural intelligence in each of us.

On a positive note, many UNPOL officers have indicated that the intercultural exchange of information was one of the highlights of their UNPOL experience. It was not enough to work in an exotic hyper-diverse environment. The participants universally enjoyed the process of learning and understanding other cultures (Sanchez, 2016).

The Refinement Stage One of the interesting elements unique to the UNPOL mission is that the intercultural atmosphere within every unit in the mission is dynamic and constantly changing. If an UNPOL officer is in a unit with UNPOL officers from the United States, Ghana, Russia, Bangladesh, Sweden, Timor Leste, and the Philippines, there is a unique transcultural environment in that unit, which is created by the interaction of all of these cultures. For example, after 2 months, the Russian UNPOL officer will get re-deployed to another job and the American officer will end his mission and go home. They are replaced with officers from Ukraine and Kenya. The intercultural dynamic changes because the components of the transcultural environment have changed. So, in an UNPOL mission, the cultural mixture is fluid and dynamic (Sanchez, 2016).

Once a new UNPOL officer opens his or her mind to creating cross-cultural communication and understanding, the remainder of the mission is spent refining that newfound sense of cultural intelligence. Each new cultural shift, or re-deployment of the UNPOL officer, which creates an entirely new intercultural dynamic, is addressed and the UNPOL officer's intercultural skills are constantly being refined. However, many UNPOL officers have conveyed that the cross-cultural dynamics of an international peacekeeping mission got easier for them as the mission went along. Also, subsequent UNPOL missions were much easier to navigate (Sanchez, 2016) (Fig. 12.2).

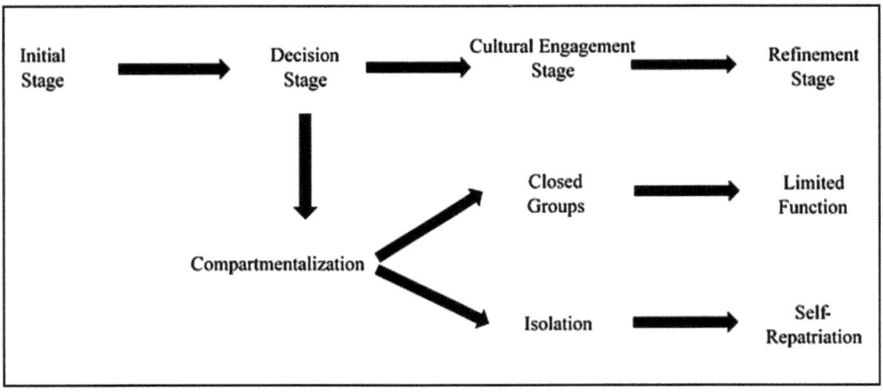

Fig. 12.2 Model of the four stages of complex acculturation (Sanchez, 2016, p. 107)

Sources of Cross-Cultural Conflict

In the hyper-diverse environment of an UNPOL mission, the potential sources of cross-cultural conflict and cultural dissonance are practically infinite. Some main areas that have been universally mentioned by UNPOL officers as areas of considerable cross-cultural conflict within an UNPOL mission are (Fig. 12.2):

Cross-Cultural Communication in an UNPOL Mission

Perhaps the most troublesome element, and the most perplexing for many UNPOL officers, was cross-cultural communication with other UNPOL officers. Although each UNPOL mission requires that all UNPOL officers speak the *mission language*, which is either English or French, non-native speakers tend to speak a second language retaining the cultural communication paradigms of their heritage language. Communication between UNPOL officers in a peacekeeping mission is far more complex and problematic than simply being understood. When communicating with people from different cultures, one must not only understand the words they are saying, but the *meaning* of those words in the context of *their* colleague's culture rather than their own.

For example, each UNPOL officer is given a performance evaluation twice per year. The Performance Appraisal Form (PAF) lists core competencies to be rated by the UNPOL officer's supervisor. One of the seemingly simplest core competencies is that of *Professionalism* (United Nations Mission in Kosovo, 2007).

So how does an UNPOL supervisor evaluate *professionalism?* Let us take two hypothetical UNPOL officers. One from a nation with a democratic police model and one from a nation with an autocratic police model. If you tell a police officer from a democratic nation to interview a subject, the officer will interview the subject, get a written statement from the subject, and write a report. If you tell a police officer from an autocratic nation to interview a subject, the officer will interview the subject and then wait for further instructions. If the supervisor is from a democratic nation and the officer is from an autocratic nation, the supervisor will say the officer is unprofessional because he did not take the initiative to get a statement and write a report. If the supervisor is from the autocratic nation and the officer from a democratic nation, the supervisor will say the officer is unprofessional because he did not wait for instructions, that the officer is a loose cannon doing whatever he wants without instruction. Both are right and both are wrong. I found that supervisors in UNPOL missions tended to assess their subordinates in the context of *their own* leadership culture, rather than in the context of the officer's national leadership culture. Something as simple as assessing professionalism in an UNPOL mission can be highly cultural and very difficult to define universally.

The second example involved a Regional Commander from a contingent from the Far East. The Regional Commander wanted to initiate an internal affairs investigation into an American UNPOL officer for gross insubordination and for insulting the Regional Commander. The Regional Commander said he had written proof of these transgressions. He then produced a printed email that the officer had sent to the Regional Commander. The first line of the email was highlighted. It said "Sir, I am not sure if you are aware of this, but an incident occurred last night in XXX village." Obviously it was difficult to understand what the problem was. The Regional Commander pointed to the highlighted statement. He finally said that by saying the Regional Commander did not know what was going on in his region, he had insulted the Regional Commander, which was gross insubordination. In the Regional Commander's culture, the autocratic nature of their leadership structure makes such a statement an insult and highly inappropriate. In American culture, such as statement is simply a preamble into explaining the incident. Even after explaining the UNPOL officer's intent, the Regional Commander *insisted* that the American officer be disciplined. One can only imagine how much energy is exerted by such communication-based cultural dissonance every day, in every unit, in every UNPOL mission.

Complex Acculturation and UNPOL Efficiency

It is possible to explore complex acculturation as a potential causal link to the chronic inefficiency in UNPOL missions. A qualitative analysis has been conducted by Sanchez (2016) that resulted in some interesting results.

At the unit level, interviewed UNPOL officers were unanimous in their assessment that much energy was expended and wasted in navigating the complex acculturation process and all of its cultural dissonance (Sanchez, 2016). There were constant interpersonal cross-cultural conflicts stemming from innumerable causes and sources.

Successfully negotiating the complex acculturation process, many UNPOL officers felt that they expended considerable energy in learning how to cope with hyperdiversity. Perhaps the most telling qualitative measurement was that all of them reported a marked and noticeable improvement in their own performance and their ability to cooperate and collaborate with other UNPOLs as they spent more time in the mission. Those UNPOL officers who served in more than one mission reported that they required almost no time to adjust to subsequent missions and that they were far more productive in those subsequent missions, even when the intercultural mixture was different. This would seem to indicate that cultural intelligence gained and refined through the complex acculturation process is retained and has a lasting effect on the UNPOL. The qualitative results clearly indicate that more research is needed to explore this question quantitatively (Sanchez, 2016).

Complex Acculturation as a Construct

It should now be determined if complex acculturation is a stand-alone construct, or a mere variant of the expatriate acculturation (simple acculturation) paradigm. Several key elements were identified that indicate that complex acculturation, as a psychological and cultural experience and as a phenomenon, is substantively different from the simple acculturation paradigm. Three main differences have been identified and will be delineated below.

No dominant subordinate relationship In the simple acculturation paradigm, there is a dominant and subordinate cultural relationship. In the hypothetical example of the American expatriate worker assigned to Tokyo, the American's heritage culture would be subordinate to the Japanese societal, workplace, and office culture. This hierarchical relationship would be understood by the expatriate worker. Management and understanding of the dominant/subordinate relationship between the two cultures would be a key element in adjusting to an expatriate assignment (Sanchez, 2016).

In an UNPOL mission, the complex acculturation paradigm, there is no dominant culture. If there is an organizational culture at all, it is a transcultural composite of the influences all of the cultures present in the particular unit. This culture would be different from unit to unit and UNPOL mission to UNPOL mission, as it is entirely dependent on the cross-cultural mixture of each particular unit or mission. Moreover, in UNPOL missions, the cross-cultural mixture is in a constant state of motion with the continuous coming and going as UNPOL officers get promoted, redeploy to different jobs, or leave the mission. All of these outcomes result in the UNPOL officer being replaced with another UNPOL. The vast majority of the time, a replacement UNPOL will be from a different nation. Thus, the cultural dynamics at every level of an UNPOL mission is in a constant state of change.

The expatriate experience in linear complex acculturation is circular The expatriate worker experience seems to be of a linear nature. The American expatriate in Tokyo must work to adjust to Japanese culture. The process is decidedly linear and moves in one direction only as seen in Fig. 12.3. Conversely, the complex acculturation experience does not have an end goal, which will also be an important element. Since the intercultural dynamic of any UNPOL unit, at any level, is constantly changing with the coming and going of UNPOL officers, the UNPOL officer does not have a specific adjustment goal per se. The adjustment target would be constantly in flux. However, in terms of the experience, the complex acculturation experience, specifically as it pertains to UNPOL missions, would be circular in nature as seen in Fig. 12.4. A comparison of the two seems to indicate that the simple and

Fig. 12.3 The linear model of simple acculturation process. (Sanchez, 2018, p. 130)

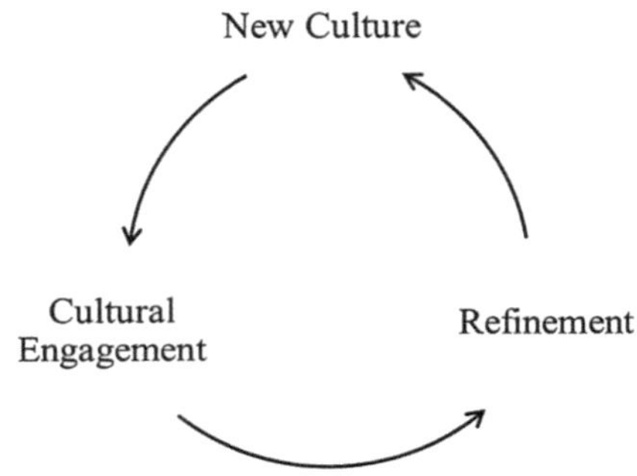

Fig. 12.4 The circular model of complex acculturation process. (Sanchez, 2018, p. 130)

complex acculturation paradigms are completely different experiences in the context of a cultural and psychological phenomenon (Sanchez, 2016).

Goals The relationship between the simple and complex acculturation experiences is most interesting when exploring the goals of each process. The simple acculturation process has a definitive and visible goal, to *adjust* (Sanchez, 2016). Adjustment is achieved when the hypothetical expatriate worker had adjusted to Japanese societal, workplace, and office culture to the extent that the expatriate worker can interact with his or her Japanese colleagues effectively and perform productively.

In the complex acculturation process, the goal is not a*djustment*; rather, the goal is ***mastery of the adjustment process itself.*** In the complex acculturation paradigm, the adjustment process *is* the goal. Since the cultural dynamic is constantly in motion, the ultimate goal of the complex acculturation paradigm is for the UNPOL officer to become increasingly intuitive and adept and quickly reading and adjusting to the cultural paradigms on new arrivals and replacement UNPOLs from a different country (Sanchez, 2016). Thus, the UNPOL officer does not learn to *adjust* per se, the UNPOL officer learns ***how*** to adjust.

These elements appear to indicate that complex acculturation, as a cross-cultural and psychological construct, is markedly and considerably different from the simple acculturation paradigm. So much so that complex acculturation appears to be a unique cultural and psychological construct in its own right. With a few minor exceptions, one only sees this level of hyper-diversity in UNPOL missions; however, with the ever-increasing globalization of the world economy, the hyper-diversification of workforces is only a matter of time (Sanchez, 2016).

Conclusion

While the identification and defining of complex acculturation were specific to the United Nation Police missions, hyper-diversity may very well describe the workforce of the future. Ever-increasing migration, diversity, and globalization will create increasingly diverse workforces, particularly in expatriate assignments. A prime example of this increasing diversity in the workforce would be an international Danish company cited by Lauring (2013). This Danish company's subsidiary office in Saudi Arabia was staffed by personnel from 14 different countries. Such examples can be seen as the leading edge of hyper-diversity in the global workforce (Sanchez, 2016).

The United Nations maintains a strong commitment to cultural sensitivity in its missions. This commitment is evidenced by the extensive training UNPOL officers undergo pertaining to the culture and societal norms of the host country. However, it would seem that the cultural dissonance born of the hyper-diverse nature of UNPOL missions themselves, and the loss of organizational effectiveness that attends tension, cultural dissonance, and intercultural conflict, has been heretofore overlooked. Research shows that expatriate failure rates are estimated to be between 25 and 40 percent due to the expatriate worker's inability to adjust to a *single* new culture. It would seem that the UNPOL officer, who must adjust to multiple cultures *simultaneously* would have an exponentially more difficult cross-cultural journey. It would appear that in assessing the productivity of UNPOL missions, the cross-cultural dissonance created by the hyper-diversity of an UNPOL mission has been overlooked as a source of poor performance in UNPOL missions and is perhaps a critical missing element in pre-deployment training of prospective UNPOL officers.

One UNPOL officer revealed that the officer's national police contingent had an informal support mechanism to help new UNPOL officers adjust to the hyper-diversity of the UNPOL mission. This national police contingent had experienced UNPOL officers explain to new officers what to expect from their UNPOL colleagues, strategies on how to deal with other cultures, and would provide informal support should the new UNPOL officer need assistance adjusting. This is, however, a singular example that has been uncovered of any UNPOL contingent or the United Nations addressing the cross-cultural challenges that consistently occur within and across the UNPOL ranks.

The complex acculturation process seems to be a self-taught, self-directed improvement of the UNPOL officer's own cultural intelligence. This self-directed training, when successful, seems to have lasting effects since all participants reported that adjustment to subsequent missions was easy. It is important to note that not all UNPOL officers work directly with the host nation's organic police force personnel; however, *all* UNPOL officers must work with *other* UNPOL officers.

This hyper-diversity within United Nations deployments has a distinctly positive effect upon UNPOL missions. Encouraging two warring factions to get along is much easier when the support mechanism is diverse in its own right. The hyper-diversity of an UNPOL mission benefits the target population, *and* to the participating UNPOL officers.

Most former UNPOL officers (including myself) attest that their UNPOL missions were among the most fulfilling and informative experiences of their careers, *because* of the hyper-diversity of the UNPOL mission. The ability to meet, work with, befriend, exchange ideas, and learn from police officers from all over the world is a multicultural experience that cannot possibly be replicated at home. Every former UNPOL officer developed lasting friendships with officers from other countries.

While there are many factors that contribute to the inefficiency of UNPOL missions, hyper-diversity and complex acculturation describe a heretofore unexplored source of interpersonal tension within an UNPOL mission that clearly would inhibit communication, cooperation, and collaboration within the ranks of the UNPOL mission. Although UNPOL officers frequently overcome the interpersonal and cross-cultural tension and dissonance, the process of overcoming these challenges saps energy from the UNPOL officer and detracts for the mission's operational effectiveness. While complex acculturation needs to be more thoroughly explored, the contents of this chapter would seem to indicate that a key element to improving the efficiency and effectiveness of UNPOL missions would be to provide extensive cultural intelligence training to new UNPOL officers as a part of pre-deployment training.

References

Bayley, D. (2006). *Changing of the guard: Developing democratic police abroad.* Oxford University Press.

Black, S. (1988). Work role transitions: A study of American expatriate managers in Japan. *Journal of International Business Studies, 19*(2), 277–294.

Çelik, A., & Çetin, H. (2013). Success and failure of international police missions operating in post conflict context: Cases of Solalia, Sierra Leone, Kosovo, and Iraq. *International Journal of Security and Terrorism, 4*(2), 95–115.

de Saint-Claire, S. (2007). *The significance, role and impact of UN police in peace operation: Regarding transnational crime, peacebuilding and normalization.* The Saint-Claire Group.

Durch, W., & England, M. (2010). *Enhancing United Nations capacity to support post-conflict policing and rule of law* (revised). The Stimson Center.

Firth, B., Chen, G., Kirkman, B., & Kim, K. (2014). Newcomers abroad: Expatriate adaptation during early phases of international assignments. *Academy of Management Journal, 57*(1), 280–300. https://doi.org/10.5465/amj.2011.0574

Greener, B. (2012). International policing and international relations. *International Relations, 26*, 181–198. https://doi.org/10.1177/0047117812438064

Hårleman, C. (2003). *An introduction to the UN system: Orientation for serving on a UN field mission.* United Nations Institute for Training and Research, Programme of Correspondence Instruction.

Heepen, P., & Freisleben, G. (2005). *United Nations civilian police: Restoring civil order following hostilities.* UNITAR Training Programme of Correspondence Instruction in Peacekeeping Operations.

Heine, J., & Thakur, R. (2010). *The dark side of globalization.* United Nations University Press.

Josien, L. (2012). Enhancing expatriate selection: Measuring the strength of acculturation. *Journal of Business Research, 11*(1), 83–92.

Kearney, J., Botzios, S., & Hadden, T. (2011). *Addressing the accountability challenges of international policing in peace support operations* (pp. 217–239). Crime, Law & Social Change.

Koveshnikov, A., Wechtler, H., & Dejoux, C. (2013). Cross-cultural adjustment of expatriates: The role of emotional intelligence and gender. *Journal of World Business, 49*(3), 362–371. https://doi.org/10.1016/j.jwb.2013.07.001

Lauring, J. (2013). International diversity management: Global ideals and local responses. *British Journal of Management, 24*, 211–224. https://doi.org/10.1111/j.1467-8551.2011.00798.x

Levine, D. (2008). *African civilian police capacity for international peacekeeping operations*. Henry L. Stimson Center.

Mobekk, E. (2005). *Identifying lessons in United Nations international policing missions*. Geneva Centre for the Democratic Control of Armed Forces.

Monk, R. (2008). *End of mission report of the seventh police commissioner of the United Nations international police in Kosovo*. This is an unpublished report and was obtained from the author.

Okpara, J., & Kabongo, J. (2011). Cross-cultural training and expatriate adjustment: A study of western expatriates in Nigeria. *Journal of World Business, 46*, 22–30.

Ram, S. (2006). *The history of United Nations peacekeeping operations during the cold war: 1945 to 1987*. United Nations Institute for Training and Research, UNITAR POCI Dag Hammarskjöld Centre.

Rotmann, P. (2011). First steps towards a police doctrine for UN peace operations (2001–2006). *Policing and Society: An International Journal of Research and Policy, 21*(1), 84–95.

Sanchez, M. (2011). *An analysis of administrative policies and procedures of the United Nations Mission in Kosovo International Police* (Master's Capstone Project). Utical College.

Sanchez, M. (2016). *A Phenomenological Exploration of Complex Acculturation in United Nations International Police Officers in Peacekeeping Missions* (Doctoral Dissertation). Northcentral University.

Sanchez, M. (2018). *United Nations international police officers in peacekeeping missions: A phenomenological exploration of complex acculturation*. Routledge.

Scheye, E. (2008). UNMIK and the significance of effective programme management: The case of Kosovo. In H. Hänggi & V. Scherrer (Eds.), *Security sector reform and UN integrated missions: Experience from Burundi, the Democratic Republic of Congo, Haiti, and Kosovo* (pp. 169–228). Geneva Centre for the Democratic Control of Armed Forces.

Silander, D. (2009). The United Nations and peace building: Lessons from the UN transitional administrations in East Timor and Kosovo. *Social Alternatives, 28*(2), 23–28.

Smith, J., Holt, V., & Durch, W. (2007). *From Timor-Leste to Darfur: New initiatives for enhancing UN civilian policing capacity*. The Stimson Center.

United Nations. (2000). *About the United Nations*. Retrieved from United Nations: http://www.un.org/aboutun/history.htm

United Nations Department of Peacekeeping Operations. (2017). *Police monitoring, mentoring and advising in peace operations*. United Nations Department of Peacekeeping Operations.

United Nations Department of Peacekeeping Operations. (2020). *Our history*. Retrieved from United Nations Peacekeeping: https://peacekeeping.un.org/en/our-history

United Nations Mission in Kosovo. (2007). *Guidelines on completion of performance appraisal form*. UNMIK Police Director of Personnel and Administration.

United Nations Police. (2019, March 15). *Police contributing countries*. Retrieved from United Nations Police: https://police.un.org/en/police-contributing-countries

United Nations Security Council. (1999). *United Nations Security Council Resolution 1244*. United Nations Security Council.

United Nations Security Council. (2004). *United Nations Security Council Resolution 1529*. United Nations Security Council.

United Nations Security Council. (2016). *United Nations Security Council Resolution 2282*. United Nations.

Chapter 13
Community Conflict Associated with PTSD and Negative Outcomes for United Nations Police Officers

Salih Hakan Can

Introduction

It is widely acknowledged that workplace stressors are associated with increased psychosocial problems for police officers such as conflict with police partners, conflict with romantic partners, and poor self-esteem (Can & Hendy, 2014; Can et al., 2008; Gershon et al., 2009; Hall et al., 2010; Liberman et al., 2002; Stevens, 2008). Specific sources of police workplace stressors have been found to include critical incidents while out in the field, department politics, daily hassles with technology or equipment, and work-home conflicts (Brown & Campbell, 1990; Can et al., 2015; Hart et al., 1994; Kureczka, 1996; Stevens, 2008; Violanti & Aron, 1993; Weiss et al., 2010). The negative psychosocial impact of police workplace stressors may be expected to be worsened when police experience widespread conflict or aggression from the community they have sworn to protect and serve. Such community aggression directed at police may take the form of protest marches, verbal assaults, physical aggression, and even murder of police officers (Anderson & Bauer, 1987). Community conflict directed at police officers has been widely publicized (Adang et al., 2018; Hunter et al., 2018; Lee et al., 2018), and in recent years it has extended to social media attacks. Extensive coverage and commentary of any cases of community–police conflict often occurs via both traditional media outlets and social media platforms. Such widespread coverage of their community difficulties may make officers feel targeted, vulnerable, and hypervigilant, which may not only affect their perceptions of workplace stressors but also produce

The original version of the chapter has been revised. A correction to this chapter can be found at https://doi.org/10.1007/978-3-030-77900-9_17

S. H. Can (✉)
Pennsylvania State University, Schuylkill Haven, PA, USA
e-mail: Hakancan@psu.edu

G. den Heyer, J. F. Albrecht (eds.), *Police and International Peacekeeping Missions*, https://doi.org/10.1007/978-3-030-77900-9_13

psychosocial problems such as conflicts with fellow officers, conflicts in their private lives such as with romantic partners, and even doubts about their own capabilities and self-esteem.

An important feature of the present study is that it examines how exposure to community conflict is associated with a variety of negative psychosocial outcomes experienced by police officers. Based on past research on other police job stressors (such as departmental politics, work-home interference), we anticipated that these negative outcomes might include symptoms of posttraumatic stress disorder (PTSD), health concerns, alcohol abuse, chronic anger, high levels of job stress, thoughts of leaving the profession, and identification with "police subculture" in which they trust and socialize exclusively with other officers (Anderson & Lo, 2011; Ballenger et al., 2011; Burke, 1994 Burke, 2016; Can & Hendy, 2014; Can et al., 2015; Chen, 2015; Ellison, 2004; Gershon et al., 2009; Ivie & Garland, 2011; Liberman et al., 2002; Menard & Arter, 2013; Violanti et al., 2011; Yun et al., 2013). Using principles of the Threat Appraisal and Coping Theory (Lazarus & Folkman, 1984), we hypothesized that a three-event sequence would be revealed for how exposure to community conflict leads to these negative outcomes for officers.

The theory suggests that if individuals experience stressors, and if they experience a sense of powerlessness (such as with PTSD symptoms of uncontrollable thoughts, body reactions, disrupted sleep and social patterns), they are at increased risk for negative outcomes. More briefly, the three-event sequence we anticipated we would find for the police officers in our study could be described as COMMUNITY CONFLICT → PTSD → NEGATIVE OUTCOMES. The benefit of documenting these three-event sequences (COMMUNITY CONFLICT → PTSD → NEGATIVE OUTCOMES) is that it may guide police departments to target their resources toward evidence-based interventions for PTSD, which serves as the "link" between community conflict and negative outcomes for their officers.

Some of the negative outcomes that may be associated with officer exposure to community conflict may be considered "maladaptive coping behaviors" in response to stressors (Lazarus & Folkman, 1984), which give the stressed individual a temporary sense of distraction or empowerment, even if these behaviors worsen later problems. Such maladaptive coping behaviors could include alcohol abuse, chronic anger, thoughts of leaving police work, and even identification with a police subculture that mistrusts anyone but fellow officers. For example, research had found that when individuals feel intense anger, they tend to feel more energized and powerful, but they also tend to view themselves as blameless and they become more accusatory of others (Herrero et al., 2010; Kazén et al., 2012), which may reduce the probability of peaceful negotiations with the target of their anger. Also, when officers respond to community conflict by identification with a police subculture that excludes family and friends, they may receive social support from peers who understand their work frustrations, but this group identity may also exaggerate their anger and hostility toward community members (Isenberg, 1986; Lamm & Myers, 1978; Myers & Lamm, 1976) Additionally, if the police subculture becomes exclusive for officers of the majority ethnicity, it may also exaggerate any racism against other ethnicities.

Another purpose of the present study was to use a new Community Conflict Scale (CCS) to examine whether community conflict served as a separate workplace stressor associated with negative outcomes for officers beyond the effects of more traditional workplace stressors from inside the organization (high demand, low support). Based on past research, negative outcomes we anticipated would be associated with community conflict were health concerns, alcohol abuse, chronic anger, and poor job satisfaction (Anderson & Lo, 2011; Can & Hendy, 2014; Gershon et al., 2009; Ballenger et al., 2011; Ivie & Garland, 2011; Menard & Arter, 2013; Violanti et al., 2011).

Additionally, using the Threat Appraisal and Coping Theory (Lazarus & Folkman, 1984) as a guide, the present study examined a three-variable sequence of experiences that could lead to increased risk for such negative outcomes in officers. The theory suggests that if individuals experience environmental stressors, and if they experience a sense of powerlessness (such as that displayed with PTSD symptoms of uncontrollable thoughts, body reactions, sleep and social patterns), they would have increased risk for negative outcomes (health concerns, alcohol abuse, chronic anger, poor job satisfaction, exclusive bonding with "police subculture" rather than family or friends): COMMUNITY CONFLICT → PTSD → NEGATIVE OUTCOMES.

The benefit of the CCS's identification of specific community conflict actions currently directed toward police would be that it guides departments in developing strategies to reduce such actions that stress officers. The benefit of documenting the three-variable sequence would be that it suggests departments invest in research-based interventions to reduce officer PTSD symptoms that link the stressor of community conflict and negative outcomes for officers.

This study also examines two possible problems associated with police subculture, i.e. seeking social support from peers is one of the most effective coping behaviors when individuals are exposed to stressors (Procidano & Heller, 1983) and police unions offer a formal support system for officers facing prosecution for their policing actions. However, the present study focused on the more informal social support that officers may find in the police subculture (Chen, 2015), where they exclusively feel trust and socialize with other officers rather than family or non-police friends. One possible problem with such a police subculture is suggested by Group Polarization Theory (Isenberg, 1986; Lamm & Myers, 1978; Myers & Lamm, 1976), which proposes that when individuals have a strong group identity, the group's influence (via modeling and/or persuasion) tends to exaggerate their emotions, beliefs, and actions. Therefore, one possible problem with police subculture is that it might exaggerate officers' anger and hypervigilance for community conflict. We hypothesized that in all three of our police samples, we would find evidence of this group polarization effect in a three-event sequence: POLICE SUBCULTURE → ANGER → COMMUNITY CONFLICT.

Another possible problem with police subculture is that, if its "membership" includes primarily the dominant ethnic group of the police department, then again by group polarization effects, it could become a social space that breeds angry and racist sentiments. As concerns about racism in police departments have been the focus of widespread community protests in support of the Black Lives Matter movement, the present study examined the effects of officer ethnicity (Black, Asian, Hispanic, White, Other) on their identification with the police subculture, controlling for other demographics (gender, age, education, years of experience). We conducted these analyses for each of our three samples of officers, which varied in the dominant ethnicity as reported by officers. Our sample of United Nations officers from 26 countries reported their ethnicity as Asian (50.4% Asian) or Other (29.0%) with these "Other" ethnicities including officers from Nepal, India, and Pakistan. We anticipated that the Asian and Other officers would report the strongest identification with police subculture because most of their fellow officers were Asian and Other ethnicity. We also anticipated that officers with less experience in various ways (younger in age, without college education, fewer years of policing) might be particularly drawn to the social support found in police subculture.

The benefit of documenting increased anger and perceptions of community conflict associated with police subculture, especially if police subculture is primarily for officers in the dominant ethnic group, is that such findings may encourage police departments to include greater ethnic diversity in their hiring procedures. Police departments also could work to reduce the formation of exclusive police subcultures primarily for officers in the ethnic majority, perhaps by developing broader socializing opportunities that is extended to all officers, their families, and even their supportive non-police friends.

Methodology

Study participants included 409 United Nations officers from 26 countries who were attending training conferences held in North East Africa, Asia, and Central Africa (mean age = 40.5 years; mean experience = 18.0 years; 81.8% males; 44.9% with college degrees; 5.9% White, 13.5% Black, 1.2% Hispanic, 50.4% Asian, 29.0% other ethnicity). Many of those reporting "other ethnicity" came from South West Asia. All officers held a "frontline" role of direct contact with the communities they served. Of the total 670 officers who received the survey, 506 (76%) of the officers responded. Of the 506 who responded, 409 (80.8%) completed all items for our most important measure of Community to Police Conflict Scale.

Study participants included 409 United Nations officers (Table 13.1) (mean age = 40.5 years; mean experience = 18.0 years; 81.8% males; 87.3% married; 44.9% with college education; 50.4% Asian, 13.5% African, 5.9% Caucasian, 1.2% Hispanic, 29.0% other ethnicity). Participants conveniently completed anonymous surveys that asked them to report demographics, responses to the new 17-item Community Conflict Scale, to measures of workplace stressors (Vagg & Spielberger, 1998), PTSD (Foa et al., 1997), health concerns (Chen et al., 1996), alcohol abuse (Christo et al., 2003), chronic anger (Spielberger et al., 1985), job satisfaction (Stanton et al., 2002), and responses to a new 8-item Police Subculture Scale that

Table 13.1 Descriptive statistics of officer demographics United Nations officers from 26 countries

	Sample (n = 409)	
Variable	%	
Gender		
Male	81.8%	
Female	18.2%	
Ethnicity		
White	5.9%	
Black	13.5%	
Hispanic	1.2%	
Asian	50.4%	
Mixed, Other	29.0%	
4-Year College degree		
Yes	44.9%	
No	55.1%	
	M	(*SD*)
Age	40.49	(5.62)
Years of police work	18.04	(5.47)

measures selective trust and socializing with fellow officers to the exclusion of others (Chen, 2015).

Measurement of Variables

The present study included measurement of eight variables relevant to frontline officers in the United Nations sample (n = 409 United Nations officers). These variables were Community to Police conflict, PTSD symptoms, health concerns, alcohol abuse, chronic anger, job stress, probability of leaving police work, and identification with an exclusive police subculture. We used published and psychometrically tested scales to measure these variables wherever possible, which were available for five of our study variables. However, probability of leaving was measured with a single item (as described below). Also, the new Community to Police Conflict Scale (CPCS) and the new Police Subculture Scale (PSS) were developed for the present study because current measurements of these variables were not available in the research literature. Table 13.2 shows descriptive statistics (mean, SD) and internal reliability (Cronbach α) of all study variables for officers in our sample. Additionally, Table 13.3 shows the bivariate correlations of all study variables.

We used SPSS 26 software for all statistical analyses of the present study, and we included only officers from each sample who had completed the new Community to Police Conflict Scale (CPCS): 409 United Nations officers from 26 countries. However, because of listwise deletion of missing data, some analyses included

Table 13.2 Descriptive statistics of study variables United Nations officers from 26 countries

	Sample (n = 409)		
Variable	α	M	(SD)
Community to Police Conflict (CPCS)	0.95	2.18	(0.79)
PTSD symptoms	0.91	1.60	(0.58)
Health concerns	0.91	1.55	(0.50)
Alcohol abuse	0.90	1.32	(0.55)
Chronic anger	0.88	1.91	(0.57)
Job stress	0.90	2.39	(0.67)
Probability of leaving police work	–	34.0%	(31.5%)
(% with some thoughts of leaving)	(74.1% of officers)		
Police Subculture (PSS)	0.80	3.30	(0.74)

slightly fewer officers if they had missing information for other study variables besides the CPCS.

The New Community to Police Conflict Scale (CPCS)

A new 17-item Community to Police Conflict Scale (CPCS) was developed for the present study. As mentioned in the Introduction, the officers were reporting the prevalence of each item of conflict directed from community members to police *before* the widespread protests against police that occurred during the summer of 2020.

The 23 items of community conflict considered for the new CPCS were gathered from a number of sources: (1) Review of past research on community–police conflict (Adang et al., 2018; Hunter et al., 2018; Lee et al., 2018); (2) Responses to the open-ended question of "What are examples of the form that public-to-police conflict may take?" when asked of 48 officers attending an informal focus group at the National Sheriffs Association meeting in Washington, DC, held in February of 2019; and (3) Review of the list of possible items by police officials from Ferguson, Michigan, and New York, New York, where widely publicized incidents had recently taken place between police and their community members. The list of 23 items considered for the CPCS included verbal, physical, and social media forms of conflict directed toward officers. Officers were asked to use a five-point rating (1 = never, 2 = rarely, 3 = sometimes, 4 = often, 5 = always) to report "How often has each community situation applied to your department during the past year?"

To identify the final items that would become the new Community to Police Conflict Scale (CPCS), we used SPSS 26 software to conduct a principle components exploratory factor analysis on the five-point ratings. To obtain scale components/dimensions as internally consistent as possible, we used the strict criteria that all items within the dimension showed factor loadings of at least 0.50, and only within one dimension. The factor analysis identified one dimension of community conflict

Table 13.3 Bivariate Pearson correlations of study variables for United Nations officers from 26 countries ($n = 409$)

COMMUNITY CONFLICT	PTSD SYMPTOMS	HEALTH CONCERNS	ALCOHOL ABUSE	CHRONIC ANGER	JOB STRESS	PROBABILITY OF LEAVING	POLICE SUBCULTURE
COMMUNITY CONFLICT	0.341***	0.257***	0.105*	0.272***	0.448***	0.115*	0.100*
PTSD SYMPTOMS		0.703***	0.436***	0.483***	0.503***	0.185***	0.144**
HEALTH CONCERNS			0.285***	0.351***	0.338***	0.045	0.078
ALCOHOL ABUSE				0.381***	0.265***	0.156**	0.087
CHRONIC ANGER					0.403***	0.127*	0.143**
JOB STRESS						0.197***	0.011
PROBABILITY OF LEAVING							0.023
POLICE SUBCULTURE							

*$p < 0.05$, **$p < 0.01$, ***$p < 0.001$

that included 17 items. The 17 items of the new CPCS included both in-person behaviors (shouting, cursing, spitting, protesting with signs) and social media attacks (accusations, videos, ridiculing officers' appearance, competence, intelligence, integrity). The CPCS showed strong internal reliability (n = 409, $\alpha = 0.95$).

PTSD Symptoms

PTSD symptoms were measured because they include the "powerlessness" in unwelcome thoughts, bodily reactions, and sleep and social life disturbances. We used the 17-item Posttraumatic Diagnostic Scale (Foa et al., 1997). Participants were asked to use five-point ratings (1 = never, 2 = rarely, 3 = sometimes, 4 = often, 5 = always) to report how often each experience applied to them during the past year. Scale items included "unwanted images," "difficulty sleeping," "body reactions (trembling, sweating)," "easily startled," "avoiding activities, places, people," and "memory loss." The score for PTSD symptoms was calculated as the mean rating for the 17 items, with higher scores indicating more PTSD symptoms.

Health Concerns

Health concerns were measured with the 16-item unnamed but psychometrically tested scale developed by Chen et al. (1996). Participants were asked to use a five-point rating (as above) to report how often each health concern applied to them during the past year. Scale items included problems in a number of body systems such as "pains in heart or chest," "trouble getting your breath," "headaches," "nausea or upset stomach," "soreness of muscles," and "sexual problems." The score for health concerns was calculated as the mean rating for the 16 items, with higher scores indicating more health concerns.

Alcohol Abuse

Alcohol abuse was measured with the 10-item Alcohol Addiction subscale from the Shorter PROMIS Questionnaire (Christo et al., 2003). Participants used a five-point rating (as above) to report how often each description applied to them during the past year. Scale items included "gulping down the first alcoholic drink fairly fast," "using alcohol as a comfort and a strength," and "drinking significantly more alcohol than I intended." The score for alcohol abuse was as calculated as the mean rating for the 10 items, with higher scores indicating more alcohol abuse.

Chronic Anger

Chronic anger was measured with the 16-item Anger Expression Scale (Spielberger et al., 1985). Participants used a five-point rating (as above) to report how often each description applied to them during the past year for their use of alcohol. Scale items included both outward displays of anger ("argued with others," "made sarcastic remarks," "slammed doors") and more internal repressed anger ("was secretly critical of others," "boiled inside," "held grudges"). The score for chronic anger was calculated as the mean rating for the 16 items, with higher scores indicating more anger.

Job Stress

Job stress was measured with the 20-item Job Stress Scale (Vagg & Spielberger, 1998). Participants used a five-point rating (as above) to report how often each description applied to them during the past year. Scale items included both high job pressure ("assigned increasing responsibility," "critical on-the-spot decisions needed," "frequent interruptions") and poor job support ("inadequate support by supervisor," "fellow workers not doing a good job," "inadequate or poor-quality equipment"). The score for job stress was calculated as the mean rating for the 20 items, with higher scores indicating more job stress.

Probability of Leaving Police Work

The officer's probability of leaving the policing profession was measured with a single item that read "What is the probability you will CHOOSE TO LEAVE police work to find other employment?" Participants were asked to respond by checking either 0%, 20%, 40%, 60%, 80%, or 100%. The score for probability of leaving was the value they checked.

The New Police Subculture Scale (PSS)

The 10 items considered for the new PSS were developed from descriptions of police subculture found in Chen (2015), from informal discussions with police officers, and from the personal observations of one of the authors when working as a frontline officer. The list of 10 items considered for the PSS included issues of exclusively trusting, socializing, and confiding with fellow officers more than with family and non-police friends. Officers were asked to use a five-point rating (1 = never, 2 = rarely, 3 = sometimes, 4 = often, 5 = always) to report "How often has each description applied to you during the past year?"

Survey Results

The goal for data analysis in this section was to examine the presence of a three-event sequence suggested by the Threat Appraisal and Coping Theory (Lazarus & Folkman, 1984) for a sequence of experiences that would link police officer's exposure to community conflict and negative outcomes for their well-being. The theory suggests that when individuals are exposed to environmental *stressors*, especially combined with a sense of *powerlessness*, they are at increased risk for *negative outcomes* for their well-being, including the use of *maladaptive coping* behaviors that bring only temporary distraction or empowerment. More specifically for the present study, we hypothesized that police officers with exposure to intense community conflict (the environmental *stressor)*, combined with intense PTSD symptoms (with its *powerlessness* of disturbed thoughts, bodily responses, sleep), would be at increased risk for six negative outcomes: health concerns, alcohol abuse, chronic anger, job stress, thoughts of leaving police work, and identification with exclusive police subculture. More briefly, this three-event sequence could be described as COMMUNITY CONFLICT → PTSD → NEGATIVE OUTCOMES.

To examine statistical significance for the proposed three-event sequences for each of the six negative outcomes, we used bootstrapping mediational analysis with SPSS 26 software and an SPSS macro provided by Preacher and Hayes (2004; www.afhyes.com, www.quantpsy.org, model 4). For these mediational analyses, 5000 bootstrapped samples were drawn from the sample (meaning that scores were randomly drawn, replaced, and then redrawn). Then, a 95% confidence interval was calculated for the distribution of 5000 *indirect effects* found for community conflict on the negative outcome when combined with PTSD symptoms. Finally, the analysis examined whether the low to high end of this 95% confidence interval did NOT include the value of 0.00 (meaning *no* effect), which led to the conclusion that the three-event sequence was supported and statistically significant ($p < 0.05$). The SPSS 26 output from these bootstrapped mediational analyses provided standardized correlation coefficients for each pair of variables, the coefficient for the indirect relationship, and values for the low and high ends of the 95% confidence interval.

The new CSS identified the specific actions of community conflict directed toward police to include both in-person behaviors (shouting, spitting, protesting with signs) and social media attacks (accusations, photos, ridiculing officers' appearance, competence, intelligence, integrity). Multiple regression comparisons of three workplace stressors (community conflict, high demand, low support) as predictors of negative outcomes revealed that community conflict was a unique contributor in explaining officer PTSD, health concerns, chronic anger, poor job satisfaction, and police subculture identification, but not alcohol abuse. Bootstrapping mediation analysis found the three-variable sequence (COMMUNITY CONFLICT → PTSD → NEGATIVE OUTCOMES) was significant for health problems, alcohol abuse, chronic anger, poor job satisfaction, and police subculture identification (Fig. 13.1).

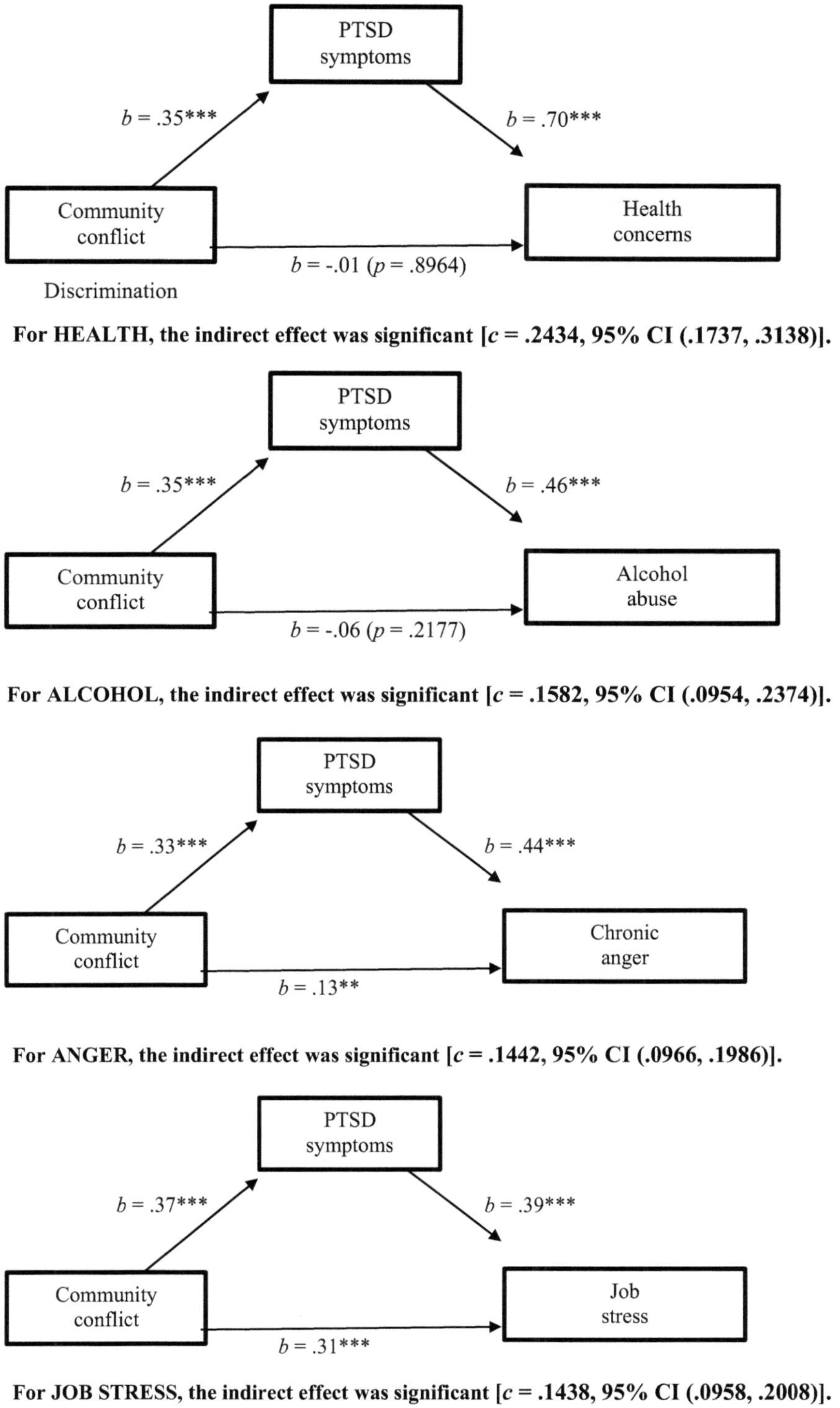

Fig. 13.1 Results for United Nations officers from 26 countries (n = 409) for bootstrapped mediational analyses to examine the three-event sequence of COMMUNITY CONFLICT → PTSD → NEGATIVE OUTCOMES for six possible negative outcomes. The b values show direct effects between pairs of variables. The c values show indirect effects of community conflict on the negative outcome, controlling for PTSD symptoms. All values are standardized coefficients (*$p < 0.05$, **$p < 0.01$, ***$p < 0.001$)

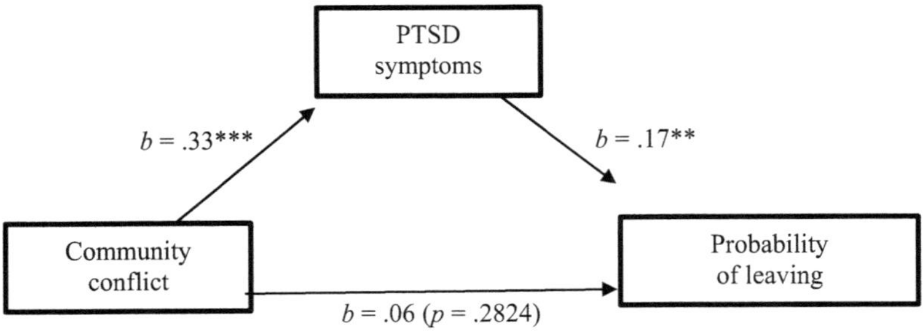

For LEAVING, the indirect effect was significant [*c* = .0545, 95% CI (.0234, .0917)].

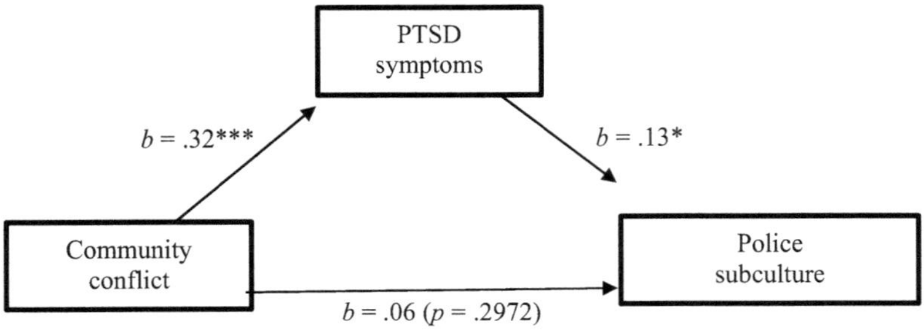

For SUBCULTURE, the indirect effect was significant [.0405, 95% CI (.0023, .0790)].

Fig. 13.1 (continued)

Conclusion

Results from the present study suggest that the current form of community conflict relevant to police officers includes both in-person and social media attacks, and that such community conflict is a predictor of negative outcomes for officers beyond those attributable to workplace stressors within the department. These findings could guide departments to develop community-relations programs to reduce the incidence or to respond effectively to these community attacks. Present results also indicate that the sense of powerlessness experienced in PTSD symptoms is a consistent "link" between such community conflicts and a variety of negative psychosocial outcomes for police officers. These findings suggest that police departments invest in research-based PTSD interventions, which may include exposure therapy (Rauch et al., 2012; Tuerk et al., 2013), medications such as sertraline (Zoellner et al., 2003), and group cognitive behavioral therapy (Becker et al., 2009). Finally, departments could develop stress-management workshops that encourage research-based healthy coping behaviors such as exercise and meditation (Burton et al., 2012; Lin et al., 2015; Sliter & Yuan, 2015; Wolever et al., 2012) to improve the health and well-being of officers.

References

Adang, O. M. J., Stronks, S., van den Brink, G. J. M., van de Klomp, M., Verbeek, P., & Peters, B. (2018). Keeping the peace or enforcing order? Overcoming social tension between police and civilians. *Peace Ethology: Behavioral Processes and Systems of Peace*, 171–190.

Anderson, A. S., & Lo, C. C. (2011). Intimate partner violence within law enforcement families. *Journal of Interpersonal Violence, 26*, 1176–1193.

Anderson, W., & Bauer, B. (1987). Law enforcement officers: The consequences of exposure to violence. *Journal of Counseling and Development, 65*(7), 381–384.

Ballenger, J. F., Best, S. R., Metzler, T. J., Wasserman, D. A., Mohr, D. C., Liberman, A., Delucchi, K., Weiss, D. S., Fagan, J. A., Waldrop, A. E., & Marmar, D. R. (2011). Patterns and predictors of alcohol use in male and female urban police officers. *American Journal of Addictions, 20*, 21–29.

Becker, C. B., Meyer, G., Price, J. S., Graham, M. M., Arsena, A., Armstrong, D. A., & Ramon, E. (2009). Law enforcement preferences for PTSD treatment and crisis management alternatives. *Behaviour Research and Therapy, 47*(3), 245–253.

Brown, J. M., & Campbell, E. A. (1990). Sources of occupational stress in the police. *Work and Stress, 4*, 305–318.

Burton, J. P., Hoobler, J. M., & Scheuer, M. L. (2012). Supervisor workplace stress and abusive supervision: The buffering effect of exercise. *Journal of Business Psychology, 27*, 271–279.

Burke R. J. (1994) Stressful events, work-family conflict, coping, psychological burnout, and well-being among police officers. *Psychol Reports, 75*(2), 787–800. https://doi.org/10.2466/pr0.1994.75.2.787. PMID: 7862787.

Burke, R. (2016). *Stress in policing: Sources, consequences and interventions*. Routledge.

Can, S. H., & Hendy, H. M. (2014). Police stressors, negative outcomes associated with them, and coping mechanisms that may reduce them. *Police Journal: Theory, Practice, and Principles, 87*, 167–177.

Can, S. H., Sever, M., & Mire, S. (2008). Police job stress and domestic violence in police families. *International Journal of Crime, Criminal Justice, and Law, 3*, 73–81.

Can, S. H., Hendy, H. M., & Karagoz, T. (2015). Law Enforcement Officer Stress Survey-Revised (LEOSS-R): Four types of police stressors and negative psychosocial outcomes associated with them. *Policing: Journal of Policy and Practice, 9*, 340–351.

Chen, K., Scheier, L. M., & Kandel, D. B. (1996). Effects of chronic cocaine use on physical health: A prospective study in a general population sample. *Drug and Alcohol Dependence, 43*, 23–37.

Chen, Z. (2015). *Measuring police subcultural perceptions: A study of frontline police officers in China*. Australian Graduate School of Policing and Security, Charles Sturt University.

Christo, G., Jones, S. L., Haylett, S., Stephenson, G. M., Lefever, R. M. H., & Lefever, R. (2003). The shorter PROMIS questionnaire: Further validation of a tool for simultaneous assessment of multiple addictive behaviors. *Addictive Behaviors, 28*, 225–248.

Ellison, K. (2004). *Stress and the police officer*. Charles Thomas Publishers.

Foa, E. B., Cashman, L., Joycox, L., & Perry, K. (1997). The validation of a self-report measure of posttraumatic stress disorder: The posttraumatic diagnostic scale. *Psychological Assessment, 9*, 445–451.

Gershon, R. R. M., Barocas, B., Canton, A. N., Li, X., & Vlahov, D. (2009). Mental, physical, and behavioral outcomes associated with perceived work stress in police officers. *Criminal Justice and Behavior, 36*, 275–289.

Hall, G. B., Dollard, M. F., Tuckey, M. R., Winefield, A. H., & Thompson, B. M. (2010). Job demands, work-family conflict, and emotional exhaustion in police officers: A longitudinal test of competing theories. *Journal of Occupational and Organizational Psychology, 83*, 237–250.

Hart, P. M., Wearing, A. J., & Headey, B. (1994). Perceived quality of life, personality, and work experiences: Construct validation of the police daily hassles and uplifts scales. *Criminal Justice and Behavior, 21*, 283–311.

Herrero, N., Gadea, M., Rodríguez-Alarcón, G., Espert, R., & Salvador, A. (2010). What happens when we get angry? Hormonal, cardiovascular and asymmetrical brain responses. *Hormones and Behavior, 3*(57), 276–283.
Hunter, R. D., Barker, T., & de Guzman, M. C. (2018). *Police-community relations and the administration of justice* (9th ed.). Pearson Education.
Isenberg, D. J. (1986). Group polarization: A critical review and meta-analysis. *Journal of Personality and Social Psychology, 50*, 1141–1151.
Ivie, D., & Garland, B. (2011). Stress and burnout in policing: Does military experience matter? *Policing: An International Journal of Police Strategies and Management, 34*, 49–66.
Kazén, M., Kuenne, T., Frankenberg, H., & Quirin, M. (2012). Inverse relation between cortisol and anger and their relation to performance and explicit memory. *Biological Psychology, 2*(91), 28–35.
Kureczka, A. W. (1996). Critical incident stress in law enforcement. *FBI Law Enforcement Bulletin, 65*(213), 10–16.
Lamm, H., & Myers, D. G. (1978). Group-induced polarization of attitudes and behavior. *Advances in Experimental Social Psychology, 11*, 145–195.
Lazarus, R. S., & Folkman, S. (1984). *Stress, appraisal, and coping*. Springer.
Lee, A. S., Weitzer, R., & Martínez, D. E. (2018). Recent police killings in the United States: A three-city comparison. *Police Quarterly, 21*(2), 196–222.
Liberman, A. M., Best, S. R., Metzler, T. J., Fagan, J. A., Weiss, D. S., & Marmar, C. R. (2002). Routine occupational stress and psychological distress in police. *Policing: An International Journal of Police Strategies and Management, 25*, 421–439.
Lin, S. L., Huang, C. Y., Shiu, S. P., & Yeh, S. H. (2015). Effects of yoga on stress, stress adaptation, and heart rate variability among mental health professionals – A randomized controlled trial. *Worldviews on Evidence-Based Nursing, 12*, 236–245.
Menard, K. S., & Arter, M. L. (2013). Police officer alcohol use and trauma symptoms: Association with critical incidents, coping, and social stressors. *International Journal of Stress Management, 20*, 37–56.
Myers, D. G., & Lamm, H. (1976). The group polarization phenomenon. *Psychological Bulletin, 83*, 602–627.
Preacher, K. J., & Hayes, A. F. (2004). SPSS and SAS procedures for estimating indirect effects in simple mediation models. Behavior Research Methods, *Instruments, and Computers, 36*, 717–731.
Procidano, M. E., & Heller, K. (1983). Measures of perceived social support from friends and from family: Three validation studies. *American Journal of Community Psychology, 11*, 1–24.
Rauch, S. A., Eftekhari, A., & Ruzek, J. I. (2012). Review of exposure therapy: A gold standard for PTSD treatment. *Journal of Rehabilitation Research and Development, 49*(5), 679–688.
Sliter, M., & Yuan, Z. (2015). Workout at work: Laboratory test of psychological and performance outcomes of active workstations. *Journal of Occupational Health Psychology, 20*, 259–271.
Spielberger, C. D., Johnson, E. H., Russel, S. F., Crane, R. J., Jacobs, G. A., & Worden, T. J. (1985). The experience and expression of anger: Construction and validation of an anger expression scale. In M. A. Chesney & R. H. Rosenman (Eds.), *Anger and hostility in cardiovascular and behavioral disorders* (pp. 5–30). Hemisphere.
Stanton, J. M., Bachiochi, P. D., Robie, C., Perez, L. M., & Smith, P. C. (2002). Revising the JDI work satisfaction subscale: Insights into stress and control. *Educational and Psychological Measurement, 62*, 877–895.
Stevens, D. J. (2008). *Police officer stress: Sources and solutions*. Pearson/Prentice Hall Press.
Tuerk, P. W., Wangelin, B., Rauch, S. A. M., Dismuke, C. E., Yoder, M., Myrick, H., Eftekhari, A., & Acierno, R. (2013). Health service utilization before and after evidence-based treatment for PTSD. *Psychological Services, 10*(4), 401–409.
Vagg, P. R., & Spielberger, C. D. (1998). Occupational stress: Measuring job pressure and organizational support in the workplace. *Journal of Occupational Health Psychology, 3*, 294–305.
Violanti, J. M., & Aron, F. (1993). Sources of police stressors, job attitudes, and psychological distress. *Psychological Reports, 72*(3), 899–904.

Violanti, J. M., Slaven, J. E., Charles, L. E., Burchfiel, C. M., Andrew, M. E., & Homish, G. G. (2011). Police and alcohol use: A descriptive analysis and associations with stress outcomes. *American Journal of Criminal Justice, 36*, 344–356.

Weiss, D. S., Brunet, A., Best, S. R., Metzler, T. J., Liberman, A., Pole, N., Fagan, J. A., & Marmar, C. R. (2010). Frequency and severity approaches to indexing exposure to trauma: The critical incident history questionnaire for police officers. *Journal of Traumatic Stress, 23*, 734–743.

Wolever, R. Q., Bobinet, K. J., McCage, K., MacKenzie, E. R., Fekete, E., Kusnick, C. A., & Baime, M. (2012). Effective and viable mind-body stress reduction in the workplace: A randomized controlled trial. *Journal of Occupational Health Psychology, 17*, 246–258.

Yun, I., Kim, S., Jung, S., & Borhanian, S. (2013). A study on police stressors, coping strategies, and somatization symptoms among South Korean frontline police officers. *Policing: An International Journal of Police Strategies and Management, 36*, 787–802.

Zoellner, L. A., Feeny, N. C., Cochran, B., & Pruitt, L. (2003). Treatment choice for PTSD. *Behaviour Research and Therapy, 41*(8), 879–886.

Chapter 14
An Analysis of the Experiences of Police Officers in Post-conflict Peacekeeping Missions: the New Zealand Police Perspectives

Garth den Heyer

Introduction

This chapter presents the findings of an electronic survey of police officers that were deployed by the New Zealand Police on international peacekeeping, monitoring, or capacity development missions between 1964 and May 2017. A link to the electronic survey was emailed in January 2018 to 928 police officers and staff, who had been identified as having been deployed on the nine missions. A list of the peacekeeping missions involving the New Zealand Police can be found in Table 3.1 in Chap. 3 of this book.

The survey was designed to examine the experiences and observations of the police members who were deployed and to find the answers to the following questions:

- The events and reasons why officers from the New Zealand Police were deployed to each mission.
- How the deployment of members of the New Zealand Police to missions furthered the strategic objectives of the New Zealand Government.
- How the members of the New Zealand Police contributed to the achievement of the objectives of each mission.

To obtain this information, a survey questionnaire that comprised of 46 questions relating to the officers' pre-deployment training, the missions they were deployed to, their role in the mission, and the objectives and achievements of the mission was emailed to the 928 police officers and staff.

The survey was based on the following two research questions: How did the deployment of New Zealand Police to various missions further the strategic

G. den Heyer (✉)
School of Social and Behavioral Science, Walden University, Havelock North, New Zealand

G. den Heyer, J. F. Albrecht (eds.), *Police and International Peacekeeping Missions*, https://doi.org/10.1007/978-3-030-77900-9_14

objectives of the New Zealand Government; and how did the New Zealand Police contribute to the achievement of the objectives of each mission.

The Survey Return Rate

Of the 928 New Zealand Police members that were sent the link to the electronic survey, 248 officers and staff completed the survey questionnaire, which was a return rate of 27 percent. While the return rate is relatively low, it is similar to other research surveys undertaken in policing (Stott & Reicher, 1998a, 1998b; Drury & Stott, 2001; Drury et al., 2009a, 2009b). The return rate was to be expected considering that questions about a sensitive, core part of policing were asked. According to Davies and Dawson (2015), a survey return rate of 35 percent is considered to be exceptional for this type of research. The deployment of police from other countries to conflict and post-conflict zones is a political and sensitive issue and creates debate from participants, media, and politicians, and can culminate in commissions or inquiries and result in the development of official reports and staff welfare problems.

Characteristics of Respondents

The first section of the survey sought to examine the experience that members had had when they were deployed on their first overseas mission and to record when they had completed the questionnaire. To answer this section, participants were asked two questions. The first question asked respondents what their rank was when they were deployed on their first overseas mission. Table 14.1 presents the results of the answers to this question. As can be seen, the largest number of respondents were first deployed as Constables or Senior Constables (102 respondents or 41.1 percent), followed by Sergeants (56 respondents or 22.6 percent) and then Detectives (32 respondents or 12.9 percent). The remaining respondents were spread

Table 14.1 Rank of Respondent when Deployed to First Overseas Mission

Rank	Number Holding the Rank	Percentage of Total
Constable and Senior Constable	102	41.1
Detective	32	12.9
Sergeant	56	22.6
Detective Sergeant	14	5.7
Senior Sergeant	18	7.2
Inspector	14	5.7
Police employee	12	4.8
Total	**248**	**100.0**

Source: Author

reasonably evenly between Detective Sergeant, Senior Sergeant, Inspector, and Police employee.

The second question in this section asked respondents their length of service with the New Zealand Police when first deployed and at the time of completing the survey. The average length of service when deployed on the respondent's first mission was 15.67 years, with the least being 3 years and the longest being 38 years. The average length of service (or when the participant had retired or resigned from the New Zealand Police) when completing the survey question was 22.66 years, the least being 7 years and longest being 44 years (Table 14.2).

The answers to the question demonstrate that the survey participants represented a reasonable spread in relation to the missions that they had been deployed on when measured by the number of repeated deployments. More than half of the survey respondents (57 percent) were deployed to the Solomon Islands and many respondents had been deployed to other missions prior to being deployed to the Solomon Islands. The second largest number of participants had been deployed to Timor-Leste (22 percent) and then Bougainville (11 percent). The largest percentage of survey respondents were deployed to the Solomon Islands because this was a large mission requiring a substantial contribution from New Zealand and was ongoing for a long period of time (2004–2017).

Table 14.3 presents the number of missions by survey respondents. The largest number of survey respondents had completed one overseas deployment (71 percent). Of the survey respondents, 99 (29%) had completed more than one mission, with 64 (18%) respondents having completed two missions (64 respondents or 18 percent) and 26 (7.5%) completing three missions. One person had completed five missions and one had completed six missions.

Survey participants were also asked about the length of their deployment. Table 14.4 presents this information by the mission number and the length in months of the deployment. The most common length of deployment was six months, with 171 respondents (54 percent) being deployed for this period. The shortest deployment was for one month, with 14 respondents being deployed for this period. The longest period of deployment was for 60 months, with 1 respondent being deployed for this period. This extraordinarily long deployment was because a senior officer chose to renew his deployment to Bougainville a number of times. The position was accompanied, which meant that the officer could take his family, and the officer retired from the New Zealand Police on completion of his final deployment to Bougainville.

Table 14.2 Length of Service

	Average Length of Service (Years)	Number of Respondents
Length of service with New Zealand Police at the time of the first overseas deployment	15.67	246
Current length of service as a member of New Zealand Police (or service at resignation/retirement)	22.66	243

Source: Author

Table 14.3 Number of Times Deployed and Countries

Mission	AF	BG	Cyprus	NM	SI	TL	Tonga	Total
1	10	22	8	2	150	55	1	248
2	3	11	2	0	33	14	1	64
3	4	4	1	0	9	7	1	26
4	0	1	0	0	5	1	0	7
5	0	0	0	0	1	0	0	1
6	0	0	0	0	1	0	0	1
Total	**17**	**38**	**11**	**2**	**199**	**77**	**3**	**347**

Source: Author
AF Afghanistan, *BG* Bougainville, *NM* Namibia, *SI* Solomon Islands, *TL* Timor Leste

Table 14.4 Number of Officers Deployed by Mission Number and Months

Months/Mission	1	2	3	4	5	6	Total
1	2	9	3	0	0	0	**14**
2	4	0	1	0	0	0	**5**
3	11	8	2	0	0	0	**21**
4	5	3	0	0	0	0	**8**
5	2	4	3	1	0	0	**10**
6	138	22	7	2	1	1	**171**
7	34	6	2	1	0	0	**43**
8	11	1	0	0	0	0	**12**
9	7	1	0	0	0	0	**8**
10	1	0	0	0	0	0	**1**
11	6	0	0	0	0	0	**6**
12	6	2	1	0	0	0	**9**
13	2	1	0	1	0	0	**4**
17	1	0	0	0	0	0	**1**
18	2	0	0	0	0	0	**2**
21	1	0	0	0	0	0	**1**
24	1	0	0	0	0	0	**1**
60	0	0	1	0	0	0	**1**
Total	**233**	**57**	**21**	**5**	**1**	**1**	**318**

Source: Author

The shorter missions that have been identified in Table 14.4 relate to officers or staff members who were deployed to fill technical roles or to cover specific operations or a specific incident. A number of tactical officers, for example, were deployed in the early 2000s to the Solomon Islands as a response to the riots that followed the results of parliamentary elections. These elections included selecting a Prime Minister, who the public viewed as being corrupt.

The third and last question in this section asked the respondents about the role they fulfilled during their deployments. The respondents identified a large number of specialist and specific roles, which have been aggregated to 18 roles, and these have been presented in Table 14.5.

Table 14.5 Roles Undertaken During Mission

Role	Role
Administration/Training	Intelligence
Capacity Development	International Monitor
CIB/Investigations	Maritime
Close Protection	Patrol
Communications/Control	Planning
Community Policing	Internal Affairs
Contingent Commander	Prosecution
DVI/Forensic	Tactical
Family Violence	Traffic

Source: Author

Table 14.6 Number of Days Training Complete Prior to Being Deployed

Days/Mission	1	2	3	4	5	6
1	2	9	3	0	0	1
2	3	0	1	0	0	0
3	11	8	2	0	0	0
4	5	3	0	0	0	0
5	2	4	3	1	0	0
6	138	22	7	2	1	0
7	34	6	2	1	0	0
8	11	1	0	0	0	0
9	7	1	0	0	0	0
10	1	0	0	0	0	0
11	6	0	0	0	0	0
12	6	2	1	0	0	0
13	2	1	0	1	0	0
17	1	0	0	0	0	0
19	2	0	0	0	0	0
21	0	0	1	0	0	0
24	1	0	0	0	0	0
60	0	0	1	0		0
Total	**232**	**57**	**21**	**5**	**1**	**1**

Source: Author

Deployment Training

The next section of the survey asked nine questions regarding mission training. The first question asked participants how many days training they had received prior to being deployed. Two hundred and thirty-two respondents answered these questions and their answers have been presented in Table 14.6. The answers have been presented by the number of missions that individuals were deployed on. The most common length of pre-deployment training given was six days, with 170 respondents

(73 percent) receiving this length of training regardless of the number of missions they had been deployed on.

The least amount of training given, pre-deployment, was for one day, with 15 respondents receiving this length of training. The pre-deployment training given over one to three days all pertain to short-term international deployments: Disaster victim identification team members, for example, who were deployed to the Solomon Islands to assist with forensic investigations and members from the Armed Offenders Squad/Special Tactics Groups who were also deployed to the Solomon Islands. Short periods of training were also given to respondents who were deployed to the Solomon Islands and Tonga to cover the riots in these locations. The longest period of training was for 60 days, with one participant receiving this length of training. This period of pre-deployment training was given to a member who was deployed to Bougainville for more than three years and the training given included extensive lessons in culture and language.

The second question was asked to identify where the pre-deployment training was given. The majority of training was undertaken at the Royal New Zealand Police College with 250 of the survey participants stating that they had completed their training at the college. The location of the pre-deployment training that was next most frequently used was a military base, with 22 participants being trained in this location. Three participants received training in-mission and nine participants did not receive any pre-deployment training (Table 14.7).

The second question asked in relation to pre-deployment training was whether the participants thought that the pre-deployment training that was given was adequate for the role that they were to undertake in-mission. Of the 296 respondents, 243 (82 percent) thought that they received adequate or appropriate pre-deployment training for their role and 53 (18 percent) thought that they did not receive adequate or appropriate training (Table 14.8).

To clarify as to why survey respondents did not think that the pre-deployment training was adequate or appropriate, the survey included a question as to which areas of the training needed to be improved. The response to this question has been

Table 14.7 Location of Pre-deployment Training

Location/Mission	1	2	3	4	5	6
Auckland	2	1				
Brindisi			1			
Brisbane			1			
RNZPC	207	30	9	3		1
Military base	16	3	3			
Christchurch	1					
Honiara		1				
In-mission		1	1			
RNZPC and Military base	3					
N/A or no training undertaken		6	2		1	
Total	**229**	**42**	**17**	**3**	**1**	**1**

Source: Author

Table 14.8 Did you feel the pre-deployment training was adequate and appropriate for the role that you were to undertake?

Mission	Yes	No	Total
1	182	45	227
2	39	7	46
3	17		17
4	5		5
6		1	1
Total	**243**	**53**	**296**

Source: Author

Table 14.9 Further Areas of Pre-Deployment Training

Area of Weakness			
Culture/history	11	Administration requirements	1
Information specific to the role	10	Specific to non-sworn	1
Threat/political	6	Computer training	1
Language	5	Firearms training	1
Information specific to the United Nations	5	Maintaining personal health	1
Disorder/riot handling training	3	More overall training	1
What to expect	2	United Nations Security Resolutions	1
Working with the AFP	1	Vehicle (maintenance/driving)	1

Source: Author

presented in Table 14.9, with the highest number of respondents suggesting that they would have liked to have received more training in relation to deployment location's culture and history. A similar number of respondents would also have liked to have received more information in relation to the role that they were assigned to during the mission. There were also a number of respondents that made comments about the lack of information provided by the United Nations and as to how to fulfill the United Nations administrative requirements. These comments were not surprising given the anecdotal comments made about United Nations peacekeeping missions. The comments usually relate to problems caused by the size of United Nations missions or because of the high number of countries that are involved.

In Mission Training

The fourth question that respondents were asked was as to whether they received any specific training when they arrived in mission. Two hundred and thirty-nine respondents (79 percent) answered that they did receive specific training when they arrived in mission and 62 respondents (21 percent) answered that they did not (Table 14.10).

To assist in understanding the weaknesses in the pre-deployment training, survey respondents were asked if they had any other comments in relation to the pre-deployment training that they had received. The majority of the comments centered on

Table 14.10 Did you receive any mission-specific training when you arrived in mission?

Mission	Yes	No	Total
1	190	41	231
2	34	14	48
3	12	6	18
4	2	1	3
6	1	0	1
Total	**239**	**62**	**301**

Source: Author

Table 14.11 Did you feel that this training was adequate and appropriate for the mission?

Mission	Yes	No	Total
1	167	47	214
2	35	4	39
3	13	2	15
4	0	0	0
6	1	0	1
Total	**216**	**53**	**269**

Source: Author

the fact that the participants had received some training and that they were grateful for this, but a number of participants thought that it may have been beneficial to have someone from a previous mission present during the pre-deployment training. Another comment was that the training given was general and not specific. However, the respondents accepted this weakness as they were aware that it was not possible to have personnel from previous missions present, owing to the fact that these were initial deployments and that the trainers would learn as the mission deployments progressed.

To complete the section pertaining to pre-deployment training, the survey respondents were asked as to whether they thought the training was adequate and appropriate for the mission to which they were to be deployed. Two hundred and sixteen respondents (80 percent) stated that they thought the training was adequate and appropriate and 53 respondents (20 percent) stated that they thought the training was not adequate and appropriate. The interesting point about this question is that only 269 respondents answered this question, compared to other questions asked, which had approximately 300 responses (Table 14.11).

Table 14.12 presents the responses to the questions as to whether participants had received any training when they arrived in mission for the role that they were to undertake. One hundred and twenty-six respondents (43 percent) answered that they did receive such training and 169 respondents (57 percent) stated that they did not receive this training.

To clarify the participants' view of the specific role training that they received in mission, respondents were asked as to whether they felt the specific in mission training was adequate and appropriate for the role that they were to undertake. One hundred and fifty-two respondents (62 percent) thought that the specific in mission

Table 14.12 Did you receive any specific training for the role that you were to undertake when you arrived in mission?

Mission	Yes	No	Total
1	90	139	229
2	22	24	46
3	11	5	16
4	3	0	3
6	0	1	1
Total	**126**	**169**	**295**

Source: Author

Table 14.13 Did you feel that the specific in mission role training was adequate and appropriate for the role that you were to undertake?

Mission	Yes	No	Total
1	112	80	192
2	25	10	35
3	12	2	14
4	3	0	3
6	0	1	1
Total	**152**	**93**	**245**

Source: Author

training was adequate and appropriate and 93 respondents (38 percent) did not (Table 14.13).

To give support to the previous question, the survey included a question as to whether members received a “handover” for the role that they were to undertake. One-hundred and sixty-eight respondents (57 percent) said that they did receive a “handover” and 127 respondents (43 percent) said that they had not (Table 14.14).

The last question relating to members training was whether the participants felt that the “handover” training was adequate and appropriate for the role they were to undertake. One hundred and forty-five respondents (57 percent) said that they thought the “handover” training was adequate and appropriate and 110 respondents (43 percent) said that it was not (Table 14.15).

Mission Role and Performance Measures

The aim of the next section of the survey was to gather information about the types of missions, the strategic goals of missions and the performance measures that were used to evaluate whether the mission achieved its goals. The first question asked was, What was the role of the mission that the member was deployed on? The survey specified four types of mission roles; mission security, mentoring of local police, capacity development, and executive policing. The answers to this question have been presented in Table 14.16. As can be seen, 93 respondents stated that the role of the mission that they were deployed on was focused on providing security, 224 stated that

Table 14.14 Did you receive a "handover" for the role that they were to undertake?

Mission	Yes	No	Total
1	133	92	225
2	23	24	47
3	9	9	18
4	3	1	4
6	0	1	1
Total	**168**	**127**	**295**

Source: Author

Table 14.15 Did you feel that the "handover" training was adequate and appropriate for the role that you were to undertake?

Mission	Yes	No	Total
1	110	89	199
2	24	15	39
3	9	5	14
4	2	0	2
6	0	1	1
Total	**145**	**110**	**255**

Source: Author

their mission was to mentor the local police, 210 defined that their mission was to contribute to the capacity development of the local police and 89 claimed that their mission was executive policing. The reason why the number of responses exceeds the total number of missions that survey respondents were deployed to is because some respondents stated that their mission had more than one strategic role.

The second question in this section of the survey comprised of two parts and asked as to whether the mission that staff had been deployed on had New Zealand or New Zealand Police objectives or goals specified and whether these had been articulated to mission members. One hundred and sixty-eight respondents claimed that the missions that they were deployed on had specific objectives articulated, 131 respondents claimed that their missions had goals that had been identified, but not articulated, and 157 respondents claimed that the objectives of goals had been articulated to members (Table 14.17).

The third question, which was similar to the second question, asked whether the mission that the respondents had been deployed on had objectives or goals that were specific to the mission and whether these had been articulated to mission members. One hundred and twenty-seven respondents stated that the mission had objectives identified, but not articulated, 103 respondents stated that the mission had goals, but not articulated, and 127 claimed that these had been articulated to mission members (Table 14.18).

The second theme of questions in this section of the survey related to mission performance measures. Survey participants were asked two sets of questions in relation to performance measures. These were asked to understand whether there were any measures stipulated by the New Zealand Police and whether any measures had been stipulated by the mission. The first question in the section asked as to whether

Table 14.16 What was the identified role(s) of each mission that was deployed on?

Mission	Mission Security	Mentoring of Local Police	Capacity Development	Executive Policing (Patrol)
1	65	176	157	67
2	18	32	39	17
3	8	12	12	4
4	2	3	2	1
6	0	1	0	0
Total	**93**	**224**	**210**	**89**

Source: Author

Table 14.17 Did the mission(s) that you were deployed on have identifiable New Zealand or New Zealand Police objectives or goals and were these articulated to mission members?

Mission	Objectives	Goals	Articulated to mission members
1	126	92	110
2	28	25	33
3	11	11	11
4	3	2	3
6	0	1	0
Total	**168**	**131**	**157**

Source: Author

the mission that respondents had been deployed on had any performance measures formulated by the New Zealand Police and whether these had been articulated to members of the mission. Forty-eight respondents stated that the mission that they had been deployed on had New Zealand Police performance measures conveyed and 45 respondents claimed that the missions that they were deployed on did not have any performance measures (Table 14.19).

To clarify the previous question, the survey asked whether the mission that respondents were deployed on had New Zealand Police performance measures stipulated, and if so, what were the measures. The results of this question have been presented in Table 14.20, and as can be seen, the types of performance measures used on the missions were basic and fundamental. Twelve respondents answered that the performance measure was based on the level of reported crime, six stated that the performance measure was the resolution or clearance rate, and 15 disclosed that the mission's performance was measured by a public satisfaction survey.

Survey participants were also asked the same two performance measurement questions in relation to whether the mission that they had been deployed on had mission performance measures stipulated. The first of these questions asked as to whether the mission that they were deployed on had performance measures and whether these were articulated to mission members. Seventy-three respondents stated that their mission had performance measures and 57 respondents stated that these performance measures were articulated to mission members (Table 14.21).

The second survey question asked if the mission did have performance measures, then what those measures specifically were. Again, respondents identified three

Table 14.18 Did the mission(s) that you were deployed on have identifiable mission specific objectives or goals and were these articulated to mission members?

Mission	Objectives	Goals	Articulated to mission members
1	98	80	94
2	20	16	22
3	8	6	10
4	1	1	1
6	0	0	0
Total	**127**	**103**	**127**

Source: Author

Table 14.19 Did the mission(s) that you were deployed on have New Zealand Police performance measures and were these articulated to mission members?

Mission	Performance Measures	Articulated to members
1	38	35
2	6	7
3	2	1
4	2	2
6	0	0
Total	**48**	**45**

Source: Author

mission performance measures: level of reported crime, the resolution or clearance rate, and public satisfaction. Twenty-one respondents stated that the mission performance measure was the level of crime, 10 respondents stated that the mission was measured by the resolution or clearance rate, and 20 respondents disclosed that it was from a public satisfaction survey of the mission (Table 14.22).

The last question in this section on mission objectives and performance measures asked whether community policing was a specific objective of the mission that the respondent was deployed on. One hundred and fifty-three respondents (64 percent) stated that community policing was an objective and 85 (36 percent) respondents stated that it was not (Table 14.23).

Mission Achievements

The last section of the survey asked two groups of two questions as to what was achieved during the mission and the personal goals of the officer. The first question asked participants whether they thought that the New Zealand Police deployment to the mission that they were deployed on assisted the mission to achieve the following four objectives: improving the level of policing delivered by the local police, increasing the resolution or clearance rate, increasing public confidence in the local police, and improving local security. Two hundred and seven respondents claimed that the New Zealand Police deployment had assisted in improving the standard of policing by the local police, 97 respondents thought that they had assisted in increasing the resolution or clearance rate, 165 respondents thought that they had assisted

Table 14.20 If the mission(s) had New Zealand Police performance measures, what were these measures?

Mission	Level of reported crime	Resolution or clearance rate	Based on public satisfaction
1	9	5	12
2	1	1	2
3	1	0	1
4	1	0	0
6	0	0	0
Total	**12**	**6**	**15**

Source: Author

Table 14.21 Did the mission(s) that you deployed on have mission performance measures and were these articulated to mission members?

Mission	Performance Measures	Articulated to mission members
1	56	43
2	10	9
3	5	3
4	2	2
6	0	0
Total	**73**	**57**

Source: Author

in increasing the public confidence in the local police and 184 in improving local security (Table 14.24).

The second question carried on the theme of the first question and asked participants whether they thought that the New Zealand Police deployment assisted the mission in improving the level of professionalism of the local police, whether it increased the use of community policing methods or increased the capability of the local police. One hundred and ninety-nine respondents thought that the New Zealand Police deployment had assisted in improving the level of professionalism of the local police, 162 respondents thought that they had assisted with increasing the use of community policing and 201 thought that they had assisted with increasing the capability of the local police (Table 14.25).

Personal Achievements

The last two questions sought to understand what survey respondents thought about their deployment. The first question asked whether they thought that the deployment had improved their skills that enhanced their policing abilities, whether it increased their knowledge of policing or increased their understanding of other cultures. Two hundred and five respondents claimed that they had improved their policing skills that would enhance their career, 153 thought that they had increased their knowledge of policing and 245 respondents thought that they had increased their understanding of other cultures (Table 14.26).

Table 14.22 If the mission(s) had mission-specific performance measures, what were these measures?

Mission	Level of reported crime	Resolution or clearance rate	Based on public satisfaction
1	14	7	15
2	3	1	2
3	3	2	2
4	1	0	1
6	0	0	0
Total	**21**	**10**	**20**

Source: Author

Table 14.23 Was the introduction of Community Policing an objective of the mission(s) that you were deployed on?

Mission	Yes	No
1	117	66
2	27	11
3	6	8
4	3	0
6	0	0
Total	**153**	**85**

Source: Author

The last survey question asked respondents whether they thought that being deployed on an overseas mission had advanced their career with the New Zealand Police. Two hundred and fifty-three participants responded to the question. Seventy-four respondents thought that working on an overseas deployment had advanced their career with the New Zealand Police and 165 respondents thought that that it had not. These results are not surprising as there are many examples where police members have not been able to use the skills that they acquired in their overseas deployment roles. There have also been a number of anecdotal stories where members, upon their return to their New Zealand Police role, have said that their deployment experience was not appreciated by their managers. A number of respondents also claimed that the deployment actually negatively detracted from their career advancement in the New Zealand Police (Table 14.27).

Conclusion

Very little is known about policing in post-conflict zones and even less about the experiences of police officers in these areas. Furthermore, there has not been any informal or academic examination or evaluation of the police role in any of the missions that New Zealand Police Officers have been deployed on. This survey is one step in starting this process.

Table 14.24 In your opinion, did the New Zealand Police deployment assist in the mission

Mission	Improving the level of policing delivered by the local police	Increasing the resolution or clearance rate	Increasing public confidence of local police	Improving local security
1	165	73	127	136
2	31	16	28	32
3	7	5	7	12
4	3	3	2	3
6	1	1	1	1
Total	**207**	**97**	**165**	**184**

Source: Author

Table 14.25 In your opinion, did the New Zealand Police deployment assist in the mission

Mission	Improving the level of professionalism of the local police	Increasing the introduction of community policing	Increasing the capability of local police
1	156	121	159
2	30	30	29
3	9	7	9
4	3	3	3
6	1	1	1
Total	**199**	**162**	**201**

Source: Author

Table 14.26 What do you feel you achieved at a personal level in-mission?

Mission	Improved skills to enhance your policing career	Increased your knowledge of policing	Increase your understanding of other cultures
1	156	115	191
2	34	26	36
3	12	10	14
4	3	2	3
6	1	0	1
Total	**205**	**153**	**245**

Source: Author

Table 14.27 Did the mission deployment assist in advancing your New Zealand Police career?

Mission	Yes	No
1	56	134
2	13	26
3	4	11
4	1	3
6	0	1
Total	**74**	**165**

Source: Author

The survey highlights a number of weaknesses and issues in the missions that the New Zealand Police have contributed staff to. Weaknesses occurred prior to deployment, during the deployment, and post deployment. To ensure that the New Zealand Police are able to contribute staff to overseas deployments in the future, they should provide suitable, adequate and culturally based pre-deployment training. Any improvement to pre-deployment training should be supported by an intelligence and operational briefing on arrival to the mission. It should also provide better support from the New Zealand based deployment team. Another area requiring review and a redefined structure is the process for when staff return to New Zealand. This process needs to ensure that being deployed overseas does not impact on a staff member's career in the New Zealand Police and that there is a method for utilizing the member's experience.

The second feature that the survey highlighted is that the majority of respondents thought that they, individually and as part of the New Zealand Police contribution, assisted with making life better for the local population of their deployment. This emphasizes that these officers have appreciated having the opportunity to be a part of a mission and that this experience has broadened their personal horizons. One of the weaknesses of this survey is that there has been no framework that has enabled individual comments to be presented in relation to specific parts of the survey or about being deployed overseas.

References

Davies, G., & Dawson, S. (2015). The 2011 Stanley Cup Riot: Police perspectives and lessons learned. *Policing: An International Journal of Police Strategies & Management, 38*(1), 132–152.

Drury, J., & Stott, C. (2001). Bias as a research strategy in participant observation: the case of intergroup conflict. *Field Methods, 13*(1), 47–67.

Drury, J., Cocking, C., & Reicher, S. (2009a). Everyone for themselves? A comparative study of crowd solidarity among emergency survivors. *British Journal of Social Psychology, 48*, 487–506.

Drury, J., Cocking, C., & Reicher, S. (2009b). The nature of collective resilience: Survivor reactions to the 2005 London bombings. *International Journal of Mass Emergencies and Disasters, 27*, 66–95.

Stott, C., & Reicher, S. (1998a). Crowd action as intergroup process: Introducing the police perspective. *European Journal of Social Psychology, 26*(4), 509–529.

Stott, C., & Reicher, S. (1998b). How conflict escalates: The intergroup dynamics of collective football violence. *Sociology, 32*(2), 353–377.

Part VII
Concluding Comments

Chapter 15
The Policing of Post-Conflict Nations and Regions

Garth den Heyer

Introduction

The first deployment of police officers to a United Nations peacekeeping mission occurred in 1960, when a civilian police contingent was included in the United Nations forces that were sent to suppress the violence in the Congo. The role of the police in this deployment was to assist the Congo Government maintain law and order while the Belgian military withdrew from the country.

In the ensuing 60 years, the majority of United Nations peacekeeping missions have included civilian police officers, and their role in peacekeeping missions during this time has changed substantially. In early missions, the role of the civilian police was generally limited to general election monitoring, the training of local police and the provision of security. In recent years, civilian policing activities have included the undertaking of patrols and developing the capacity and capability of the local police.

The deployment of police officers as a component of an international peacekeeping or assistance mission is part of a more comprehensive approach to post-conflict and state rebuilding. This approach usually encompasses other law and justice sectors, which have more specific political and developmental goals (Greener, 2009). This means that the reform of the police of a post-conflict nation is an element within a wider reform of the overarching justice sector.

The reform programs that were adopted highlighted the relationships of the police with justice institutions within a social, economic and political context (Greener, 2009). It also highlighted that police reform is not undertaken in a vacuum and that successful reform needs appropriately trained and skilled international police officers. This is one of the limitations of deploying police within peacekeeping missions. It is difficult for contributing countries to identify and deploy an

G. den Heyer (✉)
School of Social and Behavioral Science, Walden University, Havelock North, New Zealand

G. den Heyer, J. F. Albrecht (eds.), *Police and International Peacekeeping Missions*, https://doi.org/10.1007/978-3-030-77900-9_15

adequate number of trained and skilled police officers, especially from those countries who possess democratic policing values. When police officers are deployed, they should have an understanding of the types of policing that are appropriate for different cultural, historical and regional contexts, and they should have a clear understanding of the mandate of the mission. The type of policing needed during a mission will be shaped by the strategic direction and objectives of the mission (Greener, 2009).

Deployments to post-conflict nations by the countries discussed in this book have been undertaken in the context of the international community's understanding of the role that security and justice have in providing a foundation for rebuilding nations. Security and justice have been recognized as being core functions of a state and that they are particularly important for rebuilding a state and for peacebuilding in post-conflict countries where the rule of law is weak and confidence in the state and its institutions is low. The benefits of establishing security and justice organizations early in the state rebuilding process was identified by the World Bank in their 2011 World Development report, which emphasized security and justice as being key to breaking the cycle of violence and enable development (World Bank, 2011).

This chapter examines and discusses the role of the police in peacekeeping and the main problems encountered in their deployment. The chapter also reviews the issue of the security gap in peacekeeping missions and the police reform models used in post-conflict reform programs. It also discusses various methods for measuring the success of these projects. The last section of the chapter evaluates the contribution made by police to peacekeeping.

A Critique of Policing within Peacekeeping Missions

The decision to establish a peacekeeping mission by deploying military troops to a post-conflict nation creates an indefinite continuum of varying levels of security. The concept of the security continuum and gap have been presented in Fig. 15.1. The continuum starts with deployment of the military that has the capability of providing ultimate force and ends with the civilian police who provide general civilian policing services. The security gap is the time between the military being deployed and the creation of a secure environment which enables the civilian police to be deployed.

To assist a nation in its post-conflict reconstruction, the period between the cessation of hostilities and establishing a stable environment is problematic (Dziedzic & Stark, 2009). Stromseth et al. (2006) noted that the window of opportunity immediately after an intervention and on cessation of fighting should not be missed, as this is the time that security can be established. It is the military who fill the gap by providing a secure environment, which enables the police to then deploy (Greener, 2009; den Heyer, 2011). The environment must be secure and the threat of conflict diminished before civilian police are deployed.

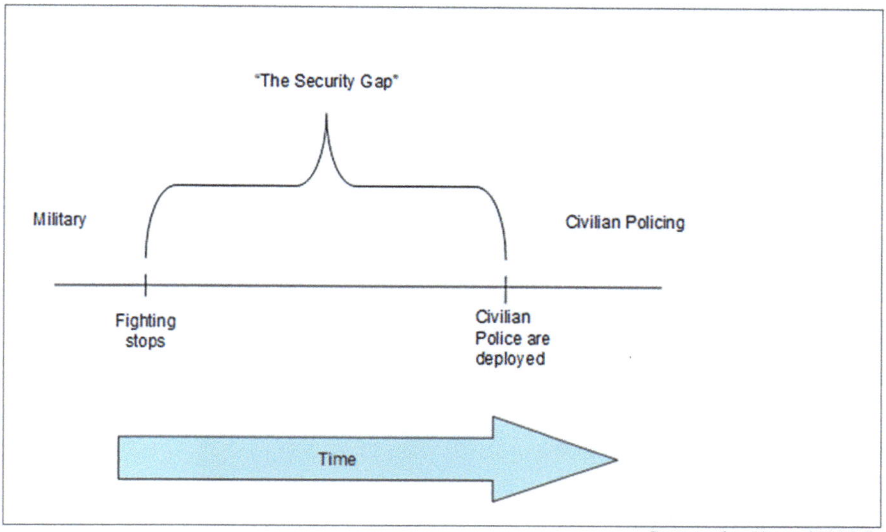

Source: den Heyer (2011a)

Fig. 15.1 The security continuum. (Source: den Heyer, 2011)

Establishing a sense of civil security is critical in rebuilding political and economic systems. The importance that has been placed on filling the security gap has been based on the argument that establishing and maintaining a stable environment is the foundation "of sustainable development, democracy, peace and security" (Hanggi & Scherrer, 2008, p. 486), and the failure to fill the security gap can negatively impact on state building, the establishment of law and order and deterring organized crime, terrorism and insurgency.

There can also be difficulties in the timing of deploying personnel, which is referred to as a deployment gap. The deployment gap occurs because there is no standing capacity of civilian police officers in a developed country. It takes time to resource, train and brief officers and arrange logistics and their travel. This means that there is often difficulty in providing a timely deployment because there are often delays between the time that the military are deployed and the time that the police can be deployed (Greener, 2009; den Heyer, 2011). As a result of this, it can be difficult to take advantage of the window of opportunity (Greener, 2009) that the cessation of hostilities provides.

Two other issues may be encountered when deploying civilian police officers as part of peacekeeping missions. The first is having the ability to deploy a large enough number of police officers. Deploying a large number of police to a post-conflict nation was advocated in research conducted by Jones et al. (2005). These researchers used nine case studies to examine the rebuilding of the security sector in post-conflict nations and claimed that the peacekeeping missions to Kosovo and East Timor were the most successful in terms of securing the environment and limiting the occurrence of violence, owing, in part, to the fact that these missions had the highest number of police officers deployed. Ensuring that an appropriate number of police officers are deployed on a peacekeeping mission is complicated by the method that is used to allocate officers to a post-conflict country (Greener, 2009). Greener (2009), claimed that deploying an appropriate number of police officers and locating them in a post-conflict country is affected by the length of the mission and the length of each rotation.

In addition to the problems encountered with deploying police officers, there are also concerns that relate to the quality and the skills of the police personnel that are available to be deployed. If police personnel are to be deployed, then their skills need to be matched to those that are required to fulfil the police tasks that have been mandated by the mission (Greener, 2009; den Heyer, 2013).

The Police Reform Model

There has been much debate in recent years about deploying police officers to oversee the reform of police institutions in post-conflict nations and the policing model that has been implemented. The reason why this issue is contentious is because deployed police primarily look to replicate the model of policing that has been used in their own country or the model that has been based on their understanding of policing in a post-conflict nation (Call, 2003). According to Greener (2009), the need to contextualize a peacekeeping or assistance mission is vital as there are different models and methods of policing, different understanding as to how to make an arrest and how to physically subdue a violent offender. The debate centres on the philosophical role of peacekeeping police and whether they should be enforcers of the law or community problem-solvers (Greener, 2009).

The policing model that is most commonly used for reforming police agencies in post-conflict nations is Community Policing. The problem is that the term Community Policing has been used too freely to describe a reform, but the reform may not necessarily comprise of all of the elements of Community Policing. Community Policing has been based on the principles of democracy. As Lum (2009) noted, owing to uncertainties in the post-conflict environment it is incorrect to argue that Community Policing is the natural definition of democratic policing just because it reflects ideals in some definitions of democracy. A more realistic approach would be to empirically examine the police transformational process during the establishment of democracy and build an appropriate theory from that (Lum, 2009). If a liberal democratic Community Policing model is to be used in the reform process, then the outcome of the reform must be one where police activities achieve what the community requires and is not one that has a rigid version of the western Community Policing model. This means that the reform model chosen must contain more than the holding and monitoring of democratic elections in weak and historically repressed countries as this "will not produce the conditions necessary for sustainable democratic police reform" or for establishing democratic institutions (Ellison & Pino, 2012, p. 208). Furthermore, the model must also take into account the fact that "levels of socio-political and economic development and police reform are intimately connected" (Ellison & Pino, 2012, p. 208)).

The most successful democratic police reform in a post-conflict nation to date, is that of the police-led Regional Assistance Mission to Solomon Islands (RAMSI). The mission signalled that the nature of the deployment was law and order focused and it removed the possibility of the mission being interpreted as an imposed colonial led model of reform. Having the police lead international intervention operations, according to Greener (2009), "assumes questions of legitimate authority have been settled in advance, and immediately indicates that the mission will have different objectives and will rely on different methods to achieve those objectives" (p. 128). This means that missions should not only include the police, but the focus of missions should be law and order.

There is a weakness, however, in basing a model of police reform on democratic principles. According to Ellison and Pino (2012), the use of democratic policing principles can lead to the further militarization of the police. This happened in South Africa and Brazil, which were not post-conflict nations, but were countries undergoing extensive national democratic reform. The reason for the increase in the militarization of the police in both countries was because the police were confronted by widespread and malevolent problems from the occurrence of crime and violence during the implementation of the democratic reforms (Ellison & Pino, 2012).

Closely tied to the issue of choosing a suitable model to reform the local police is how the organization that is to be reformed will be structured. Any structure proposed needs to suit the context of the country and be sustainable (den Heyer, 2008, 2010, 2012; Greener, 2009), but the primary issue relating to the choice of an organizational structure is the over-reliance on western models (Kaplan, 2000). According to Kaplan (2000), as a result of the use of western justice system models and their complexity and size, the focus of a reform concentrates on the material aspects of policing, rather than on the actual practice of policing.

The last problem to be discussed in relation to police reform is that of ownership of the reform process. The aim of a peacekeeping mission is for the deployed officers "to police themselves out of a job" by reforming the capacity of the local police in order for the new police agency to be self-sustaining (Greener, 2009, p. 126). It is important that the model takes the local culture into account and that the model does not slip into a modernized form of colonial policing (den Heyer, 2008, 2010, 2012; Greener, 2009). The more that the approach taken is based on the sovereignty of the post-conflict nation and relates to the concept of control and the ability to act in autonomously (Greener, 2009), the more likely that the reform will be accepted. According to Greener (2009), there are three methods for ensuring local ownership of the police reform process: consulting with local stakeholders, police and politicians; sharing the authority or management of the reform process and using local personnel to fill key positions in the project management team.

There are some weaknesses in adopting a more inclusive approach to police reform. The first is that even when the process to reform the police has been designed by members of the post-conflict nation, they inevitably draw on foreign policing models and experiences (Call, 2003). The second weakness is that few credible models of policing exist or are known within any given country (Bayley, 1995, 2006; Call, 2003). The third weakness is that most police reform efforts follow the line of least resistance and do not address larger, organizational- structure problems (Ellison & Pino, 2012). Another issue is that the policing model may be a condition that has been made by countries who are contributing development funding.

To overcome these weaknesses, a review of the lessons learned from previous peacekeeping missions was undertaken by the United Nations Development Programme. The review suggested that the reform of the police and the policing model used as a basis for a reform should draw on the input of the local police and donor countries and should be developed from using a combination of a number of international models (Call, 2003). The challenge for the police who are deployed is in fact much broader. Their advice and assistance should be crafted so that it draws on relevant models and is capable of adapting to the local environment, which builds on positive policing and justice traditions (Call, 2003).

Measuring the Success of Police Reform

How success is measured in peacekeeping varies significantly (Howard, 2008), as does the perception and understanding of performance measures. Police practitioners disapprove of performance standards that are difficult to apply or are not straightforward. Practitioners are also disinclined to favour performance measures if it is not known how comprehensive the performance measures will be. The more successful missions are, however, where peacekeepers actively learn from the environment and the culture in which they are deployed (Howard, 2008). This means that rather than instituting preconceived ideas about how the missions should be established and monitored, the mission will be at its best when the peacekeepers learn from the local population (Howard, 2008).

Two problems are encountered when developing mission and police reform performance measures. The first is when measures are designed to determine the progress made in reforming the local police and the second is determining the areas of progress that should be measured. Whether the areas of progress that a mission has a direct influence on should be included in the performance measurement framework or whether the framework should include areas that a mission does not have any direct influence on (Howard, 2008) needs to be determined. Paris (2004), argued in favour of a high standard of measure for a mission and a reform. Paris suggested that a measure of success should include the establishment of a stable and lasting peace, which has been supported by a market democracy. An opposing view is held by Downs and Stedman (2002), who suggested that a simple method of identifying peacekeeping and reform performance measures should be used. They suggested using performance measures based on:

1. whether the violence had ended, and
2. whether the peacekeeping operation completed the mandate and enabled the local police to maintain the cease-fire. In other words, that the reform had been completed to a level that the capability of the local police is self-sustaining.

The problem with the suggestion made by Downs and Stedman is that the measures that they propose may miss many of the results that arise from the actions taken by a mission (Howard, 2008). The problem is that mandates are written in detailed language, but can be open to interpretation (Howard, 2008). Furthermore, mission mandates vary from one mission to another, and as a result, do not provide an objective benchmark for comparison (Howard, 2008).

In order to capture the result of the actions taken by a mission and those areas that are not influenced by the direct control of a mission, Howard (2008), suggested two mission performance measures. The first measure is based on an examination of the success or failure of the mission in implementing its mandate and the various tasks specified in the mandate (Howard, 2008). The second performance evaluation involves a broader assessment of the state of the country and its institutions after the completion of a mission (Howard, 2008). According to Howard (2008), the measure also considers the fact that while the mission may have fulfilled its mandate, the conflict may not have ended in peace or there may have been residual problems with implementing democratic procedures in specific institutions. The strength in the second measure is that it includes a number of comprehensive measures of institution-building and those relating to the establishment of peace "but does not go so far as to say that all missions that do not result in just, stable, market democracies are failures" (Howard, 2008, pp. 7–8). The two measures are based on a survey methodology that explores whether institutions will continue to function after a mission has withdrawn (Howard, 2008). Howard (2008), describes this framework as a "structured focused comparison" (pp. 7–8).

When seeking to measure the success of a reform of local police, any change in organizational structure and processes will affect those in the organization. In a post-conflict environment, any change in organizational structure and processes will provide a basis for organizational learning for the mission (Howard, 2008). As Howard (2008), claimed, learning is "considered to be organizational learning when new ideas are manifest as change in organizational procedures, routines, strategies, structures, and goals" (pp. 15–16).

Four indicators can be used to measure the success of a mission and whether a mission has learnt from the peacekeeping operation. These indicators comprise of a mission's ability to:

1. gather and analyse information;
2. coordinate among the different divisions of the mission;
3. engage with its environment; and
4. exercise leadership in such a way that the mission commands (Howard, 2008).

Evaluation of the Police Contribution to Peacekeeping

The contribution of the police to reforming local police has been fragmented and inconsistent. This has arisen because many of the interventions and missions have been instigated as a response to emergencies or crises or because their contribution was implemented in partnership with other agencies and non-governmental organizations or because their contribution has been part of a larger and military centric mission. Each mission that the police have been deployed to was for a nation that was in a fragile state and deployments have taken place under a variety of mechanisms and mandates: United Nations mandate; regional mandate; bilateral assistance; and through joint donor mechanisms (such as the deployment to Afghanistan) (Law & Development Partnership, 2013).

The more modern contribution that has been made by the police has focused primarily on the development of the technical capacity and capability of the local police. To develop the capacity and capability of the local police, a conceptual framework has been developed by the majority of deploying institutions, which concentrates on transitioning the organizational and individual skills of the international police to assist the local police (Law & Development Partnership, 2013).

The characteristics of the approach are highly relevant to reforming the police in post-conflict countries, especially the cultural sensitivity that most police officers bring to these environments. According to a survey of New Zealand Police Officers who have been deployed undertaken by the Law and Development Partnership (2013), they were "enthusiastic, well-motivated and keen to make a difference". Such statements are indicative of police officers who have been deployed to peace missions. As noted by the Law & Development Partnership, many officers had waited "several years for the chance to go overseas and were keen to make the most of the opportunity" (p. 23).

One difficulty in relation to officers being deployed to peacekeeping mission is that any benefit gained is often constrained "by short-term deployments and an imperfect skill match of officers to roles. These weaknesses are compounded by a lack of an exit strategy. A suitable exit strategy would ensure that any improvements made would be sustainable" (Law & Development, 2013). The difficulty in resourcing is further exacerbated by a mission not achieving, or only partially achieving, what was intended. Deep-seated systemic national and social issues take a long time to resolve, are expensive and often inhibit the achievement of sustainable results.

Another difficulty is that police deployed to peacekeeping missions have relied on a technical-based philosophy to reform local police. This means that policing skills have been re-enforced at a local police officer level while providing support for the reform of the local police organization. This has been undertaken "with limited attention being given to the broader policing context, especially the mandate and legitimacy of the police" (Law & Development, 2013, p. 2).

References

Bayley, D. (1995). A foreign policy for democratic policing. *Policing and Society, 5*, 79–94.
Bayley, D. (2006). *Changing the guard: Developing democratic police abroad*. Oxford University Press.
Call, C. (2003). *Challenges in police reform: Promoting effectiveness and accountability*. Retrieved from: https://www.ipinst.org/wp-content/uploads/publications/challenges_in_police.pdf.
den Heyer, G. (2008). Evaluating police reform in post conflict nations: A Solomon Islands case study. *International Journal of Comparative and Applied Criminal Justice, 34*(1), 213–234.
den Heyer, G. (2010). Measuring capacity development and reform in the Royal Solomon Islands Police Force. *Policing and Society, 20*(3), 298–315.
den Heyer, G. (2011). Filling the security gap: Military versus civilian police. *Police Practice and Research: An International Journal, 12*(6), 460–473.
den Heyer, G. (2012). *The role of civilian police in peacekeeping 1999–2007*. Police Foundation.
den Heyer, G. (2013). Police as nation builders: Distinguishing between countries that contribute police officers to United Nations peace operations. *International Journal of Peacekeeping, 17*(1–2), 74–115.
Downs, G., & Stedman, S. (2002). Evaluation issues in peace implementation. In S. Stedman, D. Rothchild, & E. Cousens (Eds.), *Ending civil wars: The implementation of peace agreements* (pp. 43–70). Lynne Rienner Publishers.
Dziedzic, M., & Stark, C. (2009). *Bridging the Public Security Gap*. Downloaded from www.usip.org on 12 February 2009.
Ellison, G., & Pino, N. (2012). *Globalization, police reform and development: Doing it the western way?* Palgrave Macmillan.
Greener, B. (2009). *The new international policing*. Palgrave Macmillan Publishers Limited.
Hanggi, H., & Scherrer, V. (2008). Towards an integrated security sector reform approach in UN peace operations. *International Peacekeeping, 15*(4), 486–500.
Howard, L. M. (2008). *UN peacekeeping in Civil Wars*. Cambridge University Press.
Jones, S., Wilson, J., Rathmell, A., & Riley, J. (2005). *Establishing law and order after conflict*. RAND.
Kaplan, A. (2000). Capacity building: Shifting the paradigms of practice. *Development in Practice, 10*(3–4), 517–526.
Law & Development Partnership. (2013). *Strategic evaluation of police work funded under the New Zealand aid program, 2005–2011*. Wellington: New Zealand Ministry of Foreign Affairs and Trade.
Lum, C. (2009). Community policing or zero tolerance? Preferences of police officers from 22 countries in transition. *British Journal of Criminology, 49*(6), 788–809.
Paris, R. (2004). *At war's end: Building peace after civil conflict*. Cambridge University Press.
Stromseth, J., Wippman, D., & Brooks, R. (2006). *Can might make rights? Building the rule of law after military interventions*. Cambridge University Press.
World Bank. (2011). *World development report 2011: Conflict, security and development*. World Bank.

Chapter 16
Afterword: Final Thoughts About International Policing and Peacekeeping

Garth den Heyer

Introduction

The police are the primary actors in stabilizing a state. They are the key component that connects all government agencies to the democratic framework that will aid sustainable development, democracy, peace and security (den Heyer, 2008). The civilian police are pivotal to this process because they are a neutral, non-threatening entity and can move freely between all of the parties who are involved in a conflict and can assist in building confidence and trust (McFarlane & Maley, 2001). However, deployed police must understand that their role in stabilizing a post-conflict nation should be consistent with democratic policing and democratic development (Pino & Wiatrowski, 2006). Deployed police must also be aware that the reform of the local police is an important 'point of entry' for the development of the security sector and is a prerequisite for establishing democratic accountability (Griffiths et al., 2005).

Whether in a modern developed nation city or in a post-conflict environment, such as Timor-Leste, Afghanistan or the Solomon Islands, meeting the cultural, institutional and political challenges to effectively reforming police organisations is a complicated process. The challenges are immense, requiring more than just the deployment of the police and financial assistance from donor countries if the mission is to be successful (Bajraktari et al., 2006). As Bayley (1995, 2006) stated, there is much debate, enterprise, difficulty and uncertainty in reforming the police in countries that have experienced authoritarian, totalitarian and oppressive forms of governance to one of democracy.

The police have assisted a number of police agencies in post-conflict nations in their reform efforts and their transition to democratic policing. According to the Law and Development Partnership (2013), the contribution made by the police to

G. den Heyer (✉)
School of Social and Behavioral Science, Walden University, Havelock North, New Zealand

G. den Heyer, J. F. Albrecht (eds.), *Police and International Peacekeeping Missions*, https://doi.org/10.1007/978-3-030-77900-9_16

the reform of local police agencies has had a positive impact on the technical capabilities and capacities of these institutions. For example, in Afghanistan, Bougainville, Solomon Islands and Timor-Leste, the police officers from New Zealand impressed their local police colleagues and communities with their strong commitment, professionalism, impartiality and respect. There was also widespread satisfaction with the assistance provided by international police to the Community Auxiliary Police in Bougainville, the Kosovo Police, Solomon Islands and Haiti. In Timor-Leste, the contribution of the New Zealand Police to the restoration of stability and the establishment of a pilot Community Policing programme was evident. In the Solomon Islands, the New Zealand Police were seen as a crucial member of the regional police mission, which successfully restored law and order and provided assistance with the reform and capacity building of the local police. In Afghanistan, international police delivered training to local officers and helped establish a Regional Training Centre that was rated as the best police training centre in the country (Law & Development Partnership, 2013). In Kosovo, international police established the rule of law and stabilised the country.

The strengths of police officers in peacekeeping and reforming the local police is that they are responsive, democratic, flexible and locally focused. Despite their success, however, a risk remains that the reform programs in the countries discussed in this book will not be maintained by the local police on the completion of the mission.

The Weaknesses and Challenges in the Approach to Peacekeeping

Despite the accomplishments, the contribution of the police to peacekeeping and the reform of the police in post-conflict nations has only partially realised its intended outcomes. The difficulty in achieving all of the outcomes for a mission arises from the change in the usual role of assisting the local police to deliver police services to the community to one of reforming the local police. Reforming the local police has been one area in which some police officers from Western nations have performed well. However, there has been many challenges, despite Community Policing being regarded as a niche activity of Western police agencies (Law & Development Partnership, 2013). The police have been a small partner in the missions that have been discussed in this book and their level of influence and their capability has been limited in introducing Community Policing. The partial achievement of outcomes reflects the difficulty in reforming the local police in Afghanistan, Bougainville, Haiti, Kosovo, Solomon Island and Timor-Leste.

According to the Law and Development Partnership (2013), the reason why the majority of missions have been limited in achieving their goals has been because of the over-emphasis placed on instilling technical policing skills as a part of the reform of the local police and an under-appreciation of the broader political context of policing. Another reason that some mission outcomes were not achieved is because the police have not specified any objectives for their deployed staff to achieve, and if they did, there has been no system in place for monitoring them. Why objectives have not been specified may be because the deployments to Afghanistan, Bougainville, Haiti, Kosovo, Solomon Islands and Timor-Leste were initiated as a response to political emergencies and because of the complexity of a number of different national police forces being a part of a regional or international mission (Law & Development, 2013). This may help to explain the lack of forward planning documentation, but it does not explain the reason why the police did not have a comprehensive set of mission objectives, as each deployment was developed after a planning team had visited the country.

Not having any defined objectives that could be evaluated over time means that the police are not able to replicate the successful elements of previous missions. This approach is known as 'instinctive copying', (World Bank, 2011), and is a high-risk approach to managing staff and resources. This is not a criticism of any police officer who was deployed but is more of a comment on the weak planning and monitoring of deployments by the home nations of the deployed officers. This also highlights the need for the police to develop a reflective process or framework into their future deployments. This would enable any limitations in the strategies for dealing with obstacles or challenges in the reform programme to be identified and would ensure that any mission insights are translated into adjustments in the reform model. Without the ability to record insights and lessons learned from missions, the range of strategic options for the police will remain obscure, which in turn, will encourage the police to remain with a familiar product and hope that it will work in other situations. The lack of such a framework and a comprehensive monitoring process means that no matter how effective the contribution of the organisation is, it is impossible to assess with any confidence.

Suggestions for Future Police Peacekeeping Deployments

Drawing on the literature that has been presented in previous chapters and on the analysis of the results of the electronic survey of the New Zealand Police Officers, five suggestions have been made to improve future contributions to peacekeeping and police reform missions.

The first suggestion is that police need to ensure that their contribution to peacekeeping and police reform remains relevant and sustainable. To achieve this, the police need to move away from the technically based approach that is currently being used to an approach that considers the inherently political nature of policing, which includes policing within a broader security and justice context. This means that the police will need to engage those with analytical and research skills to develop a template model or methodology for analysing the political landscape for policing the country of the proposed mission. Applying a model or methodology can then be used to develop a strategic direction and specify some objectives for the proposed mission. A system that monitors a mission's progress and allows for mid-course corrections to be implemented should also be developed.

A systematic approach to planning and monitoring a deployment would enable the police to choose how it can be most effective in supporting police reform and development in transitioning or post-conflict environments.

The next suggestion is that the police make more use of the relationships that they have with other countries and use international partnerships to leverage their knowledge and experience. This would promote the role that the police can play in transitioning and post-conflict environments. It would demonstrate that the police are potentially an influential player and are capable of leveraging the knowledge and experience of their partners to provide a platform for expressing a more measured process to identify the model of reform that will be used in a post-conflict nation.

It is also suggested that if the number of peacekeeping and police reform missions increase to the same level that took place between 2000 and 2012, then Western nations should revisit the proposal to establish permanent, deployable groups of officers and staff. This would ensure that personnel would be available whenever needed.

The next suggestion is that Western nations acknowledge that establishing sustainable democratic policing practices in transitioning or post-conflict countries is 'a generational challenge' (World Bank, 2011). This means that any commitment made would be for a long period of time, which may become controversial, especially if there is an increase in crime in Western countries. If Western nations were to accept that any commitment was for the long term, then they will need to implement a more systematic approach to establishing police deployments.

If a mission is to continue for a number of years, it is important to demonstrate that progress is being made in reforming the local police, even if progress is slow. If the police develop and establish a framework for planning and monitoring deployments, this would ensure that the effectiveness of a deployment could be measured. They should also consider instituting a process for measuring how local communities perceive the reform of the local police.

Conclusions

There has been little fundamental theory developed in relation to the role and functions of the police in reforming the police in a post-conflict society and even less on how to implement a reform (Pino & Wiatrowski, 2006). There is also little evidence that police reform and capacity development efforts have resulted in sustainable outcomes (Griffiths et al., 2005). This is because effective reforms are difficult to implement and institutions take time to develop to a level where they are confident in delivering a service. Furthermore, there is no substantiation that specific programs of police reform that have been designed to improve capacity or service effectiveness have produced any measurable effects. The normal method of measuring the success of a reform programme is how the police conduct routine policing activities (Jackson & Lyon, 2002) and not on any performance measurement framework (den Heyer, 2008).

It has been the intention of this book to show that, while the police have been successful in all of their deployments to post-conflict nations, peacekeeping and democratic police reform is a complicated undertaking, and there is no one 'off-the-shelf' approach that can be adopted to ensure the success of a mission. The profession of policing is dynamic, especially since 9/11 and there is the need to understand that sometimes there may be a negative impact on the responsiveness by the police to meet the needs of the community.

While it is vital for the police to focus on the technical aspects of a police reform program, such as officer skills and organisational procedures, this will not be sufficient in countries where the governance of policing is personalised, corrupt or dysfunctional (Law & Development Partnership, 2013). Training in the technical aspects of policing is an essential part of police development programs and is fundamental to any reform effort. However, training programs need to be structured appropriately and the transfer of skills requires a comprehensive policy framework. By ensuring that programs such as these meet these requirements, the introduction of democratic policing may have a higher chance of success. This means that the reform of the local police needs to be understood as being a part of a broader engagement with the government and other institutions of states that are transiting or are post-conflict. It also means that there is a need to draw on the skills of other Western nation government agencies and that there should be a premium on acquiring the local knowledge necessary to put these reform principles into practice. According to the Law and Development Partnership (2013), taking this approach would create an argument for longer periods of deployment and would enable researchers and other academic personnel to be employed to provide support for a reform program.

The last point to be made is whether a Community Policing model is applicable for post-conflict or transitioning countries. A Community Policing model requires the local police to accept democratic policing principles. The problem with introducing Community Policing into a post-conflict nation is that the principles of such a program is based on Western assumptions as to the composition of a local community. Whether this is relevant is questionable and whether the international police have accounted for this in their approach to the reform of the local police is not known. In some post-conflict countries, a sense of shared identity, interests and mutual obligations may appear to be absent. This demonstrates that there is a need for extensive involvement in a reform programme. The perspective implies that the international police need to take a longer view of a reform program and should not avoid efforts to support the domestic demand for good policing.

There has been two objectives for writing this book. The first was to document the police contribution to peacekeeping and to critically examine their involvement. Past scholarship about the police contributions to peacekeeping and reform missions has tended to ignore members of the police and their role within a mission. Moreover, where scholarship has mentioned members of the police, the complexity and difficulty of their roles has been understated.

The findings of this book do not offer any straightforward answers to the challenges of reforming police organisations in post-conflict nations and regions. However, the police need to accept that the emphasis of peacekeeping and police reform missions has changed and that there is now a need to develop relationships with agencies across government and with all United Nations member states, international organisations and non-profit agencies who are contributing to a mission.

References

Bajraktari, Y., Boutellis, A., Gunja, F., Harris, D., Kapsis, J., Kaye, E., & Rhee, J. (2006). *The PRIME system: Measuring the success of post-conflict police reform.* United Nations.

Bayley, D. (1995). A foreign policy for democratic policing. *Policing and Society, 5*, 79–94.

Bayley, D. (2006). *Changing the guard: Developing democratic police abroad.* Oxford University Press.

den Heyer, G. (2008). Evaluating police reform in post conflict nations: A Solomon Islands case study. *International Journal of Comparative and Applied Criminal Justice, 34*(1), 213–234.

Griffiths, C., Dandurand, Y., & Chin, V. (2005). Development assistance and police reform: Programming opportunities and lessons learned. *Canadian Review of Policing Research*, Retrieved from http://crpr.icaap.org/index.php/crpr/article/view/32/40.

Jackson, A., & Lyon, A. (2002). Policing after ethnic conflict: Culture, democratic policing, politics and the public. *Policing: An International Journal of Police Strategies and Management, 25*(2), 221–241.

Law & Development Partnership. (2013). *Strategic evaluation of police work funded under the New Zealand aid program, 2005–2011.* Wellington: New Zealand Ministry of Foreign Affairs and Trade.

McFarlane, J., & Maley, W. (2001). Civilian police in UN peace operations: Some lessons from recent Australian experience. In R. Thakur & A. Schnabel (Eds.), *United Nations peacekeeping operations: Ad Hoc Missions, permanent engagement* (pp. 182–212). United Nations University Press.

McGovern, J., & Taga, M. (2009, Dec). *Review of the Bougainville Community Police Project (Phase 4).* Autonomous Region of Bougainville, Papua New Guinea: The New Zealand Agency for International Development.

Pino, N., & Wiatrowski, M. (2006). *Democratic policing in transitional developing countries.* Ashgate Publishing Limited.

World Bank. (2011). *World development report 2011: Conflict, security and development.* World Bank.

Correction to: Community Conflict Associated with PTSD and Negative Outcomes for United Nations Police Officers

Salih Hakan Can

Correction to:
Chapter 13 in: G. den Heyer, J. F. Albrecht (eds.), *Police and International Peacekeeping Missions*, https://doi.org/10.1007/978-3-030-77900-9_13

The original version of the book was published with the chapter author's name [Ata Yenigun]. This chapter author's name has been removed from the chapter due to legal reasons. The book has been updated with the changes.

The updated version of this chapter can be found at
https://doi.org/10.1007/978-3-030-77900-9_13

G. den Heyer, J. F. Albrecht (eds.), *Police and International Peacekeeping Missions*, https://doi.org/10.1007/978-3-030-77900-9_17

Index

G. den Heyer, J. F. Albrecht (eds.), *Police and International Peacekeeping Missions*, https://doi.org/10.1007/978-3-030-77900-9

MIX
Papier aus verantwortungsvollen Quellen
Paper from responsible sources
FSC® C105338

If you have any concerns about our products,
you can contact us on
ProductSafety@springernature.com

In case Publisher is established outside the EU,
the EU authorized representative is:
Springer Nature Customer Service Center GmbH
Europaplatz 3, 69115 Heidelberg, Germany

Printed by Libri Plureos GmbH
in Hamburg, Germany